Shengavit: Շենգավիթ

A Kura-Araxes Center in Armenia

This publication was made possible by a generous grant from
the Dolores Zohrab Liebmann Fund

Shengavit: Շենգավիթ
A Kura-Araxes Center in Armenia

Hakob Simonyan and
Mitchell S Rothman, editors

With contributions by Gregory Areshian, Pam Crabtree, Jennifer Piro and Douglas Campana, Nyree Manoukian, Hans-Peter and Margartehe Uerpmann, Mikayel Gregoryan, Raffi Durgaryan, and Hayk Igythyan, Roman Hovsepyan, Eliso Kvavadze and Anahit Atoyants, Khatchetor Meliksetiyan and Ernest Pernicka, Dan Rahimi, and Hovhannes Sanamyan.

Mazda Publishers

Since 1980

Costa Mesa, California
2023

Supported by contributions from
the Shelby White and Leon Levy Program for Archaeological Publications,
the Council for Research of the National Geographic Society,
the Ministry of Education, Science, Culture, and Sport of the Republic of Armenia,
the Dolores Zohrab Liebmann Fund, and Jay Carl Rothman.
Thanks also to Joseph V. Matassino, Director of Sponsored Research and
Foundation Relations, Widener University, for his willingness to help.

Mazda Publishers, Inc.
Academic publishers since 1980
P.O. Box 2603, Costa Mesa, California 92628 U.S.A.
www.mazdapublishers.com
A. K. Jabbari, Publisher

Library of Congress Control Number: 2023930911
ISBN 10: 1-56859-394-5
ISBN 13: 978-1-56859-394-4
Hardcover (alk. paper)

Printed in South Korea

*Dedicated to our friend, teacher, and colleague Gregory Areshian;
he will be missed.*

Table of Contents

Preface

For most archaeologists, the key topic of the last few decades concerned the origins of the state. As a result, the geographical focus of attention was the centers of those origins in Mesopotamia, China, Europe, and the New World. Since then questions about the theory underlying that research and a transition toward a more local and historical focus have widened our purview.

For Mesopotamia, the importance of trade in raw materials directed attention to the highland north and east. On their own, however, regions like the South Caucasus and its connections to the Eurasian steppe have emerged as a new focus independent of the Mesopotamian case. These formerly ignored regions are able to provide a very different picture of human societal evolution. They provide a counterpoint that may ever help explain the societies and cultures of the focal regions.

Perhaps, prime among the South Caucasus cultural traditions in this light is one called by local names, Shengavitian, Karaz, Pulur, Khirbet Kerak, but primarily as a group called Early Transcaucasian or today more commonly Kura-Araxes after Kuftin. That last name best describes the geographic extent of its homeland around the Kura and Araxes Rivers. This coming together of a distinct set of societal structures and cultural practices appeared at about 3500 BC, at the same time that the Mesopotamian state first formed, and it ended a millennium later.

That cultural tradition and its related societal structures is the topic of this book. As Chapter 3 will discuss, this cultural pattern was first named in the twentieth century. Locked behind the Iron Curtain, it was largely invisible to the outside world for many decades thereafter. As the Soviet empire collapsed, and as nations re-emerged as independent states, scholars recognized its potential importance.

Shengavit's first significant excavation was in the 1930's by Yevgeny Bayburtian, and then from the 1950's to 1985 by Sandro Sardarian and his son. Co-editor Hakob Simonyan began excavating the key site of Shengavit in 2000. In 2009 co-editor Mitchell Rothman joined the effort, largely with the hope to do what this book and its associated web archive are meant to accomplish; that is, make the ideas about this fascinating cultural tradition and data related to it available to as many scholars as possible. The melding of the anthropological archaeologist Rothman and the South Caucasian culture historical archaeologist Simonyan has not always been smooth— we often disagree on approaches and even how to interpret facts—, but as the reader will see, both add to an understanding of this fascinating time and place. We managed with Google translator to accomplish our task and despite occasional arguments to remain friends and produce other important articles as well.

Any project of this size is the result of many different people and institutions. First, we needed funds for tools, and supplies, diggers, and technical analysts. In this case, we were able to do our digging based on funds supplied by the Ministry of Education, Science, Culture, and Sport, Republic of Armenia, the National Geographic Council on Research, and a gift from Jay Carl Rothman. The Shelby White and Leon Levy Foundation provided most of funds for remaining technical analysis and for preparation of this manuscript. The Dolores Zohrab Liebmann Fund paid for copy editing, design, and printing, as well as the funds to translate the book into Armenian for an edition in that language.

The staff of the 2000-2008 excavations included in addition to Hakob Simonyan:

2000, Ludwig Khachatryan, Artak Gnuni, Valery Margaryan, Vahagn Hovhannisyan, Tigran Simonyan, archaeologists, Hovhannes Sanamyan, architect, Knarik Navasardyan, ceramics technologist, Kamo Mkrtchyan, geodesist, Susanna Adamyan, representative of the Shengavit Museum, Ashot Tumanyan, illustrator, Hans-Peter and Margarethe Uerpmann, archaeozoologists.

2003 Ludwig Khachatryan, Valery Margaryan, Vahagn Hovhannisyan - archaeologists, Susanna Adamyan, representative of the Shengavit Museum, Ashot Tumanyan, illustrator, Nina Manasaryan and Jenifer Piro - archeozoologists.

2004 - Ludwig Khachatryan, Artak Gnuni, Valery Margaryan, Vahagn Hovhannisyan, archaeologists, Hovhannes Sanamyan, architect, Ashot Tumanyan, illustrator, Elena Atoyants, artifact restorer, Nina Manasaryan and Jennifer Piro archaezoologists.

2005 Ludwig Khachatryan, Valery Margaryan, Vahagn Hovhannisyan, archaeologists, Hovhannes Sanamyan, architect, Ruzanna Mkrtchyan, physical

Figure i.1. Valery Margaryan and Ludwig Khachatryan.

anthropologist, Kamo Mkrtchyan, geodesist, Taguhi Hmayakyan, illustrator, Elena Atoyants and Hrachik Hakobyan, artifact restoration, Nina Manasaryan and Jenifer Piro, archeozoologists, Khachetor Meliksetian, metallurgist. Yervand Simonyan, photographer, Diana Zardaryan (2005, student), Tigran Aleksanyan (2005, student).

2006 - 2008 - Hakob Simonyan, Valery Margaryan, archaeologists, Taguhi Hamayakyan, illustrator, Elena Atoyants, artifact restoration.

Figure i.2. The 2009 excavation crew at Shengavit.

The Armenian-American team from 2009 to 2012, aside from Simonyan and Rothman (and not including workers), included: Hovhannes Sanamyan, architect, Harutyun Badalyan, Armine Hayrapetyan, Tigran Alexanyan, Meri Safaryan, G/Karen Tserecyan, Levon Mkrtchyan, Ludwig Khachatryan, Valeric Margaryan, Katherine Weber, Nyree Manoukian, Anna Sargisyan, Khacik Vardanyan, and Lusine Margaryan, archaeologists, Dan Rahimi, archaeologist and lithics expert, Khatchetor Meliksetian, metallurgist; Pam Crabtree and Jennifer Piro, archaeozoologists, Roman Hovsepyan, Eliso Kvavadze, Anahit Ayotants, archaeobotanists, Mikayel Gevorgian, Raffi Drgaryan, and Haik Igythyan, geomorphologists.

Throughout Armenuhi Simonyan acted as our translator, field student roll taker, conversationalist, and friend. Yervand Simonyan acted as driver for the 2009 and 2010 seasons and was always available thereafter to help us with all sorts of tasks from finding bags to getting shovels and small archaeological picks made. The digging was mostly carried out by students from Yerevan State University, and Simonyan's Nerkin Naver team. Working with these bright, fun young people made the intense heat and dust of our summer field seasons a lot easier to bear.

We also have to thank the staff at Hakob's lab office by the river in Yerevan. Always helpful, they tried to make sense of Mitchell's horribly insufficient Armenian. They also helped Hakob organize weekly feasts of *khorovat*, the ultimate protein-rich barbeque of beef, pig, and chicken, and vodka in the garden of the facility.

This publication is made up of two parts. The first is the volume you hold in your hand (whether the English or Armenian version). The second is a web archive that the reader can find at https://onlinepublications.uchicago.edu/shengavit. The idea of this type of publication is to be able to present the reader not only our research process and conclusions, but a far greater range of data that they might use for their own research. In usual publications, the author must present their conclusions. They will illustrate those vessels, for example, that reflect their typology. But, what if there are other patterns they did not see, or later excavations indicate as possibilities? Other researchers will not have the wherewithal to analyze them unless they travel to Yerevan. All sorts of analyses are difficult with the limited data one can put in the pages of a printed book. We therefore, as co-editor Rothman did with Hilary Gopnik for Godin Tepe, chose to provide those more detailed data in an online web archive.

There are separate Armenian and English versions. We felt it important to present it in a language most widely read and in the language of the place where the work was done.

Figure i.3. Student workers in Square J5, 2012.

Figure i.4. Our own Alexander the Great, Narek Hakobyan.

Figures

Tables

Contributors

Dr. Hakob Y. Simonyan, Professor of Art, Yerevan State University, Deputy Director, the Scientific Research Center for the Historical and Cultural Heritage, the Ministry of Culture of Education, Science, Culture, and Sport, the Republic of Armenia, haksimon@gmail.com.

Dr. Mitchell S Rothman, Emeritus Professor of Anthropology and Archaeology, Widener University; Contributing Scholar, Penn Museum, mitchellrothman@gmail.com.

Dr. Eliso Kvavadze, Institute of Palaeobiology, Georgian National Museum, e.kvavadze001@gmail.com.

Dr. Anahit Atoyants, Chair, Genetics and Cytology, Yerevan State University, a.atoyants@rambler.ru.

Dr. Gregory Areshian, deceased, former Professor of Archaeology and Armenian Studies at the American University in Armenia and University of California, Los Angeles.

Hovhannes Sanamyan, Professor, National University of Architecture and Construction of Armenia, Deputy Director for Scientific Affairs, Scientific Research Center of Historical Cultural Heritage, hovsanamyan@gmail.com.

Dr. Raffi Durgaryan, Researcher, Laboratory of Geoarcheology and Geomonitoring, Institute of Geological Sciences, Armenian National Academy of Sciences, Raffie_d@yahoo.com.

Dr. Mikayel Gevorgyan, Head, Laboratory of Geoarcheology and Geomonitoring, Institute of Geological Sciences, Armenian National Academy of Sciences, gevmikayel@gmail.com.

Dr. Hayk Igityan, Researcher, Laboratory of Geoarcheology and Geomonitoring, Institute of Geological Sciences, Armenian National Academy of Sciences, igityanhayk@gmail.com.

Dr. Pam Crabtree, Professor/ Director of Undergraduate Studies (DUS), Department of Anthropology, New York University, pc4@nyu.edu.

Douglas Campana, Archaeologist, United States Park Service, retired.

Dr. Jennifer Piro, Associate Director, Academic Programs, NYU Tandon School of Engineering.

Dr. Hans-Peter Uerpmann, Professor, Department of Geophysics, Tübingen University, hans-peter.uerpmann@uni-tuebingen.de.

Dr Nyree Manoukian, School of Archaeology, University of Oxford, nyree.manoukian@arch.ox.ac.uk.

Dr. Nina Manaseryan, Team Leader, Archeozoology, Institute of Zoology, Scientific Center of Zoology and Hydroecology, National Academy of Sciences, Armenia, ninna_man@yahoo.com.

Dr. Roman Hovsepyan, Senior Research Fellow, Archaeobotany, Institute of Archaeology and Ethnography, Republic of Armenia, roman.hovsepyan@gmail.com.

Dan Rahimi, Departmental Associate, Western Asian Section, Royal Ontario Museum. drahimi@rom.on.ca.

Dr. Khachatur Meliksetian, Director, Institute of Geological Sciences, Armenian National Academy of Sciences, Yerevan, Republic of Armenia, KM@geology.am.

Dr. Ernest Pernicka, Professor Emeritus, Department of Geosciences, University of Heidelberg; Scientific Director, Curt-Engelhorn-Center for Archaeometry University of Tübingen, ernst.pernicka@cez-archaeometrie.de.

1 | The Kura-Araxes Cultural Tradition and Shengavit

Mitchell Rothman and Hakob Simonyan

The prehistory of the South Caucasus is one of shifting populations and experiments in how the people there produced and exchanged their goods, made their tools, cooked their food, obtained raw materials, built their houses, worshipped their divine, and organized their social, political, and economic relationships. A key site of this time was Shengavit, so named because it sat in the Shengavit district of modern Yerevan. Although archaeologists had excavated parts of the site on and off since the 1930's, no one had published a full analysis of the site and its artifacts. The time was ripe, we felt, to present the material, analyze it, and provide information that future researchers could use.

The South Caucasus Region

One of those major experiments is what archaeologists call the Kura-Araxes culture, also known to scholars outside the region as Early Transcaucasian.[1] Local variants of this culture are called Shengavitian,[2] Karaz,[3] Pulur, Yanik,[4] and Khirbet Kerak.[5] Most current scholars accept "Kura-Araxes" for this cultural tradition and its related life ways. The Kura-Araxes reflects both a cultural tradition and its concomitant societal organization, and a period of time from 3500 to 2500 BC.[6] What is distinctive about that tradition is that it was carried from its homeland (Fig 1.1) across a large area east to west from the central Zagros to the Southern Levant and north to south from the Taurus to the Greater Caucasus Mountains. Researchers see the origins of this Kura-Araxes cultural tradition in a South Caucasian homeland. This region is usually defined according to modern political boundaries as Georgia, Armenia, and Azerbaijan and includes a corner of northeastern Turkey and northwest Iran.

Those areas define a highland distinct from the hills and lowlands of neighboring northern Mesopotamia. This highland is far from uniform, consisting of a wide variety of landscapes. The high mountain valleys of the northern Kura River (the Shida and Kvemo Kartli, and Samtskhe-Javakheti, including the Tsalka Plateau) of Georgia (the "Upper Province") are quite distinctive in climate, natural resources, and human adaptations from those of the Araxes River basin. The Araxes basin includes the Ararat Plain and its immediate uplands on the Kotayk Plateau, where Shengavit is located, as well as the area toward the Aragats Mountains of Armenia (the "Lower Province"). The littoral of the eastern Black Sea in Colchis varies even more than those; it lacks any traces of Kura-Araxes occupation or contact.

---

1   Burney and Lang 1971.
2   Bayburtian 2011; Simonyan 2002.
3   Işikli 2015.
4   Summers 2014.
5   Amiran 1965.
6   Batiuk 2022.

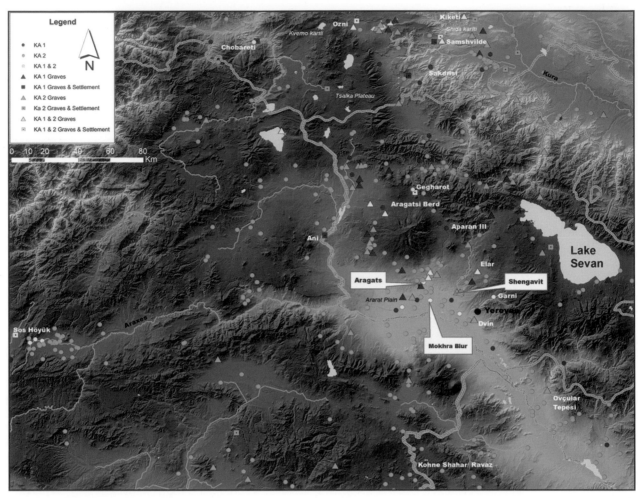

Figure 1.1. The Kura-Araxes Homeland

In a recent workshop on the Kura-Araxes in Toronto, 12 scholars discussed the best way to create a chronology for the Kura-Araxes cultural tradition. They agreed that the best chronology should use time and stratigraphy as independent variables (absolute chronology), as opposed to most current schemes that emphasize artifact, especially pottery, style (relative chronology). The time frame could then be based on radiocarbon dates from good stratigraphic contexts.[7] Those radiocarbon dates suggested the time span mentioned above, from 3500 to 2500 BC, for the Kura-Araxes cultural tradition. The name for the sub-phases the workshop attendees agreed on was KA1 (3500 to 3000 BC), and KA2 (3000 to 2500 BC). Because of the great variability in the region, beginning and end dates in each sub-region of the homeland and its migrant diaspora differed. Each sub-region had a different story to tell within the homeland and also in the diaspora sub-regions. These different pottery styles are called Yanik Ware in Iran east and south of Lake Urmia, Gray Ware in Muş /Van and the western side of Lake Urmia, South Caucasian as opposed to Central Anatolian Red Black Burnished Wares[8] in lowland Malatya, and Khirbet Kerak Ware of the Amuq Plain of the Hatay and Southern Levant. Badalyan[9] sees these differences reflected in the pottery style of the Kura-Araxes in Armenia during

---

7   Batiuk et al. 2022.
8   Batiuk 2005; Frangipane and Palumbi 2007.
9   Badalyan 2014.

the second Kura-Araxes, the KA2, period from 3000 to 2500 BC. The differing geographic zones in this style-based scheme are the Ararat Valley ("Shresh-Mokhrablur"), the highland plateau to the north and east ("Karnut-Shengavit"), and the basins of Aghstev and Debed in northeastern Armenia ("Ayrum-Teghut") (see Chapter 5e).

The Origin and Nature of the Kura-Araxes Cultural Tradition

The origin of the Kura-Araxes cultural tradition is hotly debated. Smith[10] wrote almost two decades ago that a key part of this debate involves defining what the Kura-Araxes is. In part this is because before 3000 BC people from the South Caucasus and adjoining areas began to migrate west across the Taurus Mountains and down into the Amuq and Southern Levant, southeast into the Zagros east of Lake Urmia, and northeast up along the Caspian into Daghestan.[11] In order to understand the Kura-Araxes as a whole, scholars concentrated on those features that were common to the full extent of these migrations. Therefore, its distinctive, handmade, black burnished pottery assumed a central place in the analysis of the Kura-Araxes.[12] These scholars emphasized the wares of the pottery even more than their functions.[13] As far away in distance and in ecology from the South Caucasus as the Southern Levant, the local Kura-Araxes immigrants, called Khirbet Kerak by archaeologists working there, continued to prepare and fire their pottery in much the same way as they did in Armenia hundreds of years before.[14] They even used different clay sources than the local Levantine Early Bronze III potters did (except for cooking pots). At the same time, the Armenian Kura-Araxes potters used slab construction while those of the Southern Levant used more coiling.[15] More importantly, the forms and therefore functions of Khirbet Kerak and South Caucasian Kura-Araxes potters were significantly different. The most common form in the homeland was a small, s-shaped pot that Rothman[16] interprets as an eating vessel. That form is all but absent in the Southern Levant, and plates, which are absent from the Southern Caucasian corpus, are common in the Levant. This implies a possible difference in diet and cooking, and possibly a difference between the small ethnic pockets in the diaspora and households in the homeland. In many ways the western diaspora has more in common with the KA1, certainly in its pottery style, than with the KA2 in the homeland, implying that the migrants after a couple hundred years had little contact with the homeland.

Thus, we can state that there was a common cultural tradition then, just as there is today among various ethnic groups worldwide.[17] Migrants from various ethnic groups and various regions adapt to the lifeways of the places to which they move. Yet they retain some elements of the cultural tradition of their homelands. This set of commonalities is the cultural tradition. To understand the origin of the Kura-Araxes, however, we argue that first it is necessary to define it in its South Caucasus homeland. It is there that the suite of characteristics that typify and distinguish it from earlier and contemporary cultural traditions and societal types evolved. These characteristics are what migrants then carried into its diaspora. This book will focus on those homeland sites, especially Shengavit.

The preceding Chalcolithic period in the South Caucasus was very different from what became the Kura-Araxes. Whereas pottery style alone cannot define cultural identity,[18] pottery production, function, and style can be an indi-

---

10   Smith 2006.
11   Rothman 2003.
12   Sagona 2014.
13   Palumbi 2008.
14   Iserlis et al. 2010.
15   Rothman personal observation.
16   Rothman 2011.
17   Rothman 2016, 2018.
18   Kramer 1977.

cator of cultural traditions and the degree of interaction. For post-processual archaeologists the term for this interaction is "communities of practice." The pottery production and styles of the Chalcolithic, especially the early fourth millennium BC, suggest a real break between the pre- or, as some call it, proto-Kura-Araxes, and the Kura-Araxes cultural tradition proper.[19] Two pottery wares, Chaff-Faced and Sioni (Tsopi), were the most common late Chalcolithic wares (Fig 1.2). The geographical area covered by Chaff-Faced Wares extends from the high plains and hilly country of northern Mesopotamia into the South Caucasus. More than just the pottery, however, there are indications of a cultural connection as well. At Berikldeebi Period V2[20] a building the excavators called a temple meets the criteria for a specialized Mesopotamian religious building of the Late Chalcolithic.[21] A seal from Boyuk Kesik shows this connection as well, since sealing was not part of the South Caucasian Kura-Araxes. Excavators in Georgia found other pottery matching that of Tepe Gawra in the northeastern piedmont of Iraq.[22] Some of the functional types are, however, a good match with later Kura-Araxes ones, and include the small s-shaped eating pot, although many of the other shapes are quite different.[23]

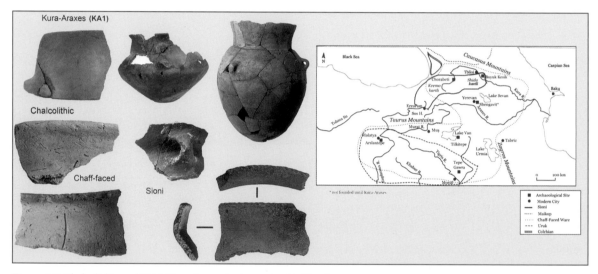

Figure 1.2 Chalcolithic and KA1 Kura-Araxes in Armenian highlands.

"There is [in the Late Chalcolithic] a limited range of generic shapes belonging to bowls and large collared jars: wide-necked jars with short out-flaring rims, either plain or moulded; holemouth jars; hemispherical bowls with turned-in lips; outrolled rims-simple, beaded, or hammer-head, depending on the site-are characteristic of larger bowls."[24]

In a narrower area inside the Southern Caucasus, a second pottery ware, the Sioni, was common in the early fourth millennium BC, especially in the Shida Kartli area.[25] Excavators found pots of Siona style in small numbers at early Kura-Araxes sites like Sos Höyük in Level VA. This might suggest a continuity, rather than a sharp break, between the two potting practices, although there were only a few sites where people built KA1 settlements on mounds with Late Chalcolithic occupations.

---

19   Sagona and Kavadze 2003; Sagona 2014; Rova 2014; Palumbi and Chataigner 2014.
20   Sagona 2014.
21   Rothman 2002, 73-74.
22   Sagona 2014.
23   Toronto Kura-Araxes workshop chronology KA1=ca. 3500-3000 BC and KA2 is ca. 2900-2500 BC.
24   Sagona 2014, 30; Figure 2.
25   Sagona 2014; Rova 2014.

The early Kura-Araxes (KA1) pottery was mostly undecorated, lightly burnished, brown, pinkish, or gray. Unlike the Chalcolithic, pots lids and handles were common. Wilkinson[26] suggests that this indicates a new kind of cooking and diet, which emphasizes stewing. That would be consistent Rothman's idea that the small s-shaped pots are for eating such liquid-based foods (see Chapter 5e). So far, the earliest appearance of this ware found is at Berikldeebi V in Georgia. By Berikldeebi IV, the Kura-Araxes cultural tradition was well established. Across the South Caucasus these KA1 wares were quite homogeneous. Some red-black wares did appear, although the supposed Kura-Araxes forms at Arslantepe may, in fact, be more related to Central Anatolia types.[27] A lot of confusion comes from the use of the same acronym, RBBW, for two different kinds of pots: the Kura-Araxes black on the outside red on the inside pots and, especially in Malatya, burnished pots with black on the inside and red on the outside, typical of Central Anatolia.

Several shapes, especially narrow necked jars with handles are typical of the KA1. The KA2 Karnut-Shengavit and Shresh-Mokhrablur pottery is mostly black and highly burnished. Some, not most, are black outside and red inside (see Chapter 5e). Ancient potters commonly decorated it with incised or raised designs. Some analysts erroneously call this raised design appliqué; it is actually made by applying a thick slip and removing enough slip to leave a raised design.

Claims of the appearance of evidence of much earlier Kura-Araxes pottery at Areni[28] and Ovçular[29] (4300-4100 BC) are problematic due to stratigraphic problems.[30] Also, as Greenberg pointed out to Marro during the Toronto Workshop, if there were people using Kura-Araxes cultural characteristics in the fifth millennium BC, what happened over the next over 600 or 700 years? Archaeologists have found no Kura-Araxes levels in that time frame.

Other cultural practices differentiate the Chalcolithic from the Kura-Araxes. One is burial practices.[31] The Late Chalcolithic practice was single inhumations in pits or large jars. A few of these internments show indications of social inequality;[32] that is, their grave goods included rare, or exotic materials. The graves at the very end of the KA1 or beginning of KA2 mostly contained groups of bodies at sites like Mentesh, where there was also a kurgan covering.[33] The grave goods were simple and locally made. Logically, if the Late Chalcolithic graves represented social differentiation, these Kura-Araxes graves represented a more egalitarian society. The earliest of these kurgans had little evidence of nearby settlements, and given the open, treeless plains around it, suggests that they represented mobile populations (see Chapter 6b).

Another marker of the Kura-Araxes is the hearth. A KA1 round hearth, found at Sos Höyük and in Shida Kartli, is flat with a small center hole. This is replaced by a deep ceramic hearth with a lobed opening or an andiron, often designed with faces and abstract designs. The latter was most common in the KA2 (see Chapter 6a).

One theory of what the Kura-Araxes tradition represented involved food (see Chapter 5b). Hovesepyan notes that the change from a broad spectrum of plants, to a narrower one with few if any pulses (lentils, peas, etc.) and a reliance on free-threshing wheat may help us find the origin point of the cultural tradition.[34] This agricultural strategy is

---

26   Wilkinson 2014.
27   Frangipane and Palumbi 2007.
28   Areshian et al. 2010.
29   Marro and 2014.
30   Palumbi and Chataigner 2014.
31   Palumbi and Chataigner 2014.
32   Lyonnet et al. 2008.
33   Poulmarc'h et al. 2014.
34   Hovsepyan 2015; Chapter 5b.

still common in the highlands of Armenia, where animals replace the protein that pulses provide. The area where such a regime is still practiced is the same as where the Sioni pottery is most often found. The exploitation of animals was mostly for meat and fat, not so much for wool or milk (see Chapter 5a). This tends to support Hovsepyan's theory. The Kura-Araxes choices for which species to grow and when to harvest them indicates a strategy meant to minimize risk and maximize returns.

The so-called Kura-Araxes cultural tradition "package" consisted of pottery style and craft techniques (Chapter 5e), ritual reflected in the hearth (see Chapter 6a), and architecture (Chapter 4a and b). Determining a pattern of architectural traditions, however, is difficult, because of the very different materials used, and the related building techniques: wattle and daub, stone foundations with mudbrick, stone, or wooden walls. Similarly, the shape of buildings—these include round, round with square ante rooms, square— all seem to have existed and mixed over geographical areas and time periods as well. Perhaps, what the observer sees is, in some ways, hiding the key factor in the Kura-Araxes practice, not building material, but interior spaces. As Whiting and Ayres[35] state, "We have found that whether a culture is settled or nomadic, the form of its family and the presence or absence of status distinctions are related to its house type, and that house type can in turn be inferred from the floor plan."

Furthermore, at its heart is the notion of house and compound. Given the geographical extent of the developed Kura-Araxes complex, it is not surprising that houses reflect regionalism in terms of basic plan (rectilinear, subrectangular, and circular houses), modes of construction (mud brick, wattle and daub, timber and stone), and spatial relationship to each other (free-standing, abutting, and terraced). This diversity, already apparent in the formative stages, surely reflects different groupings and traditions, and the specific ways of life appropriate to environmental settings. Villages of free-standing houses are more common than the complex mud brick agglomerations typical of the Near East. [...] Whereas houses would have looked different on the outside, their internal arrangement of features conveyed a clear code of practice, perhaps reflecting a shared ideology. Uniformity prevailed for the most part, with fixed points of human existence clearly delineated. The layout of the house with a circular hearth and a bench along the back wall was fundamental to the psyche of Kura-Araxes communities." [36]

That layout probably has something to do with the ideology of the Kura-Araxes people (see Chapters 6a and 6b). The hearth of the house appears to have been a focus of ritual practice.[37] With the possible exception of the red, roundhouse at Kvatschelebi (contemporaneous with Shengavit),[38] no unquestionably specialized religious building existed among the Kura-Araxes homeland sites.[39] A tower at Mokhrablur indicates a possible public ritual beyond the household, but it is not clear whether there was an actual temple building associated with it.[40] Simonyan[41] sees the Square M5 ritual installation at Shengavit as such, although other almost identical installations at Pulur Sakyol[42] are clearly present in a number of neighboring houses. The building we excavated in Square J5/J6 looks like an earlier version the M5 compound.

Another Kura-Araxes craft that researchers have written a lot about is metallurgy. Many sources of copper exist-

---

35   Whiting and Ayres 1968, 171.
36   Sagona 2014, 42.
37   Simonyan and Rothman 2015.
38   Serit Paz, Toronto Workshop.
39   Simonyan and Rothman 2015.
40   Areshian 2006; Simonyan and Rothman 2015.
41   Simonyan and Rothman 2015.
42   Koşay 1976, Chapter 6a.

ed in Armenia and neighboring Georgia, Turkey, and Iran. It was a common craft throughout the South Caucasus. Shengavit yielded evidence of significant copper smelting,[43] although the artifacts we recovered were mostly decorative rings, pins with double spirals, axes, and small blades (see Chapter 5d). The used metal axes and blades from the cache at Jrashen (whose date is not clear) were from metal ores not common in the Ararat Valley area.[44] Metals seem to have been important products, although their importance may be more because of their ability to define symbolic status than primarily as a source of weapons and craft tools. Artisans, farmers, and others mostly used tools made of ground (Chapter 5f) or chipped stone (Chap 5c) or bone (Chapter 5g). A large increase in the number and kind of metal objects in the graves of the Early Kurgan period, including ones made of gold, contrast sharply with most of the Kura-Araxes grave goods. Metallurgy could be a part of the diaspora movement, not only in terms of bringing ores, but in terms of expertise. Crafts tend to be taught not by word of mouth but by teaching techniques face-to-face.

So, in general, the suite of practices that define the Kura-Araxes include symbolic representation of pottery manufacture and style (including the complex designs of the KA2), common cuisine and cooking methods (certainly in the homeland), use of metals in some symbolic way, common layouts of houses and the correlated family structure, common burial customs, and common religious practice defined the Kura-Araxes cultural tradition. Their manufacture and exchange are indicators of the societal organization. We will investigate further how the economic activities and social structures relate to the picture we can paint of the Kura-Araxes cultural tradition and society at Shengavit.

The Mound of Shengavit

Our primary concern in this volume and the associated web archive is the site of Shengavit.[45] The site is located in the Shengavit neighborhood of Yerevan, on the bank of the river Hrazdan, now on the shore of the artificial Lake Yerevan (Figure 1.3), on a high, flat-topped cape.

Figure 1.3 Bridge over the Hrazdan River under the drained Lake Yerevan.

Located at an altitude of 930 m above sea level, it once occupied more than 6 hectares. The height of Shengavit from the Hrazdan River varies from one source to another; from 12 meters[46], 25-30 meters[47], 30 meters[48] and so on. On the map drawn by Bayburtian in the 1930s, we can clearly see 14 horizontal lines running down the river with 1 m gaps between them.[49] Now from the top of the mound to the surface of the lake is 20 meters.

---

43   Simonyan 2002.
44   Areshian 2007.
45   https://onlinepublications.uchicago.edu/shengavit.
46   Khanzadyan 1967, 80.
47   Tiratsian vol. 1, 1996, 41.
48   Sardarian 1967, 171.
49   Bayburtian 2011, 26.

To its west and south is the Ararat Valley (elevation 600 m above sea level). To its north and west is the Mount Aragats highland (2800-3400 m above sea level) and to its northeast is Lake Sevan. Our ethnobotanist, Roman Hovsepyan (see Chapter 5b), states that this region has amazing biodiversity in the plants that grew there. Most of these are wild plants. We recovered only a small number of grain and grape species .[50] Kvavadze and Ayotants' pollen analysis (Chapter 2b) and Hovsepyan's analysis of grain and chaff remains reveals a highly developed agricultural zone.

At its most extensive, we believe the site occupied 6 hectares. This estimate is somewhat tentative, because during the Soviet period authorities built a hospital in the center of the site, and later Armenian authorities allowed a bank, a petrol station, and a road to be put up along its eastern edge. An illegal orchard, now removed, had been planted in the northeast. In addition, the Soviets had a fence built along the line of the ancient wall and also built a reconstruction of architectural forms near a small wood-frame house of the 1920's and converted the house into a museum. This reconstruction (Figure 1.4), although frequently shown in illustrations, does not represent any ancient reality. It was cobbled together from different buildings at different elevations. So, now, 2.72 hectares remain open of the original 6 or more hectares.

The topography of the site has no doubt changed since its prehistoric occupation (Fig 1.5). Bayburtian, one of its first major excavators (see Chapter 3), believed at first it was a Medieval fortress, because the wall that traced along two sides of the mound and presumably surrounded it was still visible in the 20th century AD.[51] Locals called the site a "kale" or fortress. Sections through ancient strata indicate the mound was more convex, sloping from the probable high point under the hospital. Even in Square K6, the one with the whole section from the current surface to bedrock, the western section did not include the first two strata (see Chapter 3). The north side has the most acute drop down toward the river. The west side looks as if it too might have dropped acutely, although much filling in occurred during the construction of the road and probably hospital outbuildings. It is not possible today to trace the southern or eastern boundary of the original mound.

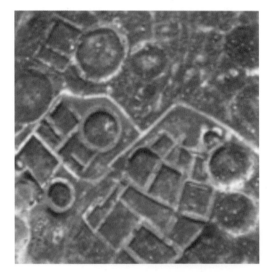

Figure 1.4 Soviet reconstruction of houses. Not likely to represent any contemporary layout.

Dating Shengavit

One of the key questions left unanswered by earlier excavators was the dating and the stratigraphic phases of the site. The question of how to date the Kura-Araxes cultural tradition in the South Caucasian homeland and across its migratory path has been challenging for many decades. In part this is because of a different use of terms like "Bronze Age" and "Chalcolithic." In part it is because there has not been a standard to correlate the various relative chronologies based on pottery typology. Table 1.1 shows how complex this problem has become, especially if one attempts to add in neighboring regions. For years the most widely accepted dating scheme was Sagona's Kura-Araks I-III.[52]

---

50   Hovsepyan 2015.

51   Simonyan and Rothman in press.

52   Sagona 1984.

Figure 1.5. Aerial photograph of Shengavit mound within Yerevan city.

More recently, twelve specialists[53] on the Kura-Araxes gathered in Toronto for a week to address a wide diversity of questions about how to understand the Kura-Araxes cultural tradition, including how to date it.[54] Our conclusion was that there were two periods: KA1 and KA2.[55] This conclusion was based on analysis of many new and corrected radiocarbon dates, as well as some relative chronologies. Tony Sagona, whose health prevented him from attending and would lead to his tragically early death, agreed with this nomenclature by email.

For Shengavit, the dates (Table 1.2) show a clear tendency to place the site within the KA2. In this, Simonyan and Rothman disagree to some degree. Simonyan points to two dates from rooms 5 and 7 (BIN 5526 and 5528) to indicate that the site had a KA1 level. He also recovered three out-of-context painted sherds he attributes to the Mesopotamian Chalcolithic (see Chapter 5e). These, if relevant, would likely put the earliest levels in the early fourth of even late fifth millennium BC. Rothman argues that the three radiocarbon dates from very secure find spots just above the bedrock in Square K6 (BETA 387474, BETA 387469, and UCL 136275) are amazingly tightly clustered, and they all indicate a founding date at the latest of 2885 BC cal. In addition, there are two dates from room 7(g). One is the early date, but the other (BIN 5527) agrees with the dates from above bedrock. It is hard to see how one room (7) could have lasted for over 400 years. Simonyan argues that there was evidence of occupation under his lowest "horizon" from his 2000 season (Chapter 3). Rothman analyzed a few pots of the 1541 diagnostic and 750 body sherds from secure proveniences that fit Badalyan's Elar-Aragats style group that were typical KA1 types, although

53   Stephen Batiuk, Karim Alizadeh, Ruben Badalyan, Philip Graham, Rafi Greenberg, Roman Hovsepyan, Bertille Lyonette, Sarit Paz, Giulio Palumbi, Mitchell Rothman, Savash Sameii, (by e-mail, Tony Sagona).
54   Batiuk et al. 2022.
55   Batiuk et al. 2022.

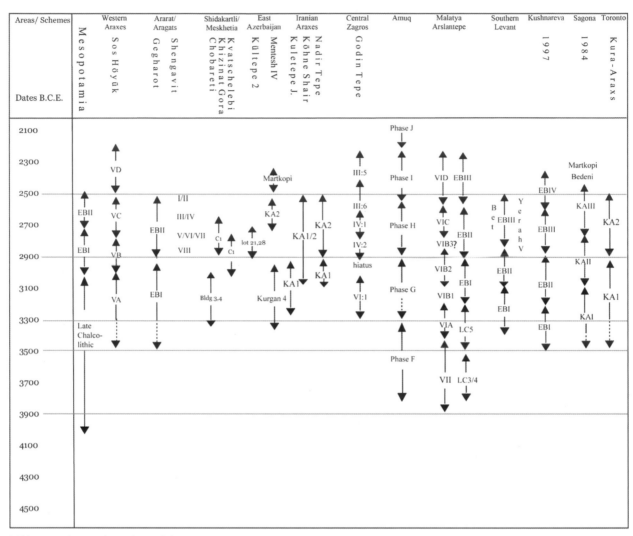

Table 1.1 Relative Chronology of the Kura-Araxes.

there are only a few. The early dates can be explained because they were corrupted. UCL 136276 from meters above the three early dates in K6 gives an early fourth millennium date. This inexplicably early date from a sample inside a clay hearth/ ojagh, can be attributed to its exposure to cigarette ash. The night watchmen clearly were looking at it while smoking before the sample was taken. A similar case is illustrated by a Middle Bronze tomb dug near Lake Sevan. A friend of Simonyan's asked him to run some radiocarbon samples, which gave an age much earlier that the expected late third millennium BC dates. When asked, the friend admitted that his diggers smoked when they were working. In any case, a date for the beginning of the site either way is most likely near or after 3000 BC. Our latest date (BIN 345981), not counting the MB pit in Square J5 (BETA 283206) and a similarly disturbed pit in K6 (BETA 387471), is from the Square M5 room. This date suggests an end of the Kura-Araxes at Shengavit from 2568-2450 BC cal. A Bedeni styled sherd from that context (see Fig 5e. 14) suggests that a date near 2450 BC is consistent with the finds there. In the Near East generally the radiocarbon curve is wiggly for this period, making a finer differentiation within the period from 2900-2600 BC cal. hard to make. Within the KA2, carbon dating cannot give absolutely clear sub-phases.

The georadar survey (see Chapter 4d) confirms that the deposition is three and a half meters over bedrock, as we found in our excavation in Square K6. Nowhere on the site have excavators dug deeper than that.

So, another question is how many phases, horizons, strata, or architectural levels are found within the three and a half meters of deposit. The basic stratigraphic unit is a stratum, a unit with a distinct break in the nature of the fill. An architectural level, as we use it, is a unit that is made up of one or more strata that are associated with one set of architectural remains. A horizon can be an architectural level or a set of architectural levels that share similar architectural or artifactual types. A phase is basically the same as a horizon. So, in the case of Badalyan, "For most of the above schemes, the basis of the

Oxcal v. 4.2.3 Bronk Ramsey (2013) McCall 3 Atmospheric curve

Lab/ number	Locus	BP +/-	BC cal 95.4	Depth *	
Beta 283206	J5 2017	3710/40	2270-1977	10	pit from surface
Beta 387471	K6 1036	3760/30	2287-2044	76	pit into gray surface
LE 672	?	3770/60	2455-2025	?	Sardarian
Beta 387472	K61060	3820/30	2448-2144	166	deep pit ?burned building
Beta 387467	J5 2047	3930/30	2558-2300	167	at base of main building
Beta 345981	M5 24020	3930/30	2568-2300	100	seeds from pit room 2
Beta 328809	M5 24027	3950/30	2617-2488	80	M5 ojagh
Beta 387473	K6 1083	4020/30	2620-2471	93	bricky fill end Building 1 NS wall
Beta 345980	M5 24012	4030/30	2623-2473	80	"cult corner"
UCI 136275	J5 2072	4090/15	2840-2574	146	above timbers room 2 with bone
LE 458	?	4020/80	2871-2307	?	Sardarian
Bin 5527	OS11 21	4040/10	2881-2306	65	Room 7 (g)
Beta 345982	M5 24027	4080/30	2857-2496	100	M5 ojagh
Beta 387468	K6 1155	4140/30	2874-2621	334	Building 6 floor 4 layers from bedrock
Beta 283205	K4/L4	4147/40	2876-2586	245 ?	round building
Beta 387474	K61168	4160/30	2880-2632	345	above bed rock
UCI 136275	K6 1170	4185/20	2885-2680	340	above bed rock
Beta 387469	K6 1171	4170/30	2882-2636	350	above bed rock
BIN 5526	OS11 52	4390/100	3366 2790	100	room 7(g)
BIN 5528	OS11 14	4400/100	3366-2876	120-70	room 5(e)
UCI 136276	K6 1125	4960/15	3782-3702	129	ojagh room 5

3600 3400 3200 3000 2800 2600 2400 2200 2200
Calibrate date (cal BC)

Table 1.2 Shengavit radiocarbon dates.

stratigraphic division of the cultural layer the settlements were served only by ceramics and represented by a limited number of samples."[56] Sardarian suggested three horizons,[57] while Bayburtian proposed four. Simonyan, based on his analysis of the depth of building dug by Bayburtian, proposes that Bayburtian's excavation had five architectural levels. K6 had six architectural levels and eight strata. The K6 section (Figure 1.6) illustrates the complexity of these different terms. There appear to be eight distinct strata, including Stratum II, a large working floor that extends over significant parts of squares K6, K5, and J5 and is over 100 m2. This stratum with pits throughout had a series of re-laid floors with some sort of vegetation matting between each re-plastering. So, in this case Stratum I and II equal Architectural Level 1. Architectural Level 1, the final one, contained a large building contemporaneous with the building in Square I14 and with the building that contained the Square M5 ritual emplacement (see Chapter 3). Stratum III, Architectural Level 2, contained two buildings, a square one (Building 2) and a round one with square antechambers (Building 3). Stratum IV, Architectural Level 3, contained a burned Building 4 (square?) over which Building 3 sits, and the rectangular Building 5 at the bottom of a large modern pit. The remaining Strata V-VIII consisted of a series of round buildings, 6a-d, one on top of the other and, from Strata VI-VII, another square Building 7 resting on rubble above bedrock. These represent Architectural Levels 4-6. The re-working of Building 6— each re-working had different sized bricks (see Chapter 3)— Architectural Levels 5 and 6. Residents raised Building 7 in Stratum VII, and it lasts through Stratum VI. This illustrates the complexity of the stratigraphy on the mound as four distinct strata of Building 6 are matched by only three Architectural levels, since Building 7 was whole only during strata 5 (see Chapter 3).

---

56   Badalyan et al. 2015, 225 (translated from the Russian).
57   Simonyan 2015, Chapter 3.

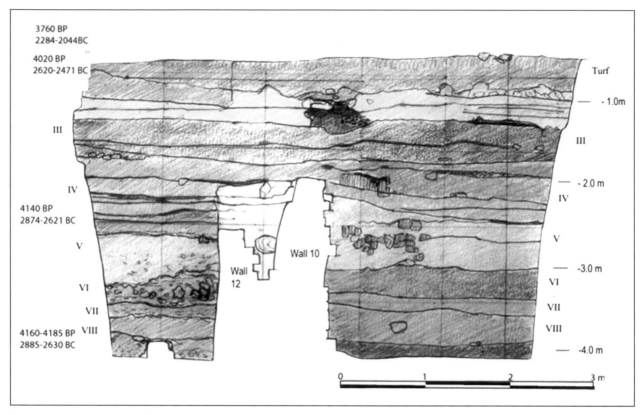

Figure 1.6. Square K6 east balk section.

So, Bayburtian never reached Architectural Level 6, and Stratum I was missing in some areas. In general, as we describe in Chapter 3, the site is so continuously occupied and tightly packed, the sorts of clear demarcation between "horizons" provided by hiatuses does not exist.

Societal Context of Shengavit in KA2

The likelihood that Shengavit was occupied in the KA2 places it in a period of great societal and, as described above, environmental change (see Chapter 2). The KA2 saw significant population growth, especially in the Ararat Plain and adjoining areas, [58] although some sites may have been abandoned and even reoccupied within the KA2, indicating a lower number of occupied hectares.[59] In addition to the growth in the number of sites, individual sites grew in size. The larger sites seem to have been the centers of sets of smaller sites.[60] Many of these central sites were fortified. Walled sites include Mokhrablur and Adablur in the Ararat Plain, Dzyanberd, Shengavit, Shresh Blur, Shaglama, Karnut, and Gudbertka.[61] The citadels at Köhne Shahar (Ravaz)[62] and at Elar[63] were also walled, but not the whole site. The sizeable walls indicate that some, at least temporary, coordinating organization was necessary. Feeding larger population also suggests the need for coordination and storage of significant amounts of staple foods. At Shengavit

---

58   Areshian 2007.
59   Batiuk in press.
60   Areshian 2007.
61   Kushnareva 1997, 55, 61.
62   Alizadeh et al. 2013.
63   Kushnareva 1997, 59.

Simonyan found a series of very large lined storage pits in the northern end of the mound with evidence of grain in them.[64] The estimated volume of these pits would outstrip the needs of the population at the site. The need to intensify production of basic foodstuffs is also indicated by sizeable irrigation works found in the Ararat Valley near Mokhrablur.[65] While the Ararat Valley centers grew, the upland plateaus saw few sites. Areshian[66] proposes that pastoral nomadic peoples occupied that area, although no direct evidence of them exists to date. The salt deposits around the Ararat Valley sites may indicate that their occupants did not plan for appropriate fallow and drainage as they intensified agricultural production. The same sort of problem may have caused the abandonment of other upland sites. Like Southern Mesopotamian sites in the second millennium BC,[67] their fields became so saline that the sites were no longer viable. At that point, and as climate became wetter and warmer, centers were moved to sites like Shengavit and Köhne Shahar. These sites were centers not only of local control. They were also centers of the production of goods and trade. Such specialized production is evident in the walled citadel of Köhne Shahar.[68] Shengavit may, too, have provided agricultural products and other goods for local and more distant populations. One hard to document resource that may have been used as a trade item was salt, large deposits of which lie very close to the site.[69] Yanik Tepe, on the eastern side of Lake Urmia, was also located near a salt source.[70] Salt is essential for both humans and animals.

The Contents of this Volume

Our intent is to investigate all elements of the life of the people who lived at Shengavit in the early third millennium BC. Chapter 2 sets the environmental background of the Shengavit area. The natural environment in which the people of Shengavit lived is essential background. As Adams[71] points out, macro-environments are one thing, but farmers and herders live in micro-climates of their fields, orchards, and pastures. Especially in a region as environmentally diverse as the South Caucasus, ground level analysis is essential to understand the practices of local residents. The results of pollen analysis in Chapter 2 clarify the agricultural, weed, and other plants that were in the environment around the site.

Chapter 3 reviews in more detail the stratigraphy of the site from the 2000-2012 seasons, with comments on Bayburtian and Sardarian's results. In our analyses, we emphasized finds from primary and secondary proveniences. Primary ones are floors of buildings, or clearly marked surfaces in open areas of the mound. Secondary ones are those directly filled by the occupants: trash middens, destruction fill, recent fill over floors, etc.). Tertiary ones are materials moved out of context by construction (for example, terracing or pitting used for constructing mud brick) or by ancient or modern pitting. Explaining our stratigraphy is a basis to establish the quality of the data we use. This material is supplemented in the web archive by reproducing the field notes of square supervisors and many more photographs and drawings than we could ever hope to put in a printed volume.

Chapter 4 presents in detail the built and unbuilt environment of the Kura-Araxes and specifically of Shengavit. As we discussed above, the layout, and the construction of houses reflect deeper mental models of how the people of

64   Simonyan 2002.
65   Areshian 2005, 2007.
66   Areshian 2005.
67   Jacobsen 1982.
68   Alizadeh 2015.
69   Simonyan 2002.
70   Summers 2013.
71   Adams 1981.

Shengavit constructed their world. It also reflects the social and political organization of the site and the area in which the people lived.

Chapter 5 is actually a series of sub-chapters that present the analyses of the economic activities of the residents. What did they produce? How does the production process reflect the deeper social and political organization of the site and its area, what material basis was there for exchange locally and in the larger region? Again, the web archive will include many more details and much more raw data than this printed volume could provide. These include reports on plants and animal utilization, tools and objects made of metal, ceramics, ground stone, and bone. It also includes small finds that can be understood as jewelry, including beads, amulets, hair pieces, and the like.

Chapter 6 investigates the ideology of the people, so important in creating their mental map of their and the divine world. It begins with their use of symbols in ritual. These include the decorations of pots, many of which we recovered from ritual contexts, the description and interpretation of ritual places, and of figurines. The ideology of societal structures is perhaps best symbolized in their treatment of the dead and their ritual practices. This chapter will detail and interpret those practices.

Chapter 7 brings together all the economic, the residential, and the ideological patterns as they reflect economic, social, and political organization. These patterns are essential for telling the full story this ancient community. First, we look at the various functions of each of the major buildings we excavated. Do they indicate anything about occupational specialization, difference in status, differential access to goods? What does Shengavit say about Shengavit as a Kura-Araxes center and about the Kura-Araxes more generally? What prospects are there for the future? What questions do we still need to answer?

The web archive can be found at https://onlinepublications.uchicago.edu/shengavit. It is organized first around the basic information on our fieldwork. These include the field notes from the square supervisors, and photographs and drawings of what we found. The rest contain information on different classes of artifacts with lists, data matrices, photographs, and drawings. The last grouping are articles and books on Shengavit.

References

Adams, Robert McC 1981 *Heartland of Cities.* Chicago: University of Chicago Press.

Alizadeh, Karim, H. Eghbal and Siavash Samei 2015 Approaches to social complexity in Kura-Araxes Culture: A View from Köhne Shahar (Ravaz) in Chaldran, Iranian Azerbaijan. *Paléorient* 41(1):37-54.

Alizadeh, K., Siavash S., Mohammadkhani, K., Heidari, R., and Tykot, R. 2018 Craft Production at Köhne Shahar, a Kura-Araxes Settlement in the Iranian Azerbaijan. *Journal of Anthropological Archaeology* 51: 127–143.

Areshian, Gregory 2007 From extended families to incipient polities: The trajectory of social complexity in the Early Bronze Age of the Ararat Plain, in *Social Orders and Social Landscapes*, edited by L. M. Popova, C. W. Hartley and A. T. Smith, 26–54. Cambridge: Cambridge Scholars Press.

Areshian, G. 2005 Early Bronze Age settlements in the Ararat Plain and its vicinity, *Archaeologische Mitteilungen aus Iran und Turan* 37: 71–88.

Areshian, G., Gasparyan, B., Avetisyan, P., Pinhasi, R. Wilkinson, K., Smith, A., Hovsepyan, R., and Zardaruan, D. 2012 The Chalcolithic of the Near East and South-eastern Europe: Discoveries and New Perspectives from the Cave Complex Areni-1, Armenia. *Antiquity* 86:115–130.

Badalyan. R. 2014 New Data on the Periodization of the Kura-Araxes Culture in Armenia. *Paléorient* 40(2):71-92.

Badalyan, R. and Avetisyan, P. 2007 *Bronze and Early Iron Age Archaeological Sites in Armenia. Volume I Mt. Aragats and Surrounding Region.* Oxford: BAR International Series 1697.

Batiuk, S. in press The Spatial Matryoshka Doll: New perspectives on the settlement dynamic of the Kura-Araxes. Badalyan festschrift.*Aramazd*.

Batiuk, S., Rothman, M.S, Samei, S., and Hovsepyan, R. 2022 Unraveling the Kura-Araxes Cultural Tradition across Time and Space. *Ancient Near Eastern Studies* 59:236-325.

Bayburtian, Y. E. 2011 *The Sequence of the Oldest Cultures of Armenia on the Basis of Archaeological Material.* Yerevan: History Museum of Armenia. (in Russian)

Connor, W.E. and Kvavadze, E. 2014 Environmental Context of the Kura-Araxes Culture. *Paléorient* 40(2):11-22.

Frangipane, M., Di Nocera, G.-M., Andreas Hauptmann, A., Morbidelli, P., M. Palmieri, A., Sadori, L., Schultz, M., and Schmidt-Schultz, T. 2001 New Symbols of a New Power in A "Royal" Tomb from 3 000 BC Arslantepe, Malatya (Turkey). *Paléorient* 27(2):105-139.

Fragipane, M. and Palumbi, G. 2007 Red-blackware, pastoralism, trade, and Anatolian-Transcaucasian interaction in the 4th-3rd millennium BC, in *Les_Cultures du Caucase*, edited by B. Lyonnet, 232–255. Paris: CNRS Editions.

History of the Armenian People 1971, vol. 1, 129.

Hovsepyan, R. 2015 On the Agriculture and Vegetal Food Economy of Kura-Araxes Culture in the South Caucasus. *Paléorient* 41(1): 69-82.

Iserlis, M., Greenberg, R., Badalyan, R. and Goren, Y. 2010 Beth Yerah, Aparan III, and Karnut I: Preliminary comments on Kura-Araxes homeland and diaspora ceramic technology, *TÜBA-AR* 13:245–262.

Jacobsen, T. 1982 *Salinity and Irrigation Agriculture in Antiquity*. Malibu: Undena Publications.

Kalantar, A. 1994 An ancient irrigation system in Armenia, in *Armenia: From the Stone Age to the Middle Ages* (Civilisations du Proche-Orient, Serie 1, Archeaologie et Environnement), edited by G. Karakhanian, 29–35. Neuchatel: Recherches et Publications.

Kavadze, T. and Sagona, A. 2003 On the Origins of the Kura-Araxes cultural Complex, in *Archaeology in the Borderlands: Investigations in Caucasia and Beyond*, edited by Adam Smith and Karen Rubinson, 95-110. Los Angeles: Cotsen Institute of Archaeology.

Khanzadyan, E. 1967 *Culture of the Armenian Highlands in the 3rd millennium BC*. Yerevan (in Russian).

Kleiss, W. and Kroll, S. 1979 Ravaz und Yakhvali, zwei befestigte Platze des 3. Jahrtausends, *Archaeologische Mitteilungen aus Iran* 12: 27–47.

Koşay, H. 1976. *Keban Projesi Pulur Kazisi 1968–70*. Ankara: METU.

Kramer, C. 1977 Pots and Peoples, in *Mountains and Lowlands*, edited by T.C. Young and L. Levine, 91-112. Malibu: Bibliotheca Mesopotamia 7.

Kushnareva, K.Kh. 1997 *The Southern Caucasus in Prehistory*. Philadelphia: University Museum Press.

Kushnareva, K.Kh. 1954 Copper Age Monuments in Nagorno-Karabakh. *Soviet Archaeology* 20: 165-179. (in Russian)

Lyonnet, B., Akhundov, T., Almamedov, K., Bouquet L., Courcier A., Jellilov, B., Huseynov, F., Loute, S., Makharadze, Z., and Reynard, S. 2008 Late Chalcolithic Kurgans in Transcaucasia. The cemetery of Soyuq Bulaq (Azerbaijan). *Archaeologische Mitteilungen aus Iran und Turan* 41:27-44.

Marro, C.,.Bahshaliyev, V., and Berthon. R. On the Genesis of the Kura-Araxes Phenomenon: New Evidence from Nakhichean (Azerbaijan). *Paléorient* 40(2): 131-154.

Munchaev, R. M. 1975 *The Caucasus at the Dawn of the Bronze Age. Neolithic, Eneolithic, Early Bronze*. Moscow: Nauka; 1975. (in Russian).

Palumbi, G. 2008 *The Red and the Black*. Rome: Università di Roma, Sapienza.

Palumbi, G. and Chataigner, C. 2014 The Kura-Araxes Culture from the Caucasus to Iran, Anatolia, and the Levant: Between Unity and Diversity. A Synthesis. *Paléorient* 40(2):247-260.

Poulmarc'h, M., Pecqueur, L. and Jalilov, B. 2014 An Overview of Kura-Araxes Cultural Practices in the South Caucasus. *Paléorient* 40(2): 231-246.

Rothman, M. S 2018 Modelling the Kura-Araxes Cultural Tradition. in *Context and Connection*, edited by A. Batmaz, G. Bedianashvili, A. Michalewicz, and A. Robinson, 125-146. Leuven: Peeters.

Rothman, M. S 2016 Explaining the Kura Araxes. in *Fitful Histories and Unruly Publics*, edited by K. Weber, E. Hite, L. Katchadourian, and A. Smith, 217-257. Leiden: Brill.

Rothman, M. S 2011 Migration and Resettlement: Godin IV Period. in *On the High Road: The History of Godin Tepe, Iran,* edited by H. Gopnick, and M. S Rothman, 139-208. *Toronto:* Royal Ontario Museum/ Mazda Press.

Rothman, M. S 2003 Ripples in the Stream: Transcaucasia-Anatolian Interaction in the Murat/Euphrates Basin at the Beginning of the Third Millennium B.C. in *Archaeology in the Borderlands: Investigations in Caucasia and Beyond*, edited by A. Smith and K. Rubinson, 95-110. Los Angeles: Cotsen: Institute of Archaeology, UCLA.

Rothman, M. S 2002 *Tepe Gawra. the Evolution of a Small, Prehistoric Center in Northern Iraq*. Philadelphia: The University of Pennsylvania Museum Publications.

Rova, E. 2014 The Kura-Araxes Culture in the Shida Kartli Region of Georgia: An Overview. *Paléorient* 40(2):47-69.

Sagona, A. 2014 Rethinking the Kura-Araxes Genesis. *Paléorient* 40(2): 23-46.

Sagona, A. 1984 *The Caucasian Region in the Early Bronze Age*. Oxford: British Archaeological Reports, International Series No. 214.

Sardarian, S. H. 1967 *The Primitive Communal System in Armenia*. Yerevan: Mitk (in Armenian, English and Russian summaries).

Simonyan, H. 2015 Observations of the Armenian-American Joint Expedition of Shengavit. *Fundamental Armenology*. http://www.fundamentalarmenology.am/issues/9/ISSUE-2,-%C2%A0-2015.html

Simonian, H. 2002 The Stratigraphy, Building and Construction Principles of Shengavit. in *The Ancient Culture of Armenia: the Scientific Forum Devoted to Emma Khanzadian's Jubilee*. Gitutyun' Nas, RA, Yerevan.

Simonyan, H. and Rothman, M. S 2015 Regarding Ritual Behaviour at Shengavit, Armenia. *Ancient Near Eastern Studies 52: 1-46.*

Simonyan, H. and Rothman, M. S in press New Data on the Construction and Meaning of the Shengavit Settlement Wall. Badalyan festschrift. *Aramazd*.

Smith, A. 2005 Prometheus unbound: Southern Caucasia in prehistory. *Journal of World Prehistory* 19: 229–279.

Summers, G. 2013 *Yanık Tepe Northwestern Iran, the Early Transcaucasian Period: Stratigraphy and Architecture*. Leuven: Peeters.

Tiratsian, G.A. 1996 *History of Armenian Architecture*. Yerevan (in Armenian)

Whiting, J. and B. Ayres. 1968. Inferences from the Shape of Dwellings, in *Settlement Archaeology*, edited by K.C. Chang, 117-133. Palo Alto CA: National Press Books.

Wilkinson, T. 2014 The Early Transcaucasian Phenomenon in Structural-systemic Perspective: Cuisine, Craft, and Economy. *Paléorient* 40(2): 203-246.

2a | Natural Setting of Shengavit During the Kura-Araxes

Mitchell Rothman

Shengavit is located on the Koytak Plateau of the Lower Province of the Kura-Araxes homeland. The Lower Province runs along the axis of the Araxes River, which flows from Erzurum and the Pasinler Plain in the west through the Ararat Valley into the Mughan Steppe bordering the Caspian Sea to the east. The more important northern tributaries, particularly the Kasakh and Hrazdan Rivers, snake from the highlands, connecting the Lesser Caucasus mountains along the foothills of Mount Aragats to the Ararat Plain and the Araxes River basin. The Hrazdan River originates in Lake Sevan. Shengavit lies on a bluff above the Hrazdan River, which was recently dammed up to create the artificial Lake Yerevan. The Upper Province is defined largely by the Kura River basin and its adjoining highlands.

Moving to the north, the Upper Province is on the southern slope of the Greater Caucasus mountain range.[72] The geography is highly diverse, because the Alpine geo-synclinal region creates many up-thrust and subsidence zones. A series of long narrow valleys, each a distinct ecotone, marks this northern area. A wide valley along the western side of the Kura River, Kvemo Kartli, has a concentration of Kura Araxes sites on the western side of the Kura River (see Fig. 1.1). Shida Kartli on the east side of the Kura River, north of the Tsalka Plateau defines

Figure 2.1. The landscape of the Lower Province.

the western part of this sub-region. A considerable number of Kura-Araxes sites existed there. Surveyors of the lowlands near the Black Sea, ancient Colchis, found no Kura-Araxes sites. The geography funneled travelers along the rivers mostly east and west, with only a few passageways north and south. The Tsalka Plateau marks the place where the Lesser Caucasus Range verges into the Armenian high plateau or Armenian highlands that extend through the current borders of modern Armenia into modern Turkey and Iran.

Geographically, the Armenian highlands are delimited on the west along a line from Muş north to Erzurum, and

---

72   Sagona 1984, 22f.

on the east along a line defined by the western coast of Lake Urmia. The Armenian highlands are divided into three areas. The westernmost are unsubmerged mountain folds. This area is defined by the drainage of the Kara Su and Murat Rivers and the area north of Lake Van in the Ağrı, Patnos, and Kars provinces of modern Turkey. The second and largest area is an undulating, treeless, volcanic plateau 2800 to 3400 meters above sea level. It stretches from the Aparan Plain near Lake Sevan in the east to the Arpa River in the west.[73] The Aragats Mountains lie in its middle. The third area consists of steep-sided basins, the largest of which is the Ararat Plain from 900 to 600 meters above sea level. This was one of the most highly populated area in the time of the Kura-Araxes.[74]

The Lower Province was a system of higher and lower elevation sites. The altitude gradient ranges from 2100 m above sea level (asl) at Gegharot to 990 m asl at Shengavit to below 800 m asl in Naxçivan. However, many settlements were located in the alluvial zones of the Ararat Plain (c. 600–900 m asl), as well as the high intermontane valleys, gorges, and plateaus (1700–2200 m asl). These sites are primarily found in three locations: 1) on natural hills or terraces along the edges of river valleys (e.g., Duzdağı, Gegharot, Ovçular Tepesi, Shengavit, Köhne Shahar); 2) on natural, elevated bluffs, , and volcanic outcrops (e.g. Armavir Blur, Metsamor); and 3) on alluvial flatlands, valley floors, and floodplains (e.g. Aygavan, Jrahovit, Maxta, Kültepe I/II, Mokhrablur, Sev Blur, Dvin, and Voske Blur). All three areas provided residents with easy access to reliable water sources. The choice of bluffs and hilltops may have had the advantage of a more defensible position, although armed conflict is not well documented for the Kura-Araxes. The elevation from Shengavit to Gegharot in the Aragats Mountain area represents a distance of only 75 km, yet the difference in the agricultural and pastoral landscape is evident in their differing preferences in animal breeding crop choice (see Chapters 5a and 5b).

Settlement during KA1 in the Lower Province was primarily concentrated in the Ararat Plain, on the tributaries of the Araxes River (on either side of the river), and in the highlands adjoining Mount Aragats. By the KA2, many of the Ararat Plain sites were abandoned, as occupation shifted to the higher

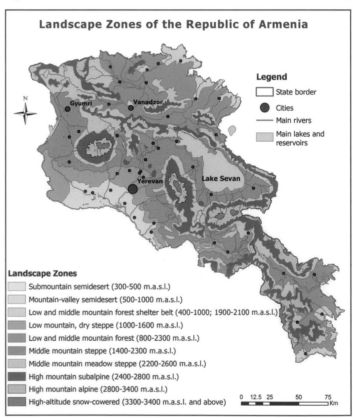

Figure 2.2. Landscape zones of the Republic of Armenia.

terraces around the valley, and farther north into the intermontane plateaus of the Lesser Caucasus Mountains, such as the Kotayk Plateau and the Iğdır, Doğubeyazıt, and Çaldıran highland plains. One possible reason was salinization of the soils in the Ararat Plain bottomlands, making agriculture less productive.[75]

---

73   Badalyan and Avetisyan 2007.
74   Areshian 2007.
75   Areshian 2005.

The area's climate is framed by the mountains at its edge. These mountains encircle a subtropical zone. They block humid air masses, so the higher elevations receive 800 mm of rain annually compared to the lower plains that receive on average 300 mm or less of precipitation per year. The weather is typified by hot, dry summers and cold, wet winters and springs. Climatic factors vary across the homeland region. In the Kotayk Plateau to the north most rain comes in April and May, and there is a dry period from July to September. On the Tsalka Plateau and near Tbilisi most rain falls in May and June, and a typical dry period lasts from December to February.

The soils, too, vary from light brown alluvial soils with little humus in the Ararat Plain to richer and darker ones in the highlands, and black chernozem soils in the high steppe. The region is one of volcanic outcrops. The need to clear volcanic rocks from the soil limits the hectares of field available for farming. Residents utilized the lower elevations for agriculture, horticulture, and animal husbandry, whereas the higher elevation plateaus, intermontane valleys, and the piedmont zone could be exploited for more limited farming, as well as pasture for animal herding. As Figure 2.2 illustrates, the Koytak Plateau is in an area of low mountains, dry steppe, while the Ararat Plain is considered sub-mountain semidesert.

Rainwater for agriculture would have been sufficient in most years. Drought, however, is not uncommon now, nor was it unlikely in the past. Drought would certainly affect the Ararat Valley most of all. For Shengavit, canal construction from the river to the flat at the site's base should have been possible if the height of the water were sufficient (see Figure 1.3). Bucket irrigation would have been an alternative strategy. So, in general,

> "Vegetation in many parts of the region follows an altitudinal zonation, from semi-desert steppes in the lowlands, to xerophytic scrub vegetation in the foothills, grading into oak forests at middle elevations, dense beech forests in the upper forest belt, open oak, pine or birch woodlands at the upper tree line and then into mountain steppes. These patterns vary depending on slope, aspect, climate, soils and past human activity. The highest elevations, where not covered with permanent snow, harbour alpine vegetation. The intermixture of the Euro-Siberian and Irano-Turanian floras combines with steep climatic gradients, rugged topography and a long history geological isolation to create extraordinary levels of plant biodiversity, making the Caucasus a global biodiversity hotspot."[76]

The climate during the Kura-Araxes times was somewhat different than today. Evidence of a drying phase in the Eastern Mediterranean from 3300 to 3000 BC may have affected the South Caucasus. However, after 3000 BC pollen evidence indicates a large-scale increase in deciduous trees in the highlands, which corelates with a warmer and wetter climatic regime. Mountain grasslands with thicker deciduous-coniferous forests existed in the northern stretches of the South Caucasus. Pastureland in the higher areas of the north were pushed out by forest expansion. The Mount Aragats area was much like it is today. Samples from Shengavit indicate a more open environment with fewer trees, perhaps a reason for the increased number of sites in the south in the KA2.[77]

Overall, these changes in climate created a very different set of what ecologists call patchy environments; in this case, ones that are good for agriculture and those that are less optimal for agriculture, but good for animal pasture. These areas were not optimum landscapes for agriculture compared to adjoining lowland regions and limited their carrying capacity.

A key factor in the adaptation of peoples in this topography and climate is transportation. Movement across

---

76   Connor and Kvavadze 2014, 14.
77   Areshian 2007.

the region from west to east is easier than in the Zagros Mountains to the east. However, it is not as easy as in the steppes of Eurasia. Further, the snow and ice that typifies the region limit travel for months at a time. The multiple contemporaneous Urartian fortress centers of the first millennium BC may have been adaptations to this lack of movement and communication.[78]

A more detailed picture of the natural environs of Shengavit analyzed from pollen and non-pollen palynomorphs by Kvavadze and Atoyants follows in section 2b below. They affirm the general conclusion of palynologists and climatologists that after 3000 BC, the climate around the Ararat Plain was warmer and wetter, and the forests of hardwood trees expanded significantly from the earlier KA1.[79]

---

78   Rothman 2000.
79   Connor and Kvavadze 2014.

2b | Palynology of Shengavit

Eliso Kvavadze and Anahit Atoyants

Introduction

One of the tools we have to discover what the environment was like is the analysis of pollens and non-pollen palynomorphs that blew in or are part of the fill in the excavations. The use of palynological analysis in archaeology started in the second half of the last century and initially was not widely used. However, subsequently palynology gradually has taken root in archaeological research and became as a separate discipline: "archaeological palynology."[80] American palynologists first noticed organic remains that archaeologists could find in artifacts.[81] For example, palynological studies of vessel contents were used to clarify issues related to paleodiets. Later, palynologists studied kitchen utensils, the thin coating of skeletal teeth, the remains of organic food left in the abdominal cavity of skeletons, microscopic remains on hand mills and mortars for the same purpose.[82]

Material and Method

From 2008 to 2012, the directors of the Shengavit excavations sent 16 samples for analysis. Missing, unfortunately, were samples taken from the deepest strata, VI-VIII, which might have indicated changes in climate over half a millennium. Seven of the samples are the contents of different types of pottery, four are from deposits of hearths, three are from refuse pits, and two are from the floors of cultural layers of the settlement. The material was processed using standard methods.[83] Part of the material was processed in the Palynological Laboratory of the National Museum of Georgia (Tbilisi), and the other part in the Laboratory of General and Molecular Genetics of the Scientific Research Institute of Biology of the Yerevan State University. We conducted the identification and calculation of the material under the microscope "Olympus BX 43" in the National Museum of Georgia and SWIFT MIOL in the Research Institute of Biology of Yerevan State University. We conducted static processing of pollen and non-pollen palynomorphs (NPP), as well as charting of diagrams using the program Tilia.[84]

Results

At the first stage of research, this by Kvavadze, analyzed two samples from the latest Architectural Level 1 (Stratum II, at Shengavit, samples 1 and 2). Sample 1 came from pot bag 1294, however, Sample 2 is a piece of plaster from

---

80   Bryant and Holloway 1983.
81   Bohrer 1968; Hevly 1970; Bryant and Holloway 1983.
82   Bortenschlager and Oeggl 2000; Kvavadze and Narimanishvili 2010; Moe and Deggel 2013; Kvavadze et al. 2015, 2020.
83   Erdtman 1960; Moore et al. 1991.
84   Grimm 2004.

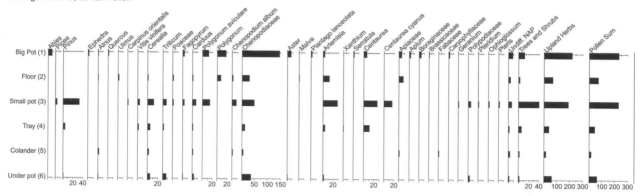

Figure 2.3. Quantities of the Pollen Species Discovered by E. Kvavadze.

Analyzed by Eliso Kvavadze

Shengavit 2010, 2012. NPP

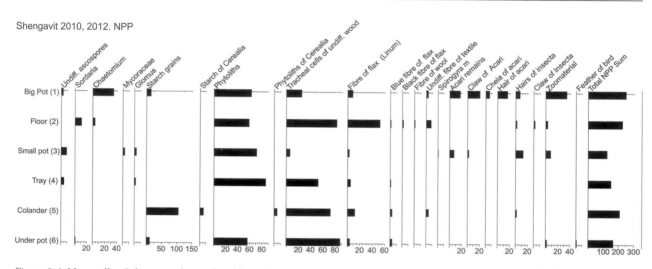

Figure 2.4. Non-pollen Palynomorphs Analyzed by E. Kvavadze

Analyzed by Eliso Kvavadze

the upper floor (Square K6, Locus 1015, Level I, Stratum I). Excavators also sent four samples from earthen vessels of the Shengavit Necropolis. The graphical images of the species appear in two palynological diagrams. On the first of them (Fig 2.3) I show the quantities of the pollen and spores in them, and in the second diagram (Fig 2.4) I graph the quantities of the non-pollen palynomorphs' character.

Following are the analyses of each sample by E. Kvavadze.

Sample 1. This sample was recovered in the Shengavit settlement from a big vessel, Bag 1294 (Square K6, Locus 1035). The total content of the pollen is poor here. We have estimated only 18 taxons of highest plants. There is a scarcity of trees and bushes. We have only detected pollen grains of *Pinus, Ephedra procera, Quercus,* and *Alnus.* Among grass plants Chenopodiaceae are the most common. There is a great amount of weed pollen, such as *Centaurea, Serratula, Fagopyrum, Polygonum aviculare, Polygonum.* Also, I found pollen grains of *Plantago* and *Ranunculus,* as well as pollen grains of *Apium* and other Apiaceae. I haven't found spores of forest fern (Polypodiaceae) in the palynological specters of the samples studied.

Among non-pollen palynomorphs there are a lot of phytoliths among them those of Pooideae. I also detected tracheal cells of wood. In a small number there are fibers of flax textile and spores of *Chaetomium* fungus destroying the flax fibers. I also found undetermined textile fibers. In the specter there are a lot of micro-remains of ticks (hairs, claw, chela) and various insects.

Sample 2. This sample was from the plaster of the Stratum I (sq. K6, locus 1015) and is characterized by the low content of tree (arboreal) pollen. Pollen grains of alder (*Alnus*) and elm (*Ulmus)* are rare. Among grassy (herbaceous) plants there are a lot of Cichorioideae, Chenopodiaceae, and *Artemisia.* There is also pollen of cereals (Poaceae), including cultivated ones (Cerealia). We have also noted such weeds as *Carduus, Malva, Chenopodium album, Polygonum.*

In the group of fossils of non-pollen palynomorphs, phytoliths of cereals are the most numerous; there are also a lot of tracheal arboreal cells (wood parts). There is a very high number of flax textile fibers in the content, among them some dyed fibers. There is a small number of spores of *Chaetomium* fungus. We have found fibers of dyed wool cloth, also there are unidentified fibers of unidentified type of dyed textile. I found almost no micro-remains of insects.

During the excavation of the Shengavit site, excavators sent me six samples for pollen analysis. Several of those samples came from the excavations

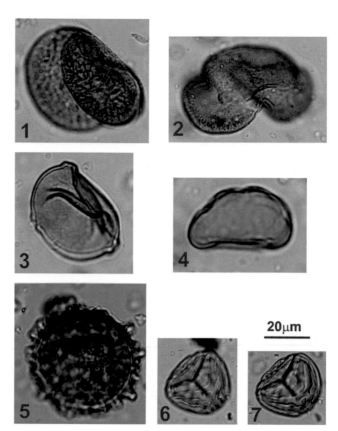

Figure 2.5. Shengavit settlement, small vessel from necropolis, sample No 3. Forest elements of pollen spectra: 1-*Picea*; 2- Pinus; 3-*Carpinus*; 4- Polypodiaceae; 5- *Ophioglossum*; 6,7 – *Pteris*.

of the Shengavit Necropolis (2008). Simonyan's crew recovered Sample 3 from a small vessel and Sample 4 from the bottom half of a vessel. In addition, they took some organic remains from the openings of ceramic sieves. This is Sample 5. Sample 6 they took from organic material from under a ceramic vessel.

Sample No 3 (SHGT, pot, Necropolis, 2008). The contents of this small vessel contained a lot of pollen and plant spores (Fig 2.3). I found fossils of many non-pollen palynomorphs (Fig 2.4). Pollen of pine (*Pinus*) were most numerous among woody and shrub plants (Fig 2.3 and 2.5). There were also pollen of spruce (*Picea orientalis)*, hornbeam (*Carpinus orientalis*) and common grape vine (*Vitis vinifera* (Fig 2.6)). There were a lot of weeds of grain fields in the group of pollen of herbaceous plants (Fig 2.7, 2.8). Among them I found cornflower (*Centaurea cyanus*), lesser knapweed (*Centaurea nigra* type), white goosefoot (*Chenopodium album*), common knotgrass (*Polygonum aviculare*), buckwheat (*Fagopyrum*), and so on. I also observed pollen of wheat (*Triticum* (Fig 2.6)) and other cultivated cereals (Fig 2.3, 2.8). In addition, the palynological spectrum contained a lot of pollen of weeds: wormwood (*Artemisia*) and various kinds of goosefoot (Chenopodiaceae), plumeless thistle (*Carduus*). Spores of forest

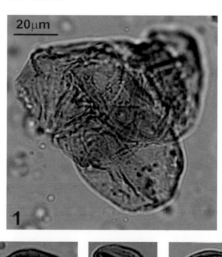

Figure 2.6. Shengavit settlement, small vessel from necropolis, sample No 3. 1- Pollen of *Triticum*; and 2,3,4 - *Vitis vinifera.*

ferns (Fig 2.3) came from the aforementioned vessel. These were also adder's-tongue (*Ophioglossum vulgatum*), brake (*Pteris*), bracken (*Pteridium*), and undefined single-rayed spores of ferns (Polypodiaceae).

Phytoliths of cultivated cereals were greatest in number among the group of fossil non-pollen palynomorphs, followed by insects and ticks (Fig 2.4). I also identified spores of mold fungi (Mucoraceae), *Glomus,* and other

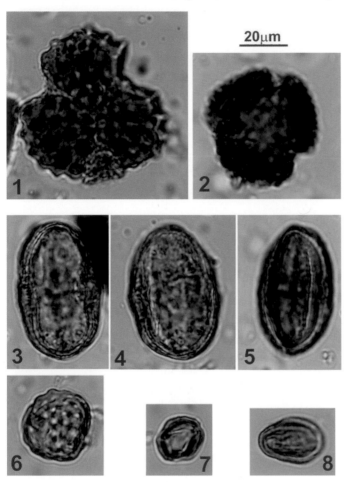

fungi in the vessel, and small number of fibers of flax (*Linum*) textile, tracheal cells of wood and remnants of freshwater algae *Spirogyra.*

Sample 4 (SHGT tray, Necropolis 2008) came from the bottom half of a vessel. The material did not contain much pollen, but there were many fossils of non-pollen palynomorphs. I also found pollen of pine (*Pinus*) and common grape vine (*Vitis vinifera*), but, in general, pollen from weeds of wheat fields were most common, including centaury (*Centaurea*). Pollen grains of wheat and other cereals were also present in the palynological spectrum, but in a small amount. In addition, there were ruderal elements growing in yards, on roadsides, in garbage places, etc. These were absinth (*Artemisia*), cocklebur (*Xanthium*), goosefoot family (Chenopodiaceae), plumeless thistle (*Carduus*).

Phytoliths and the starch from cultivated cereals dominated the group of fossil non-pollen palynomorphs, followed by the charred tracheal cells of wood. Spores of the fungus *Glomus* and other fungi were present in small amounts. I observed some fibers of linen cloth, including those dyed blue.

Figure 2.7. Shengavit settlement, small vessel from necropolis, sample No 3. Pollen of weeds of Cerealia fields: 1-Carduus; 2-Centaurea;3,4,5-Centaurea cyanus; 6-Chenopodium album; 7-Artemisia; 8- Polygonum aviculare.

Sample 5 (SHGT Necropolis 2008) came from the openings of a clay sieve. It is more like a "colander" for straining liquid than a sieve, since it had the shape of a perforated bowl. There are very few pollen grains in the palynological spectrum, but the number of fossil non-pollen palynomorphs was quite large, especially that of starches (Figs 2,4; 2.9-2.12). The only woody plant pollen I discovered was alder (*Alnus*). The group of herbaceous plants included weeds of grain fields. These are plumeless thistle (*Carduus*), white goosefoot (*Chenopodium album*), and other species of goosefoot family (Chenopodiaceae). Fossil non-pollen palynomorphs were abundant with starch grains of wheat and other cultivated cereals, followed by phytoliths of cultivated cereals (Figs 2.4, 2.10, 2.12). Charred tracheal cells of wood remained in considerable numbers. Fibers of flax cloth were significant as well. Fluff of insects and fibers of unidentified cloth also came from this sample. What was this sieve used for? We can deduce that some product made from grains or flour was strained through it, but this product was cooked, as there are many charred microscopic cells of wood in the openings. These would have gotten there from the fire on which this product was cooked (Fig 2.11). Phytoliths and numerous starch grains of cultivated cereals adhering to the sieve are proof that the product was made of grains or flour of cereals. I also found pollen grains of cultivated forms of the cereals themselves (Fig 2.12). Thus, I suppose that most likely the remains came from noodles or pasta, which are made of thin layers of dough, and might have been strained through the sieve.

Sample 6 (SHGT, Necropolis 2008) archaeologists collected this sample from under a ceramic vessel. The spectrum contains no pollen grains of shrubby plants at all, but I observed a lot of pollen of herbaceous plants. Wheat (*Triticum*) and weeds were well represented. This was pollen of centaury (*Centaurea*), plumeless thistle (*Carduus*), white goosefoot (*Chenopodium album*), and buckwheat (*Fagopyrum*). In this sample I also found pollen of other cultivated cereals. Besides, there were many pollen of goosefoot family (Chenopodiaceae) in the palynological spectrum, many of which, as it is known, belong to the edible plants (Fig 2.3). There were pollen grains of ruderal vegetation growing near human dwellings in the sample. I also saw spores of forest ferns.

Charred tracheal cells of wood dominated the group of fossil non-pollen palynomorphs (Fig 2.4), followed by phytoliths of herbaceous plants, including those of cultivated cereals. I observed starch grains of cultivated cereals as well (Fig 2.4). I found fibers of flax and remnants of feathers of birds. Zooepidermis and spores of dung fungus *Sordaria* were extremely rare.

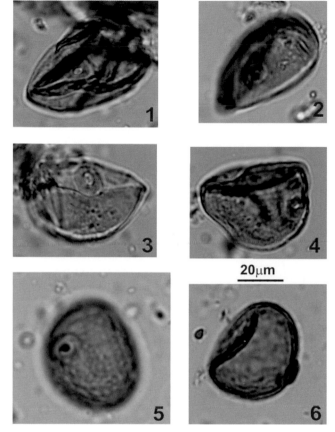

Figure 2.8. Shengavit settlement, small vessel from the Necropolis, sample No 3. Pollen of different type of Triticum.

In the next stage of investigation samples were taken from locus 24013, 24017, 24020, 24022 from the Square M5 of the Shengavit settlement, which were analyzed by Anahit Atoyants. This square is the one that contained the ritual emplacement (see Chapter 6a). The results of the palynological analysis are presented in two diagrams (Figs 2.13, 2.14).

Sample No 1 (M5, Locus 24244, hearth). Overall, I studied 447 pollen and spores. In the sample pollen of herbaceous plants (81%) dominated. The share of the pollen of tree species accounted for only five percent. In the palynological spectrum the pollen of trees includes representatives of the nut family (Fig 2.13), such as walnut (*Juglans regia*), alder (*Alnus*), pine (*Pinus*), and oak (*Quercus*), which were the highest in number.

The herbaceous group were far more numerous. In the composition of the herbaceous plants goosefoot family (Chenopodiaceae) represented 43.5 percent, and the share of white goosefoot or (*Chenopodium album*) was seven percent (Fig 2.14). The latter is noteworthy, because young leaves and shoots of goosefoot are edible both raw and cooked. This plant is also known to be used in traditional medicine for treating sore throat or stomach pains, and as an ingredient in making red paint. The share of the pollen of grain plants (Poaceae) accounted for 29 percent, including five pollen of cultivated grains (Cerealia). These included pollen of families of buckwheat (Polygonaceae), sorrel (*Rumex*), Asteraceae, also pollen grains of wormwood (*Artemisia*), and single pollen of cornflower (*Centaurea*) and groundsel (*Senecio vulgaris*).

I found pollen grains of greater plantain (*Plantago*), which grows on foot paths and other trampled out places. Observers would find it as a leafy weed in pastures. Quite often, I also observed 15 grains of pollen of the flax family (*Linum*), its stalks being used as a fiber in making cloth, and its seeds in making oil. In addition, I found single pollen grains of the families of carnation (Caryophyllaceae), ranunculus (Ranunculaceae), and foxtail lilies (*Eremurus*).

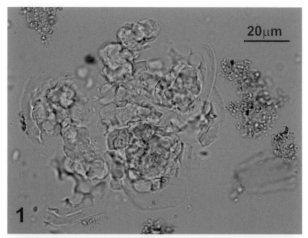

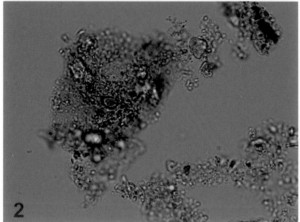

Figure 2.9. Shengavit settlement, necropolis, organic remain from sieve, starch grains.

Among the flora I noted spores of club moss (Lycopodiaceae) and many cells of green algae. In addition to these samples there were a large number of starch grains, possibly mineral particles (perhaps, phytoliths of plants), as well as hairs of insects and their epidermis. There were fibers of flax textile, some even dyed. I also found a large number of pieces of charcoal (parenchimal cells of charred wood).

Sample 2 (Square M5 locus 24245, hearth). In total, I examined 523 pollen grains and spores. Taxonomically, the pollen spectra were rich. Besides pollen, the sample contained a large number of particles of charcoal, other vegetable remains, and epidermal remains of insects. In general, as in the previous sample, pollens of grass plants were the most numerous.

This sample was also characterized by a great number of species of tree pollen. Among them were most often pollen of walnut (*Juglans regia*) and elm (*Ulmus*) trees. In addition, there were pollen of birch (*Betula*), hazel (*Corylus*), lapina (*Pterocarya*), oak (*Quercus*), plantain (*Platanus*), and pine (*Pinus*). Many destroyed microfossils remained in this sample.

Among herbs, pollen of cereals and goosefoot (*Chenopodium*) were the most numerous (36 and 37 percent, respectively). Also, there were pollen of goosefoot family (Chenopodiaceae). Pollen from the buckwheat (Polygonaceae) family was represented by several types, in particular, knotweed (*Polygonum*) and sorrel (*Rumex*). Also, in this spectrum I found fixed pollen of the Asteraceae family, including varieties of wormwood (*Artemisia*) and pollen grains of cloves (Caryophyllaceae), buttercup (Ranunculaceae), flax (Linaceae), rosaceous (Rosaceae), geranium (*Geranium*), plantain (*Plantago*), umbellate (Apiaceae) and legumes (Fabaceae).

Besides pollen, I found spores of ferns (*Polypodiaceae*) and club mosses (*Lycopodiaceae*) in quite large numbers.

Among non-pollen palynomorphs, the most common were phytoliths of herbs and especially cereals as well as unclassified colorless fibers of textiles. In this sample were many microscopic particles of mineral origin. I noted grains of starch from cultivated cereals, which are always present in seeds. A few cells of freshwater algae also occurred. Spores of *Glomus* fungi were included in the spectra. *Glomus* grows on the cultivated loose soil and in this case is a good indicator of agriculture.

Sample No. 3 (Square M5 locus 24246, hearth). Overall, I analyzed 496 pollens and spores. The overall composition, as in the previous samples, was dominated by the pollen of herbaceous plants (89 percent). The percentage of tree species accounted for six percent of pollen.

Among the tree species in the sample there were nine pollen grains of pine and 29 of alder. I saw a single pollen each of spruce, elm, walnut, hazel, and oak.

Among the herbaceous plants the pollen of grasses and goosefoot were most frequent. I found a sizeable number of goosefoot pollen, which suggests that they grew close to the site. It is possible that the plants could be from the vessel itself. I also identified 44 pollen grains of goosefoot (*Chenopodium*). The pollen of buckwheat (Polygonaceae) occurred in small numbers, including knotweed and sorrel.

I recovered pollen of the lily (Liliaceae) family and eremure (*Eremurus*, 5%). The roots and leaves of eremure are now used for dying wool and silk in pink, yellow, and olive-green colors. In the same way, they could be used as the basis for the adhesive, polysaccharide eremure. The young leaves and shoots of eremure are edible. A small number of pollen grains of the Asteraceae families, clove family (Caryophyllaceae), and geranium (Geraniaceae) occurred. In this sample there was fixed pollen of the fire-weed (Onagraceae) family. It is well known that this weed is the first to populate an area after fire. In the Caucasus people used the roots of the fireweed

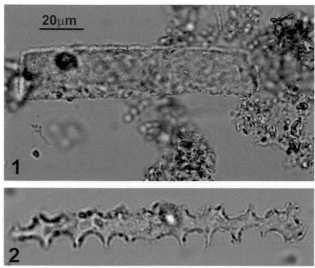
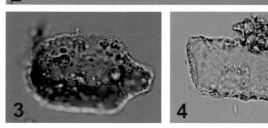

Figure 2.10. Shengavit settlement, necropolis, organic remain from sieve: phytoliths of Cerealia (2) and Pooideae (1,3,4) with starch grains.

to make flour and bake bread. When fermented, it is an alcoholic drink. Young and fresh shoots and roots and leaves form are suitable for making vitamin-rich salads; when boiled they can be used in food instead of asparagus or cabbage.[85] Fireweed has properties of the fiber crop, providing 15 percent of the output of the fiber. The fibers in Russia, for example, were used to make ropes and produce tissues. The lint, which is very rich in the fireweed when in bloom, is used in the manufacture of cotton wool, used as a filler for pillows and mattresses.

Among the cryptogrammic plants—the general composition of them in this version was among the fewest I observed— were club-mosses (*Licopodium*).

In the group of fossils of non-pollen palynomorphs, I observed mineralized particles most frequently, maybe phytoliths of cereals and other representatives of grass. In this sample I also discovered ascospores of *Glomus* and *Sordaria*.

Sample 4 (Square M5 Locus 24282, hearth). In total, I examined 300 pollen grains and spores. There was not enough pollen from tree species in this sample to permit me to define them accurately. I identified pollen of alder, grapes, pine, fir-trees. I recorded the remains of coniferous plants, actually microfossils.

There were a lot of plant epidermis remains. There were parenchyma cells of charred wood; also twisted,

---

85   Thamm 1997.

presumably, linen fibers, dyed pink. In addition, the sample contained a large number of starch grains and mineralized particles (possibly plant phytoliths), as well as insect hairs and their epidermises.

Sample No. 5 (M5 loc.24084, soil). In total, I examined 470 pollen grains and spores. A significant difference of this sample from others was the presence of a large number amount of pollen from cultivated cereals. There was pollen of the families of goosefoot (Chenopodiaceae), buckwheat (Polygonaceae), cloves (Caryophyllaceae), and flax (Linaceae). Just like in the previous sample, many pollen grains were noted here. Thus, in the spectrum of this complex I saw pollen belonging mainly to various weeds. There were single pollen grains of the families of eremure (*Eremurus*), rosaceous (Rosaceae), plantain (*Plantago*), and battercup family (Ranunculaceae).

Sample No 6 (2012, M5, Loc. 24013, altar). I examined 689 pollen grains and spores in all. Pollen of herbaceous plants are the largest group in this sample. Actually, this is true of all the samples I analyzed. The share of pollen of woody species is about four percent and that of spore plants is two percent.

Palynological spectra of the contents stood out by the prevalence of pollen of representatives of the goosefoot family (Chenopodiaceae). What is more, pollen grains differed in type, which speaks to variety of genera and species of this family. Pollen of wild cereals (Poaceae) was the second most frequent. I observed five pollen grains of cultivated cereals. There was a lot of pollen of the aster family (Asteraceae), among them those of wormwood (*Artemisia*), sow thistles (*Sonchus*), groundsel (*Senecio vulgaris*), beggarticks (*Bidens*), saw-wort (*Saussurea*), centaury (*Centaurea*). Pollen of various species of the buttercup

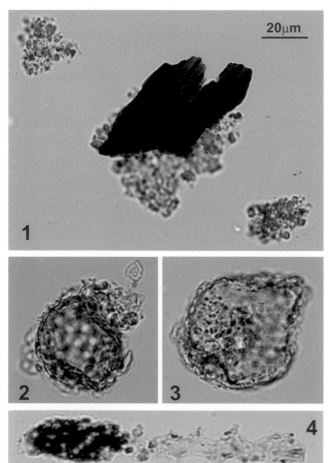

Figure 2.11. Shengavit settlement, necropolis, organic remain from sieve: 1-starch grains with parenchimal cells of wood; 2-pollen of Chenopodiacea with starch; 3-phytolith of Pooidea with starch; 4-phytoliths of Cerealia with starch.

(Ranunculaceae), knotweed (Polygonaceae) and crucifers (Brassicaceae) families was also present. Thus, the spectrum of this complex contains pollen, belonging mainly to various weeds.

The spore-pollen spectrum was also characterized by the presence of pollen of woody species. These included pine (*Pinus*), spruce (*Picea*), alder (*Alnus*), birch (*Betula*) and elm (*Ulmus*).

Ground pines (Lycopodium) and ferns (Polypodiaceae) were rarely observed in the spore group. I found many fossil non-pollen palynomorphs in the form of of phytoliths of cereals and other herbaceous plants. The sample included unidentified species of spores of mold fungi (Mucoraceae). There were many microscopic particles of mineral origin, various parenchymal cells of plants, that is, starch grains. Remnants of green algae existed. Besides that, fibers of flax cloth were numerous as well. Many of them are twisted, but colorless.

Sample No7 (2012, M5, Loc. 24017, pit No. 3). I identified 515 pollen grains and spores here. The palynological spectra of the contents of the Sample No. 7 is characterized by a large amount of pollen of woody and spore plants, in comparison with the spectra of the previous samples. Herbaceous plants account for 79 % of the spectrum.

The woody species were represented by a varied composition of different families of trees and shrubs. I observed alder (*Alnus*), pine (*Pinus*), spruce (*Picea*), and alm (*Ulmus*). I noted pollen of grape vine (*Vitis vinifera*), as well as isolated cases of pollen grains of fir (*Abies*), oak (*Quercus*), and walnut (*Juglans*).

Poaceae was most numerous among herbaceous plants, among which were eight pollen grains of cultivated cereals. There was also a lot of pollen of the goosefoot (Chenopodiaceae), knotweed (Polygonaceae), and aster (Asteraceae) families. In the aster family (Asteraceae), plants of the species *Senecio vulgaris* occurred. It is an invasive weed and is most often found on row and grain crops in gardens and vineyards. There was also pollen of the buttercup family (Ranunculaceae) or rather the genus meadow-rue (*Thalictrum*). I also note the discovery of pollen of the rose family (Rosaceae). Pollen grains of Brassicaceae, Apiaceae, *Turgenia*, *Eremus*, *Linum* occurred in isolated cases.

In another category, I identified spores of ferns (*Polypodium*) and ground pines (*Lycopodium*). Of the group of fossil non-pollen palynomorphs, I found green algae (Chlorophyta), spores of the fungus *Glomus*. In archaeological material, *Glomus* is an indicator of cultivated soil or soil erosion. Spores of mold fungi (Mucoraceae) were numerous. There were also a lot of phytoliths of cereals and other herbaceous plants among the fossil non-pollen palynomorphs. Charred parenchymal cells of wood were in the sample

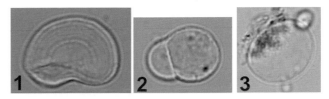

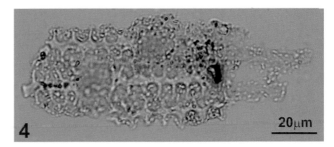

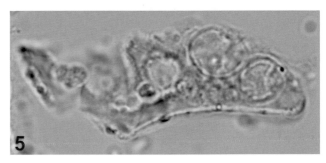

Figure 2.12. Shengavit settlement, necropolis, organic remain from sieve: 1,2,3,5-starch of Triticum; 4-phytoliths of Triticum.

in great numbers. Microscopic particles of the epidermis of cereals were also present. The ancients likely stored grains of cultivated cereals in this pit.

Sample N 8 (2012, M5, Loc. 24020, No. 5 stone lined pit in adjoining room). I counted 519 pollen grains and spores from this sample. There was a low content of pollen of woody and spore plants here. I identified pollen grains of pine (*Pinus*), walnut (*Juglans*), hornbeam (*Carpinus*), alder (*Alnus*), and hazel (*Corylus*). Pollen from alder, which mainly grows in floodplain forests, was the most common.

The goosefoot family (Chenopodiaceae) dominated the herbaceous plants in the sample. Garden orache, which is a weedy plant found in orchards, was identified up to species level. The rest of the pollen varied both in size and in number of spores, indicating that it belongs to other genera of this family. Pollen of the representatives of the knotweed family (Polygonaceae) is present in a small quantity, including that of knotgrass (*Polygonum*) and sorrel (*Rumex*). In addition, I identified pollen of the aster family (Asteraceae), including that of the genus ragwort (*Senecio*) and the species of common groundsel (*Senecio vulgaris*), as well as wormwood (*Artemisia*). Also occurring were pollen of the plantain (Plantaginaceae) and carnations (Caryophyllaceae). I recorded pollen of foxtail lilies (*Eremurus*) as well.

Mineralized particles, phytoliths of cereals and other herbaceous plants, were most numerous in the group of fossil non-pollen palynomorphs. Insect hair and epidermis and fibers of linen cloth, including those dyed, also existed.

Sample N9 (2012, M5, Locus 24022, pit). Counted 595 pollen grains and spores in this sample.

Among woody species, I found pine (*Pinus*), walnut (*Juglans*), hornbeam (*Carpinus*), alder (*Alnus*), oak (*Quercus*), elm (*Ulmus*), joint-pine (*Ephedra),* and common grape vine (*Vitis vinifera*).

Knotweed (Polygonaceae) and goosefoot (Chenopodiaceae) families were most frequent among herbaceous plants. There was a lot of cereal pollen: namely, that of wheat (*Triticum*) and other forms of cultivated cereals (Cerealia). Pollen of representatives of the aster (Asteraceae) and pink (Caryophyllaceae) families is five percent. There are rare instances of pollen grains of the buttercup (Ranunculaceae), rose (Rosacea), foxtail lilies (*Eremurus*) families.

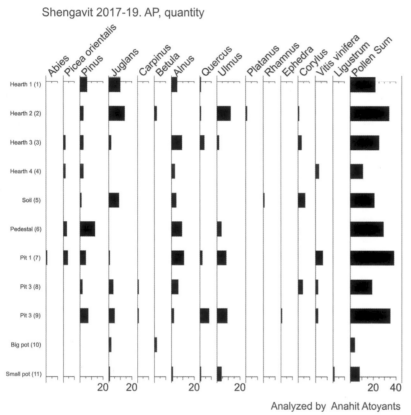

Figure 2.13. Quantities of Species from Samples Analyzed by Atoyants.

Among spore plants, I noted rare spores of ferns (*Polypodium*) and ground pines (*Lycopodium*). From the non-pollen palymorph group came the remnants of green algae. This may indicate a damp place, that is, moisture could have been accumulated here, which would have been a favorable environment for developing of these representatives. Phytoliths of herbaceous plants were most common among the non-pollen palynomorphs. I found early undyed, unidentified textile fibers as well. This sample contained many microscopic particles of mineral origin, siliceous sand. The preparation is polluted with the coal residues.

Sample NN10, 11. I examined the pollen samples from two samples of vessel contents from the buildings of Shengavit. Both samples contained pollen sufficient for the statistical processing. Apart from pollen, the samples contained a large amount of other plant remains and coals. All pollen were poorly preserved and highly mineralized, which in many cases did not make it possible to identify pollen reliably. The most frequent pollen was from the goosefoot family (Chenopodiaceae), which has very characteristic and noticeable diagnostic features, and allowed me to determine its association reliably. In both samples, this pollen was most common in palynological spectra, accounting for 86 percent in the large vessel and 68 percent in the small one (Fig 2.13, 2.14). The pollen detected varied both in size and in number of spores; this was the proof of its belonging to different genera of the family. Accumulations of this pollen occurred rather often (Fig 2.14), testifying to the presence of the flowers of this plant. Lumps of glued pollen grains are found only in flowers. Lumps of pollen grains in an archaeological vessel diagnose the presence of honey, or a honey drink.[86] Apart from pollen of the goosefoot family (Chenopodiaceae), in both

---

86   Kvavadze 2016; Kvavadze et al. 2020.

samples I identified pollen of the chicory (Cichorioideae) and aster (Asteroideae) subfamilies, including the genus centaury (*Centaurea*). Pollen of the carnations (Caryophyllaceae), celery (Apiaceae), crucifers (Brassicaceae), and rose (Rosaceae) families were present in small amounts. Pollen of the knotweed family (Polygonaceae) appeared frequently, but its amount in the small vessel was much higher. Almost all representatives of the knotweed family are melliferous (produce honey). For example, pollen of sorrel (*Rumex*), which is melliferous, was contained in the small vessel. Along with it, the spectrum contained a lot of pollen of such melliferous plants as Centaurea, Apiaceae,

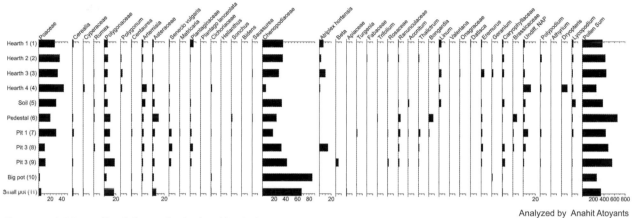

Figure 2.14. Non-pollen Palymorphs Analyzed by A. Atoyants

Rosaceae, and Asteraceae. Privet (Ligustrum) is a wonderful melliferous plant as well, pollen of which occurred in the small vessel (Fig 2.14). Based on these facts, the small vessel probably served to store honey.

As for the large vessel, people kept either groats of the representatives of the goosefoot family in it, or a porridge groats was cooked in it.

Discussion

Overall Climatic Pattern

The results of the palynological study enable us to reconstruct both the paleoclimatic conditions and the ancient landscape in the environs of the Shengavit settlement. In the era of the Kura-Araxes, climatic conditions here, as has already been noted above, were considerably warmer and more humid in comparison with the present day. Climate warming had a global character at that time and spread not only throughout the South Caucasus, but also across a considerable part of Eurasia as well.[87] The existence of viticulture around the Shengavit settlement at an altitude of 800 m above sea level was possible because of the warm climate. Both walnut and hazel groves existed across a wide area 5000 years ago; they are thermophilic plants: that is, ones that thrive at higher temperatures. The existence of walnut and hazel groves here is evidenced by material from the palynological study of lacustrine-marsh sediments of the Vanevan section (Armenia), located at an altitude of 1898 m above sea level.[88] In the era of the Kura-Araxes culture in the territory of neighboring Georgia walnut groves and viticulture were widespread in the mountains of Javakheti and Meskheti at altitudes of 1800 above sea level and higher.[89]

---

87   Kvavadze and Connor 2003; Connor and Kvavadze 2008, 2014; Connor 2011; Kakhiani et al. 2013; Sagona 2014, 2018.
88   Leroyer et al. 2016.
89   Kakhiani et al. 2013; Kvavadze et al. 2020.

An important argument in favor of the existence of the warm climate is provided by the archaeological material, in which pollen of broad-leaved tree species such as hornbeam, plane-tree, oak, elm, and spores of forest ferns (*Ophioglossum vulgatum, Pteridium, Athiriun*) characteristic of thermophilic, broadleaved forests are evident. According to palynological data here, in addition to broad-leaved mountainous forests, a significant territory was occupied by floodplain forests such as the alder trees that grew around lakes and along river valleys. In the nearby mountains grew birch and coniferous trees, such as pine, spruce and fir. The existence of similar forests in Armenia 5000 years ago is also evidenced by the results of palynological study of swamp sediments of the Vanevan section.[90]

The leveled relief and fertile soils of the environs of the Shengavit settlement, formed on bedrocks of volcanic origin, contributed to the development of agriculture along with favorable climatic conditions. Agriculture must have been of the slash-and-burn type, where farmers burned off forests to prepare fields.

Details from Samples

We have learned a lot from the individual samples. The ceramic vessel in Square K6 Locus 1035, Bag 1294 (Sample 1) was mainly used for storing groats of the goosefoot family. A similar use for a vessel is evident in M5 Sample 10/11. Both the abundance of pollen of these plants and the remains of insects and ticks, which eat stored cereals, confirm this conclusion. An analogous spectrum was also evident in the small vessel from the Necropolis (Sample 3). This ceramic vessel was filled with dry, raw grains during burial, since in the spectrum, along with pollen of wheat and other cultivated cereals, their phytoliths are present in abundance. We recovered the remains of insects and ticks, which destroyed the wheat in the vessel. Only with the help of palynology could we have discovered their microscopic particles, invisible to the naked eye.

In another sample of the half vessel (Sample 4), discovered in the Necropolis, participants put sweet wheat porridge cooked with grape juice into the vessel during the burial of the deceased. Grape (*Vitis vinifera*) pollen grains, which are always present both in the grape juice and grape wine, indicate this.[91] A good argument for determining the presence of porridge in a vessel, apart from pollen of cultivated cereals, is the abundance of their phytoliths and charred cells of wood, which wind up in the vessel in the process of cooking porridge over an open fire.[92] Porridge made of wheat was also present in the sample No 6, taken from under the ceramic vessel. Goosefoot was mixed into this porridge (Fig 12.3). Phytoliths of cultivated cereals and charred cells of wood represented the highest percentage of the palynological spectrum here as well.

The palynological spectrum of organic remnants from the sieve in Sample 5 is extremely interesting. The ancients boiled noodles made of wheat flour and strained them through the sieve. Starch, which is always contained in flour, remained in the openings of the sieve.[93] Phytoliths of cereals, also contained in flour, occupy second place in terms of percentage. There were many charred tracheal cells of wood in the palynological spectrum of organics from the sieve and noodles from the same stove or fire over which the porridge was cooked. Evidence existed for grains of flour starch and dough, stuck both to wood cells and to phytoliths of cereals and plant pollen (Fig 2.11 and 2.12). Some fibers of flax were also polluted with starch.

The results of the palynological study of deposits from the bottom of stoves, or hearths (Samples 1-4) and refuse pits (Samples 7-9) analyzed by Atoyants, are quite interesting and rich. In the spectra from the bottom of hearths

---

90   Leroyer et al. 2016.
91   Rosch 2005; Kvavadze et al. 2010, 2014, 2019; McGovern et al. 2017.
92   Kvavadze et al. 2012.
93   Torrence and Bartom 2006.

existed the largest percentage of wood pollen, which entered the stove together with wood, branches of trees and bushes, and their brushwood. Shells of walnuts, hazelnuts, and other household remains were also thrown into the stove fire. Because of this, there is much walnut pollen in this spectrum. Elm-tree wood predominates in its content. Pine wood only occurred in the hearth spectrum. The presence of alder pollen, which is a good fuel, was rather high as well. Analysis showed pollen grains of spruce, pine, birch, and oak that apparently got there from wood for burning.

The fact that the largest amount of pollen of edible plants and especially parts of the plants on grape vines came from refuse pits, is of great interest. It suggests an idea that stone-lined pits served as storage units, where food could have been kept for rather a long time. There was also a lot of pollen of medicinal herbs in the spectra of these pits. These include, for example, plantain (*Plantago*), sorrel (*Rumex*), and joint-pine (*Ephedra*).[94] Foxtail lilies (*Eremurus*), present among the remains in the pits. They have long been used in folk medicine. Foxtail lilies are used for treating inflammatory disorders.[95] Its vine is also regarded as a medicinal herb.[96] Its dry and crushed leaves treat such illnesses as anemia, epilepsy, allergies, etc.

The analyzed palynological samples of the contents of the vessels and refuse pits, first of all, reflect the type of human activity, in which agriculture prevailed. They also contain information on human diet in the era of the Kura-Araxes culture. Goosefoot groats or grains of wheat and other cultivated cereals were stored in large ceramic vessels at the Shengavit settlement. The results of the palynological analysis show that a good indicator of the presence of grain in a vessel, apart from pollen of cultivated cereals and their weeds, is a significant number of phytoliths of cereals in a spectrum. The evidence of the presence of grain in spectra is also microscopic remains of those insects and ticks, which, during long-term storage, destroy grain in a vessel.[97] This is clearly shown in the Figure 2.4 from Shengavit (2010, 2012, NPP).

Pollen of elements of horticulture and viticulture also testifies to the strong development of agriculture. Of all the samples analyzed, almost everywhere pollen of walnut, hazelnut, as well as pollen grains of weeds characteristic of cultivated fields, existed. It should also be noted that pollen of common grape vine occurred in almost half of the material examined. This also indicates that viticulture was practiced in the surroundings of the Shengavit settlement during the Kura-Araxes. Viniculture would have been impossible without warm climatic conditions.

In all likelihood, flax cultivation was developed at a high level; that would also have been possible only in a humid climate. This is indicated not only by the abundance of fibers of flax textile, but its pollen grains as well. The paucity of wool fibers may or may not mean that the ancients wore woolen cloth less frequently than flax-based cloth.

Cattle raising is present at Shengavit, but sheep/goat raising exceeds that by a wide margin (see Chapter 5a). The spectra contain only a small amount of pollen of pasture plants. Spores of a dung fungus were also present in small numbers. This is significant, because palynological spectra of the present-day soils of pastures in the territory of Armenia, where cattle breeding dominates, differ radically from the spectra of the Shengavit settlement. In the spectra of present-day pastures pollen of wild cereals is most common one, and in the group of non-pollen palynomorphs, spores of fungus *Alternaria* dominate. Here, there are quite a lot of spores of such dung fungi as *Podospora*, *Sporormiella*, *Arnium*, *Cercophora*.[98] Cattle and sheep remained close to the site and were not those of nomadic pastoralists.

---

94   Fortini at al. 2016; Eissa et al. 2013; Abourashed et al. 2003.
95   Gaggeri et al. 2015.
96   Adams et al. 2009, 2012; Hayta et al. 2014.
97   Kvavadze et al. 2015, 2016, 2020.
98   Hayrapetyan et al. 2020.

The pollen evidence therefore paints a picture of an agricultural society with a developed agricultural regime of cereals and a wide variety of other plants used. Fuel was mostly from locally grown trees more than from dung.

References

Abourashed, E., El-Alfy, A., Khan, I., Walker, L. 2003 Ephedra in perspective: a current review. *Phytoteteraphy Research* 17(7): 703-712.

Adams, M., Berset, C., Kessler, M., and Hamburger, M. 2009 Medicinal herbs for the treatment of rheumatic disorders: A survey of European herbals from the 16th and 17th century. *Journal of Ethnopharmacology* 121: 343–359.

Adams, M., Schneider, S. V., Kluge, M., Kessler, M., and Hamburger, M. 2012 Epilepsy in the Renaissance: A survey of remedies from 16th and 17th century German herbals. *Journal of Ethnopharmacology* 143: 1-13.

Areshian, G. 2007 From extended families to incipient polities: The trajectory of social complexity in the Early Bronze Age of the Ararat Plain, in *Social Orders and Social Landscapes*, edited by L. M. Popova, C. W. Hartley and A. T. Smith, 26–54. Cambridge: Cambridge Scholars Press.

Areshian, G. 2005 Early Bronze Age settlements in the Ararat Plain and its Vicinity. *Archaeologische Mitteilungen aus Iran und Turan* 37: 71–88.

Bohrer, V. L. 1968 *Paleoecology of an archaeological site near Snowflake. Arizona.* Ph.D. dissertation, University of Arizona, Tucson.

Bortenschlager, S. and Oeggl, K. (eds.). 2000 *The Iceman and His Natural Environment: Paleobotanical Results.* New York: Springer.

Bryant, V. M. and Holloway R. G. 1983 The role of palynology in archaeology, in *Advances in Archaeological Method and Theory*, edited by D. Schiffer. Volume 6: 191-224. New York: Academic Press.

Connor, S. E. 2011 A Promethean Legacy: late quaternary vegetation history of Southern Georgia, the Caucasus. *Ancient Near Eastern Studies*. Supplement 34. Leuven: Peeters.

Connor, S. and Kvavadze E. 2008. Modelling Late Quaternary changes in plant distribution, vegetation and climate using pollen data from Georgia, Caucasus. *Journal of Biogeography* 36: 529-545.

Connor, S. E. and Kvavadze, E. 2014 Environmental context of the Kura-Araxes Culture. *Paléorient* 40.2: 11-22.

Eissa, T. A. F., Palomino, O.M., Carretero, M.E., and Gómez-Serranillos, M.P. 2013 Ethnopharmacological study of medicinal plants used in the treatment of CNS disorders in Sinai Peninsula, Egypt. *Journal of Ethnopharmacology* 151: 317–332.

Erdtman, G. 1960 The acetolysis method. *Svensk Botanisk Tidskrift* 54: 561-564.

Fortini, P., Di Marzio, P., Guarrera, P.M., and Iorizzi, M. 2016 Ethnobotanical study on the medicinal plants in the Mainarde Mountains (central-southern Apennine, Italy). *Journal of Ethnopharmacology* 284: 208-218.

Gaggeri, R., Rossi, D., Azzolina, O., Leoni, F., Ahmed, K. M., Avanzini, A., Mantelli, M., Gozzini, D., Paolillo, M., and Collina, S. 2013 Anti-inflammatory properties of ethanolic root extract of Eremus persicus (Jaub and Spach) Boiss, a Kurdish herbal remedy. *Journal of Medical Plants Research* 7:1730-1735.

Grimm, E. C. 2004 *T. G. View 2.0.2*, Illinois State Museum, Research and Collections Centre, Springfield, USA.

Hayta, S., Polat, R., and Selvi, S. 2014 Traditional uses of medicinal plants in Elazığ (Turkey). *Journal of Ethnopharmacology* 154: 613-623.

Hayraperyan, N. A., Kvavadze, E. V., Shatilova, I. I., and Gabrielyan, I. G., Bruch, A. W. 2020 Subfossil palynological spectra from the surroundings of the village Tsovinar (Lake Sevan, Armenia). *Biological Journal of Armenia. Experimental and theoretical articles* 3 (72): 52-58.

Hevly, R. H. 1970 Botanical studies of sealed storage jar cached near Grand Falls, Arizona. *Plateau* 42: 150-155.

Kakhiani, K., Sagona, A., Sagona, C., Kvavadze, E., Bedianashvili, G., Massager, E., Martin, L., Herrscher, E., Martkoplishvili I., Birkett-Rees J., and Longford C. 2013 Archaeological Investigations at Chobareti in Southern Georgia, the Caucasus. *Ancient Near Eastern Studies* 50: 1-138.

Kvavadze, E. 2019 Das organische Material aus dem Kurgan Nr. 3 von Ananauri. in *Gold & Wein Georgien sälteste Schätze*, edited by L. Giemsch and S. Hansen. 190-195. Frankfurt: Archaeologisches Museum Frankfurt.

Kvavadze, E. 2016 Palynological study of organic remains from the Ananauri Kurgan. in *Ananauri Big Kurgan N3*, edited by Z. Makharadze, N., Kalandadze, and B. Murvanidze. 156-196. Tblisi: Georgian National Museum Press.

Kvavadze, E., Martkoplishvili, I., and Chichinadze, M. 2020 *Ancient human activity and environment palynological date from Early Bronze Age of Georgia, Caucasus*. Tbilisi: Cesanne Printing House. (in Georgian and English).

Kvavadze, E., Boschian, G., Chichinadze, M., Gagoshidze, I., Gavagnin, K., Martkoplishvili, I., and Rova, E. 2019 Palynological and Archaeological Evidence for Ritual Use of Wine in the Kura-Araxes Period at Aradetis Orgora (Georgia, Caucasus). *Journal of Field Archaeology* 44(8): 500-522.

Kvavadze, E., Jalabadze, M., and Sagona, A. 2016 Tetritskaro (Nadarbazevi) Burial Mound 2: Bread, Ruck and the Bedeni Period. *Proceedings of the International Workshop: Aegean World and South Caucasus*. 128-138. Tbilisi.

Kvavadze, E. Sagona, A., Martkoplishvili, I., Chichinadze, M., Jalabadze, M., and Koridze, I. 2015 The hidden side of ritual: New palynological data from Early Bronze Age Georgia, the Southern Caucasus. *Journal of Archaeological Science: Reports* 2: 235-245.

Kvavadze, E., Martkoplishvili, I., Chichinadze, M., Babaev, I., Kakhiani, K., Gambashidze, I., Chikhladze, V., and Mindiashvili, G. 2012 Non-Pollen Palynomorphs in vessels from archaeological sites – an important index for the reconstruction of human diet. *Abstracts of 5th Workshop on Non-Pollen Palynomorphs*. 31. Amsterdam.

Kvavadze, E. and Narimanishvili, G. 2010 The Palaeolandscapes of the Tsalka Plateau in the Late Pleistocene and Holocene (in the light of palynological data from archaeological and geological material). In Rescue Archaeology in Georgia: The Baku-Tbilisi-Ceyhan and South Caucasus Pipelines, edited by M. Vickers, 573-606. Tbilisi: Georgian National Museum Press.

Kvavadze, E., Jalabadze, M., and Shakulashvili, N. 2010 Arguments indicating the presence of wine in Neolithic pots from Georgia using the method of palynology and chemical analysis. *Proceedings of 33rd World Congress of Vine and Wine 8th General Assembly of the OIV 20-25 June.* Tbilisi (OIV online).

Kvavadze, E. and Connor, S. 2003 Zelkova carpinifolia (Pall.) Dipp. in Holocene sediments of Georgia as a climatic optima signal. *Review of Palaeobotany and Palynology* 133: 69-89.

Leroyer, C., Joannin, S., Austin, D., Ali, A.A., Peyron, O., Olliver, V., Tozalakyan, P., Karakhanyan, A., and Jude, F. 2016 Mid Holocene vegetation reconstruction from Venevan peat (south-eastern shore of Lake Sevan, Armenia). *Quaternary International* 395: 5-18.

McGovern, P., Jalabadze, M., Batiuk, S., Callahan, M.P., Smith, K.E., Hall, G.R., Kvavadze, E., Maghradze, D., Rusishvili, N., Bouby, L., Failla, O., Cola, G., Mariani, L., Boaretto, E., Bacilieri, R., This, P., Wales, N., and Lordkipanidze, D. 2017 Early Neolithic Wine of Georgia in the South Caucasus. *Proceedings of the National Academy of Sciences of the United States of America* 114(48): 10309-10318.

Moe, D. and Oeggl, K. 2013 Palynological evidence of mead: a prehistoric drink dating back to the 3rd millennium B.C. *Vegetation History and Archaeobotany* 23(5): 515-526.

Moore, P.D., Webb, J.A., Collinson, M.E. 1991 *Pollen Analysis.* Oxford: Blackwell Scientific Publications.

Piperno, D. R. 2006 *Phytoliths: A Comprehensive Guide for Archaeologists and Paleoecologists.* New York: Alta Mira Press.

Rosch, M. 2005 Pollen analysis of the contents of excavated vessels- direct archeobotanical evidence of beverages. *Vegetation History and Archaeobotany* 14:179-188.

Rothman, M. S 2000 Environmental and Cultural Factors in the Development of Settlement in a Marginal, Highland Zone. In *The Archaeology of Jordan and Beyond: Essays in Honor of James A. Sauer,* edited by L.E. Stager, J.A. Greene, and M.D. Coogan, 429-43. Winona Lake, Ind: Eisenbrauns.

Sagona, A. 2014 Rethinking the Kura-Araxes Genesis. *Paléorient* 40(2): 23-46.

Sagona, A. 2018 *The Archaeology of the Caucasus: From Earliest Settlements to the Iron Age* (Cambridge World Archaeology). Cambridge: Cambridge University Press.

Thamm, E.A. 1997 On the anti-inflammatory effect of alcoholic extracts of narrow-leaved fireweed. *Abstracts of the 4th International Conference on Medicinal Botany,* 489-490. Kiev.

Torrence, R. and Bartom, H. (eds.) 2006 *Ancient starch research.* Walnut Creek, California: Left Coast Press.

3 | The History of the Shengavit Excavation, Architectural Remains, and Stratigraphy

Hakob Simonyan and Mitchell Rothman

The archaeological recognition of Kura-Araxes cultural remains began over 150 years ago. In 1869 in the surroundings of the village of Zaglick workers uncovered the first tomb of this culture during the exploitation of lime mines.[99] Archaeologists discovered artifacts of the Kura-Araxes culture in 1879 in a tomb from the mound of Armavir,[100] in 1887 in the village of Metechli in Kars province,[101] in 1893 on the western slope of Aragats mountain,[102] and in 1897 in Nagorno-Karabakh.[103] Lalayan discovered Early Bronze Age sites in 1904 at Mokhrablur, in Naxçivan, at Shresh Blur in the village of Nizh in 1913, and at Vardashen in Noukhi region, as well as in on the western shores of Lake Sevan.[104]

Shengavit Excavation History

"In 1935 quarry workers in search of road fill excavated three areas. In one of the diggings the workers suddenly came across a stone wall, which they destroyed. In the back dirt there was a lot of broken pottery and several fragments of clay hearths. The rumor reached the museum workers, and in the spring of 1936 the site was inspected and once again registered by them as an ancient city-site of Shresh Blur type.

Taking into consideration the scientific significance of the study of a city-site of this type, the Department of the Preservation of Monuments decided to carry out trial excavations, which began on June 14, 1936."[105]

Bayburtian was in charge of the expeditions of the Committee for the Preservation of Historical Monuments.[106] In three seasons of work spanning 1936-38, Bayburtian determined that it was a prehistoric site with a culture he called "Shengavitian."[107] His work was stopped, because the Soviets accused him of anti-government activities. He was transferred to Moscow and later died in Russia. His fieldnotes[108] and a sample of his finds found their way into the National History Museum (see his areas of excavations in Fig 3.1). In 2011, the Institute of Archaeology and Ethnography of Armenia published Bayburtian's dissertation draft which had been stored at the National History

---

99   Kuftin 1944.
100   Kuftin 1944; Munchaev 1975; Lalayan 1919.
101   Kuftin 1944, 93, fig. 40, tab. XVII1; Munchaev 1975, 15.
102   Marr 1934 tab. VII, fig. 8; Munchaev 1975, 15.
103   Piotrovsky 1949 c. 39; Kushnareva (1954) XXI, 165-167; Munchaev (1975), 15.
104   Lalayan 1919, 38, 43-44; Lalayan 1931.
105   Bayburtian fieldnotes.
106   The full dissertation published in Russian by the Institute of Archaeology in 2011 as Bayburtian (2011).
107   Bayburtian 2011, 26-37.
108   see them in the web archive.

Museum.[109] The artifacts he excavated are housed there, as are his field notes, which are mostly represented in his dissertation.

In 1958 Sandro Sardarian began the excavations again. Pictures exist (not currently available to us) in the archives of the small Shengavit Museum showing him digging while the Soviets were building a hospital in the middle of

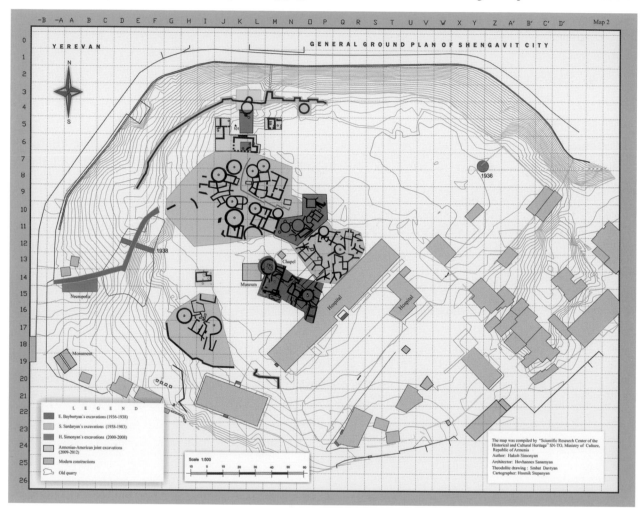

Figure 3.1. Topographic map of Shengavit Mound with areas excavated by various teams.

the mound. He and his son continued this work until 1964 and again from 1965-1983.[110] Much of the time he used the site to train Yerevan State University students. Sardarian's strength was as a synthesizer, and his works have covered a wide range of archaeological cultures in Armenia. He brought many different materials to the Shengavit Museum, which was, in a way, his personal repository. Many of these potsherds and other finds were moved to the Erebuni Museum; they were all classified as from the site of Shengavit, although some clearly were not. A guard at the Shengavit museum, who dug with him, told us that Sardarian only kept big or beautiful potsherds and other artifacts. So, what is housed at the Erebuni Museum and to some extent at the Yerevan City Museum and at the National History Museum do not represent a full sample of what he unearthed. Although rumors about his fieldnotes have

---

109   Bayburtian 2011.
110   Sardarian 1967, 171-182.

circulated for years, none have ever appeared. At the Erebuni Museum[111] the catalog sometimes states "1 meter down" or "2 meters down," but that is all. His daughter offered us notes of where he dug, but not the stratigraphy. She also offered us drafts of his two books, the latter of which she wrote from these notes.[112] Sardarian dug more area than any other excavator (see Figure 3.1), but we know little about the contexts from which his finds came. Ruben Badalyan et al. completed a catalogue of the Shengavit collection in the National History Museum, consisting of Bayburtian's and some of Sardarian's collection.[113] Parts of Sardarian's collection are also housed at the Erebuni Museum, the Shengavit Museum, and at the City Museum.

The site Sardarian found was covered with trees and bushes (Fig 3.2). In the earlier part of the 20th century AD, the top of the mound housed a series of small workers' cabins, the one that remained became the small museum for the site. In 1938 "the surface of the settlement is strewn with river pebbles and fragments of ancient pottery. From the western side you can see the traces of the fortress wall of unprocessed stone blocks laid in one row, and over the entire

Figure 3.2. Shengavit mound in the 1950's.

area circles of stones are barely visible, leaving the impression of cromlechs or burial places. In early spring and late autumn, when the settlement is covered with young grass or exposed, these circles remain bare and clearly visible."[114]

The Soviets built a hospital in the center of the mound, partially on top of Bayburtian's excavations, and various buildings for use of the hospital (Fig 3.3). Locals built two restaurants on the northern edge of Lake Yerevan, and a bank and gas station on its southern edge. An illegal garden in the northeast destroyed another approximately 200 m². Thirty-five percent or so of the original mound is available for excavation. As mentioned, the Soviets established the small Shengavit Museum and cemented a sample of round houses, used to illustrate the site and built cement walkways. Based on the depth of some of the exposed sides, these houses were not likely occupied contemporaneously. No such plan ever existed at Shengavit.

Figure 3.3. Shengavit mound 2021.

Since 2000 the expedition of the Historical and Cultural Heritage, Scientific Research Center, headed by Hakob Simonyan, continued the study of the site. The excavations began in 2000 with a re-excavation and expansion of one of Sardarian's trenches near the small museum to determine whether Sardarian's 3 phases fit the actual stratigraphy.[115] Simonyan also worked in squares K5, K/L 3/4, L6 nearer the northern edge of the mound, and in an necropolis

---

111   Our attempt to document the finds at the Erebuni Museum were abandoned due to administrative problems at the museum.
112   Sardarian 1967, 2004.
113   Badalyan et al. 2015.
114   Bayburtian 2011.
115   Simonyan 2015.

Figure 3.4. Shengavit Building 2 from Bayburtian excavations.

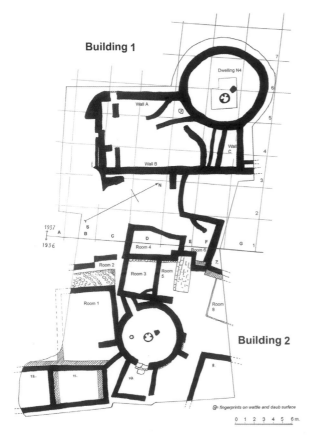

Figure 3.5. Excavations of Bayburtian 1936-37.

beyond the wall and down the western side of the mound's slope.[116] We believe that the multiple-person graves excavated by Sardarian are from this necropolis area.[117]

In 2009 Mitchell Rothman joined Simonyan. The goal was finally to publish the remains of the site. Few Kura-Araxes sites in all of the South Caucasus have been fully documented and published. Without that, progress on understanding this important ancient cultural tradition and societal type is not possible. What was apparent to Simonyan and Rothman was that some additional excavation was necessary to give a context to earlier material. Only Bayburtian had a complete sequence from the top to bedrock, but his description does not permit a precise understanding of the stratigraphy. Finer stratigraphic control had to be extended to a wider area than Simonyan's team had dug in the earlier years. Over three digging seasons in 2009, 2010, and 2012 these goals were fulfilled. In Square K6, supervised by Rothman, the team reached bedrock (see below). In J5 a team supervised by Dan Rahimi and then by Armine Hayrapetyan opened a stratigraphically comparable series of levels and excavated an important building. Kgaren Tseretsyan supervised the continuation of earlier excavation in squares K/L 3/4. A team that was tasked with opening more tombs in the Necropolis only reached the top of the tomb in the last few days of the season. Another team from the Geophysics Department at Yerevan State University directed by Mikayel Gevorgyon and Raffie Durghayah conducted a geo-radar survey (see Chapter 4c) before digging began in 2012. Arkhady Karakhanyan begun that project, but sadly passed away before it was completed. That survey identified a number of "hot spots." Based on that georadar survey, excavation in two identified "hotspots," Squares I14 and M5, yielded very important results. Hakob Simonyan with the aid of Levon Mkrtchyan, and Meri Safaryan supervised excavations in these squares and added much new information.

In the following a number of terms related to stratigraphy will be used. Stratum defines a major change in the nature of the fill. Architectural level is a stratum or strata that is associated with a single building levels superimposed

---

116   Simonyan 2002.
117   Sardarian 1967, 2004.

on top of other buildings. So, a single architectural level may contain more than one stratum. A horizon, sometimes called a phase, are one or more architectural levels that are lumped together based on the cultural style content of the remains. So, a horizon is, for example, all the architectural levels with small, free-standing round houses, as opposed to all those with round houses associated with square outhouses or open courtyards. The first two terms, stratum and architectural levels are stratigraphic links to particular time periods. Horizon or phase lumps architectural levels according to common artifact style or cultural changes.

Shengavit, because it's architecture is so tightly packed and one stratum sits immediately on top of another, can be confusing. It is less like a layer cake than a circular staircase in which at times stratigraphy seems to mix levels.

Excavations of Y. E. Bayburtian

In 1936 when Bayburtian began his excavations many round buildings were evident in the short grass. The pottery was similar to that he encountered at Shresh Blur, Kültepe I, and Franganots; that is, material of the KA2 period after 3000 BC. He claims that there were three architectural levels of round buildings, but he noted many re-buildings. One building he described as having an 80 cm high wall. Based on the K6 deep sounding, the site was very tightly packed, and the odds of finding an 80 cm high wall that was a single architectural level are few (Fig 3.4). Building 1 is drawn as if it were contemporaneous with the surrounding walls of square enclosures. That conclusion does not match the pictures or descriptions we have. The square rooms of Building 2 (Fig 3.5) are actually

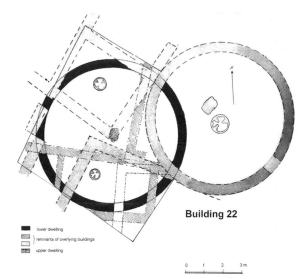

Building 22

■ lower dwelling
▨ } remnants of overlying buildings
▢
▨ upper dwelling

0   1   2   3 m.

Figure 3.6. Excavations of Bayburtian 1938.

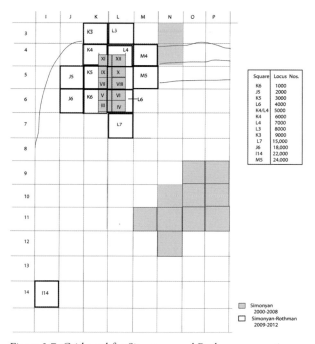

Square	Locus Nos.
K6	1000
J5	2000
K5	3000
L6	4000
K4/L4	5000
K4	6000
L4	7000
L3	8000
K3	9000
L7	15,000
J6	18,000
I14	22,000
M5	24,000

▨ Simonyan 2000-2008
▢ Simonyan-Rothman 2009-2012

Figure 3.7. Grid used for Simonyan and Rothman excavations.

a meter beneath the round building. A three-part division may be too simple, as our deep operation indicates (see Square K6 below). Throughout his excavations he saw very little difference in the ceramic typology or other artifacts. He noted that, as in Square K6 (see below), round buildings tended to be reconstructed on the same plan (see Chapter 4b). The free-standing round buildings with one course of bricks were three and a quarter to eight meters in diameter. At the highest elevation they had attached square rooms or open courtyards (Fig 3.6). Bayburtian asserts that builders made the foundations of the walls with larger field stones on the outside and smaller ones on the inside (see K6 Building 3 below for which Rothman proposes the inner stones may be the base for a bench). Bedrock in his excavations, as in Square K6, was at about three and half meters. Again, like Square K6, layers of ash were evident at 1.2 meter and 1.75 meters, suggesting that fire consumed some of the houses. Overall, we agree

Figure 3.8. Open area of the mound before 2000 excavations.

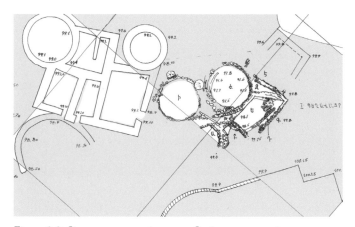

Figure 3.9. Simonyan excavations near Soviet reconstruction.

with his conclusion that the site was continually occupied and rebuilt without a central plan in mind. In 1937 Bayburtian dug 7.3 meters from the earlier 1937 excavations (see Fig 3.1). There he uncovered a section of the settlement wall with an adjoining quadrangular building that abutted the settlement wall. At 14.5 x 7.5 meters it resembled Building 1 (Level I) in Square I14 and Building 1 in Square K6 (see below). Bayburtian suggests that the two graves (Fig 3.5) were modern; he calls them "Christian" and pointed to an iron wristlet on one of the skeletons. The wall surrounding them, therefore may not be contemporaneous with the other walls of Building 1.

Mostly, Bayburtian excavated round buildings, near the top with square additions (Fig 3.5) and below without (Fig 3.6). Three-lobed hearths were typical features (see Chapter 6a). Some of the additions seem to have been integrated into the round buildings. One question we had is whether the top level Bayburtian excavated was the original top level of the site. We know that buildings like the one made into a museum covered this area. The large rectangular buildings we excavated are near the surface in the north (Square K6), and west along the settlement wall.[118] On the other hand, I14 looks like it should be in the same topographic position as Sardarian and Bayburtian's round houses, unless just by luck it was in an open area. What is also unclear is whether the square rooms were all roofed. None from Bayburtian have hearths, although there is a hearth in a subsidiary small square room in Square K6 (see below). They certainly are not like the Kvatschelebi houses with mudbrick for the main room, and wattle and daub, short annex or covered porch (see Chapter 4a). The likelihood is that they were not roofed, but they were courtyards for craft activity or corals for domesticated animals.

Generally, the pictures show diggers with shovels. Bayburtian may have missed quite a few ancient floors using them as his primary digging tools.

The artifactual contents and functions of these buildings are discussed below in Chapter 7.

Simonyan 2000 to 2008 Excavations

Simonyan began his excavation adjoining Sardarian's in the area we renamed M to P, 9 to 12 (Figure 3.7). He later worked in 5 x 5 meter squares, numbered IV, VI, VIII, X, XI, and XII (Site 2). These crossed the updated grid in L6, K5, K4, and L4. His team also dug in the necropolis down the western slope (see Chapter 6b). In 2021, Simonyan expanded into Squares N2-3 to explore the settlement wall. The area around Sardarians's excavations Simonyan labeled as Site 1, the area in the north as Site 2.

---

118   Bayburtian 1938.

His team dug with shovels and trowels. Most fill was not screened until 2009, when the Armenian-American team screened his northern squares' back dirt.

M-P9-12

The first excavation site covered an area of 250-300 m², about 10 to18 meters north of the museum building. There previous excavations created a large depression (Fig 3.8). Their task was to use the latest methods to identify semi-destroyed structures and undamaged areas of the artifact-rich cultural layers, to recover previously unknown structures in the expanded areas, and to determine the stratigraphy and correlation of architectural levels and cultural horizons in this section of the site. Excavations revealed that, despite previous work, there were still wall bases and intact cultural strata, and the construction and stratigraphy of Shengavit was much more complex than had been presented by Sardarian and Bayburtian. We can assume that Sardarian dug from the surface in a fairly narrow excavation on the northern part of the basin, and the large pit was formed as a result of erosion of the adjacent cultural strata that covered the untouched lower horizons with their rubble. The reconstruction of buildings by the Soviets clearly used stone from deeper levels as well, since the round building in the middle of Figure 3.8 did not have stone walls in antiquity and so they built up earlier building to appear on the surface of their reconstructions.

The oldest living quarters Simonyan excavated in the central area of the settlement sat on river pebbles cemented with lime lying on sterile soil. Its elevation was 285 to 300 cm below the surface of the surrounding area.[119] Note that the surface of the ground at this site was partially demolished and leveled as a result of modern construction works (Fig 3.9). For this reason, the ground level at the first excavation site was 30-50 cm lower than the northern site. This makes sense in terms of the K6 sounding which was 3.5 meters deep, and the likelihood that Stratum I in Square K6 was destroyed before we began excavating. In the Square K6 deep sounding excavators reached bedrock, but bedrock is not apparent in the rest of the excavations.

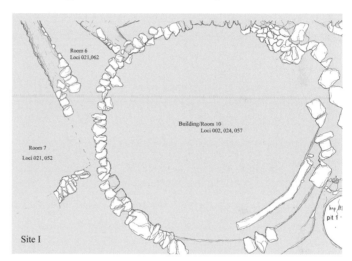

Figure 3.10. Simonyan excavation of Building (Room 10).

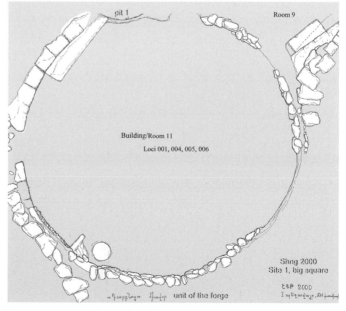

Figure 3.11. Second round Building (Room 11).

---

119   Note that the elevation for the 2000-2008 buildings and for 2009-2012 Squares I14, M5, and K/L 3/4 was measured from the surface at the beginning of excavating a square. Squares J5 and K6 elevations were based on the same datum, a point on the metal geological marker in the north.

Figure 3.12. Round Building 11.

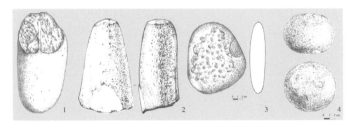

Figure 3.13. Ground stone tools in pit related to Building 11.

From the surface in Site 1 Simonyan's team excavated two round buildings with a diameter of 570 to 580 cm (Fig 3.10 and 3.11). In contrast to the upper horizons, when the ancient workmen built the foundation of stones and the walls of mudbricks, here they used a combination of different building materials on the horizontal levels. Some of the walls were made of mudbricks and the other half of the wall of flat stacked river stones and torn basalt (Fig 3.12).

Building (Room) 10 sat in the central part of the excavation area (see Fig 3.1). The diameter of the room was 570 cm. Partially warped walls in two to five rows consisted of river stones, some basalt, mudbrick, and small gravel mixed with clay mortar on which there were traces of clay capping. The hard and level floor consisted of an area covered with clay. They found an arc-shaped long trench 25-40 cm wide and 15 cm deep between the floor and the east and north walls. By the southwestern wall lay an oval, fired clay griddle fixed with a protruding partition in the middle and a deep recess in the rim. The griddle was probably intended for baking *lavash*-like flatbreads and had many cracks, probably caused by high temperatures. More than 70 artifacts lay on the floor, including fragments of pottery, mortars and smoothers, the rim of a basalt vessel, a fragment of red tufa, and other objects.

The use of different building materials to build the walls of the same house indicates that the builders used any available material and did not attach much importance to the design and durability of the house. They tried to finish it as quickly as possible. This fact shows that contrary to the round houses of the upper layer, the lower houses of

Figure 3.14. Red stone "button."

a similar layout were not central structures among the structures of a large complex.[120] Nor was there a strict building code defined by the Kura-Araxes culture tradition at this time (see brick size below).

Building (Room) 11 was relatively well preserved to five courses of stones on the east (height 50 cm, width 60 cm). The western and southwestern walls of the Building 11 stood to only one or, in some places, two courses of flat river stones. The other walls had three or four courses of 20 to 40 cm high stones. Builders made the foundation with small stones on top of which they laid stone walls with clay plaster lining on the inside. The north wall of the room, 280 cm long and 70 cm wide, was constructed with mudbricks in a double row of 150 cm and a single row of 130 cm. Some parts of the wall consisted of river stones, basalt, and mudbricks mixed together. The southern wall included a part of an earthen partition, which divided the room into two uneven parts. The floor had a level of river sediments covered with yellow sand and plaster.

---

120   Dzhavakhishvili 1973; Kushnareva 1997.

On the east side of the dwelling lay a triangular, solid structure made of small stones mixed with clay mortar. In the center was a rectangular (30 x 40 cm) depression of 10 cm. Under the west wall of dwelling 10 and the west side of dwelling 11 was a hole 40 cm in diameter and 10 cm deep.

Between the circular of the lower elevation houses, on the northeast side of Building (Room) 10 and the west wall of Building (Room) 11 remained the lower part of the round hole dug in the solid ground with a diameter of 140 cm, 20 cm deep.

On the north-west side of circular Building 11 sat a door 70 cm wide. We uncovered a household pit filled with soft, gray earth and river stones, among which the team found tools (Fig 3.13). This semi-circular pit had traces of clay coating on the walls, which the builders had set in hard sediments. The southeastern wall of the pit contained river rocks of different sizes stacked in five rows. The pit contained 14 tools of basalt and river stones: a saddle quern of porous basalt, mortars, one of which had a polished surface, basalt smoothers, spherical mortars, a four-sided grinding stone, reddish black polished pottery with red-gray overlays and with hemispherical lugs (locus 50a). This pit also contained numerous animal bones.

On the south-west side of the dwelling 11 Simonyan's team dug another pit,. It was 100 cm

Figure 3.15. Deposit of metal working debris.

Figure 3.16. Copper crucible and pots with smelted copper.

Figure 3.17. Second building horizon.

deep and 110 cm in diameter. Builders coated its walls and floor with plaster. For the clarification of Shengavit stratigraphy this pit is of great importance, because the foundation of southwestern wall of Building 11 lay over the southeastern part of the pit. This room was one of the earlier structures of Shengavit built on the mound, and the pit existed before the construction of Building 11. Consequently, we can propose that before the construction of the first solid dwellings made of stone and mudbrick in this part of the mound people lived on Shengavit, possibly in houses made of materials that did not survive for archaeologists to find. The pit contained river stones, half of a basalt saddle quern, and two pieces of worked yellow tufa, one of which may be a fragment of the tufa pit cover of the pit (Fig 3.13). We recovered 80 potsherds of various Kura-Araxes pottery types with black-red, thick-walled, rough exteriors with mottled gray and brown, and brown exteriors. Two fragments of black and brown gray exterior pottery had fragments of ornamentation. One has a raised design (see Chapter 5e), the other had fine incised designs (locus 051). Also found in the pit were pieces of obsidian with outside of the pebble flaked off as a crusher, or chisel (Fig 3.13, 1), a "button" of red stone (Fig 3.14), charcoal, and a large number of bones of various animals (locus 51).

Building (Room) 11 yielded more than 70 potsherds: fragments of a storage jar, closed serving forms, intermediate types, open forms, etc. (Locus 50). Potters decorated the surface of some of them with raised, deep patterns. They had black, red, or red-brown surfaces. We also found thick-walled pots of brown and gray, red pottery with rough surface treatment, as well as obsidian fragments and small, rounded ground stones.

We excavated an additional area of 3 x 2.5 m on the western side of the Building (Room) 11, between the wall of the dwelling and the western part of the earlier excavations. Here we found a large amount of pottery, mostly black with red interior (locus 55). Under the artifact-laden layer, at a height of 30 cm from the surface was a rounded clay podium, covered with a 15-20 cm thick hard layer of ash, which continued westward, beyond the limits of the excavation. On the west side of Building (Room) 11, at a height of 30 cm from the surface, was a rounded clay podium covered with a 15-20 cm layer of ash, which continued westward beyond the limits of the excavation (Fig 3.15). It was here that the team unearthed a large quantity of charcoal, slag, and seven fragments of thick-walled pottery (Locus 055). Three of these ceramic vessels were crucibles covered with infusions of green copper oxide residue (Fig 3.16), and the rest showed signs of a fire. We found two more fragments with copper embedded in the walls near the podium. A metal worker must have been smelting here and tried to pour some of the molten product into pots that then broke. According to our calculations, this operation produced 150 kg of smelted copper for making items in molds not found where we excavated.[121] Molds did appear elsewhere (Chapter 5d). In this layer we have the oldest radiocarbon dating of the Shengavit settlement, analyzed in the laboratory of the German Archaeological Institute in Berlin (Bln-5526: 4462±47BP, 3350BC (90.1%) 3010BC).[122] We could not excavate most of the area, because of rules preventing us from removing the stone structure of the upper horizon. Under the western section of excavation at a depth of 280-300 cm from the surface near the bottom of the occupation diggers unearthed a terracotta bull statuette and fragments of a cult stand with ram's head limbs (Locus 61).

At an elevation of 100-120 cm from the topsoil and 180 cm below the day's starting elevation a second architectural level appeared (Fig 3.17). The foundations of all structures of it were at the same elevation. This suggests that the first building

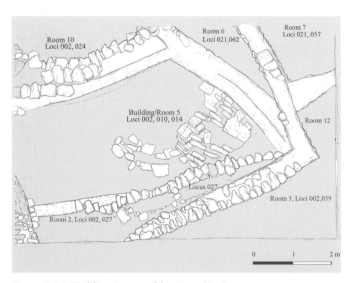

Figure 3.18. Building in second horizon, Site I.

Figure 3.19. Wall construction with stone and thick clay mortar.

---

121 Simonyan 2013, 14; Simonyan 2018, 7-8.

122 But see comments in Chapter 1 on some contradictions in those dates, which imply that this date is too early.

horizon in an area of at least 250-300 square meters was leveled and residents created a second building phase on the resulting flat area.

Buildings (Rooms) 2, 5, 7 and 9 belonged to the second architectural level (Fig 3.18). The walls of Building 9 were made only of mudbricks of different sizes. The wall was preserved to the height of 1 m. Only part of one wall was excavated in this room, as the other walls had been destroyed by previous excavations or erosion. Judging by the preserved wall fragment, this room was rectangular in plan.

Builders also made the walls of the enclosed courtyard or trapezoid Building (Room) 5 of mudbricks. We excavated this room in its entirety except for the southern part, which was under the wall of the upper horizon, built of river stones. The northeast wall had a length of 400 cm preserved to a height of 40 cm and a thickness of 60 cm. On this wall builders laid the mudbricks in two rows on a stone foundation. According to the excavation supervisor Ludwig Khachaturyan's diary, the outer side of this wall consisted of river stones and mortar, while the inner side consisted of mudbricks. The longitudinal walls of the corridor made of raw bricks had thinner walls.

Figure 3.20. Narrow Corridor 5 and Building (Room) 7 with stone foundation stones on walls. (Room 7).

Figure 3.21. Brick-making in Room (courtyard) 7.

In front of the northern wall of corridor 5, almost adjoining it, at an acute angle ran the southern wall of Building (Room) 7, whose walls were made of river pebbles, which builders seemed to have thrown into a soft clay mass bounded on both sides by a rim. This wall both outside and inside was covered with clay plaster (Fig 3.19). The remaining walls of Building (Room) 7 lay outside the excavation area. Between walls of constructions 5 and 7 there was a narrow, triangular, closed space (Fig 3.20, 3.18). Simonyan suggests that Building (Room) 7 had been built earlier, and there was no free space to build the northern wall of the corridor 5 properly. For this reason, the northern wall of the corridor 5 the ancients constructed obliquely, as a result of which the corridor-yard had the shape of an irregular trapezoid.

Surprising, they put together the top of the eastern longitudinal wall with river stones in one row. In all likelihood, after the partial collapse, they repaired the mudbrick wall as well as they could. The structure of the wall gives us reason to believe that it was not a classical structure, the walls of which could support a roof. Most likely it was a walled courtyard without a roof. Bayburtian dug a similar structure of larger size.[123] It is no coincidence that in the northern part of the room on the floor there was a cluster of raw bricks standing on their sides (Fig 3.21). From this

123   Bayburtian 2011, 29, 31.

Figure 3.22. Objects in Courtyard 5.

Figure 3.23. Andiron of ram's heads from Courtyard 5.

we can suggest that it was a brick making yard. They had put finished bricks on the side to dry, and they remained as they were until our excavations.

To the south of Room 5 lay a northwest corner of Building 2, the western wall of which consisted of mudbrick. Builders of the northeastern and western sides of Building 2 made upper layer walls of fluvial and chopped basalt stones. On the east, the wall lay along the border of the excavation and on the south was a cluster of stones of a partially destroyed round wall, which Simonyan's team did not have time to excavate in 2000. As a result of this situation, Simonyan's team could only excavate the northwest corner of Building (Room) 2. The mudbrick wall extending southward from the west wall of Courtyard 5 at an obtuse angle could have been a continuation of the courtyard. In this case open Area 5 in the plan takes the form of a a partial space. In this small space were many artifacts (Fig 3.22): a whole basalt saddle quern, a stone grinding stone, a bifurcated movable, horseshoe-shaped andiron made of fired clay with ram horns similar to the one from locus 61 (Fig 3.23).

To the second architectural level belonged a building also made of mudbrick and round in plan. This was excavated in our second excavation square in the northwest corner of the Square XII in 2000 at a depth of 210 cm from the ground surface.

This architectural level is second from the bottom, so in terms of the one continuous stratigraphic column in Square K6 (see below) it was probably contemporaneous with K6 Architectural Level 4. Summarizing the data of the second architectural level, we can state that a) all rooms of the second building horizon had a rectangular layout, and b) a variety of building technologies is evident. That is to say, 1) builders made walls of mudbricks on a stone foundation, 2) they also used irregularly cut basalt stones, 3) sometimes, they built only with mudbricks, and 4) sometimes, they built walls from river stones cemented by thick clay mortar, probably with a narrow opening in the wall with spaces defined on both sides by wooden and other movable partitions, filled with clay mortar into which they pressed river stones. Naturally, in the Kura-Araxes the ancients could not get flat surfaces, so after construction they covered the walls with a thick layer of clay plaster inside and outside. In contrast to the lower, first architectural level (K6 Architectural Level 5), where they used different building materials together to build the walls, in the second building horizon they made each house of the same material, but they used different materials in different houses.

Above these clearly defined architectural levels, the stratigraphic situation becomes less clear (Fig 3.24). The third building horizon (K6 architectural level 3) begins approximately 140 to 150 cm above the base of the earliest buildings at a depth of 150 to160 cm from the surface of the ground. The third building horizon refers to the rectangular Building (room) 4 of the first site, built of river stones on clay mortar. As noted, the ancients covered their walls outside and inside with clay plaster. Only the northeast corner remained intact. Interestingly, a single row of large river stones was subsequently laid on top of the east wall. As the corner of this room was slightly higher than the Room 5, and it repeated the layout and structure of the wall, we propose that Building (Room) 4 would have housed the same activities. Fragments of preserved floors of tamped clay and a perfectly polished surface in the square XII of Excavation Area 2 near

Figure 3.24. Horizons or architectural levels from Area I.

the triangulation tower in the northern part of the mound also belong to this building horizon.

The fourth architectural level (K6 Architectural Level 2) corresponds to the upper building horizon defined by Bayburtian, in which he excavated 12 buildings with rectangular layout and Buildings 1 and 2 with circular layouts. As Bayburtian writes, the foundations of these premises were located at a height of 234 cm from the lowest level that he reached and at a depth of 100 cm from the ground surface.[124] Most structures excavated by Sardarian belong to this building horizon, especially the rectangular room built of river stones at the western edge of his first excavation, the foundations of which were 60 cm below the modern surface of the ground.

Building (Room) 3 on the first excavation site has an area of 6.5 x 3 m, with its footing at 100 to110 cm from the surface. It belonged to the 4th architectural level (K6 Architectural Level 2). At a depth of 30 to 40 cm from the surface, the entire area of the room revealed a hard, light yellow-colored clay floor with a thickness of 10-15 cm. Under the floor lay soft earth with lenses of ash preserved to a depth of 100 to 110 cm. Simonyan's team excavated in their entirety the southern and southeastern walls, both from the inside and the outside. The total length of the fully excavated southern wall of the Building (Room) 3 was 570 cm, the preserved height 100 cm and its width 60 cm. The

ancients built this two-course wall with river stones set in clay mortar. There were fragments of clay plaster on some parts of the wall. A thick layer of clay 60 cm wide and 120 cm long remained on top of the masonry of the southern wall. Builders made the northern wall of the room using the same technique, but mudbricks also constituted the masonry of the northern wall.

In the central part of Building (Room) 3 at a depth of 40 cm from the surface sat a platform measuring 190 x 200 centimeters, 30 centimeters high from the floor and built of mudbricks, basalt stones, and clay connected to the northern wall. On the walls of this platform rested two

Figure 3.25. Building (Room) 1 Square IV.

124   Bayburtian 2011, 28-33.

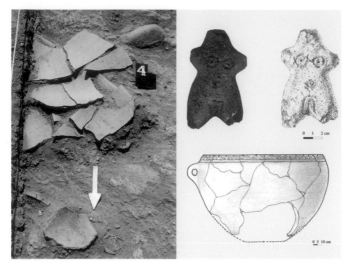

Figure 3.26. Artifacts from Square IV.

Figure 3.27. Stoned lined pits in Squares IV and XII.

potsherds with remnants of molten copper on the interior. At a depth of 40-60 cm inside Room 3, the team found a stone spindle whorl with notches probably for setting ornamental stones and a model of a red tufa wagon wheel.[125] The team also found many stone tools, including obsidian blades with retouched cutting edges, querns of porous basalt, graters, etc. (Locus 52). On the southern side of Room 3, in a small triangular area surrounded by walls on three sides, they found a peculiar storeroom, in which lay a flint sickle element, a saddle quern of porous basalt, and mortar of river pebbles (Locus 059). The pottery was mainly ornamented with obliquely shaded raised lines that formed continuous rows of triangles. Similar ornamentation was also common on ceramics from the cult emplacement we excavated in 2012 in Square M5.

A partially preserved upper wall of mudbrick, erected above the southern wall of Room 9 on fine gravel foundation, as well as partially excavated Building (Room) 7 with walls of mudbrick on stone foundation in the northern part of the first excavation, also belong to the 4th architectural level.

The crew found rich archaeological material (more than 70 artifacts) in a triangular, enclosed space between the walls of Buildings (Rooms) 5 and 7 at a depth of 60 to 80 cm from the surface (Locus 21). Among the ceramics are: a) a fragment of a black polished body with a gray interior, ornamented with a broad raised pattern, around which finely carved geometric motifs, b) a fragment of a bowl rim, ornamented with a finely incised pattern, c) a potsherd of a black polished thin-walled bowl, ornamented with broad oblique lines, and d) the hemispherical handle of the black-polished vessel. The team also recovered fragments of obsidian and tools of porous basalt and river stones from this room.

The circular Building (Room) 1 in the square IV of the Excavation Area 2 also belongs to the 4th architectural level. It was at a depth of 100 to 110 cm from the surface (Fig 3.25).[126] Builders made the walls of this room from flat river stones bound with clay mortar, while they laid a mat soaked in clay mortar on the surface every 4 rows (see

---

125 Although these models of wagons with oxen common, the wheels without the rest of the model may be spindle whorls
126 Editor's note: since we know that the surface of the site was disturbed in different ways in different parts of the mound, depth from surface can be somewhat different from area to area.

Chapter 4b). This construction technique, not yet recorded in the sites of the Kura-Araxes culture, gave the walls elasticity and resistance to tectonic shifts. In other words, it was an ingenious protection against earthquakes, which were a frequent phenomenon in Armenia since ancient times. A storage jar lay crushed in place (Fig 3.26) along with a female statuette of black tufa on the eastern side of this room.[127] In Squares IV and XII of Excavation Area 2 at a depth of 50 to 60 cm from the surface emerged skillfully constructed grain-storage pits with cylindrical entrances, lined with river stones and tightly covered with disk-shaped tufa covers (Fig 3.27). [128]

This architectural level also represents a rectangular in plan built of two rows of river stones in square L6 (earlier XII) and a rectangular in plan room in square VI of the Area 2 excavation (Fig 3.7), which was built of mudbricks on a foundation of river stones. During the 2009-2012 excavations, we found that this was part of the large Building 1, which extended into squares K6, L6, and L7 (see below).

The fifth, uppermost architectural level (Architectural Level 1 in K6) was preserved in the form of utility pits and individual walls of large worked stones, which ancient workers used to build spacious houses with a rectangular layout. Such walls were uncovered in Excavation Area 1 during the 2003 excavation, and in Square X of Excavation Area 2 during the 2000 excavation (Fig 3.28). Only the lower rows of walls remained of the upper horizon dwellings on the surface of the settlement. The pottery was still within the tradition of Early Bronze Age Kura-Araxes, but there are also innovations characteristic of the Early Kurgan culture, which formed during the Kura-Araxes/ Early Kurgan

Figure 3.28. Architecture from the transitional Kura-Araxes/Early Kurgan top layer.

transition.[129] In all likelihood, the ornaments from the ruined burial ground discovered during the 2009 excavations in the J5 square as well as some of the burials in the necropolis also belong to the transitional Kura-Araxes/Early Kurgan transition, the fifth architectural level or K6 Architectural Level 1.

The stratigraphy of the Area 2 is represented by a Harris matrix (Fig 3.29).

Summarizing the results of the 2000 to 2008 excavations, we suggest that there were 5 architectural levels in Shengavit in the areas Simonyan's team excavated, four of which belonged to the Early Bronze Age, and the fifth, partially destroyed upper layer belongs to the transition period from Kura-Araxes to the Early Kurgan times, Stratum 0. That layer existed elsewhere on the site (see below). As discussed in the next section, in the deep sounding in Square K6 we unearthed eight clear strata representing six architectural levels. K6 architectural level 6 is missing in the earlier work of Simonyan's team. That deepest architectural level 6 from Square 6 sat on clean bedrock. We cannot be absolutely certain whether Bayburtian reached bedrock at all, although he may have been close. Sardarian clearly did not go much deeper than Architectural Level 2. In general, a kind of circular stratigraphy is evident at Shengavit,

---

127   Simonyan 2004, 59-61.
128   Simonyan 2013, 11.
129   Simonyan 2013, 41.

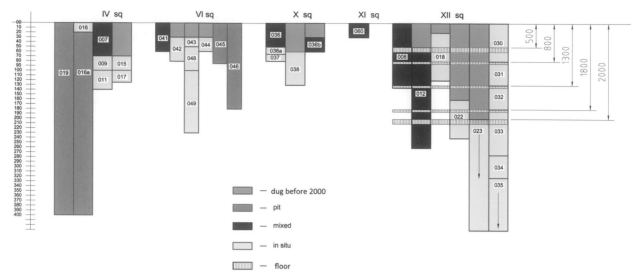

Figure 3.29. Harris matrix of Shengavit excavation at Site 2 north 5 x 5 m squares.

by which we mean that there were not clear breaks in the sequence and when buildings were abandoned in some areas, people moved and built new buildings creating not a flat layer cake with clear distinctions, but rather a rather messy agglomeration of layers that break through each other, creating a kind of zigzag or, again, circular, stratigraphy.

Although most levels are clearly KA2, a few individual artifacts like a hand ax flint tool (Fig 3.30) remind us of the late KA1 (earlier called Eneolithic) horizon from sites in Georgia (Shulaverisgora, Odishi, from Abkhazia). These comparable artifacts are displayed in the Museum of Georgian History. Also, individual potsherds, originating from Pit 2 under circular Building (Room) 11 consist of typical KA1 artifacts. It is possible that they come from layers of the lower horizon, of which undisturbed layers have not yet been identified. Perhaps, it was during the KA1 period that the Shengavit settlement was founded in a limited area. But drawing this conclusion from a few artifacts is not sufficient without extensive excavations of the lower levels of the settlement.

Figure 3.30. Artifacts from pit 2 in the lowest horizon.

Simonyan-Rothman 2009 to 2012

The focus of these excavations was primarily to establish the dated stratigraphy of the site in order to make sense of the earlier work before large-scale publication. Our focus was squares emanating from the settlement wall line in the north, Squares K6, J5, J6, K/L3/4 (Fig 3.7, 3.1), plus the two squares identified as hotspots in the georadar survey: Square I14 and M5 (see Chapter 4c).

Our method of digging relied mostly on small picks and trowels. We used larger picks only for moving tertiary deposits like the modern pit fill in Square K6. All deposits were put through quarter inch (.635 cms) screens, and in some loci, like hearth contents, through finer screens. We used a locus system and bag numbers; the latter served as a kind of sub-locus or lot designation. Each category of artifact, mostly ceramics, animal bone, obsidian, and ground stone received a separate bag number, as did any special or whole artifact like tools, figurines, whole pots, etc. So, every locus tended to have two or more bag numbers for the same category of artifact. If we later discovered we missed a context, we could still distinguish its artifacts from other contexts by bag numbers. We took large bags of fill (up to ten liters) for flotation where we had a primary or good secondary context. Most of these samples came from Squares K6 and M5. Unfortunately, our student workers were of variable screening ability, and square supervisors had little time to supervise, so the sample is good, but not perfect. The old Russian leveler we used for taking elevations was not as accurate as we would have hoped. Within each operation that took daily elevations (Squares K6 and J5), the relative elevations are good, but they are not always precisely matched from square to square.

Based on Square K6, the only modern excavated square at Shengavit to bedrock, we propose that not counting the few Early Kurgan Period materials found here and there across the site, there were eight Kura-Araxes strata (see Fig 1.5).

Square K6

This square adjoins the stones of a round building's foundation to the south, the initially unexcavated Square J6 to the west, the partially excavated Square L6 to the east, and previously excavated Square K5 to the north. Whether the round building was a Soviet creation or not is unclear, but a concrete path built by the Soviets runs between Square K6 and that nearest round building. The southern 35% of the square consisted of a modern pit into which presumably these Soviet planners dumped artifacts, and modern tin cans, window glass, and metal nails to a depth of about two and a half meters from the datum (the crossbar of a metal geological mapping marker).

On 4 July 2009 we began excavation of this square. Below the turf at .98m below the datum, a

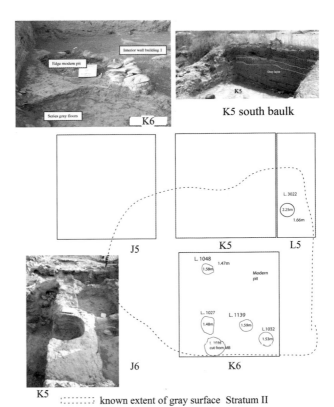

Figure 3.32. Stratum II, the gray layer.

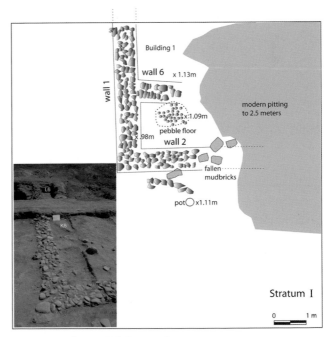

Figure 3.31. Square K6, Stratum I.

stone foundation appeared. It clearly was part of the same building whose wall was exposed years before in Square L6 (Fig 3.31). The foundation was made up of unmodified river pebbles of sandstone, set in a thin clay base on top of the white plaster surface of Stratum II. A few fallen mudbricks in the west indicates that the foundation was

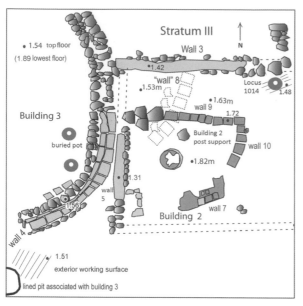

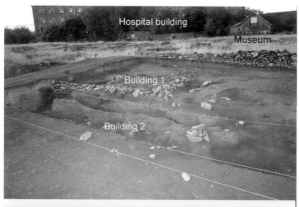

Figure 3.33. Stratum III with a piece of Stratum IV.

Figure 3.34. Building 1, 2, and 3 and the place of Strata I-IV.

the base for a mudbrick wall, which no longer remained. The floor was made up of small pebbles, similar to the same stratum in Square J5 (see below), and in a round building Bayburtian unearthed. The two radiocarbon samples from Building 1 date it to between 2620 and 2468 BCE (see Table 1.2), so it existed in the final Kura-Araxes times at Shengavit. Nothing from the building can be considered to be in a primary context. Modern glass and metal are mixed with it. Stratigraphically, we propose that Building 1 in Square I14, the M5 room with a ritual installation, and a pebble floor without evidence of architecture in J5, are contemporary. They represent the first stratum from the top. It is not really possible to equate it with anything in Sardarian's excavations. From what we see of Bayburtian's excavations, he did not find Level I, except perhaps the building by the settlement wall, but we do not have a drawing. The details of its loci, their placement in the square, and their details are available in our web archive.

Shengavit residents put the foundation of Stratum I on the second stratum. It is a series of hard gray to white plaster floors and pits of various sizes, mostly small (Fig 3.32). In one (Locus 1036) Early Kurgan people cut a pit down into the stratum. Radiocarbon samples date that pit to 2287 to 2044 BC. Interestingly, a kind of green plant matting was placed between each floor in Stratum II. To access every other succeeding bit of architecture in Square K6, much of Square K5 and a corner of Squares J5 and J6 the gray layer had to be removed. Its placement in the square, and their specifics are available in our web archive.

We do not consider Stratum II to be a separate architectural level, but part of architectural level 1.

Stratum III contained two major buildings. Building 2 is represented by three to four layers of mudbrick over a stone footing (Fig 3.33, 3.34). North of Wall 3, we found piles of fallen mudbricks. We also found remains of matting on top of the stone foundation stones onto which the builders piled up the mudbricks for the walls. The east-west Wall 3 ran into the eastern baulk. A piece of the north-south Wall 5 remained.

The southern east-west wall must have been destroyed by the modern pit. The other structure is Building 3, a round building with two parallel courses of mudbrick over a stone foundation. As Bayburtian found, a third course of mudbrick and small stone foundation rested inside the outer mudbrick wall. In both Building 2 and Building 3 large storage jars (*karaz*) were set beneath the floor (Fig 3.35). An analysis of spawls from their interior suggest a resonated wine, although this is not one hundred percent clear.[130] In addition, an exterior hard packed earthen work floor existed in the south with remains of animal bone and plants inside it. The floors of Building 2 and 3 were light plaster, frequently re-laid. A lined storage pit existed inside this floor.

Part of the problem of figuring out the strata III and IV (see below) is that Stratum IV was a burned building. The local people raised Building 3 on the top of a pit in which people dumped the remains from the burned building below.

A room with a ceramic hearth, defined by Walls 9, 10, and 7, appeared in the square (Fig 3.33). Since the top of Wall 9's elevation puts it below the floor level of Building 2, we think it likely that it really belongs in Stratum IV. Wall 8 appeared below that and is probably the top of a building of Stratum IV or V. Again, we did not have time to explore some of these issues. We also were somewhat limited by the local Ministry Cultural Preserve of Yerevan, whose leadership felt that removing walls of upper levels to access lower levels was inappropriate, as these buildings were "monuments." We were permitted to remove the stone foundation of Building 1, which gave us access to rich remains from Building 2, but it created quite a controversy in Yerevan.

Stratum IV, as discussed above, was largely

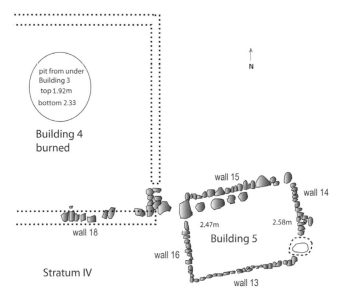

Figure 3.35. Storage jars set under the floors of Buildings 2 and 3.

Figure 3.36. Square K6 Stratum IV.

Figure 3.37. Square K6 Buildings 5,6,7.

---

130   The analysis was by Patrick McGovern of the Penn Museum.

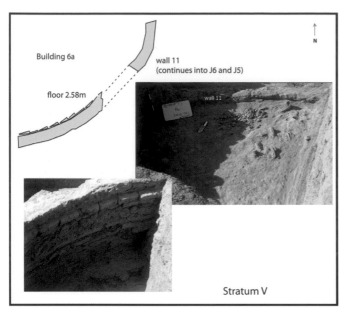

Figure 3.38. Square K6 Stratum V with the full Building 6 wall and the Building 6a floor.

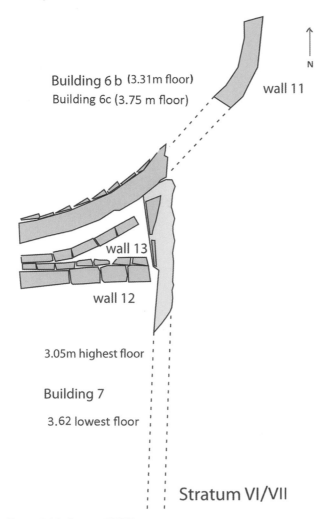

Figure 3.39. Stratum VI/VI.

burned (Fig 3.36). It is clearly evident as a separate stratum in Figure 1.5. The remains of Wall 18 suggest that the burned Building 4 was square. As discussed above, the likelihood is that Room 5 with the ceramic hearth was Stratum IV as well. Unlike any other room, we found the hearth sealed with clean white plaster and completely cleaned out of any artifacts, as if it were desacralized after a fire.

At the bottom of the modern pit we found another square structure, Building 5. We dug it to the floor, but what we did find was fairly disturbed by the modern pit. Its exact stratum is also hard to say definitively, as we had no direct connections between it and any other building. The depth of its foundation at 2.47 m under datum would put it in the Stratum IV part of the western section in Fig 1.5 (see Fig 3.37), but the mound was significantly curved, so we cannot be certain.

Given the Yerevan Cultural Preserve's insistence on not removing any wall, we dug the remaining strata starting with Stratum V west of Wall 4 of the round Building 3. Wall 11 emerged under the burned layer. We found short stretches of this same wall in squares J5 and J6, helping us to date the building in J5 (see below). This same wall was one that defines four rebuilding phases from a mud platform sitting directly on bedrock. Each rebuilding had somewhat different shaped bricks.

Inside of Wall 11 (Fig 3.38) was a floor with animal mandibles, a horn, and a pile of talc stones and a lithic knapping kit (see Fig 5f.18). We suspect that residents did some flint knapping, bead-making, and maybe bone craft work on this floor.

Under this floor, we encountered a pile of mudbrick, indicating a flattening of the Building 6b wall before the rebuilding of Building 6a.

Stratum VI is the one with Building 6b (Fig 3.39). A second building (7), emerged at this level. The exact nature of this building is a bit hard to determine. As is evident in Figure 3.40, the wall of Building 7 seems to curve to abut the wall of Building 6. Cutting into this wall are two separate walls, 12 and 13. The brick size in each is different. Between Wall 13/12 and the wall of Building 6 was a thick deposit of ash. Neither Wall 13/12 nor the original wall of Building 7 extended all the way to bedrock. In neither case was there a stone foundation. The one theory we proposed was that Building 7 was built first on the remains of Stratum VIII (Fig 3.41). It burned down. Residents then cleaned it out and built Wall 12, then 13 as buttresses to the building. Two distinct strata are represented by the two floors in the building. An original window or small door was built into the eastern wall. The full size of the building is not clear. These two strata, VI and VII, to us represent one architectural level number 5.

Stratum VIII rests on bedrock. The final floor of Building 6d is in this stratum (Fig 3.42). Building 7 and Wall 13/12 end at the same level as the bottom of stratum VII. Underneath Building 7 lay a small pisè semi-circle (Fig 3.43). Its function is not clear as we found almost no artifacts in it.

In sum, Square K6 had eight strata (Fig 1.5, Table 3.1). Interestingly, even in Square K6 the slope of the site did not include Level I all the way across the K6 square. We suspect that this top level was missing in a number of places on the mound, including in Bayburtian's excavation.

We feel of these strata only six architectural levels existed. We do know that there is evidence of Early Kurgan Period people using the site as temporary settlement, or a place to store foodstuffs, or bury their dead. We have no building from this period. We therefore are calling it Level 0. Clearly, Shengavit continued to be a place of some symbolic importance for the Early Kurgan population, suggesting a connection to memories of their Kura-Araxes past.

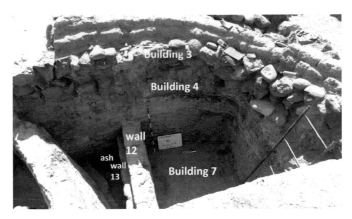

Figure 3.40. Building 7.

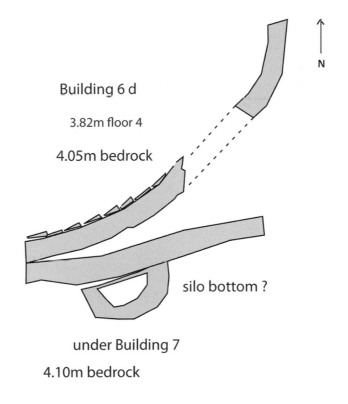

Figure 3.41. Stratum VIII.

Square J5 and J6

Squares J6 is west of K6, and J5 is north of J6 along the settlement wall line. In both J5 and J6 the top level was cut by many pits. Many of these pits appear to be post-Kura-Araxes, Shengavit 0. The first clear sign of a Kura-Araxes

Stratum	Buildings	Top elevation (from datum) meters	Bottom elevation (from datum; subtract .6 m for from surface) meters	Levels
0	Early Kurgan pits/graves	-	-	0
I	1	.98	1.13 (bottom floor)	1
II	Gray surface (starts immediately under stone foundation of Building 1, and immediately on top of the walls of Buildings 2 and 3).	1.14	1.35/1.44 (over area)	1
III	Buildings 2 and 3. We did not dig below Square Building 2. Building 3 was built on top of the burned Stratum IV/ Level III remains. It probably lasted longer than building 2, as there were many rebuilt floors. A square alcove with a ceramic hearth may be associated with Building 3 or 4.	1.45	1.66/1.88	2
IV	Building 4, 5 and a wall of possible Building 8. Building 4 seems to have been square. A line of its walls remains. Building 5 appeared at the bottom of the modern pit. It contents we did not have time to explore, as they were likely mixed with the pit fill. A piece of the wall of Building 3 appeared in J6, establishing its size. Preservation in that square dominated by Early Kurgan pits is very limited.	2.21	2.58	3
V	The top layer (3th rebuilding) of Building 6 (6a), a series of rebuilt buildings on the same plan.	2.54	3.31	4
VI	This stratum includes a 2nd rebuilding of Building 6(b) and the top of building 7.	3.31	3.62	5
VII	This stratum includes the first rebuilding of Building 6 (c) and the bottom of Building 7. Strata VI and VII seem to us to be one Level.	3.62	3.82	5
VIII	The original building of Building 6 directly on bedrock, and the area under Building 7 with a small circular structure, perhaps the base of something in Building 7.	3.82	4.1	6

Table 3.1 Stratigraphy of Square K6.

level is a stretch of pebble floor, very much like the floor in Building 1 of Square K6 (Fig 3.44). Presumably, it is also like the floor that Bayburtian observed. A few scattered mudbricks also suggest that a building had been nearby. The fill, however, is badly mixed with modern glass and iron pieces. Locus 2002 in the southern half had four pits with soft fill. Locus 2003 had a patch of small river stones (Fig 3.45). Under Locus 2003, we found in Pit 3 (Locus 2008) a pair of earrings made of polished obsidian and gold foil (see Chapter 5i). Rothman and Hayrapetyan believe it to be part of a burial pit from Shengavit 0, post Kura-Araxes. Under it was what Hayrapetyan describes in her fieldnotes as "a firm packed platform." She questions whether it was modern, but stratigraphically it matches Stratum II of Square K6. North of Wall W001A a series of hard floors may also be equivalent to Square K6 Stratum II (Fig 3.46).

We found Strata I and II, Architectural Level 1 in Square J5, as it had been in Square K6 (Fig 3.47). Underneath the hard surface of Stratum II, a significant building emerged that was apparently rebuilt and refurnished a number of times. Under it, the round wall of Stratum V (W007) in Square K6 continued into Square J5. This means that the larger building was later than Stratum V; therefore, likely contemporary with Strata III and probably IV. As we will discuss in Chapters 6a, this rectangular J5 building may have shared elements of the ritual function similar to shrine room of Stratum I in Square M5. One such element is the central room (Room 1) and an adjoining Room 2, again much like the Square M5 building.

In Square J5, in strata III and IV, we focused

Figure 3.42. Building 7 with a window or small door.

Figure 3.43. Round structure under Building 7.

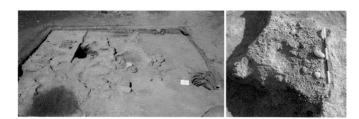

Figure 3.44. Level I, Square J5 with pits and pebble floor base in the southwest.

on three different areas: the major building, that the excavators called Room 1, an adjoining room that the excavators called Room 2, and an apparently outdoor space bordered by Wall W003 (Fig 3.47). Room 1, Wall W002 the ancients built on top of an earlier wall, indicating a considerable period of use and re-use. To some degree the building seems to have been cleaned out before it was abandoned. Room 2 was also occupied for a long time. The lowest level had an unusual wooden floor (Fig 6a.10). It was lower than the lowest floor in Room 1, which does not mean there were not lower floors in Room 1. The stratigraphy within the two rooms is quite complex. Firm packed

Figure 3.45. Possible grave cover.

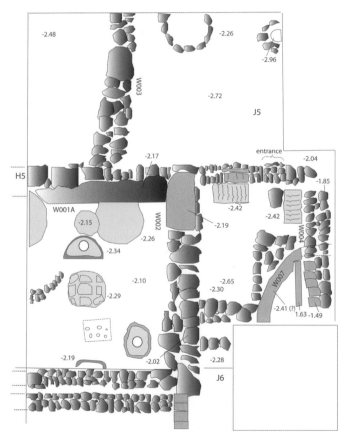

Figure 3.46. Strata III to IV.

surfaces alternated with lenses of ash and tumbled stones. These fills were rich with pottery, bone, and botanical remains. A series of loci north of the Square J5 wall W001A (Loci 2035, 2045, 2047, and 2050 [see web archive for placement of loci]) have the look of a trash deposit, presumably from the Square J5 rooms. The animal remains do not look like those from a feasting center, according to Crabtree (Chap 5a). A number of pits cut the west end—we did not dig the west wall beyond the bulk— of the big building. Inside the ritual room, a few of the pits, including Locus 2071, contained grain and other stored goods. Hayrapetyan claims it was below the building, but it is as likely that it was from the building (her fieldnotes do not specify the elevation from which the pit was cut).

J6, whose excavation Katherine Weber and Nyree Manoukian supervised, was very badly cut by pits similar to the uppermost strata of J5. The turf and area under it were filled with modern remains mixed with some Kura-Araxes pottery and tools, such as a flint sickle blade. The excavators divided the square into four sub-squares. In the northwestern sub-square (A) a small square of fieldstones very much like locus 2003 in square J5 (Fig 3.x15) covered pit 3, Locus 18022. Human remains were not found there. There were, however, quite a few animal bones, including sheep/goat and cattle. There were 13 such pits, none other covered in stones. Under this layer of pits in sub-square A was the southern wall of the J5 Stratum III/IV building at approximately 2 meters below datum. Aside from animal bones, ceramics, and ground stone, excavators recovered a large chunk of obsidian just south of the wall in Locus 18041 at 2.2 meters below datum. Sub-square J6c adjoined the southern half of Square K6. At 1.54 meters below data a small stretch of Wall 4 from the K6 Building 3 and a small stretch of the floor associated with it at 1.43 meters under datum appeared. The fill was mixed. Locus 1061 from Square K6, a grain pit continued into Square J6, as did the foundation of the square wall of Building 4 at 1.65 meters below datum. This was all that we did in Square J6.

Square I14

The georadar study (Chapter 4c) identified Square I14 as one of three "hotspots." As with Square M5, the choice of I14 proved auspicious. What the excavators uncovered was a large rectangular building with an annex at one end, like Building 1 from Square K6 (Fig 3.48) (see above). Pottery, ground stone, and lithic tools appeared very close under the turf. Pitting from above and also within the room also occurred. A surface north of the annex seems like it had a surface typical of a floor, but it was not clear where the defining walls would have been. About 42 to 63 centimeters from the surface a hard-plastered floor appeared, although it did not remain across the whole room.

Square M5

Square M5 is located along the northern edge of the mound (Fig 3.49). A layer of turf covered it, which Saerdarian had excavated somewhat. Simonyan interprets this as a separate horizon with distinct pottery styles. There was pitting clear in the section of the eastern side of Room 1 where the ritual emplacement was located (Fig 3.50).

In the upper layer of Square M5, at a depth of only 5 to 10 cm from the surface, in 2012 we uncovered upper rows of walls of a structure consisting of at least two sections (Fig 3.51). The western one was a room of dimensions 6 x 4.5 m outside (Room 1). Another rectangular room (Room 2) adjoined it to the east. We did not excavate the eastern and southern walls of the Room 2, as they were outside the excavated area. Someone had disturbed the western and northern walls of Room 1 earlier, so the upper masonry of row-brick was completely destroyed. Fortunately, the previous digger stopped his excavations at this level, so the rest of the walls and the interior of the room remained intact.

Builders carefully planned out Room 1 with rectangular layout had a north to south orientation. The main walls, 75 to 77 cm wide, they laid out in three rows

Figure 3.47. J5 Strata III/IV, Architectural Level II ritual building.

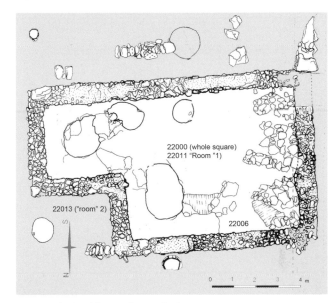

Figure 3.48. Building in Square I14.

Figure 3.49. Placement of Square M5 on the Shengavit mound.

Figure 3.50. Section drawing of the east side of Square M5, Room 1.

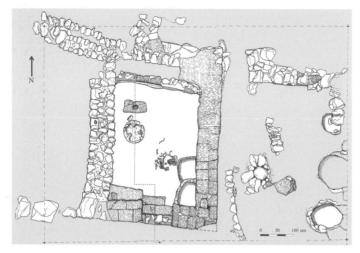

Figure 3.51. The M5 building, Rooms 1 and 2.

Figure 3.52. Excavations in Squares K/L 4/5.

of river stones and chopped basalt, the front row consisted of large stones and the inner one of smaller stones. [131]

In buildings of the Kura-Araxes cultural tradition, including Shengavit, workmen usually built the walls of stones and mudbrick in one or two rows. Three-row walls are rare. This peculiar masonry seemed to foreshadow the special significance of this building. Another peculiarity regards the foundation masonry. The basalt unworked large stone on the southwest corner stood out sharply for its large size (Fig 3.51). Simonyan sees in this a continuity to later temples. He writes, "The symbol of ancient man-made temples was stone, to which supernatural power was ascribed. It found its reflection in written sources of later eras, for example: '... And this stone, which I have set up as a pillar, shall be the house of God...".[132] Christ said to Peter, "And I tell you that you are Peter, and on this rock I will build my church, and the gates of hell shall not prevail against it.'[133]" A large stone also rested at the northern end of the J5 building.

The northern wall was one and eight tenths meters thick. Excavations have shown that it consisted of two layers. It is likely that the northern wall was rebuilt during the long operation of the temple. A new wall had been built inside, which resulted in a smaller room. Unfortunately, previous excavations destroyed the upper part of the brick row of the north wall and destroyed the stone base. Therefore, it is difficult to obtain a reliable image of the northern wall. Judging by the position of the surviving stones, we can conclude that there was a hidden entrance in the northern wall. There was an empty space between the outer wall and the inner wall. This allowed the priest or his confidant to enter unnoticed and address the worshippers from his hiding place with the name of the deity.

The two rooms in Square M5 appear to be like a similar ritual building in J5 (see above). The floor level of

---

131   Simonyan 2014, 24.
132   Bible, King James Version, Genesis 28:22.
133   Matthew 16:18.

the buildings was well preserved with a ceramic hearth set in the floor, a clay altar in the "ritual corner" (see Chapter 6a). Based on the pottery recovered from there the date of the building is K6 Stratum I. Perhaps, like the J5 building, the ritual emplacement lasted for a long time. It is also possible that the Bedeni pot was in the pit, presumably of Stratum 0 date. Simonyan's team excavated nothing below that stratum in this location.

Square K5

Square K5 is made up of Simonyan's team 2000 and 2003 5 x 5 meter (old-) Squares IX and VII in the eastern half of the square (Fig 3.7), and excavation in the western half to Stratum II in 2010 after Rothman joined the team. As it crosses into Square K4, we will discuss details of sub-Square VII in the next section.

Square K/L 3/ 4

In the Simonyan team's excavation, particularly in 2003, digging crossed Squares K4 and L4 and a bit of Square K5 (Fig 3.52). K5 is represented by an area with no architectural remains in the south in old Square VII a stone-lined grain pit under the Stratum II hard surface. A part of Square K4, represented by old-Square XI consists of a number of strata (Figs 3.53 and 3.54).

Figure 3.53. Old Square XI, New K4, 2003.

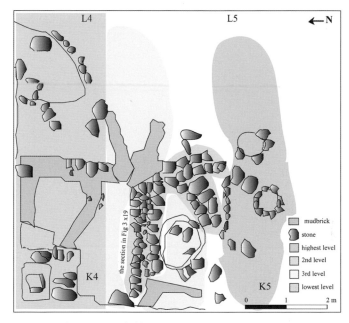

Figure 3.54. Drawing of old Square XI, new Square K4.

There were at least four major architectural layers, and as the southern section shows, a number of floors within those sections. Its position is indicated on the drawing (Fig 3.54). Above it, the edges of the stone-lined pit are visible (Fig 3.55).

Beneath the K4 material excavated in 2003, the outline of a sizable round building (1) appeared. We better defined the shape of the building and exposed its floor in 2009 and 2012 (Fig 3.56).[134]

As Simonyan's 2003 fieldnotes state, the crews needed to open Square L4 (old Square XII, Fig 3.7) to complete exposing its outline. The settlement wall should have run over the top of the Round Building 1. Since Rothman provisionally dates the beginning of the settlement wall to Strata III or IV, he suggests with some assurance that the lowest buildings, which were both round houses, predate that event. An apparently straight stone foundation of a

---

134   see Fieldnotes in our web archive.

Figure 3.55. Section on the south in Square K4.

Round Building 1

Figure 3.56. Round Building 1 in Squares K3/4 and L3/4.

Figure 3.57. Grain pits on the inside are from the settlement wall.

building wall lay on top of it. We did not find the northern part of the Round Building 1 wall, made of pounded mud with a stone intermixed in Squares K/L 3. A burned level is apparent in the section at the south of the building (Fig 3.55).

In the new 2021 excavations intended to clarify the construction and date of the settlement wall in Squares N1 and N2 (see Chapter 4b) the extent of grain pits became ever clearer (Fig 3.57).

Thus, the excavation of Shengavit proves a complex puzzle of architecture in strata and architectural levels spanning the KA2 into the Kura-Araxes and possibly including some Early Kurgan material in Stratum 0. Simonyan believes there was a small area with earlier KA1 deposits, but the evidence is very limited to this date. The following Chapters 4a and b will investigate the architecture of the site further.

References

Anonymous *History of Armenia*. Yerevan: National Museum of History of the Republic of Armenia (in Armenian).

Badalyan, R.; Hovsepyan S., Khachatryan, L. 2015 *Shengavit: Catalog of Archaeological Materials and 3 Collections of the Museum of History of Armenia*. Yerevan.

Bayburtian, E. 2011 *The Sequence of the Oldest Cultures of Armenia on the Basis of Archaeological Material*. Yerevan: History Museum of Armenia. (in Russian)

Dzhavakhishvili, A.I. 1973 *Construction Work and Architecture of South Caucasian Settlements in the Fifth to the third millennia B.C.* Tbilisi. (in Russian).

Kuftin, B.A. 1944 A Urartian "Columbarian" at the foot of Ararate and Kura-Araxes Eneolithic. *Bulletin of the State Museum of Georgia XIII:* 1-172. (in Russian with Georgian and English summaries).

Kushnareva K. 1997 *The Southern Caucasus in Prehistory. Stages of cultural and socioeconomic development from the 8th to the 2nd millennium BC.* Philadelphia: University of Pennsylvania Museum Press. (translated by H. Michael).

Lalayan, E.A. 1931 *Excavation of Graves in Soviet Armenia*. Yerevan: (publisher unknown)

Lalayan, E.A. 1919 Excavations in the Village Below Vardashen. *Proceedings of the Caucasian Branch of LEA.* 43-44.(in Russian)

Marr, N.I. 1934 *Ani; History of the city according to literary sources and the excavations of the ancient city.* Leningrad: Gosudarstvennoe Sotsial'noekonomicheskoe Izdatel'stvo. (in Russian).

Munchaev, R. M. 1975 *The Caucasus at the Dawn of the Bronze Age. Neolithic, Eneolithic, Early Bronze.* Moscow: Nauka; 1975. (in Russian).

Piotrovsky, B. B. 1949 *Archeology of Transcaucasia*. Leningrad: Publishing House of Leningrad State University. AA Zhd¬nova. L 12 (in Russian).

Sardarian, S. H. 1967 *The Primitive Communal System in Armenia*. Yerevan: Publishing House "Mitk."

Sardarian, S.H. 2004 *Armenia, Cradle of Civilization*. Yerevan: Hamalsarani Hratarakjch'ut'yun. (in Armenian).

Simonian, Hakob 2002 The Stratigraphy, Building and Construction Principles of Shengavit. In *The Ancient Culture of Armenia: the Scientific Forum Devoted to Emma Khanzadian's Jubilee*. Yerevan: Gitutyun' Nas, RA,.

Simonyan, Hakob 2015 Observations of the Armenian-American Joint Expedition of Shengavit. *Fundamental Armenology*. http://www.fundamentalarmenology.am/issues/9/ISSUE-2,-%C2%A0-2015.html.

4a | Architecture of the Kura-Araxes

Gregory Areshian

The architecture and town plans of Kura-Araxes settlements are full of potential to help us understand the societal structure of its various regions and sub-regions. Mostly, archaeologists have recovered houses. There are a few buildings that may have a public function, like the Red, Round Building of Kvatskhelebi,[135] perhaps a building adjoining the raised platform with a standing stela at Mokhrablur,[136] and the public building at Godin Tepe IV:1.[137] However, for the most part the buildings appear first and foremost to be residential constructions. Based on their shape, construction, and artifactual content, we can discover clues for reconstructing the activities and societal structure of Kura-Araxes domestic units.

Considering the fact that archaeologists have studied the settlement patterns, architectural designs, and construction techniques of the Kura-Araxes much less than its pottery and metalwork, we will present an analysis in this chapter of the architectural assemblage of Shengavit within a framework of broader analysis of the architecture of the Kura-Araxes culture area, addressing in particular details in terms of: (1) the spatial-temporal dynamics of particular features and traditions of Kura-Araxes architecture and patterns of those features at different sites; (2) principles of their settlement planning as indicators of the character of the sociopolitical organization of the Kura-Araxes societies; and (3) household architecture and construction techniques as reflections of lifeways of groups inhabiting settlements. For Shengavit, this third issue will be discussed in greater detail by mapping artifacts in key architectural spaces in Chapter 7.

The Kura-Araxes Homeland in the KA1

The assertion that architectural assemblages and their transformations, together with their artifactual contents, are to a significant degree useful to define the Kura-Araxes cultural tradition requires us to show correlations of distinctive features representing the early stage of the Kura-Araxes in space and time. As was suggested in the 1970s and early 1980s[138] and confirmed by multiple statistically reliable sets of radiocarbon dates obtained in the course of the following decades,[139] such appearance of more or less uniform early Kura-Araxes (KA1) assemblages should be dated to ca. 3500-3000 BC. Many of these components found their origins in earlier sites from different regions where the Kura-Araxes cultural tradition appeared throughout Eastern Anatolia, the North and South Caucasus, and western

---

135   Sagona 1984; 2018.
136   Areshian 2006; Simonyan and Rothman 2015.
137   Rothman 2011.
138   Djavakhishvili 1973, 229-269; Areshian 1981:51; Areshian 1996/1985, 33-35.
139   Badalyan 2014, 78, Fig 4.

Iran.[140] We consider as the origin point of the Kura-Araxes the geographic distribution of mostly uniform assemblages dating to the second half of the fourth millennium BC.

One of the sites that, according to our present knowledge, represents the uniformity of features of the early Kura-Araxes homeland is Norabats near Yerevan in the Ararat Plain.[141] Excavations there exposed an area of near one thousand square meters, and radiocarbon dates firmly place it in the third quarter of the fourth millennium BC. This site provided all of the major elements of a Kura-Araxes artifact assemblage: an abundant repertoire of ceramics, the settlement layout and architecture, cultic paraphernalia and art, lithics, etc. The pottery assemblage of Norabats is characteristic of the so-called "Elar-Aragats group," characterized by Badalyan[142] as "the stage of homogeneity of the Kura-Araxes" pottery in Armenia during the Kura-Araxes. But the Elar-Aragats group differs very little from the Didube-Kiketi pottery assemblage,[143] identified in the Kura River Basin to the north and northwest from the Ararat Plain in the geographic regions of Kvemo Kartli and Shida Kartli in eastern Georgia. From the standpoint of artifacts, besides the pottery, that characterize the uniformity of the early Kura-Araxes homeland, the Didube-Kiketi repertoire is also represented at Khizanaant Gora level E.[144] This is a settlement that had cultic assemblage and architectural planning quite similar to those found at Norabats, although with minor differences. These could be attributed either to an internal diversity of artifact typology within the Kura-Araxes heartland or to slightly different dates.

The settlement of Norabats[145] is represented by one single building level, within which it was possible to identify a sequence in construction of individual structures forming two stratigraphic, chronological phases (Fig 4a.1). The most salient feature of the architectural layout is the complete absence of rectangular structures. All of the eight early Kura-Araxes houses excavated at Norabats had a circular plan with their external diameter varying between

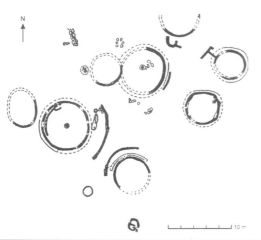

Figure 4a.1. Norabats architecture.

140   for the multisource origins of the Kura-Araxes ceramics repertoire during the Late Chalcolithic see: Kiguradze and Sagona 2003, 40-44, 51-59; Areshian et al. 2012, 127-128.
141   Areshian 1980; 2006; 2007, 31-32; Areshian et al. 1981.
142   Badalyan 2014, 73.
143   Kiguradze and Sagona 2003, fig. 3,15-3:36.
144   Kikvidze 1972.
145   Areshian 1996/1985, 35-36; Areshian 2005.

4.8 and 7.5 meters. Two round houses had small external annexes used for utilitarian purposes (most likely for storage), one of which had a rectangular plan with internal partitioning, while the plan of the other was irregular. House 8 was of exceptional interest, since its circular wall, preserved to a substantial height, was curving toward the center of the circle starting from the level of the floor. The curvature was shaped by laying down each consecutive row of mudbrick masonry with a slight recess toward the center of the structure, which created a corbelled ("false") dome and, on completion, the bell- or "beehive"-shaped design of the house. Besides the overwhelming predominance of round structures, another characteristic feature marks three of the excavated houses (3, 5, and 7). In those, the main, internal circular wall is surrounded by an external, also circular, concentric wall creating a corridor encompassing the main room. In House 5 the external circular corridor was wide enough to become an important area of daily household activities, such as storage, grinding flour, maybe making flint tools. Alternatively, this could have been a screen against wind and cold, as wood or stone screens against wattle-and-daub houses could have been added.

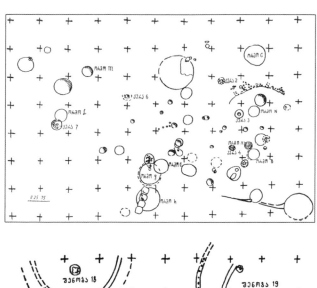

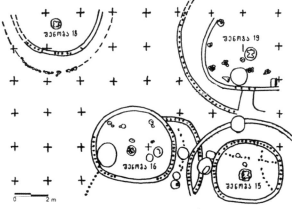

Figure 4a.2. Khizanaant Gora E and D architecture.

Khizanaant Gora's levels D and E display the same principle of circular planning of houses (Fig 4a.2). More than that, the round houses of Level D had a circular external corridor, closely resembling the architectural design found at Norabats.[146] But there is an obvious difference in construction techniques between the round houses of Norabats and Khizanaant Gora. The houses of Norabats were built exclusively of mudbricks, whereas the structures of Khizanaant Gora had wattle-and-daub walls. This difference raises the question whether construction technique could be viewed as diagnostic in the analysis of early differences in the Kura-Araxes homeland. The predominance of wattle-and-daub versus mudbrick buildings seems to mark more highland from lowland occupation. Archaeologists uncovered stone foundations of a building that had concentric walls displaying a plan analogous to the houses of Norabats and Khizanaant Gora at Samshvilde[147] in association with a pottery assemblage characteristic of the Didube-Kiketi group typical of the KA1 in the Kura-Araxes homeland. Yet another similarity between Norabats and Khizanaant Gora was the distinctive uniformity in the architectural design characteristic of the Kura-Araxes homeland; that is, the placement of a round cultic hearth in the center of circular buildings. In addition to these two sites, this is also attested at other settlements representing the homeland and is frequently recorded in KA2 levels of Shengavit (see Chapter 6a).

---

146 Areshian 2005.
147 Gobedzhishvili 1978.

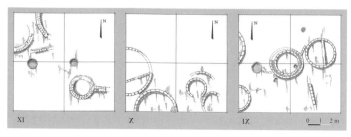

Figure 4a.3. Mokhrablur Strata XI-IX.

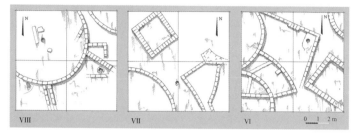

Figure 4a.4. Mokhrablur Strata VIII, VII, and VI.

Another site, whose lowest levels contain remains of settlements representing the uniformity of the early Kura-Araxes homeland is Mokhrablur (Fig 4a.3). Like Norabats it was located in the Ararat Plain. The more than seven-meter-thick Kura-Araxes deposits of Mokhrablur contained nine building levels (third through eleventh, counted from top to bottom), several of which (fourth and fifth) were formed by a number of construction phases. The recorded changes in architectural design and construction techniques have led me[148] to subdivide the Kura-Araxes deposits into four consecutive architectural levels as follows. First, Period I contained the earliest three building strata (XI, X, IX) (Fig 4a.3). Period II contained Strata VIII, VII, and VI (Fig 4a.4). These are equivalent to a time from KA1 into the beginning of KA2. Radiocarbon dates of Period I coincide with those of Norabats, placing it somewhere in the third quarter of the fourth millennium BC. My description of the pottery includes early KA2 forms; namely, the double carinated intermediate 1 types (see Chapter 5e). Although the three levels of Period I were excavated within the limited surface of the stratigraphic trench that was less than 60 square meters at the bottom, it is possible to conclude that the pottery and fragments of cultic artifacts are very similar to those found at Norabats and Khizanaant Gora Level E. The same could be said about the remaining architectural remains of that period. All of the buildings excavated in the ninth and tenth levels had a circular plan. The diameter of small structures that could have been used for storage varied between 1.8 and 2.5 meters, but, besides those, archaeologists excavated larger, round houses with a diameter up to four meters. Only in the earliest level, XI, did archaeologists recover a solidly built rectilinear wall. Its width was formed by two rows of square bricks (measuring 0.16 x 0.16 m).

To the southeast of the Ararat Plain, further downstream the Araxes River on the Naxçivan Plain, Abibullaev excavated the tell nowadays known as the Kültepe I (Fig 4a.5). He subdivided its stratigraphic sequence into levels according to the cultural assemblage contained in each layer. The second, 8.5-9.5-meter-thick level contained Kura-Araxes assemblages and was subdivided in its turn into 14 building horizons.[149] The pottery of the second level was not fully published, but there can be no doubt that its major part belongs

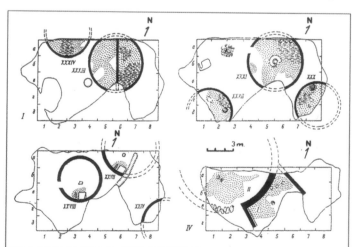

Figure 4a.5. Kültepe I architecture.

148   Areshian 1996/1985:34-35.
149   Abibullaev 1982.

to the uniform typological repertoire of the Kura-Araxes in Armenia, as does the category of cultic artifacts. We can thus say that Naxçivan was part of the homeland. The architectural patterns revealed by the twelve levels that comprised the lower four meters of the Kura-Araxes sequence of the Kültepe I are also consistent with the tradition of circular buildings characteristic of Norabats, Khizanaant Gora E and D, and Mokhrablur's Architectural Periods I and II. Out of 40 excavated structures, 28 had a circular plan, while the remaining 12 were small rectangular annexes attached to the round buildings.

One finds, not surprisingly, the combination of features characteristic of the Kura-Araxes heartland across the Araxes River on the Iranian side of the modern border, where it was identified in the stratigraphic Trench II excavated on Kul Tepe near Jolfa. The two-meter-thick remains of Period V provided a pottery repertoire identical to that of Norabats. Also identical were cultic artifacts (cultic circular clay hearths), a circular mudbrick structure, and, importantly, radiocarbon dates within the range of 3350-3000 BC.[150] The round houses with inner partitions excavated in Level VIII of Haftavan Tepe could easily be found in the aforementioned sites, particularly Mokhrablur Period I; however, three features of the associated pottery—these include "rail" rims, ribbed semi-globular lugs, and angular sharp transition between the upper and lower parts of jars' bodies— make it quite unlikely that the date of that level is ca 3000-2900 BC.[151] The Urmia Lake basin sites probably were not within the homeland zone.

How far the Kura-Araxes core extended toward the east is not clear. To date archaeologists have found no settlement of the last third of the fourth millennium BC in the mountainous Karabagh area. Several large clusters of Kura-Araxes sites (about 50), explored in the southern part of the Mil Steppe along the tributaries of Araxes River near the Caspian Sea, need more investigations and radiocarbon dating.[152]

The Origin and the Disappearance of the Round House

The appearance of mud-brick round-plan houses in the Altınova (Harput or Kharberd) Plain ca. 2700 BC is attested at Norşuntepe Horizon 24, where they are associated with the appearance of a tradition of Kura-Araxes pottery representing a KA2 phase of its development.[153]

One may conclude with confidence that the round plan of houses is the most distinctive feature of architecture of the Kura-Araxes KA1 for two obvious reasons: (a) its spread is strongly correlated with the pottery typologically characteristic of the KA1 (i.e. "Elar-Aragats" and "Didube-Kiketi" typological groups), and (b) the tradition of building those round-plan houses could be found nowhere else in the Near East after the end of the sixth millennium BC, except the Armenian Highlands occupied by the Kura-Araxes KA1 cultural tradition populations.

Yet, the conclusion that the round-plan houses represent a distinctive feature of the Kura-Araxes core suggests at least three additional research questions: (1) where should we look for the origins of the round plan in the domestic architecture of the Kura-Araxes; (2) did other designs in house planning, such as rectangular ones, coexist with the round plan during the KA1 period of the Kura-Araxes, (3) what was the destiny of round houses in the processes of divergences in architectural traditions, which followed with the balkanization and heterogeneity of the KA2; and (4) is there an advantage to the different shapes of houses?

Four decades ago, before the massive accumulation of calibrated radiocarbon dates and discovery of new sites,

---

150   Abedi and Omrani 2015, 57-58, 60-62.
151   Summers 2014:159-162.
152   Ismailov 1963.
153   Hauptmann 2000:421-423, 428, pl. 1, 4-5.

the answer to the first question would have seemed much simpler than it is today. In those days the newly discovered Shulaveri-Shomutepe culture of southeastern Georgia and the western part of the Republic of Azerbaijan (not Iranian Azerbaijan) and Teghut in the Ararat Plain of Armenia [154] presented a pattern of only circular plans in domestic construction.[155] Keeping in mind that these sites were thought to be Chalcolithic, dating to the fifth to fourth millennia BC and preceding the Kura-Araxes without a major time gap, it was easy to assume that the round-house planning of the latter was derived directly from the Neolithic Aratashen-Shulaveri-Shomutepe architectural tradition. But a major accumulation of new data since that time has made the interpretation of the origins of round-house planning in the Kura-Araxes KA1 more complex.

On the one hand, the newly obtained series of radiocarbon dates and the discovery of Halaf pottery at the settlements of Aknashen and Masis Blur in the Ararat Plain representing the Aratashen-Shulaveri-Shomutepe culture require a drastic revision in the chronology of that culture, currently re-dating it to ca. 6100-5300 BC; that is, more or less synchronous with the Halaf and the radiocarbon dates from Masis Blur.[156] This resulted in a re-attribution in the course of the last three decades of the Aratashen-Shulaveri-Shomutepe to the Late Neolithic and created an almost two millennium-long gap between the probable end of the Aratashen-Shulaveri-Shomutepe culture sometime around 5300 BC and the formation of the Kura-Araxes KA1 ca. 3500-3300 BC. On the other hand, the excavations of Chalcolithic settlements, dated from the last part of the sixth through the middle of the fourth millennium BC, which presented patterns of complex rectangular house plans, have been gradually, but still only partially, filling this gap. The discovery of a large rectangular public building in Level V2 at Berikldeebi, located not far from Khizanaant Gora, [157] affirms its connection to Northern Mesopotamia.[158] Excavations of rectangular multi-room complexes at Adablur near Ejmiacin in the Ararat Plain, [159] the settlement plan composed of similar multi-room rectangular buildings of Alikemek-tepesi Level I in the Mil steppe of the Republic of Azerbaijan,[160] and the architectural layout of Leilatepe indicate beyond a reasonable doubt that a northern Mesopotamian influence occurred on an architectural tradition represented by rectangular (oftentimes multi-room) buildings sometime in the course of the fifth millennium BC. The area covered by Chaff-Faced Ware pottery confirms the connection of the two regions.

Whether that replacement of the earlier "Halaf-Shulaverian" architectural style had been more or less dominant, or the construction of circular buildings continued here and there as a lingering residual form in the course of the fifth and first half of the fourth millennium BC is unclear. Despite the dominating development of complex rectangular architectural planning in sites of the period dug so far, the limited number of Chalcolithic sites excavated mean this question can only be clarified by future excavations. Yet, there are some indications that might speak in favor of such a continuing tradition. The excavations of the Late Chalcolithic site at Gödedzor located in the gorge of the Vorotan River in the mountainous zone of the Syunik' Province of Armenia uncovered the foundations of a small circular structure built of large undressed rocks. Excavators also uncovered fragments of other circular foundations. A sequence of radiocarbon dates firmly places these remains within the period from 3650 to 3350 cal. BC. [161] A very similar stone

154   Torosyan 1976.
155   Djavakhishvili 1973.
156   Badalyan and Harutyunyan 2014:175, fig. 6.
157   Javakhishvili 1998.
158   Sagona 2014.
159   Areshian 1991.
160   Narimanov 1987:57-58.
161   Chataigner et al. 2010:382; Palumbi and Chataigner 2014:251-253.

foundation of a circular structure measuring 3.5 m in diameter was attributed to Period VIA (Late Chalcolithic 3) in Trench II at Kul Tepe Hadishahr dated by two radiocarbon samples between 4037 and 3792 cal. BC.[162]

Another exception is represented by the Teghut settlement near Ejmiacin in the Ararat Plain where a single-layer settlement that existed for no more than few decades consisted exclusively of scattered single-room semi-subterranean round houses and free-standing round storage bins with walls built of pounded-earth (pisé) or sun-dried mudbricks.[163] The date of the Teghut settlement is quite important to our discussion and, although no radiocarbon dates exist so far for this site, artifactual remains suggest it existed after the end of the Aratashen-Shulaveri-Shomutepe culture and before the Late Chalcolithic of the first half of the fourth millennium BC, represented in Armenia by such sites as Gödedzor and Areni-1. Contrary to other opinions, my suggestion that the Teghut settlement could be dated within the second half of the fifth millennium BC[164] may still be valid, especially in light of our current knowledge concerning the trajectory of development of the chipped-stone artifact production in Armenia from the Neolithic through the Bronze Age. Chalcolithic Adablur, located in the same Late Neolithic-Early Bronze Age group of settlements as Teghut on the Kasakh River, provides us with an obsidian chipped-stone industry based on the production of long blades derived from the Aratashen-Shulaveri-Shomutepe tradition,[165] whereas Teghut's data suggest an advanced stage of change in that tradition. From this one could plausibly, although roughly, attribute Adablur to the timespan somewhere between the end of the sixth millennium and the middle of the fifth millennium BC and place Teghut between the middle and the very end of the fifth millennium BC. Beyond any doubt, such a dating is highly provisional at this time, but it suffices to support my hypothesis that the tradition of round house building, although temporarily replaced by some rectangular domestic architecture during the Chalcolithic Chaff-Faced Ware stage, still survived as a local cultural tradition from the end of Aratashen-Shulaveri-Shomutepe times throughout the fifth and first half of the fourth millennium BC. They were then resurrected as the norm in the Kura-Araxes KA1.

I can suggest two hypotheses, which are not necessarily mutually exclusive, with regard to general historical and sociocultural conditions that lead to the emergence and expansion of the architectural tradition of round house building among the societies of early farmers in the Near East. First, the round house plan may have replicated the plan of round shacks built of tree branches, twigs, sometimes skins of large animals and reeds characteristic of mobile hunter-gatherers beginning at least from the Upper Paleolithic and surviving up to the ethnographic present.[166] In the case of the Kura-Araxes KA1 it could also have been a reproduction of round tents of mobile pastoralists, i.e. in both cases the formation and development of round house planning among agriculturalists would have been related to, or maybe even caused by processes of sedentism.[167] However, the association of wattle-and-daub houses with mobile populations may also not be sustainable. Wattle and daub houses can last a very long time. They require some skill to manufacture, and in England and Germany some wattle-and-daub houses have stood for centuries. (Fig 4a.6). One of the major differences is in the roofing. To build a flat roof or a solid beehive-shaped roof, one needs the strength of a mudbrick base. Most wattle-and-daub houses use thatch roofs or require large logs as supports inside the walls. Also, most nomadic pastoral tents are square and quite a lot larger than most Kura-Araxes houses of any shape. The

162   Abedi and Omrani 2015:57-58.
163   Torosyan 1976:21-43.
164   Areshian 1996/1985:28.
165   Areshian 1991.
166   Djavakhishvili 1973:207
167   Cribb 1991.

Figure 4a.6. Construction of A. wattle-and-daub houses, B. Medieval English wattle-and-daub house.

layout of typical Baluch tents reflects the complexity of the space created for nomadic pastoral household, which moves seasonally, but then settles for months at a time (Fig 4a.7). In addition, wattle-and-daub houses are more likely to survive earthquakes than mudbrick houses.[168]

The second hypothesis is connected to the corbelled bell-shape or beehive-shape dome building technique in the Aratashen-Shulaveri-Shomutepe period building tradition and the architecture of the Kura-Araxes KA1. The construction of corbelled domes could hardly be derived from simple shacks of a round plan, since it required imagination and empirical knowledge of properties of the building material (sun-dried bricks and clay mortar and plaster) and of the structural internal forces producing downward and outward thrusts in the brick masonry. Djavakhishvili[169] already stressed the specific role of mortar which had a deliberately harder composition than the bricks in the Shulaveri-Shomutepe architecture, thus creating stronger properties and structural stability to the entire building. The acquisition of such knowledge could have been stimulated by environmental conditions of severe scarcity of construction wood in the areas where such architecture had originated and developed.[170] However, new environmental evidence suggests that the forests were expanding during the Kura-Araxes, so such a reason is not very likely.[171] Further, whereas the square building has more floorspace, the round ones have advantages. They are better able to withstand winds and earthquakes, retain heat and cool better, and are acoustically superior to square buildings.[172] In none of these buildings were roofs used as working or sleeping spaces, as they were in Mesopotamia.

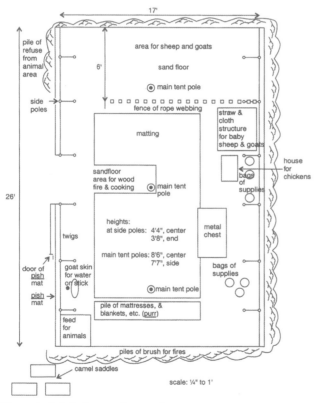

Figure 4a.7. Baluch nomad pastoral tent.

168   Dutu et al. 2018.
169   Djavakhishvili 1973:208.
170   O'Kane 1995.
171   Connor and Kvavadze 2014.
172   https://www.econation.co.nz/blog/the-benefits-of-round-houses/

Did other designs in house planning, such as rectangular shapes, coexist with the round plan already during the period of the Kura-Araxes KA1? Before addressing this question, one needs to reexamine an existing opinion that round house planning was characteristic of settlements built on the flatlands of plains in river valleys, whereas houses of rectangular plan were constructed in mountainous areas on hilltops and slopes. These sites are located on the flatland edge of the first terrace surrounding the Ararat Plain. Kura-Araxes round houses in the mountainous zone also were attested at Elar, and the Vanadzor cluster of Kura-Araxes settlements. One can conclude with sufficient confidence that roundhouses appeared in all the geographic zones during the period of the KA1. So, this correlation of geographical zone and round houses is not supported by the currently available data. After the KA1 the situation is even more variable. For example, the settlement at Garni, built in the mountain zone and representing the KA2 regionalization of the Kura-Araxes, had a pattern of large roundhouses with rectangular annexes, but also squares buildings, characteristic of the contemporaneous building levels at Shengavit (see Chapter 4b) and Franganots. Another variation is evident at Pulur Sakyol and Godin Tepe [173] at the southeastern and western edge of the Kura-Araxes diaspora in the KA2 (Fig 4a.8). Most Kura-Araxes buildings were free standing. But builders at these sites made a combination of square buildings with adjoining walls in a round shape, which they also combined with freestanding, square building types at Godin.

The end of the unity of the Kura-Araxes KA1 and the transformation to a heterogeneous corpus of artifacts in the KA2 (ca. 3000-2500 BC) is reflected in clear changes in architectural patterns and trends, ending in either a complete disappearance or small percentage of round houses. The contrast is evident at Mokhrablur. There see Period III the fifth and fourth strata, Period IV the third or last Kura-Araxes building stratum (Fig 4a.9).

At least three patterns of architectural change are identifiable with regard to the relationship between circular and rectangular planning of domestic archi-

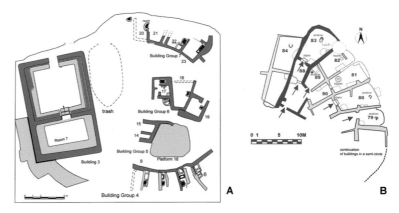

Figure 4a.8. Kura-Araxes (KA2) architecture at Godin Tepe (A) and Pulur Sakyol (B).

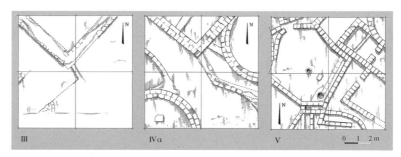

Figure 4a.9. Mokhrablur Strata III and IV.

tecture in the course of regionalization of the Kura-Araxes. First, a complete replacement of roundhouses with rectangular plans in the architectural layouts of entire settlements is identifiable both in settlements built on a previously unoccupied terrain and within stratigraphic sequences of multi-level sites. Second, rare cases existed of the possible coexistence of two separate, but more or less synchronously built areas, one consisting predominantly of round houses, while the other of rectangular buildings within the boundaries of a single settlement located on a more or less flat terrain. This is evident at Arslantepe VIB1 (3200-3100 BC), the only time a clearly Kura-Araxes presence

---

173   Koşay 1976; Rothman 2011.

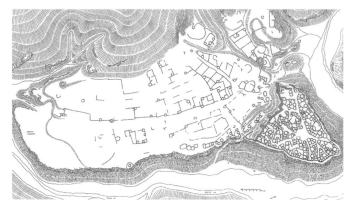

Figure 4a.10. Köhne Shahar (Ravaz) town plan.

existed at the site.[174] This might just be a case of mixed ethnicities. At Shengavit at least these later round houses had thicker walls, benches, and may not have had beehive roofs (see below). The third is the most complex and diverse pattern of gradual transformation from architectural layouts primarily consisting of roundhouses to those dominated by rectangular planning observable throughout the stratigraphic sequences of multi-level settlements. The first and third patterns are identifiable throughout all the geographic areas initially occupied in the Kura-Araxes KA1 and in its vicinity subjected to the processes of regionalization.

The possibility of synchronous coexistence of two differently built areas within a single settlement, one consisting predominantly of round houses, and the other of rectangular complexes, can be seen at Köhne Shahar, also known as Ravaz (Fig 4a.10), located to the northwest of the city of Chaldran in Iranian Azerbaijan[175] and Shengavit Architectural Level 2 (see Chapter 3). The modern borders may present a false image of where Köhne Shahar was located, as it lies within the homeland zone near the Araxes River, although within the borders of modern Iran. The radiocarbon determinations and similarity of pottery matches the time at the transition of the KA1 and KA2 and the whole of the KA2.[176] This large settlement consists of two distinctively different parts. One is the inner town (named "the citadel" by the excavators) surrounded by a fortification wall with round towers with densely built round houses, some of which had rectangular annexes, and the outer town consisting of freestanding, rectangular complexes with some circular structures.

The pattern of replacement of round houses with rectangular layouts within a single site is visible in the transition

Figure 4a.11. Kura-Araxes architecture at Norşuntepe (A/B are KA2, C is pre-Kura-Araxes Chalcolithic).

---

174   Palumbi et al. 2017.
175   Kleiss and Kroll 1979: 31-34,37-47, fig. 5-7; Alizadeh 2015:91-257; Alizadeh, Eghbal and Samei 2015; Areshian 2007:45-46, fig. 2.7.1.
176   Batiuk et al. 2022.

between the whole architectural designs of the levels belonging to the Early Bronze Phase I and Phase II at Yanik Tepe, Godin Tepe, Norşuntepe, and Shengavit. At Godin Tepe, Yanik Tepe, and Norşuntepe this may represent the transition to post-Kura-Araxes societies.[177] At Shengavit it represents the final stage of society near the end of the Kura-Araxes occupation of the site in a transitional phase with the Early Kurgan Period. The change in building style coincides with the change in the repertoire of pottery style and graves with KA2 and Early Kurgan pottery.[178] Yet, the transition between the two phases also reveals continuity with regard to the organization of house interiors and some features of ceramics.[179]

A good illustration of a striking replacement of architectural tradition within the area of Kura-Araxes expansion due to a migration of its carriers during the period of regionalization in the KA2 is provided by the aforementioned stratigraphic sequence of Norşuntepe on the Altınova Plain in the Taurus Mountains (Fig 4a.11).[180] Kura-Araxes houses and associated pottery and other artifacts appear in KA2 houses containing a mixture of Syrian and Kura-Araxes pottery assemblage in Horizon 24 at the beginning of what the excavators call the Early Bronze IIA Period (FBIIA, KA2) of that site (around ca. 2700 BC). This architectural level overlaid Horizon 25 composed of single-room rectangular houses containing a "Syrian-style" pottery (including samples resembling Amuq H) and was succeeded by horizons 23-14 predominantly formed by the remains of wattle and daub houses associated with a pottery assemblage consisting of approximately 50% of local versions of Kura-Araxes types. It is quite obvious that Norşuntepe displays two consecutive replacements of architectural traditions, both resulting from migrations of the Kura-Araxes-related populations.

Another case of relatively rapid, yet not abrupt transition from the round house plan of the Kura-Araxes KA1 to a rectangular planning of houses organized in a new type of settlement layout during the period of regionalization is demonstrable in the sites of Shida Kartli. There, the round house plan of the lowest building at Level E Khizanaant Gora, still representing the phase of the KA1, was replaced in subsequent levels by rectangular houses with rounded corners and internal partitioning that developed very soon into a new "standard" plan of rectangular bipartite houses consisting of a small front room and the main back room. This plan is evident at Kvatskhelebi meticulously excavated by A. I. Djavakhishvili and L. Glonti.[181] That transformation of dwelling plans was achieved by using wattle and daub construction technique or a combination of mudbrick and wattle-and-daub. That technique was at times free standing, but at times the outer wall was made of large wooden posts or stone, bracketing the wattle and daub (Fig 4a.12).[182]

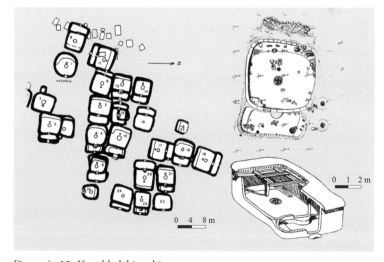

Figure 4a.12. Kvatskhelebi architecture.

---

177   Rothman 2011.

178   Simonyan and Rothman in press.

179   Burney 1961; Burney 1962; Burney 1964; Summers 2013.

180   Hauptmann 2000.

181   Kikvidze 1972; Djavakhishvili and Glonti 1962; Djavakhishvili 1973:113-149.

182   Sagona 2018, 230f.

A gradual transformation of a settlement composed of free standing, mostly small round houses characteristic of the Kura-Araxes KA1 into a densely built space in which large roundhouses become the central room in a multi-room assemblage is well attested in the stratigraphy of Mokhrablur in the Ararat Plain (Fig 4a.4 and 6).[183] The architectural Period I (building levels XI through IX) of this site predominantly represented by small and medium size round houses (Fig 4.3) was followed in Period II by large round houses reaching seven meters in their internal diameter with rectangular external annexes (e.g. house no. 37 in the eight building level) (Fig 4a.4). The gradual development of the household architecture at this site is evinced by the fact that the walls of those large roundhouses of the eight level are as thin (only 0.25 m) as the walls in the preceding Strata IX through XI, being composed by a single row of sun-dried mudbricks laid in a way that their width (0.22 m) formed the width of the wall. The structural inadequacy between the thin walls and large size of the room made the whole building unstable and prone to collapse, this was overcome in consequent Architectural Periods III and IV by doubling the width of house walls through an addition of a second row of mudbrick masonry (Fig 4a.9). The seventh building level excavated in the stratigraphic trench at Mokhrablur presented a substantial innovation in house planning ushered by the appearance of a free-standing rectangular, almost square building (structure no. 33), with internal measures of 2.08 x 2.01 meters that was not an annex to round houses. A major development is reflected in the uncovered pattern of transition from architectural Period II to Period III (i.e. from building level six to building level five). Domestic structures of the fifth and fourth building levels (Architectural Period III) clearly display a qualitative increase in the massiveness of architecture composed of complexes dominated by a large round building forming the core of a dwelling complex and surrounded by multiple rectangular and polygonal annexes. This development is causally related to the dramatic increase in the thickness of building levels. The thickness of a building level containing the remains of Periods I and II (Building Levels XI through VI) varied between 0.4 and 0.7 meters, whereas the thickness of Building Level V recorded in the stratigraphic trench amounted to 1.6 meter, and of the Level IV 1.8 meter. The wall of roundhouse no. 7 in Building Level IV was 0.68-0.70-meter-thick. So, it is not surprising that Building Levels XI through VI are represented by a single construction phase, while two construction phases with two sub-phases in each were recorded in five and four phases in Level IV. The change between phases within each level was determined by the rebuilding of the roundhouse, the flattened wall of which was used as a socle for raising a new wall exactly replicating the contour of the preceding wall. The same pattern is evident in square K6 at Shengavit (see Fig 4b.6). So, the plan and the size of the roundhouse remained the same, while the layouts of annexes have changed from one phase to another. Within one building level, a round house of an earlier phase was dutifully replicated in the next phase, but the same approach was not followed with regard to annexes. The stratigraphic borderlines of Levels V and IV were determined by shifts in the location of round houses, which were built in new places together with the rebuilding of annexes. An architectural pattern similar to Mokhrablur Period III was uncovered by Khanzadyan at Jrahovit, [184] but on a much larger scale; this unfortunately remains largely unpublished. The increase in massiveness of architectural remains attested in the transition from Mokhrablur Period II to Period III was also recorded by Abibullaev in the change of the character of debris from the 12th to the 13th building horizons, i.e. in the uppermost part of the second (i.e. Kura-Araxes) cultural level of Naxçivan's Kültepe I. The last, fourth architectural period in the Kura-Araxes sequence of Mokhrablur represented by only a single building, Level III, is dated to the timespan ca. 2700-2500 BC. This level demonstrates the pattern of an increased number of rectangular and polygonal plans in domestic architecture at the expense of the total space occupied by roundhouses.

---

183   Areshian 1996/1985,39-41.
184   Khanzadyan 2003.

A more detailed pattern of the transformation of domestic architecture dominated by round house construction in the times of the Kura-Araxes KA1 into layouts characterized mainly by rectangular plans, particularly toward the end of that cultural tradition, is revealed in the extensive excavations at Shengavit.

These patterns of free-standing single brick round houses of KA1 is followed by clear changes both in the forms and heterogeneity of all classes of artifacts in the KA2. Similar buildings continue into the KA2, but then marked changes occur. Round buildings had at least two brick-wide walls and may not have the beehive shaped roofs. Among the new forms in KA2 are round and square buildings with square antechambers like at Shengavit, or ones with covered porches like at Kvatskhelebi C. At Shengavit the round form disappeared, and larger rectangular buildings took over. For more detail on Shengavit, see Chapter 4b.

In conclusion, the shape and size of building of sites under the umbrella of the Kura-Araxes cultural tradition have a general tendency to go from free-standing round buildings to rectangular buildings. However, an apparent lack of central planning meant that all sorts of combinations of the round, round with square adjoining rooms, and free-standing rectangular buildings is mixed in a pattern that shows no consistency through time and place.

References

Abedi A. and Omrani, B. 2015 Kura-Araxes Culture and North-Western Iran: New Perspectives from Kul Tepe Jolfa (Hadishahr). *Paléorient* 41 (1): 55-68.

Abibullaev, O. A., 1982 *The Aeneolithic and Bronze Age in the Territory of the Nakhichevan Autonomous Soviet Socialist Republic.* Baku: "Èlm" Press. (in Russian).

Alizadeh, K. 2015 *Social Inequality at Köhne Shahar, an Early Bronze Age Settlement in Iranian Azerbaijan.* Doctoral dissertation, Harvard University.

Alizadeh, K., Eghbal, H, .and Samei, S.. 2015 Approaches to Social Complexity in Kura-Araxes Culture: A View from Köhne Shahar (Ravaz) in Chaldran, Iranian Azerbaijan. *Paléorient* 41(1): 37-54.

Areshian, G. 1980 Norabats – a New-found Site of the Bronze Age. In *Archaeological Discoveries of 1979*, edited by B. A. Rybakov, 423. Moscow: "Nauka" Press. (in Russian).

Areshian, G. 1981 Cultural Traditionalism Exemplified by the Kura-Araxes Culture. In *Proceedings of the Methodological Seminar of the Leningrad Division of the Institute of Archaeology*, edited by V. M. Masson and V. N. Borjaz, 49-52. Leningrad: "Nauka" Press. (in Russian).

Areshian, G. 1991 Excavations at Adablur. In *Concise Reports of the Conference Devoted to the Results of Archaeological Fieldwork in Armenia, 1989 – 1990*, 8-11. Yerevan: Publishing House of the Academy of Sciences of Armenia. (in Armenian).

Areshian, G. 1996/1985 The Architecture of the Armenian Highland and Adjacent Regions of the Early Bronze Age. In *A History of Armenian Architecture, Vol. I: The Architecture of Armenian Highlands from the Earliest Times to the 3rd Century AD,* edited by G.E. Areshian, K.K. Ghafadaryan, K.L. Hovhannisian and A.A. Sahinian, 33-67. Yerevan: "Gitut'yun" Press of the Armenian National Academy of Sciences. (in Armenian).

Areshian, G. 2005 Early Bronze Age Settlements in the Ararat Plain and its Vicinity. *Archäologische Mitteilungen aus Iran und Turan* 37 (2005): 71-88.

Areshian, G. 2007 From Extended Families to Incipient Polities: The Trajectory of Social Complexity in the Early Bronze Age of the Ararat Plain (Central Near Eastern Highlands). In *Social Orders and Social Landscapes: Proceedings of the 2005 University of Chicago Conference on Eurasian Archaeology*, edited by L.M. Popova, C.W. Hartley, and A.T. Smith, 26-54. Newcastle upon Tyne: Cambridge Scholars Publishing.

Areshian, G., S. H. Devejian, and H. R̄. Israyelyan. 1979 Excavations of Sites between Norabats and Nerk'in Charbakh Villages. In *Proceedings of the Conference Devoted to the Results of Archaeological Fieldwork in Armenia, 1979 – 1980*, 25-27. Yerevan: Publishing House of the Academy of Sciences of the Armenian SSR. (in Armenian).

Areshian, G. B. Gasparyan, P. Avetisyan, R. Pinhasi, K. Wilkinson, A. Smith, R. Hovsepyan, and D. Zardaryan, 2012 The Chalcolithic of the Near East and Southeastern Europe: Discoveries and New Perspectives from the Cave Complex Areni-1, Armenia. *Antiquity* 86 (331): 115-130.

Badalyan, Ruben, 2014 New data on the periodization and chronology of the Kura-Araxes culture in Armenia, *Paléorient*, 40 (2): 71-92.

Badalyan, R., Lombard, P., Avetisyan, P., Chataigner, C., Chabot J., Villa, E., Hovsepyan R., Willcox G., and Pessin H. 2017 New Data on the Late Prehistory of the Southern Caucasus. The Excavations at Aratashen (Armenia): Preliminary Report. In *Les culture du Caucase (VIᵉ-IIIᵉ millénaire avant notre ère. Leurs relations avec le Proche-Orient)*, edited by B. Lyonnet, 37-61. Paris: CNRS Éditions.

Badalyan, R. and Harutyunyan, A.. 2014 Aknashen – the Late Neolithic Settlement of the Ararat Valley: Main Results and Prospects for the Research. In *Stone Age of Armenia: A Guide-book to the Stone Age Archaeology in the Republic of Armenia, edited by* B. Gasparyan and M. Arimura, 161-176. Kanazawa (Japan): Kanazawa University.

Batiuk, S. 2005 *Migration Theory and the Distribution of the Early Transcaucasian Culture.* Ph.D. dissertation, Department of Near and Middle Eastern Civilizations, University of Toronto.

Batiuk, S., Rothman, M. S, Samei, S., and Hovsepyan R. 2022 Unraveling the Kura-Araxes Cultural Tradition Across Space and Time. *Ancient Near Eastern Studies.* 59:235-325.

Bayburtian, E. 1937 A Cultic Hearth from the Excavations of the Shengavit Settlement. *Journal of Ancient History* 2 (in Russian).

Bayburtian, E, 2011/1938 *The Sequence of Earliest Cultures of Armenia Based on Archaeological Data*, edited by R. Badalyan. Yerevan: Museum of History of Armenia. (in Russian).

Burney, C. 1961 Excavations at Yanik Tepe, North-West Iran. *Iraq* 23 (2): 138-153.

Burney, C. 1962 The Excavations at Yanik Tepe, Azerbaijan, 1961, Second Preliminary Report. *Iraq* 24 (2): 134-152.

Burney, C. 1964 The Excavations at Yanik Tepe, Azerbaijan, 1962, Third Preliminary Report. *Iraq* 26 (1): 54-61.

Chataigner, C., Avetisyan, P., Palumbi, G., and Uerpmann, H-P. 2010 Gödedzor, a Late Ubaid-related Settlement in the Southern Caucasus." In: *Beyond the Ubaid: Transformation and Integration in the Late Prehistoric Societies of the Middle East, edited by* R.A. Carter and G. Philip, 381-398. Chicago: Oriental Institute of the University of Chicago. (*Studies in Ancient Oriental Civilization* 63).

Connor S, and E. Kvavadze. 2014 Environmental context of the Kura-Araxes culture. *Paléorient*. 40(2): 11-22.

Cribb, R. 1991 *Nomads in Archaeology*. Cambridge: Cambridge University Press.

Dutu, A., Niste, M., Spatarelu, I., Dima, D. I., and Kishiki, S. 2018 Seismic Evaluation of Romanian Traditional Buildings with Timber Frame and Mud Masonry infills by In-plane Static Cyclic Tests. *Engineering Structures* 167: 655-670.

Djavakhishvili, A. I. 1973 *Building Construction and Architecture of Settlements in Southern Caucasus in the 5th-3rd millennia BC*. Tbilisi: "Metsniereba" Press. (in Russian).

Djavakhishvili (Javakhishvili), A. I. 1998 Ausgrabungen in Berikldeebi (Shida Kartli). *Georgica* 21: 7-21.

Frangipane, M. 2000 The Late Chalcolithic - EB I Sequence at Arslantepe. Chronological and Cultural Remarks from a Frontier Site. In *Chronologies des pays du Caucase et de l'Euphrate aux IVe-IIIe millénaires*. Actes du Colloque d'Istanbul, 16-19 décembre 1998, *Varia Anatolica* 11:439-471, Istanbul: Institut Français d'Études Anatoliennes- Georges Dumézil.

Frangipane, M. and Palumbi, G.. 2007 Red-Black Ware, Pastoralism, Trade, and Anatolian-Transcaucasian Interaction in the 4th-3rd Millennium BC. In *Les culture du Caucase (VIe-IIIe millénaire avant notre ère. Leurs relations avec le Proche-Orient)*, edited by B. Lyonnet, 233-256. Paris: CNRS Éditions.

Gobedzhishvili G. E. 1978 *The village of Tetri-Tskaro*. Tblisi: Metsniereba. (in Georgian).

Hauptmann, Harald. 2000 Zur Chronologie des 3. Jahrtausends v. Chr. am oberen Euphrat Aufgrund der Stratigraphie des Norsuntepe. In *Chronologies des pays du Caucase et de l'Euphrate aux IVe-IIIe millénaires*, edited by C. Marro and H. Hauptmann, 419-438. Istanbul: Institut Français d'Études Anatoliennes- Georges Dumézil.

Ismailova, G. S. 1963 *From the History of the Ancient Culture of Western Azerbaijan (Copper-Bronze Age)*. Teblisi: Avtoref nauk. (in Russian).

Javkhishvili, A. I., and Glonti, L. I. 1962 *Urbnisi I: Archaeological Excavations Carried Out in 1954-1961 at the Site of Kvatskhelebi*. Tblisi. (in Russian).

Khanzadyan, E. 2003 Jrahovit. in *Ancient Culture of Armenia 3: Materials Session, dedicated to the 70th Year of Telemak Khachaturian*. 13-19. Yerevan: Mughni. P. (in Armenian).

Kiguradze, T. and Sagona, A., 2003 On the Origins of the Kura-Araxes Cultural Complex. In *Archaeology in the Borderlands. Investigations in Caucasia and beyond*, edited by A. T. Smith and K. S. Rubinson, 38-94. Los Angeles: University of California, Cotsen Institute of Archaeology (Monograph 47).

Kikvidze, J. A. 1972 *The Early Bronze Age Settlement of Khizanaant-gora*. Tbilisi: "Metsniereba." (in Georgian).

Koşay H. 1976 *Keban Project Pulur excavations 1968-1970*. Ankara: Middle East Technical University.

Narimanov, I. 1987 *The culture of the most Ancient Agricultural-pastoral Population of Azerbaijan: The Epoch of Aeneolithic*. Baku: Èlm. (in Russian).

O'Kane, B. 1995 Domes. *Encyclopaedia Iranica*, Vol. VII, Fasc. 5: 479-485.

Palumbi, G. 2008 Fourth Millennium Red-Black Burnished Wares from Anatolia: A Cross-Comparison. In *Ceramics in Transitions. Chalcolithic through Iron Age in the Highlands of the Southern Caucasus and Anatolia*, edited by K.S. Rubinson and A. Sagona, 39-58. Leuven-Paris-Dudley: Peeters (*Ancient Near Eastern Studies Suppl.* 27).

Palumbi, G. and C. Chataigner. 2014 The Kura-Araxes Culture from the Caucasus to Iran, Anatolia and the Levant: Between Unity and Diversity. A Synthesis. *Paléorient*, Vol. 40, No. 2:247-260.

Palumbi G., Alvaro, C., Grifoni, C., Frangipane, M.. 2017 A 'communal' building of the beginning of the Early Bronze Age at Arslantepe-Malatya (Turkey); Spatio-functional analysis and interpretation of the archaeological context. *Paléorient*. 43(1): 89-123.

Rothman, M. S 2011 Migration and Resettlement: Godin IV Period. In *On the High Road: the History of Godin Tepe, Iran*, edited by H. Gopnick and M. S Rothman, 139-208. *Toronto:* Royal Ontario Museum/ Mazda Press.

Sagona, A. 1984 *The Caucasian Region in the Early Bronze Age*, Vols. 1-2, British Archaeological Reports, International Series, no. S214. Oxford: BAR Publishing.

Sagona, Antonio, 2000 Sos Höyük and the Erzurum Region in Late Prehistory: A Provisional Chronology for Northeast Anatolia. In *Chronologies des pays du Caucase et de l'Euphrate aux IVe-IIIe millénaires, edited by C. Marro and H. Hauptmann,* 329-373. Paris: DeBoccard.

Sagona, A. 2018 *The Archaeology of the Caucasus*. Cambridge: Cambridge University Press.

Salzman, P. 2000 *Black Tents of Baluchistan*. Washington, CD: Smithsonian Institution Press.

Simonyan, H. and M. S Rothman. 2015 Regarding Ritual Behaviour at Shengavit, Armenia. *Ancient Near Eastern Studies 52: 1-46.*

Summers, G. D. 2013 *Yanik Tepe, Northwestern Iran: The Early Trans-Caucasian Period. Stratigraphy and Architecture*. Leuven: Peeters Publishers (*Ancient Near Eastern Studies Supplement Series*, 41).

Summers, Geoffrey D. 2014 The Early Trans-Caucasian Culture in Iran: Perspectives and Problems. *Paléorient*, Vol. 40 (2): 155-168.

Torosyan, R. 1976 *Early Agricultural Settlement of Teghut*. Yerevan: Publishing House of the Academy of Sciences of the Armenian SSR (Archaeological Sites of Armenia 14). (in Armenian).

4b | The Architecture of Shengavit

Hakob Simonyan and Hovhannes Sanamyan

Introduction

Builders are crafts persons in the same sense as are potters, flintknappers, or metal-workers.[185] They have a variety of materials from stone to wood to thatch to earth (mudbrick, daub, pisè, plaster) to work with. From these materials they have to construct interior and exterior spaces that 1) allow a set of activities to be performed by residents, 2) fulfill the cultural expectations of people, and 3) factor in different ecological conditions.

This chapter will discuss the actual plans and construction of the buildings at Shengavit, all of which fit into the KA2 period. Details of especially KA1 and some KA2 buildings across the Kura-Araxes homeland appeared in Chapter 4a. The activities represented by artifacts in buildings and the site plan we will discuss in Chapter 7.

Shengavit is important as a key case study and data source for the Kura-Araxes period in the South Caucasus, particularly the Lower Province south of the Lesser Caucasus Mountains along the Araxes River. It represents the Kura-Araxes cultural tradition (the Early Bronze Age) on the Koytak Plateau above the Ararat Plain. Architectural elements of that tradition found at Shengavit include a sequence of building types (see Chapter 3) and special constructions like a massive settlement wall complete with a secret passage to the Hrazdan River (see below), and an unusually large number of stone-lined grain storage pits.

The Characteristics of Buildings at Shengavit

Among each of the six architectural levels and eight strata (based on our complete section of Square K6), excavators found buildings of similar sizes and with similar construction techniques. In general, there is a progression over time of small, free standing round houses to round houses with adjoining square annexes to large rectangular houses. There are exceptions to this pattern as in Architectural Level 2 (Stratum III) in Square K6. There free-standing rectangular and round buildings existed side-by-side. The same pattern is evident at Mokhrablur Level IV (Fig 4a.9). Other variations include buildings with smaller rectangular rooms side-by-side in squares J5 and M5,[186] Architectural Levels 2/3 and 1 respectively.

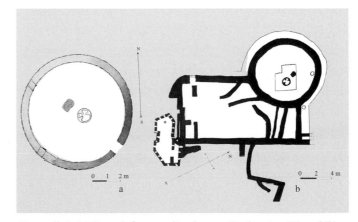

Figure 4b.1. (a) Round, free-standing houses (Bayburtian 22) and (b) round houses with square adjoining room (Bayburtian Building 1).

---

185 Wright 2001.
186 Rothman 2017; Simonyan and Rothman 2015.

The free-standing round buildings range from 6[187] to 10 meters in diameter (28 to 50 m² in area) (Fig 4b.1). The smaller ones are the buildings with a single course of mudbricks, while the later round, free-standing buildings had two courses of brick and often an interior bench. They tended to be bigger.[188] The round rooms with square adjoining rooms were at times smaller than the free-standing ones. Bayburtian draws one such room at only 3.25 m in diameter

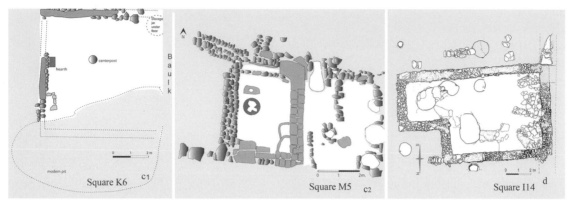

Figure 4b.2. (c) Rectangular building, large square building, d) Rectangular building with an annex.

(8 m² in area).[189] Most seem to be about 6 m in diameter. The assumption has been that the square rooms were all roofed. A number of authors have suggested that this was not always so. Such a large hall required beams for its roof, but excavators found no bases or post holes for these beams, whereas stone bases for roof beams were common in the round buildings and the rectangular Building 2 in Square K6. Parenthetically, that base was flat on the top, but builders had put small stones and potsherds under it to make sure it was stable and flat. Also, according to Bayburtian, in these rectangular spaces they found no ceramics.[190] From this Bayburtian suggests that this building had no roof and could only serve as a courtyard.[191] Others suggest that it was a fenced yard[192] or even a stable (cattle yard).[193] Rothman suggests that the artifacts found there imply that productive activities dominated the walled, unroofed space (see Chapter 7). Flintknapping, which is evidenced there, is normally an activity conducted outdoors, because the flakes scatter and are sharp under foot. On the other hand, the rhomboid-shaped room to the right of Bayburtian's Building 11 may well be a roofed storage room because of its storage vessel and macehead and the size of the space.

We recovered few complete rectangular rooms (Fig 4b.2). Among them are a building in K6 Architectural Level

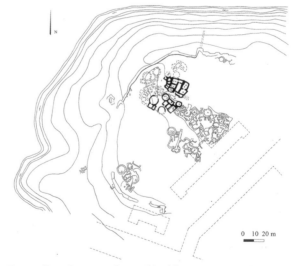

Figure 4b.3. Square and round buildings uncovered by Sardarian.

187   Bayburtian 2011, Figure VI.
188   Fig 3.33.
189   Bayburtian 2011, Figure V.
190   In Bayburtian's fied notes in the National History Museum, one storage pot is listed.
191   Bayburtyan 2011, 31.
192   Kushnareva, 1991, 2.
193   HAA, 1996, 43.

2 (Stratum III), and the two ritual rooms in Squares M5 and J5. Sardarian appears to have found at least one building made of small square rooms (Fig 4b.13). One of these, Building 2 in Square K6, was at least 7 x 7 meters (more than 49 m² in area). M5 was 2.5 x 3.5 meters on the outside (6 m² in interior area). Larger rectangular buildings with annexes existed in Squares I14 and K6. The building in I14 was 7 x 12.5 meters on the outside (81 m² in interior area). The Square K6 Building 1 is longer (14 meters) with an additional 14 m² in area inside.

Details of Building Construction

MATERIALS

The basic materials of the walls of buildings at Shengavit are fairly consistent over time. Dwellings' walls were set on a foundation of ground stones up to 0.9 m high and 40 to 70 cm wide on which builders set mudbrick walls.[194] An exception is Building 7 in Stratum VII of Square K6, which sat on rubble from Stratum VIII (see Chapter 3). The lower levels tended to have river-worn stones in their foundations, whereas builders in later levels used basalt as the most frequent material for foundations.[195] According to S. Sardarian, "As before, people lived in circular dwellings with stone foundations and adobe walls, and square dwellings adjoining circular houses, that is, houses with stone foundations and adobe walls formed dwellings in all four cultural horizons."[196] In K6, we recovered remains of straw matting with mortar, which was used as a base for setting the mudbrick on the stone foundation (Fig 4b.4). Between re-laid plaster floors we found a green algae-like substance in Squares K6 and K5.

These constructions had to meet two very different seasonal weather profiles. In summer, they had to maintain the cool of night during hot days and to dispel the heat.[197] In winter they had to retain the heat. Mudbrick as a material is efficient for both seasons. The walls of the single brick round dwellings were 40 cm thick and survived up to 2 m high.[198]

At a depth of 1 m from the surface in the upper architectural levels builders laid river stones in two rows, as well as untreated small stones[199]. Builders constructed most excavated dwellings exclusively of mudbricks. Excavators

Figure 4b.4. Reed matting on foundation stones as a base for mudbricks.

did find a few walls with stone walls set in clay at a depth of 2 m, the outer masonry of which consisted of relatively large stones, while the inner side of the wall was composed of small stones (Fig 4b 5), (see a modern example in Fig 4b.10).[200] The masonry of some dwellings was stepped in to make a domed roof.[201]

---

194 Bayburtian 2011, 34; Khanzadyan, 1967, 9-10.
195 Bayburtian 2011.
196 Sardarian 1967, 174.
197 Szabo and Barfield 1991, 137.
198 Sardarian 1967 27.
199 Sardarian 1967 27, 29, 36.
200 Sardarian 1967, 27, 34.
201 Sardarian 1967 29.

Figure 4b.5. Wall made of stones set in clay.

Figure 4b.6. Mudbricks from Square K6, Building 7 (below), Building N2 (2000) (above).

The entire surface of the wall of Bayburtian's Round dwelling 22 was covered outside with clay; fingerprints are visible in the clay.[202] The same thick clay with signs of fingers pressing it into the wall joins occurred in Square K6, Building 7 (Fig 4b.6). Bayburtian interprets the fingerprints recorded here below the floor as "irrefutable evidence that the floor of the dwelling was arranged above the level of the ground of that era."[203] In our opinion, Bayburtian did not consider the fact that sturdy houses were repeatedly repaired at the times they built new floors. As our excavations show, many buildings had several layers of floors.[204] In a number of instances in Bayburtian's and our work, we found round buildings where they rebuilt it a number of times. One can see the process of rebuilding in Figure 4b.7. The old wall was flattened by knocking the top bricks off onto the old floor and scraping the top surface. New bricks— the size of bricks for each rebuilding were different— were placed on top and a new floor was constructed over the old one with mudbricks as a foundation of the floor.

Our excavations of 2000, as well as those of the Armenian-American expedition in squares K5, K6, and J5, confirm that builders covered the walls inside and outside with clay plaster and painted them black or blue in some houses.[205]

The excavations of 1937 recorded two main sizes of raw bricks: 28 x 20 x 10 cm. and 29 x 40 x 10 cm.[206] There were also bricks 12 cm high.[207] The bricks of K6 were 30 x 40 x 10 cm. (Building 2), 30 x 40 x10 (Building 3), 23 x 29 x 10 cm. (Building 5), 28 x 28 x 10 cm. (Building 6, Stratum V), and 26 x 41 x 10 cm. (Building 7). Sardarian mentions dimensions of 38 x 18 x 10, 52 x 22 x 10 and 30 x 30 x 10 cm.[208] In Shengavit in 2003, we found bricks 30 cm long and 12 cm wide in the upper layer of central part at the depth of 60 cm.[209] Bricks of different sizes occurred in different levels in Mokhrablur; for example, on the lowest XI building horizon the bricks were square with dimensions of 16 x 16 cm, in Levels X and IX the width of the bricks

202 Bayburtian 2011, 31, 35.
203 Bayburtian 2011.
204 Simonyan 2002, pp. 20, 21; Simonyan and Rothman, 2015.
205 Areshian et al. 1996, 43.
206 Bayburtian 2011, 32.
207 Bayburtian 2011, 29.
208 Sardarian, 2004, 272.
209 Simonyan, Khachatryan 2005, 57.

is 21 x 22 cm, which corresponds to the width of bricks from sites in Iğdir. In Mokhrablur Levels V and IV, the bricks were 36 x 27 x 9 cm., and in the last Level III, 32 x 32 x 8 cm. Two types of clay bricks were noted in Norabats: (a) convex ones in the upper level bricks of 40 to 60 cm long, 22 to 23 cm wide and 10 to 12 cm thick, and (b) rectangular bricks measuring 48 x 22 x 10/12 cm. in the lower levels. The mud bricks from Shengavit are identical in size to the bricks from the second layer of Kültepe I in Naxçivan: 40 x 20 x 10, 42 x 18 x 12, 42 x 22 x 12, 42 x 24 x 12, 44 x 20 x 12, 44 x 22 x 10, 50 x 24 x 10 cm respectively, although here the bricks used for each individual house were the same size.[210] So, the bricks do not seem to be of a standard size anywhere. Perhaps, each builder over time used a preferred size brick.

Figure 4b.7. Rebuilding of Stratum VII Square K6 Building 6.

Figure 4b.8. Domed houses with square outhouses in modern Afghanistan.

ROOFING

Roofing round and rectangular houses posed different technical problems for builders. Areshian (Chapter 4a) believes that many of the round buildings with one course of bricks had a domed roof of brick with a hole in the center to let smoke out. Such buildings still exist in modern Afghanistan and elsewhere in the Middle East (Fig 4b.8.). They create enough space for basic family life in the cold of winter and the heat of summer. In Figure 4b.8 they are attached to squared rooms. An alternative form of roofing is slant roofs with a center post (Fig 4b.9). In round buildings near the hearths were flat large stones, which, according to Bayburtian, served not so much as surfaces to put pots on from the hearth,[211] but as bases for wooden poles to support the roof of the round dwellings.[212] This assumption is based on the fact that the stones were usually placed near the center, while the hearths were placed at the sides of the stones. On the other hand, during the excavations of 1938, they found only a flat stone without a hearth in the center of the lower dwelling.[213]

Bayburtian's arguments about supporting pillars in the center on flat stones to hold up the roofs of round houses are not confirmed by further excavations; however, they found such flat stones in rectangular rooms (Fig 4b.2, c1).

An alternative explanation has to do with the framework for a

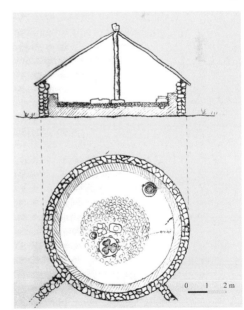

Figure 4b.9. Roofing of round house suggested by Bayburtian.

---

210 Areshian et al. 1996, 38.
211 Ishoev and Greenberg 2019 claim that andirons were not placed over the fire, but to its side to receive pots off the fire.
212 Bayburtian 2011, 30-31, scheme 1.
213 Bayburtian 2011, 30.

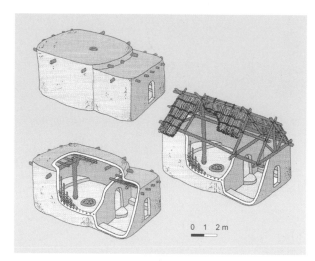

Figure 4b.10. Alternative roof construction in partially wattle and daub walled houses.

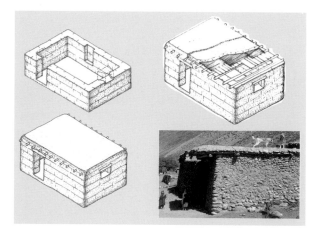

Figure 4b.11. Modern construction of roofing on a rectangular, free-standing building of mudbrick or stone in highland Afghanistan.

Figure 4b.12. Piece of clay from Square K6 roof with impressions of reeds and sticks.

roof (Fig 4b.10). As Sagona draws them (Fig 4b.9),[214] the cross beam does not need to be supported by a base in the very center, and there could be a center hole for venting smoke in the center, unless the roof were slanted. In that case builders would not include a center hole. Note also that the wooden poles resting on flat and massive stones would be stable only under heavy roofs of thick logs. As shown by the excavations at Mokhrablur, Shengavit, and other excavated settlements of the Kura-Araxes in the South Caucasus, dwellings had ceilings of thin rods, which, in turn, builders covered with a layer of reeds. It was no coincidence that the supporting pillars were sunk into holes dug to support the light roof, as borne out by the architecture of Kharberd-Malatia. According to Sanamyan, the pits dug in the rock tufa at Agarak were intended for supporting wooden pillars.

The problem with just using reeds is how it performed in a snowy winter to protect the house and keep it warm. One possible advantage of the free-standing round buildings with multiple courses of mudbrick is that the walls could support larger logs. Like rectangular structures they might have had flat ceilings.[215] As Figure 4b.11 illustrates, builders placed large cross beams at the top of the wall. They then put reeds over the wood lattice and smeared clay on top of the reeds. The stone house with this type of roof (Fig 4b.10) is typical of high elevation farmer-herder settlements in modern Afghanistan. A piece of the roof from Square K6 reflects this construction technique (Fig 4b.12).

At Shengavit, most likely early round buildings had domed mudbrick roofs or the kind of clay over reed roofs illustrated in Figure 4b.10.

DOORWAYS

For many of the dwellings we found no clear evidence of a doorway, but in as many cases we did not have the full building or only had the foundation stones and perhaps one or two courses of mudbrick. This was true of all the buildings in Square K6.[216] Some of the round buildings Sardarian excavated had entrances from the round room into a rectangular adjacent room, as

---

214 Sagona 2018, 233.
215 Bayburtyan 2011, 31; Sardarian 1967, 174; Tiratsian 1996, p. 43.
216 Unless what we took as a window in Fig 4b.5. was a crawl door.

did the round buildings in Figure 4b.1 (Fig 4b.13). According to Szabo and Barfield,[217] having doors turned in the same direction is often a sign of cold weather. If the buildings in Figure 4b.11 were contemporaneous, it would therefore be odd that the doors literally open in every direction. Perhaps, some of the buildings were semi-subterranean like the ritual room in Square M5 (Fig 4b.14).[218]

BENCHES

Builders often attached benches to the inside of the wall with a width and height of 45 cm, which were built of clay and mudbricks.[219] One such bench we uncovered in Square K6, Building 3 (Fig 4b.15). It rested right by the openings of two large storage jars (*karas*) sunk under the floor, and near a bear's skin rug (see Chapter 5a). Benches of this type are common at other Kura-Araxes sites like Kvatskhelebi and Godin Tepe.[220]

FLOORS

Plastered floors are a common trait of Kura-Araxes builders throughout the extensive landscape in which people carrying that cultural tradition lived.[221] These floors were laid and pounded to make them even and flat. As mentioned above, at times builders made the underlayment for these floors with mudbricks and at time pebbles. The floor itself may have worn away over some of these underlayments, but they were re-laid a significant number of times. Bayburtian may have misunderstood this process when he wrote that the floor of room No.5 was made of clay bricks. It is likely that the floor noted by Bayburtian was a layer of broken mud bricks from the upper walls which had been used to fill the interior of the outdated house on the platform of which a new house was built, often according to the design of the old house, as is illustrated in Figure 4b.7.

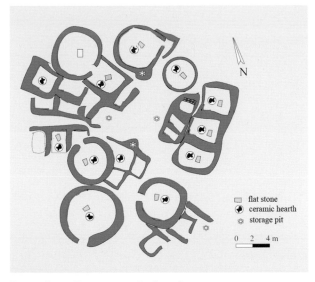

Figure 4b.13. Doorways in Sardarian's excavations.

Figure 4b.14. Steps down into Square M5 ritual room.

Figure 4b.15. A clay bench in Square K6, Building 3.

217   Szabo and Barfield 1991, 137.
218   Bayburtian 2011, 27, 29; HAP 1971, 129; Simonyan 2013.
219   Bayburtian 2011, 33; History of the Armenian People 1971, 129; Simonyan 2013.
220   Rothman 2011.
221   Rothman 2011, 29.

The Settlement Wall

The bluff on which Shengavit sat was surrounded by a substantial walls of unworked, large basalt stones filled with smaller stones on the interior (Fig 4b.16). On the western and southern edges of the site the wall had three sections and was 10 meters wide.[222] On the northern edge of the mound facing the bluff and the Hrazdan River below the wall was narrower. Parallel to Squares J5, K5, L5, M5, N5, builders constructed rectangular buttresses and an underground passage leading to the river Hrazdan (Fig 4b.17),[223] and on the southern, most accessible side also a trench.[224] Sardarian writes that the settlement wall of Shengavit was founded during the 3rd horizon of the settlement and functioned during the 4th horizon until the settlement was abandoned.[225] Some archaeologists have doubted that the excavated fortress wall was built in the Early Bronze Age[226]. Our research in 2021 not only confirmed that the settlement wall belonged to the Kura-Araxes culture, but also allowed us to conclude that the builders erected it in at least 2700 BC, [227] although Rothman sees it as being 2700 to 2600 BC and Simonyan 2900 to 2700 BC.

The results of that excavation revealed that, indeed, the Shengavit settlement wall was built with a rather complicated technique. Initially, builders erected the front part with two layers of large stones, river boulders on the outside and roughly processed basalt stones on the inside. These stones were attached to one another with clay mortar.

On the inner side of the masonry builders constructed a clay platform with a width of at least three meters; the clay platform continued to the south and entered an uninvestigated section of the site to a height of more than 100 cm (Fig 4b.18). The front part of the masonry of the settlement wall rested on this platform. This made the wall more stable.

Figure 4b.16. The western side of the Shengavit wall, excavated by Bayburtian.

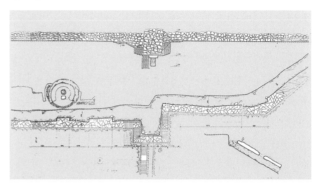

Figure 4b.17. Drawing of passageway to the river.

Figure 4b.18. Shengavit north wall with clay platform.

---

222 based on a note contemporaneous with Bayburtian (see Chapter 7).
223 Sardarian 1967, 171; *History of Armenian People* 1971, 129.
224 Bayburtyan 2011, 18; Sardarian 1967, 171.
225 Sardarian 1967, 171; Sardarian 2004, 196:
226   Kohl 2007, 90.
227 Simonyan and Rothman in press.

The construction of what we found was as follows. These two components of the wall were erected almost simultaneously. First, the builders laid out the stones, and then a platform-support was formed from poured clay. Later, they built rectangular rooms made of mudbricks on this clay base. The preserved buttress on the front side had a third, randomly laid out row of large pebbles. In all likelihood, it was laid later to secure an important part of the wall. It was later on that work crews built this clay platform and rectangular rooms of mudbrick.

Conclusion

The construction and plan of buildings at Shengavit shows that there were changes in shape and size over time. In general, round, free-standing buildings were earliest and large rectangular buildings with annexes were latest. In the middle a mix of round buildings with square, often unroofed adjoining buildings and a combination of sturdier round and square buildings typified the site.

Throughout, builders seemed to be less concerned with the plan or the construction of walls (see Chapter 3), but they wanted to build a building quickly using the techniques they were most familiar with. No standardization of brick size or even what they made the walls out of existed. The construction of the walls seemed to be at the whims of particular builders.

References

Armenian Soviet Encyclopedia 1979 book 5, Yerevan. (in Armenian).

Areshian, G., Ghafadaryan, K. K., Hovhannisian, K. L., and Sahinian, A. A. (eds.) 1996 *A History of Armenian Architecture, Vol. I: The Architecture of Armenian Highlands from the Earliest Times to the 3rd Century AD*. Yerevan: "Gitut'yun" Press of the Armenian National Academy of Sciences. (in Armenian).

Atkin, T. and Rykwert, T. 2005 Building and Knowing. in *Structure and Meaning in Human Settlements*, edited by T. Atkin and T. Rykwert, 1-12. Philadelphia: University of Pennsylvania Museum.

Bayburtian, E. 1938 Working tools in ancient Armenia (According to the newer of the Armenian National Academy of Sciences), *Bulletin of the Institute of History and Literature of the USSR*, book I: 193-231. (in Armenian)

Bayburtian, Y. 2011 *Sequence of Ancient Cultures of Armenia on the Basis of Archaeological Material*. Yerevan: Armenian Museum of History. (in Russian).

History of the Armenian People 1971 Armenia at the period of primitive communal and slave-owning systems, book 1, Yerevan: "Publishing House of the Academy of Sciences of Soviet Republic of Armenia." (in Armenian).

Ishoev S, Greenberg R. 2019 Khirbet Kerak Ware (Kura-Araxes) Andirons at Tel Bet Yerah: Functional Analysis and Cultural Context. *Tel Aviv* 46: 21–40.

Khanzadyan E. 1967 *The culture of the Armenian Highland in the III mill. BC*, Yerevan: "Publishing House of the Academy of Sciences of Soviet Republic of Armenia." (in Armenian).

Sardarian S. H. 1967 *Primitive society in Armenia*. Yerevan: "Mitq" publisher's, Yerevan (in Armenian with Russian and English summaries).

Sardarian S. H. 2004 *Armenia – cradle of civilization*, Yerevan: Yerevan University Publishers. (in Armenian).

Simonyan H. Ye. 2000. Formation of early agricultural and producing culture in Armenia// Theses of series of talks *Armenian civilization from ancient times to the adoption of Christianity*, 37-39. Yerevan. (in Armenian).

Simonyan H. Ye. 2001 Excavations of 2000 at Shengavit. *Ancient culture of Armenia*", theses of the conference devoted to the memory of Haroutyun Martirosyan, 33-34. Yerevan. (in Armenian).

Simonyan H. Ye. 2012 Temple of Fire at Shengavit. *International symposium devoted to the 125th anniversary of birth of the academician Hovsep Orbeli Directions of talks*, 103-106. Yerevan: "Gitutyun" publisher's at the AS of RA. (in Armenian).

Simonyan H. Ye. 2018 Shengavit – Ancient Settlement of Yerevan. «*Yerevan 5*». *Collection of Scientific Articles* edited by A. Melkonyan, E., Minasyan, and H. Simonyan, 3-13. Yerevan,

Simonyan H. Ye., Gnuni A. 2002 The communal structure in the EBA (according to archeological sources) *Towards the celebration of the 1600th anniversary of the creation of Armenian letters*, 50-51. Oshakan:"*Mashtots readings IV*" (in Armenian).

Simonyan H. Ye., Khachatryan L. 2005 Excavations of Shengavit in 2003. in *"Culture of ancient Armenia", XIII, materials of republican scientific conference*, 56-59. Yerevan (in Armenian).

Simonyan, H. and Rothman, M.S in press New data on the construction and meaning of the Shengavit settlement wall in Paradise Lost: Collection of papers in honour of Ruben S. Badalyan on the occasion of his 65th birthday, edited by A. Kosyan, P. Avetisyan, K. Martirosyan-Olshansky, A.Bobokhyan, and Y. Gekyan. *Aramazd* XVI (1/2): 406-428.

Szabo, A. and Sekler, E. 1991 *Afghanistan: An Atlas of Indigenous Domestic Architecture*. Austin: University of Texas.

Wright, H. Cultural Action in the Uruk World. in *Uruk Mesopotamia and its Neighbors*, edited by M. S Rothman, 123-148. Santa Fe: SAR Press.

4c | Results of the Ground Penetrating Radar (GPR) Survey of the Shengavit

R. Durgaryan, M. Gevorgyan, H. Igythyan

The Method and Examples

The ability to excavate a large percentage of the remaining Shengavit mound area is limited. One approach is to discover the places with the greatest potential to dig. This technique permits the evaluation of landscape dynamics, and the location of objects that are often buried under layers of sedimentation. The GPR surveying enables us to reconstruct remains of historical interest concerning human activity and the impacts of natural phenomena on the human environment.

A number of remote sensing techniques exist. Magnetometers, for example, measure magnetic fields by bouncing a signal into the ground and recording the response. It picks up anomalies that can mean activity that occurred in the past. The limitation of that method is that it tends to bounce off the architectural features that are nearest the surface.

Georadar surveys use the application of geophysical techniques for the discovery of archeological remains. It is based on the physical properties of the object and the surrounding fill and features, including, but not limited to, electromagnetic features, electrical conductivity, elastic parameters, density, etc. Unlike magnetometry, it can penetrate deep into the ground, revealing anomalies at differing depths.

Use of these methods in the field of archeology is not new; it has a decades-long history.[228] Rapid development of technical data processing software tools in recent years has greatly contributed to the improved accuracy of the geophysical techniques, enabling resolution of most complex archeological problems. GPR surveying is related to such geophysical methods. The GPR system analyzes electromagnetic pulses, and records signals reflected from layer boundaries within the investigated medium. It defines sediments and objects with different electro-physical properties; thus its main usefulness is that it determines the thicknesses of layer boundaries and layer bedding depths. The benefits for its use in a stratified archaeological site are therefore clear.

The GPR sounding technique operates in a continuous mode and its resulting data informs users on the location, position, and dimensions of an object that is not homogeneous with its surrounding matrix. It has proved to be an efficient tool in locating places to excavate or other archeological information when excavation is not possible.

There are two stages. The two-dimensional survey helps to identify anomalies that may be of historical and cultural importance. Analyzing two-dimensional survey data, similar anomalies can point the excavators to promising areas. To study the latter in detail, three-dimensional GPR survey is used. This enables delineating the entire structure of an anomalous body, estimating depth of its occurrence, and understanding its geometry. The findings of GPR survey are correlated with the evidence of archeological investigation, and excavators can select the areas for archeological excavation.

---

228 Fouache 2007.

We implemented similar activities in the Republic of Armenia, Egypt, and in other countries. As an example, we describe below the studies we did at Luxor, Egypt. This city is famous for its temples of Amon-Ra, Mut, and the temple of Amenhotep III, decorated with sculptures and bas-reliefs. The geo-archeological surveys were carried out at the site of Pharaoh Amenhotep III's temple, located on the western bank of the Nile River in the outskirts of the modern city of Luxor. Two giant Memnon statues stand at the temple entrance, one missing its arm section. The famous Memnon Colossus is 18m high. As a result of a strong earthquake, the Northern Colossus was fractured. According to tradition it had been giving some specific sound with the first sunrays touching it at dawn. Restorers repaired the monument in the third century and since then the sounding of the statue had ceased.[229] There are many studies and extensive evidence about the site from Strabo's account (27 BC) until the present day.

To discover, map, and model archeological objects, we conducted a GPR survey in the area of the Temple of Amenhotep III. Based on the GPR survey data, we discovered fragments of quartzite and mapped the area adjacent to the Memnon Colossus (Figure 4c.1.,a and 1., b) and the three-dimensional pattern was plotted at the next stage (Figure 4c.1., c).

The complex geophysical and archeological analysis, which considered that the Memnon Colossi and the discovered fragments were made of quartzite, suggested that the fragments could have belonged to the damaged parts of the statue. With this assumption archaeologists proposed to excavate the anomaly site. The excavation unearthed the shoulder section of the Memnon Colossus statue consisting of three fragments (Fig. 4c. 1., d).[230]

In the course of the studies, the analysis of GPR survey data helped to identify more than 70 promising sites, which were excavated by archeologists and confirmed the credibility of the GPR survey data.

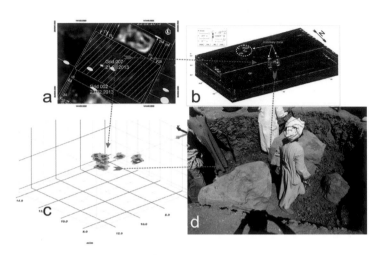

Figure 4c.1. The area of the first sub-site within the Temple of Pharaoh Amenhotep III. a) layout of factual materials and anomaly locations; b) three-dimensional GPR survey; c) three-dimensional model of the surveyed anomaly; d) the excavated shoulder section of the Memnon statue.

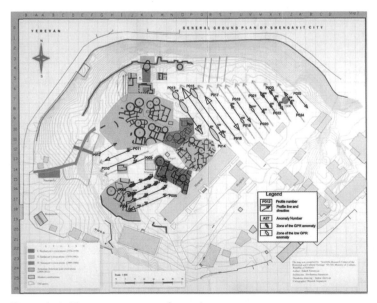

Figure 4c.2. The vector patterns of georadar survey.

229   Hamilton and Falconer 2015, book 17, v. 3, chap. 1, para. 46, pp. 261–262.
230   Gevorgyan 2015; Karakhanyan et al. 2014.

Shengavit

We conducted the archeo-geophysical studies in two stages within the selected areas of the Shengavit settlement. To implement the three-dimensional (3D) GPR survey and collect detailed information the site was subdivided into three regular geometrical surfaces, each consisting of individual profiles set 2 meters apart, taking into account the dimensions of the identified structures (Fig 4c.2). In some sectors of the sites, the relief, existing archeological excavations, and utility lines limited the results to two-dimensional surveying alone. This method is good for discovery, but for the most part cannot be used for reconstruction of what is under the surface. For that a more intensive effort with much closer runs of our georadar antenna is necessary.[231]

The study involves running a cart with the georadar "antenna" over the ground and recoding the signal that bounces back (Fig 4c.3). This signal is then analyzed by the geomorphologists, and they can create colored diagrams showing anomalies.

Some of the areas studied were of interest in view of the varied geophysical fields, as well as rich bulk of accumulated materials. We noted that first the entire area studied has a rich diversity of archeological structures deteriorated to different degrees. This made GPR analysis difficult, as in many cases conflicting results were generated depending on the rate of deterioration of individual elements in a structure or the density of the architectural material. Therefore, we identified areas of archeological interest versus the general field with great caution and reservations.

Two sites that might guide future archeological investigation were selected and mapped only upon comprehensive analysis. The excavators chose two of those "hot spots,'" Squares I14 and M5. Excavations unearthed a large rectangular building of Stratum I in Squares I14 (see Chapters 3 and 7), and M5 (Chapter 3, 6a, and 7), the latter of which revealed a very significant ritual emplacement and associated room described in detail in Chapter 6a. Excavators did not have time to explore the hotspot in Square V7.

An additional problem the excavators wanted to address was the settlement wall along the northern edge of the mound (Chapter 4b). Various scholars have proposed widely divergent dates for its construction.[232] The georadar analysis indicted a maximum depth of two meters (Fig 4c.4). There were a number of factors that made it impossible

Figure 4c.3. Cart with "antenna" to make the readings for georadar.

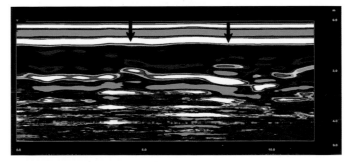

Figure 4c.4. Georadar image of the northern part of the settlement wall.

---

231   Seth Price and Eileen Ernenwein, personal communication.
232   Kohl 2007; Sagona 2018; Simonyan and Rothman 2015.

to give the full detail of the wall using georadar. Nonetheless, the georadar suggested that builders made the wall in the strata dating from 2700 to 2600 BC.[233] In 2021 Simonyan conducted excavations to better date the wall.[234] It confirmed what the preliminary georadar study had suggested.

In general, the georadar study we conducted revealed three main depth ranges that seem to suggest three main areas. The first, from 0-1.2 meters below the surface primarily includes archaeological objects, modern utility lines or concrete, strata. The second stratum is limited to the interval of 1.2-2.8 m, representing the greatest interest, and encompasses archeological features such as walls, voids and other features. It is possible to discern almost vertically oriented cylindrical bodies in this stratum, which may be walls. The last third stratum is filled mainly with dense sediments, and in places contains fragments of elements that could be of archeological interest. The interval of interest spreads mostly up to 3.5 m deep over the entire area studied, and the deepest intact or undisturbed interval, containing preserved floors of archeological structures or their walls, spans 2 meters. The three-dimensional models plotted up to this depth depict underground man-made (anthropogenic) voids where we could identify cylindrical walls and floors.

The joint analysis of the GPR and archeological evidence resulted in identification of anomalies that were promising in view of archeological excavations. This kind of analysis helped to identify more than 20 likely buildings or walls within the studied site. The actual excavation suggests multiple strata within these areas that georadar studies identified. It agrees with the proposed depth of the humanly laid materials over a layer of bedrock on a natural bluff starting three and half meters under the least disturbed areas.

We concluded that the use of georadar at Shengavit provided indications of where to dig. The trial excavation that was carried out at the sites mapped by the GPR survey data was promising in terms of archeology and confirmed the credibility of the GPR survey findings completely. (The full reports with illustrations are published in the Shengavit web archive). The technique also gave us valuable information about the settlement wall on the north by the slope.

References

Fouache E. 2007 What is Geoarchaeology? *Geodinamica Acta*, 20; I-II; 2007, DOI: 10.3166/ga.20.I-II.

Gevorgyan, M. 2015 The usage of Georadar Survey for paleoseismological investigations in the territory of Memorial Temple of Amenhotep III. in *Collection of Scientific Articles of YSU SSS, Materials of the Scientific Session dedicated to the 95 th Anniversary of Yerevan State University*, 86-93. Yerevan: Yerevan State University Press.

Hamilton, H.C. and Falconer, W. 2015 *The Geography of Strabo, 1854–1857*. US: Andesite Press.

Karakhanyan, A., Avagyan, A., Sourouzian, H., Lopez Roa, C., Gevorgyan M. 2014 Evidence of a Strong Earthquake in the Period Between 1200 and 900 BC Identified in the Temple of Amenhotep III and in Other Temples of the Ancient Thebes. *Archaeological Heritage and Multidisciplinary Egyptological Studies* 1: 321-344.

Kohl, P. 2007 *The Making of Bronze Age Eurasia*. Cambridge World Archaeology. Cambridge: Cambridge University Press.

Sagona, A. 2018 *The Archaeology of the Caucasus*. Cambridge: Cambridge University Press.

Simonyan H. and Rothman, M.S 2015 Regarding ritual behaviour at Shengavit. *Ancient Near Eastern Studies* 52: 1–45.

Simonyan, H. and Rothman, M. S in press New Data on the Construction and Meaning of the Shengavit Settlement Wall in *Paradise Lost: Collection of papers in honour of the 65th birthday of Ruben Badalyan*, edited by A. Kosyan, P. Avetisyan, K. Martirosyan-Olshansky, A.Bobokhyan, and Y. Gekyan. Aramazd XVI (1/2): 406-428.

---

233   Simonyan disagrees with this dating, suggesting construction from 2900-2700 BC.
234   Simonyan and Rothman in press.

5a | Faunal Remains of Shengavit

Pam J. Crabtree, Jennifer Piro, and Douglas Campana (with data added from
Nina Manaseryan, Hans-Peter and Margarethe Uerpmann, and Nyree Manoukian)

Introduction

This chapter will present the results of studies of the animal bone remains recovered from the Shengavit excavations, especially those excavated between 2009 and 2012. Jennifer Piro did the initial analysis on the 2009 material. Pam Crabtree joined the project during the final excavation season in 2012 and completed the identification of the 2009-12 material during the summer of 2013 (Fig 5a.1). Our work builds on a long history of archaeological and zooarchaeological research that has been conducted at Shengavit since the 1930s. Nina Manaseryan examined the faunal remains that were recovered from the 1965-1980 and 2003-2007 excavations.[235] These results were presented at the 2015 meeting of the Archaeozoology of Southwest Asia and Adjacent Areas (ASWA) working group in Gröningen, Netherlands. Hans-Peter Uerpmann and Margarethe Uerpmann wrote an additional report for this volume based on animal bones recovered from the 2000 excavation season.[236] A report on the fish remains by Nyree Manoukian is also included here. We presented an initial report on the faunal remains from the 2009-12 season at the 2017 meeting of ASWA in Cyprus.[237]

Figure 5a.1. One locus' animal bone sample.

Our chapter has three goals. The first is to present a detailed study of the faunal remains that were recovered from Shengavit between 2009 and 2012 (plus summary tables from earlier analyses) in order to understand the economy of animal husbandry and hunting at the site. Our first goal is to examine the ways in which the inhabitants obtained meat and other animal products. This we will do first by calculating the relative counts of the various animal species and their distribution across the site. Second, we will calculate the age profiles for the sheep and goat remains that make up the majority of the faunal remains recovered from Shengavit. Thirdly, we want to use these data to address broader questions about the food-getting and animal products economy for the Kura-Araxes

---

235 Manaseryan 2018.
236 Uerpmann's full report will appear on our web archive. The raw database on animal remains from Crabtree and Piro's research will will appear there as well.
237 Crabtree and Piro 2021.

cultural tradition in the ancient Near East. In addition, our recent paper[238] discussed the issue of mobile (nomadic) pastoralism in the Kura-Araxes culture. There we argue that Kura-Araxes sites are associated with a range of settlement patterns and subsistence systems. This chapter includes additional comparative data from sites that are currently under excavation and earlier excavations at sites that have recently been published. Finally, we want to use our data to address the question of the possible presence of domestic horses in the Kura-Araxes.

Materials and Methods

Crabtree examined a total of 35,647 animal bones and fragments from the 2009-2012 seasons. The vast majority of these bones were small, unidentified fragments of mammal bone (N = 28,132). While the bones were generally in quite good condition, the careful recovery procedures through excavation with small picks and trowels and systematic screening guaranteed that a large number of small, unidentifiable fragments of mammal bone would be recovered (Fig 5a.2). In 2009 Piro examined a total of 1,933 fragments, of which 1,241 were unidentified. The details of the identified materials are presented below.

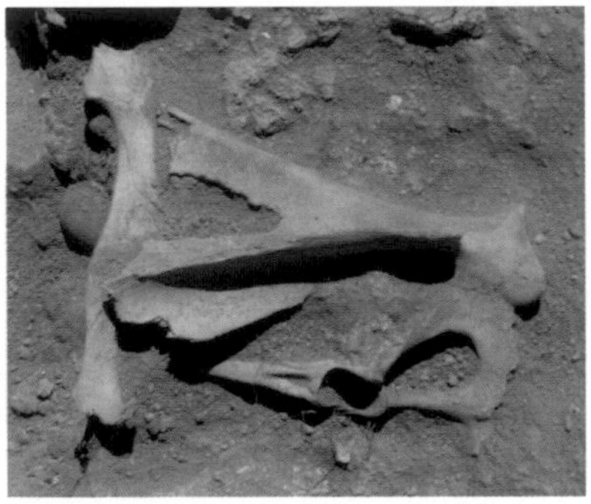

We identified the bones to species or higher order taxon, following the methods described in Crabtree.[239] Sheep were distinguished from goats following the recommendations of Boessneck,[240] Payne,[241] Halstead,[242] Zeder and Pilaar,[243] and Zeder and Lapham.[244] We used measurement data following Boessneck[245] to distinguish domestic cattle (*Bos taurus*) from wild cattle (*Bos primigenius*) (Table 5a.1). Bone measurements also indicated that a small number of the Shengavit sheep were, in fact, wild sheep (*Ovis orientalis*). We also identified a number of possible wild cattle. Species ratios were based on NISP (number of identified specimens per taxon) following Lyman.[246]

We planned to use dental morphology following Eisenmann[247] to distinguish horses (*Equus caballus*), donkeys (*Equus asinus*), and onagers (*Equus hemionus*). Hite's research using both dental morphology and ancient DNA indicated that the morphology of the mandibular cheek teeth was an effective method for distinguishing the three species from the

Figure 5a.2. In situ bones from Square K4

	Mean	Min.	Max.	s.d.	c.v.	N
Cattle (*Bos*)						
Tibia Bd	64.5	64.3	64.7	0.3	0.1	2
Astragalus GLl	67.8	60.1	76.6	4.7	21.8	8
Astragalus Bd	46.7	41.9	52.8*	4.1	16.5	6
Metatarsus Bd	62.9	58.2	69.4*	4.9	24.2	4
Metacarpus Bd	71.3	70.8*	71.8*	0.7	0.5	2
Metacarpus Bp		69.6*				1
Sheep (*Ovis*)						
Tibia Bd	29.7	23.9	35.4	2.6	6.9	35
Humerus BT	32.6	27.5	37.8	2.4	5.6	26
Radius Bp	35.5	30.2	45.3**	4.7	22.5	13
Astragalus GLl	31.8	26.4	38.0	2.4	4.6	48
Metacarpus Bd	25.4	24.1	27.7	1.1	1.3	9

Table 5a.1 Summary of selected measurements of sheep and cows.

238   Piro and Crabtree 2017.
239   Crabtree 1990, 5.
240   Boessneck et al. 1964.
241   Payne 1985.
242   Halstead et al. 2002.
243   Zeder and Pilaar 2009.
244   Zeder and Lapham 2010.
245   Boessneck 1995.
246   Lymaan 2008.
247   Eisenmann 1985.

site of Godin in Iran.[248] Piro identified three teeth as donkey from the 2009 excavations. Domestic donkeys dated to about 3000 BC are known from Abydos in Egypt,[249] and donkeys appear to have been domesticated around 5000 to 4000 BC in Africa[250] and were present in Mesopotamia during the fourth millennium.[251] Domestic donkeys are known from Syria, Iraq, and Iran dated to between 3500 and 2500 BC,[252] so donkeys could be at Shengavit during the Early Bronze Age.

Unfortunately, the Shengavit 2009 to 2012 material studied by Crabtree produced no equid mandibles or mandibular teeth and only a single very poorly preserved maxillary cheek tooth. As a result, we used postcranial measurements to try to identify the equid species present.[253] We recorded measurement data following the recommendations of von den Driesch.[254]

The cattle, sheep, goat, and equid measurements are shown in Table 5a.2a-d. Crabtree and the Uerpmann's agree that the true domesticated horse is unlikely to have appeared at Shengavit during the KA 2 period despite Manaseryan's assertion. Newer research makes her identification of true horse unlikely. Recent research based on aDNA indicates that domestic horses did not appear in Eurasia until the late third millennium at the earliest.[255] They assert (summary report in web archive), "In addition, there are some finds which belong to the horse - either wild or domestic.

However, it is also not unlikely that the horse bones are intrusive. Radiocarbon dating of a horse tooth from the studied Shengavit collection provided a date of 900 to 810 cal BC (2σ). Similar observations were made for horse-finds from the Early Bronze Age levels at Mokhrablur and Horom.[256] According to our present knowledge the oldest horse remains in Armenia derive from graves at Nerkin Naver, where a horse bone yielded a radiocarbon date of 2285-2070 cal BC.[257] Up until now there does not seem to be secure evidence for an occurrence of the wild horse in this region.

We recorded ageing data using both dental eruption and wear and epiphyseal fusion of the long bones.[258] The state of eruption or wear on each mandibular tooth we recorded following Grant,[259] and the mandibles we grouped into categories

measurements	Lower 3rd molar		Metacarpus		Astragalus	
	LM3	BM3	Bd	Dd	LI	BC
mean	36,64	15,77	68,1	35,8	68,10	47,2
std.-dev.	9,76	1,04	5,80	2,82	5,80	5,73
n=	10	10	4	4	14	12
LM3 - length of the M3 BM3 - breadth of the M3			Bd - distal breadth Dd - distal depth		LI - lateral length BC - breadth of the caput	

Table 5a.2a Summary of cattle (*BOS*) osteometry

measurements	mandible	teeth	scapula	astragalus		calcaneus
	LTR	LM₃	SLC	LI	BC	GL
mean	77,2	24,1	21,9	30,9	19,9	62,1
std.-dev.	2,48	0,99	1,29	1,72	1,24	4,43
n=	5	25	11	45	44	6
LTR - length of the tooth-row LM3 - length of the M₃			SLC - smallest width of the collum	LI - lateral length BC - breadth of the caput		GL - greatest length

Table 5a.2b Summary of Sheep (*Ovis*) Osteometry

248 Hite 2008.
249 Russel et al. 2008.
250 Kimura et al. 2013: 86.
251 Wright 2001.
252 Wright 2001; Russel et al. 2008; Vila 2006; Zeder 1986.
253 see, for example, Davis et al. 2008.
254 von den Driesch 1976.
255 Lobrado et al. 2021.
256 Uerpmann and Uerpmann 2010, notes on page 241.
257 Uerpmann and Uerpmann 2010:214.
258 Silver 1969.
259 Grant 1983.

following Payne.[260] Traces of butchery, bone-working, and animal gnawing were also noted (Fig 5a.3). Campana entered Crabtree's animal bone data into FAUNA, a specialized database manager for zooarchaeology.[261] FAUNA allowed us to sort the bones by context and by stratigraphic levels.

Mammal Bones from Shengavit

The mammal species identified from the entire 2009-12 assemblages studied by Crabtree and Piro are shown in Table 5a.3a. The results of analysis by Uerpmann and Uerpmann and by Manaseryan from earlier excavations and the fish bone analysis by Manoukian appear in Tables 5a.3b, 5a.3c and 5a.3d respectively. In terms of the numbers of identified specimens or NISP,[262] caprines are the most common species with sheep outnumbering goats by a ratio of more than two to one. The same general pattern is evident in animal remains from earlier excavations (Tables 5a.3b and c). Cattle were second in number, but, given their larger size, they would have provided the bulk of the meat consumed at Shengavit during the Early Bronze Age. For the 2009-2012 sample, there is no clear evidence for extensive traction pathologies on the cattle remains from Shengavit,[263] indicating that the cattle samples represented primarily sources of meat. Despite the lack of unambiguous evidence for traction pathology, clear evidence of cattle drawn carts and figurines with two cows harnessed together at Shengavit make their use as traction animals likely. Uerpmann and Uerpmann also state, "A large proportion of the cattle remains display 'stress markers,' morphological alterations caused by using the animals for labor.[264] There is also clear evidence for the presence of *Bos primigenius*

measurements	mandibular teeth		Astragalus			
	LM₃	BM₃	Ll	Lm	Dm	BC
mean	23,3	8,8	27,9	26,7	16,6	18,4
std.-dev.	2,08	0,55	1,24	1,65	1,07	1,36
n=	5	5	8	9	8	8

LM3 - length of the M₃
BM3 - width of the M₃
Ll - lateral Length
Lm - medial length
Dm - medial depth
BC - breadth of the caput

Table 5a.2c Summary of Goat (*Capra*) Osteometry

Scapula							
	1	2	3	4	5	6	7
	60,7	–	–	43,5	–	–	–

1 - smallest cranio-caudal neck-width
4 - width of the articular surface

Tibia							
	1	2	3	4	5	6	7
–	44,8	–	–	–	–	(40,0)	31,0

1 - distal depth
6 - smallest shaft width
7 - depth of the shaft at 6

Astragalus							
	1	2	3	4	5	6	7	
EQSI/ 5	53,3	51,4	25	49,5	42,8	29,5	41,7	–

1 - Greatest height
2 - Length of the medial verticillus
3 - Distance of the verticilli
4 - GB - Greatest width
5 - BFA - Width of the distal articular surface
6 - GD - Depth of the distal articular surface
7 - Greatest medial depth

Metatarsus III							
UNIT/Nr,	1	2	3	4	5	6	7
EQSI/ 13	43,2	41	–	25	27,4	26,1	–

1 - distal breadth of the shaft
2 - distal breadth of articular surface
4 - smallest depth of the lateral distal condyle
5 - largest depth of the medial distal condyle
6 - smallest depth of the medial distal condyle

Phalanx 1, posterior							
UNIT/Nr,	1	2	3	4	5	6	7	8
EQSI/ 14	37,6	30,3	23,9	21,1	(16,2	)–	–	–

1 - Proximal width
2 - Proximal depth
3 - Smallest shaft-width
4 - depth of the shaft at 3
5 - smallest depth of the shaft

Table 5a.2d Osteometry of the Onager (*Equus hemionus*).

---

260 Payne 1973.
261 Campana 2010.
262 see Lyman 2008.
263 following Bartosiewicz et al. 1997.
264 Bartosiewicz 2008.

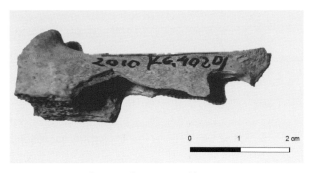

Figure 5a.3. Butchery marks on animal bone.

as well, the wild ancestor of domestic cattle. In some cases a separation of the two forms was not possible." Domestic pig is comparatively rare. Hunting played a relatively small role in the Shengavit food economy. However, the analysts identified onager (*Equus hemionus*), red deer (*Cervus elaphus*), roe deer (*Capreolus Capreolus*), hare (*Lepus sp.*), fox (*Vulpes vulpes*), badger (*Meles meles*), brown bear (*Ursus arctos*), otter (*Lutra lutra*), wild boar (*Sus scrofa* L), wild sheep, (*Ovis orientalis*), wild goat (*Capra aegagrus*), aurochs (*Bos primigenius*), fish (Table 5a.1d), birds, turtle (*Testudo graeca*), gazelle (*Gazella subguttosa*), beaver (*Castor fiber L.*), weasel (*Mustela nivalis*), and wolf (*Canis lupus*) in the faunal assemblage. A riparian (riverine) environment and salt flats on which domestic animals grazed is evident in the residue analysis of pottery.[265] As mentioned, measurement data suggest that the Shengavit assemblage also included a small number of wild cattle (*Bos primigenius*) and wild sheep (*Ovis orientalis*).

While the Shengavit economy is based primarily on domestic animals including cattle, sheep, and smaller numbers of goats, the range of wild animals suggest that the hunters who supplied the town were exploiting a variety of different environments. Red deer, roe deer, bears, and wild cattle are forest dwellers, and environmental data suggest that the immediate area around Shengavit was probably treeless, but the Koytak plateau as a whole was not. Hares are often found around cultivated fields, and the initial pollen data from Shengavit (Chapter 2b) indicate that agriculture was well developed. Today foxes are the primary predators for hares, so foxes are likely to be found near cultivated fields as well.[266] Onagers would have favored grasslands, while wild sheep are likely to be found at higher elevations. Otters, of course, are aquatic, and must have lived in the Hrazdan River.

The summary measurement data for cattle from Shengavit are shown in Table 5a.1. One astragalus with a distal breadth of 52.8 mm falls just within the range of wild cattle (51.0-69.0 mm), but the greatest lateral length (GLl) of the same individual at 76.6 mm is just below the

Species	Piro	Crabtree	Total	%
Cattle (*Bos taurus*)	108	1016	1124	20
Sheep (*Ovis aries*)	154	397	551	10
Goat (*Capra hircus*)	40	178	218	4
Sheep/goat	232	3,076	3,308	59
Pig (*Sus scrofa*)	8	119	127	2
Dog (*Canis familiaris*)	10	225	235	4
Equid (*Equus* sp.)	3	47	50	1
Domestic species totals	555	5,058	5,613	100
Red Deer (Cervus elaphus)	2	24	26	13
Roe deer (*Capreolus capreolus*)	3	1	4	2
Hare (*Lepus* sp.)	1	18	19	10
Fox (*Vulpes vulpes*)		11	11	6
Badger (*Meles meles*)		2	2	1
Otter (*Lutra lutra*)		1	1	0.5
Bear (*Ursus arctos*)		4	4	2
Bird	2	21	23	12
Fish	5	79	84	43
Amphibians		1	1	0.5
Testudines (turtles)		19	19	10
Wild species totals	13	181	194	100
Large Mammal "cattle-sized"	33	523	556	
Small Mammal "sheep-sized"	91	1,756	1,847	
Unidentified Mammal	1,241	28,132	29,373	
Total samples	1933	35647	37,580	

Table 5a.3a. Species identified from the 2009-12 excavations at Shengavit (Crabtree/Piro).

265 Manoukian, personal communication.
266 Dimirbaş 2015.

Taxa	n	n%	w(grams)	w%
Domestic cattle, *Bos*	1037	46	26472	67
Domestic sheep, *Ovis*	343	15	4506	11.5
Domestic goat, *Capra*	63	3	942	2.4
Domestic sheep or goat,	699	31	6564	17
Domestic pig, *Sus*	34	1.5	475	1
Dog, *Canus*	46	2	333	1
Domestic chicken, *Gallus*	6	.025	34	0.9
Domestic animals total (87% total n, 84% by weight)	**2228**	**100%**	**39325.8**	**100**
Wild or Domestic cattle	15	13.5	556	22.5
Wild or Domestic sheep	14	12.6	287	11.6
Wild or Domestic sheep or goat	15	13.5	171	7
Wild or Domestic pig	1	1	4	0.2
Wild or Domestic horse	5	4.5	281	11
Equidae indetermined	49	44	965	39
Wolf or Dog	11	10	185	7.5
Canidae indet.	1	1	16	0.7
Domestic or Wild animals (4% total n, 5% total weight)	**111**	**100%**	**2465**	**100%**
Hare, *Lepus Capensis/europaeus*	2	1	3.4	0.07
Fox, *Vulpes vulpes*	14	6.5	804	17
Carnivora indet., small	2	1	12	0.3
Carnivora indet., medium	10	5	98	2
Carnivora indet., large	2	1	46	1
Equus hemionus	10	5	412	8.5
Wild boar, *Sus scrofa*	3	1.5	42	1
Red Deer, *Cervus elaphus*	50	24	1052	22
Roe Deer, *Capreolus capreolus*	1	0.5	16	0.3
Aurox, *Bos primigenius*	18	8.5	561	12
Gazelle, *Gazella subgutturosa*	7	3	9	0.2
Wild Goat, *Capra aegagrus*	7	3	214	4.5
Wild Sheep, *Ovis orientalis*	53	25	1139	23.5
Caprinae indet.	24	11	315	6.5
Wild mammals total (8% total n, 10% total weight)	**211**	**100%**	**4829**	**100%**
Identified Mammals total	**2550**	**91.7%**	**46619**	**95**
Unidentified mammals	219	8	2486	5
Unident. Birds, (*Aves* indet.)	8	0.3	33.5	0.07
Unident. Turtle (*Testudinae* indet.)	1	0.04	7	0.01
Unident. Fish (*Salmonidae?*)	1	0.04	1	0
Unident. Molluscs	2	0.07	8	0.02
Unidentified total (8% total n)	**231**	**8.31%**	**2535**	**5%**
unidentified, small	6	2.5	22	1
unidentified, medium size	3	1.5	1	0.05
unidentified, medium to large size	6	3	37	1.5
unidentified, large	204	93	2416	98
unidentified total	**219**	**100**	**2477**	**100.00%**
Faunal remains total	**2781**	**100,0**	**49154**	**100.0%**

Species	1958-1980	2003-2007	Total	%
Cattle – *Bos taurus* L.	821	513	1334	38
Domestic Goat – *Capra hircus* L.	80	15	95	2.5
Domestic Sheep – *Ovis aries* L.	60	23	83	2
Ovis aries or *Capra hircus*	1056	623	1679	47
Pig – *Sus domesticus* L.	41	37	78	2
Horse – *Equus caballus* L.	128	47	175	5
Ass – *Equus asinus* L.	11	-	11	0.3
Dog - *Canis familiaris* L.	57	8	65	2
Domestic animals total	**2254**	**1266**	**3520**	
Brown hare – *Lepus europaeus* Pall.	1	-	1	0.2
Beaver – *Castor fiber* L.	1	1	2	0.4
Fox – *Vulpes vulpes* L.	40	39	79	14
Wolf – *Canis lupus* L.	28	-	28	5
Canis lupus or *Canis familiaris*	170	73	243	44
Marten – *Martes foina* Erxleben.	2	1	3	0.5
Weasel – *Mustela nivalis* L.	1	-	1	0.2
Marbled polecat – *Vormela peregusna* Gueldenst.	1	-	1	0.2
Badger – *Meles meles* L.	17	3	20	3.5
Wild ass – *Equus hemionus* Pall.	2	-	2	0.4
Roe deer – *Capreolus capreolus* L.	4	6	10	2
Red deer – *Cervus elaphus* L.	53	44	97	18
Wild pig – *Sus scrofa* L.	2	-	2	0.4
Gazelle, *Gazella subgutturosa* Gueldenst.	2	-	2	0.4
Moufflon – *Ovis orientalis* Gmel.	16	4	20	3.5
Bezoar goat – *Capra aegagrus* Erxleben.	-	2	2	0.4
Fish – *Pisces*	1	1	2	0.4
Tortoise – *Testudo* sp. or *Testudo graeca*	1	1	2	0.4
Birds – *Aves*	-	33	33	6
Wild animals total	**342**	**208**	**550**	
Grand Total	**2596**	**1474**	**4070**	

Table 5a.3b. Species from the 2000 excavations at Shengavit (H-P. and M. Uerpmann)

wild range (77.0-07.0 mm). This individual is either a large domestic cow or a small aurochs. The measurements on three metacarpi and one metatarsus fall within the range of wild cattle. The fauna of Shengavit was dominated by domestic cattle (*Bos*). These animals belonged to a rather large breed,[267] which seems to have been characteristic for other sites of this period in the South Caucasian area as well.[268] Besides favorable environmental conditions this might have been the result of conscious human selection of particular cattle types. [269]

Two sheep radii may represent wild sheep, but the vast majority of the sheep are domestic animals (Table 5a.1). The metrical data for the Shengavit equids identified by Crabtree indicate that these animals are onagers. The one exception is a fragmentary first phalanx. Based on the data published by Davis,[270] this fragment probably represents a donkey, but it falls at the very small end of the onager range.[271] There is no evidence in the 2009-12 faunal assemblage for either domestic or wild horses. Wild horses are well documented in the Chalcolithic period in central Anatolia,[272] but not in Armenia.

Chronological Analysis

Not all the Shengavit fauna could be assigned to one of the main strata. For example, 102 of the dog bones and fragments identified by Crabtree appear to be surface finds and may not date to the Early Bronze Age. The animal bones that could be identified to a specific chronological

---

267 Uerpmann, M. 2006, Fig. 7, 291
268 Uerpmann and Uerpmann 2010, Fig. 3, p. 240.
269 Uerpmann and Uerpmann report.
270 Davis et al. 2008.
271 see Crabtree and Piro under review.
272 see, for example, Crabtree in press

Species	1958-1980	2003-2007	Total	%
Cattle – *Bos taurus* L.	821	513	1334	38
Domestic Goat – *Capra hircus* L.	80	15	95	2.5
Domestic Sheep – *Ovis aries* L.	60	23	83	2
Ovis aries or *Capra hircus*	1056	623	1679	47
Pig – *Sus domesticus* L.	41	37	78	2
Horse – *Equus caballus* L.	128	47	175	5
Ass – *Equus asinus* L.	11	-	11	0.3
Dog - *Canis familiaris* L	57	8	65	2
Domestic animals total	**2254**	**1266**	**3520**	
Brown hare – *Lepus europaeus* Pall.	1	-	1	0.2
Beaver – *Castor fiber* L.	1	1	2	0.4
Fox – *Vulpes vulpes* L.	40	39	79	14
Wolf – *Canis lupus* L.	28	-	28	5
Canis lupus or *Canis familiaris*	170	73	243	44
Marten – *Martes foina* Erxleben.	2	1	3	0.5
Weasel – *Mustela nivalis* L.	1	-	1	0.2
Marbled polecat – *Vormela peregusna* Gueldenst.	1	-	1	0.2
Badger – *Meles meles* L.	17	3	20	3.5
Wild ass – *Equus hemionus* Pall.	2	-	2	0.4
Roe deer – *Capreolus capreolus* L.	4	6	10	2
Red deer – *Cervus elaphus* L.	53	44	97	18
Wild pig – *Sus scrofa* L.	2	-	2	0.4
Gazelle – *Gazella subgutturosa* Gueldenst.	2	-	2	0.4
Moufflon – *Ovis orientalis* Gmel.	16	4	20	3.5
Bezoar goat – *Capra aegagrus* Erxleben.	-	2	2	0.4
Fish – *Pisces*	1	1	2	0.4
Tortoise – *Testudo* sp. or *Testudo graeca*	1	1	2	0.4
Birds – *Aves*	-	33	33	6
Wild animals total	**342**	**208**	**550**	
Grand Total	**2596**	**1474**	**4070**	

Table 5a.3c. Species identified from the 1958 1980, 2003-2007 excavations at Shengavit (after Manaseryan 2018).

layer are shown in Table 5a.4. With the exception of the relatively small assemblage from Stratum IV, all the chronological units are dominated by the remains of caprines, followed by smaller numbers of cattle, and very few pigs. Equids are also quite rare. The species ratios for cattle, sheep/goat, pigs, and equids for layers that included more than 100 identified elements of these species are shown in Table 5a.5. There is no clear evidence for changes through time in the Shengavit assemblage.

Ageing Analysis

Since sheep and goats make up the majority of the identified faunal remains from Shengavit, we wanted to identify how the residents of the site obtained these animals. Were these animals raised locally, or were they obtained from pastoral specialists who may have kept their flocks some distance from Shengavit for substantial portions of the year? The age profiles for the complete and nearly complete sheep and goat mandibles from Shengavit are shown in Figure 5a.4. From that figure it

YEAR	SQUARE	LOC.	BAG#	CLASS	SPECIES	AGE
2010	K4/L4	5051	5127	Actiropterygii	Salmonidae	N/A
2010	K4/L4	5051	5127	Amphibia	Bufonidae	Young
2010	K4/L4	5051	5127	Amphibia	Bufonidae	Young
2010	K6	1057	1394	Actiropterygii	Salmonidae	N/A
2010	J5	2047	2552	Actiropterygii	small fish	N/A
2010	L4	8003	?	Actiropterygii	Large fish - Salmonidae	N/A
2010	J5	2050	2657	Actiropterygii	Salmonidae	N/A
2010	J5	2038	2377	Actiropterygii	Cyprinus carpio	N/A
2010	I 4	7058	7106	Ave	Small bird	N/A
2010	J5	2045	2504	Indeterminate	Small mammal?	N/A
2010	J5	2039	2429	Actiropterygii	Salmonidae	Adult
2010	J5	2025	2310	Actiropterygii	Salmonidae	Young
2010	K6	1041	1342	Actiropterygii	Salmonidae	Adult
2010	L6	4001	4002	Actiropterygii	Salmonidae	Adult
2010	J5	2031	2341	Actiropterygii	Small fish- Salmonidae?	Young
2010	J5	2050	2686	Actiropterygii	Cyprinus carpio	Young
2010	J5	2050	2686	Actiropterygii	Salmonidae	Young
2010	J5	2034	2486	Actiropterygii	Large fish - Salmonidae	Large - Adult
2010	J5	2039	2368	Actiropterygii	Large fish - Salmonidae	Adult
2010	L6	4007	?	Actiropterygii	Small fish- Salmonidae?	Adult
2010	L6	4007	?	Actiropterygii	Small fish- Salmonidae?	Adult
2010	J5	2045	2549	Actiropterygii	Salmonidae	Adult
2010	L6	4001	4004	Actiropterygii	Salmonidae	Adult
2010	L6	4001	4004	Actiropterygii	Salmonidae	Adult
2010	L6	4001	4004	Actiropterygii	Salmonidae	Adult
2010	L6	4001	4004	Actiropterygii	Salmonidae	Adult
2010	L6	4001	4004	Actiropterygii	Salmonidae	Adult
2010	J5	2055	2624	Actiropterygii	Large fish - Carp	Adult
2010	J5	2055	2624	Actiropterygii	Large fish - Carp	Adult
2010	K6	1062	1472	Actiropterygii	Small fish	N/A
2010	K6	1062	1472	Actiropterygii	Small fish	N/A
2010	K6	1030	1214	Actiropterygii	Salmonidae	Young
2010	L6	4017	?	Actiropterygii	Salmonidae	Young
2010	K6	1080	1546	Actiropterygii	Salmonidae	Young
2010	J5	2045	2566	Actiropterygii	Large fish	N/A
2012	K6	1138	1839	Gastropoda	Indeterminate	N/A
2012	L6	4008	1910	Actiropterygii	Salmonidae	Young
2012	K6	1127	1832	Actiropterygii	Cyprinus carpio	Mid-Adult
2012	K6	1127	1832	Actiropterygii	Cyprinus carpio	Mid-Adult
2012	K6	1127	1832	Actiropterygii	Cyprinus carpio	Mid-Adult
2012	K6	1127	1806	Actiropterygii	Cyprinus carpio	Young
2012	K6	1127	1806	Amphibia	Bufonidae	Young
2012	K6	1127	1806	Amphibia	Bufonidae	Young
2012	K6	1127	1806	Amphibia	Bufonidae	Young
2012	K6	1110	1573	Actiropterygii	Salmonidae	Young
2012	K6	1110	1573	Actiropterygii	Salmonidae	Young
2012	K6	1102	1595	Actiropterygii	Salmonidae	Young
2012	K6	1127	1782	Actiropterygii	Small fish	N/A
2012	K6	1127	1782	Actiropterygii	Salmonidae	Adult
2012	K6	1126	1774	Actiropterygii	Salmonidae	Adult
2012	K6	1126	1774	Actiropterygii	Salmonidae	Adult
2012	K6	1115	1745	Actiropterygii	Small fish	Indeterminate
2012	K6	1115	1745	Actiropterygii	Small fish	Indeterminate
2012	K6	1127	1806	Actiropterygii	Salmonidae	Adult
2012	K6	1127	1806	Actiropterygii	Salmonidae	Adult
2012	K6	1127	1806	Actiropterygii	Salmonidae	Adult

Table 5a.3d. Fish Remains from 2009-2012 (Nyree Manoukian).

Species	Stratum I	M5	Stratum II	Stratum III	Stratum IV	Stratum V	Stratum V-VI	Stratum V-VII	Stratum VI	Stratum VII	Stratum VIII
Cattle (*Bos taurus*)	90	55	134	164	80	22	14	11	3	1	18
Sheep (*Ovis aries*)	26	24	74	56	4	9	14	4	5		24
Goat (*Capra hircus*)	25	22	17	18	2	4	2	2	1		13
Sheep/goat	214	165	554	453	49	47	35	39	23	2	92
Pig (*Sus scrofa*)	5	11	21	26		1	2	2			
Dog (*Canis familiaris*)	15	5	18	17	9	4	1	6			
Equid (*Equus* sp.)	3	1	8	3		1	3	4	2		1
Red Deer (*Cervus elaphus*)	1	1	3	6	1	1		4			
Roe deer (*Capreolus capreolus*)	0			1							
Hare (*Lepus* sp.)	1	2	3	3			2				
Fox (*Vulpes vulpes*)	1			2		1	1				
Badger (*Meles meles*)		1			1						
Otter (*Lutra lutra*)											
Bear (*Ursus arctos*)		1		3							
Large Mammal "cattle-sized"	32	32	74	78	27	22	7	7	2	1	7
Small Mammal "sheep-sized"	125	95	397	222	22	19	23	15	28		63
Unidentified Mammal	2607	1590	5541	3643	1013	384	314	309	171	4	433
Bird	4	2	3	2		1	3				
Fish	1	31	9	6	8	2					2
Amphibians						1					
Testudines		1		9			6				
Total	3150	2039	6856	4712	1216	519	427	403	235	8	653

Table 5a.4: Animal bones identified from each archaeological layer at Shengavit.

is clear that substantial numbers of animals were culled during the later first and second years of life, but there were no animals under the age of 6 months in the entire Shengavit assemblage. An assemblage that is dominated by the remains of younger animals may represent a subsistence that is focused on meat, milk, and herd security.[273] The Shengavit assemblage, however, also includes a substantial number of older animals that may have been kept for secondary products such as wool and hair. However, the Shengavit age profile provides no clear evidence for specialized wool production. While young sheep provide fine wool, wool production generally peaks in sheep that are about 5-7 years old.[274] If the Shengavit sheep were specialized wool producers, we would expect to see larger numbers of sheep culled at older ages (between 4 and 8 years of age). In addition, castrated male sheep are excellent wool producers, so we would not expect to see a large kill-off in the first two years of life in a specialized wool-producing flock. The Shengavit age profile seems to focus on a more generalized use of sheep and goats with an emphasis on meat production. The absence of very young animals and the diverse age range represented in the faunal assemblage could indicate that the inhabitants of Shengavit were supplied with meat and other animal products by pastoral specialists. It is also possible that some of the animals were supplied by the inhabitants of other nearby sites. Finally, a variety of producers who lived at the site might have raised the animal themselves. The current

Species	Stratum I	M5	Stratum II	Stratum III	Stratum IV	Stratum VIII
Bos sp.	24.8	19.8	16.6	22.5	59.3	12.2
Ovis/Capra	73.0	75.9	79.8	73.6	40.7	87.2
Sus scrofa	1.4	4.0	2.6	3.6		0.0
Equus sp.	0.8	0.4	1.0	0.4		0.7

Table 5a.5: Species ratios for cattle, caprines, pigs, and equids for each archaeological layer that produced more than 100 bones of these species.

273 Redding 1984.
274 O'Connor 2010, 12.

data do not permit us to say for certain which possibility is the most likely, although the pollen studies suggest this (Chapter 2b).

We recovered only 6 cattle mandibles that could be used for aging analysis from the Shengavit excavations, and not all of them could be aged closely. We looked at the epiphyseal fusion data to see whether we could find information on the patterns of cattle management. The epiphyses were grouped into early fusing (by one and a half years), middle fusing (by three years), and late fusing (by four years) elements (see Table 5a.6, Fig 5a.4). Almost none of the cattle that were consumed at Shengavit were killed during the first year and a half of life, and only about 17% were killed before three years of age. Cattle reach bodily maturity between about four and five years of age, and 62.5% of the Shengavit cattle were killed by age four, most of them between three and four years of age. These data suggest that the Shengavit cattle were raised primarily for meat production. As noted above, older cattle can also be used as traction animals to pull carts and plows, but the Shengavit cattle from 2009-2012 show no clear evidence of traction pathologies, suggesting that they were probably raised primarily for meat rather than secondary products. They could have been grazed in the pasture areas along the river.

Fish

Fish are rarely mentioned in analysis of animal remains. They certainly represent a significant part of the ancient diet. Excavators at Shengavit recovered bones of two families of fish, Salmonidae and Cyprinidae (Table 5a. 3d). The former include fresh water salmon, trout, chars, whitefish, and graylings. The latter include a variety of carp. Ancient Kura-Araxes people appear to have fished with hooks and nets; for the latter we have ground stone sinkers (see Chapter 5f). The association of Kura-Araxes and fishing with hook and line fish is indicated by the first appearance of them in the Southern Levant Early Bronze III, when Kura-Araxes, locally known as Khirbet Kerak Ware people, appeared at sites like

	Fused	Unfused
Early Fusing		
D. Humerus	0	5
D. Radius	0	2
P 1st Phalanx	1	59
P 2nd Phalanx	0	54
Total	1	130
Middle Fusing		
D Tibia	4	12
D Metacarpus	1	9
D Metatarsus	1	9
D Metapodial	1	4
Total	7	34
Late Fusing		
P Calcaneus	5	1
P Femur	3	5
D Radius	2	2
D Ulna	4	0
D Femur	3	0
P Tibia	1	1
Total	15	9

Table 5a.6. Aging by epiphyseal fusing of joints.

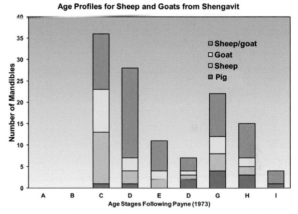

Figure 5a.4. Age profile (following Payne 1973) for sheep and goat remains from Shengavit.

Species/ Buildings	B 1-2	B. 2	B. 3	B. 4	B. 5	B. 6a	B. 6b	B. 6c	B. 6d	B. 7
Cattle (Bos taurus)	18	24	56	63	9	2	1	1	8	2
Sheep (Ovis aries)	3	13	23	1	1		2		13	1
Goat (Capra hircus)	2	2	6	1					10	
Sheep/goat	24	69	160	27	8	5	7	2	56	7
Pig (Sus scrofa)	3	5	2							
Dog (Canis familiaris)	5	3	2	6	1					
Equid (Equus sp.)			3				1		1	1
Red Deer (Cervus elaphus)		1	5	1						
Hare (Lepus sp.)		1	1							
Badger (Meles meles)					1					
Bear (Ursus arctos)			2							
Large Mammal "cattle-sized"	5	15	33	18	9	4	1	1	5	
Small Mammal "sheep-sized"	12	62	86	13	6	1	1		27	9
Unidentified Mammal	428	692	931	561	299	37	31	4	224	71
Bird		1								
Fish		7		3	5				2	
Testudines (turtle)	2	1	1							

Table 5a.7a Building-by-building summary of the faunal remains recovered from Shengavit Square K6.

Tel bet Yerah.[275] Fish have the advantage of being easily salted to keep them for times when other meat is less available. Salting in large basins was a common practice in Greek and Roman times.[276] It could easily have been so during the Kura-Araxes, especially with sources of salt close at hand. Unlike the Greeks and Romans, excavators probably have not been looking for the salting pools for the Kura-Araxes.

Building-by-Building Analysis

The faunal remains that could be assigned to particular buildings, other than the two shrines of M5 and J5, are shown in Table 5a.7a and b. Some of the assemblages are quite small. The largest faunal collections were recovered from Square K6 Buildings 2, 3, and 6d. Caprines dominated most of the assemblages in the Square K6 buildings, except for Building 4, which produced far more cattle bones than sheep and goat remains. Building 4 was represented largely by a pit into which builders threw its burned remains. It is not, therefore, a completely representative collection. Cattle and pig bones are completely absent from K6 Buildings 4, 5, 6, and 7, and equid remains are also quite rare in those buildings. An unusual find were the bones of bear paws on the floor of Building 2. Our interpretation was that a bear skin lay on that floor near the two buried large jars (see Chapter 3)(Fig 5a.5).

The faunal remains from Building 1 (Square I14) of Stratum I are shown in Table 5a.7b. The assemblage is dominated by the remains of caprines, including equal numbers of sheep and goats. Most of the rest of the identifiable remains were those of cattle. The assemblage also produced small numbers of pig, dog, and red deer bones.

RITUAL INSTALLATIONS

One of the most striking features of the Early Bronze Age at Shengavit is the presence of two ritual emplacements. Previous analysis of the faunal remains from the M5 ritual shrine and associated room revealed a faunal assemblage with species ratios that mirrored those seen at other buildings of the site. The contexts associated with the M5 hearth yielded the remains of cattle, sheep, goats, pigs, fish, and a single fragment of red deer antler, probably a ritual symbol. The species identified from the M5 hearth are shown in Figure 5a.6. Most of the faunal remains are caprines with smaller numbers of cattle and a few bones of other species.[277] The second ritual space from J5 excavated in 2012 also yielded

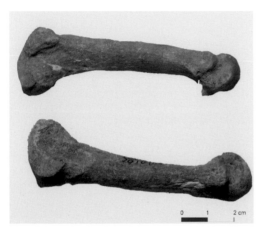

Figure 5a.5. Bones of bear paws from the floor of Square K6 Building 2.

Species	NISP
Cattle (*Bos taurus*)	78
Sheep (*Ovis aries*)	22
Goat (*Capra hircus*)	22
Sheep/goat	161
Pig (*Sus scrofa*)	3
Dog (*Canis familiaris*)	11
Red Deer (Cervus elaphus)	1
Fox (*Vulpes vulpes*)	1
Large Mammal "cattle-sized"	24
Small Mammal "sheep-sized"	80
Unidentified Mammal	1728
Bird	4
Fish	1
Total	2136

Table 5a. 7b: Animal Bones Identified from Building 1, Square 114

275   Lernau et al. 2021.
276   Højte 2005.
277   see also Crabtree and Piro 2021.

species ratios that mirrored those of the site as a whole, although when we added in an apparent trash deposit just north of the north wall (Table 5a.8a and b, Fig 5a. 7) , in the Minimum Number of Individuals (MNI) the building had a higher percentage of pigs and fewer cattle and sheep than the average (Fig 5a.7).

One question the excavators had, given the feasting found at KA2 Kura-Araxes Godin Tepe,[278] and KA1 Arslantepe,[279] was whether these ritual sites were also feasting centers. In those sites, the proposed feasting was marked by specialized buildings; in the Godin case, it was marked by a large kitchen and, at Arslantepe, by very young animals with a higher concentration of the best meat cuts from sheep.

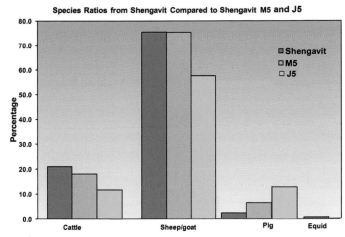

Figure 5a.6. Species identified from the assemblage associated with the Squares M5 and J5 ritual emplacements.

At Shengavit we might expect a feasting center to have a large number of bones from a small number of individuals. We would expect to see all the body parts represented relatively equally. When we look at the body part distribution for the sheep and goats (we used this to calculate the MNI), we do not see the kind of distribution that we would expect from feasting. The body part distribution is relatively uneven, and the most commonly represented bones are those that survive best in the archaeological record: tibias (TIB), mandibles (JAW), teeth (e.g., 18 upper molars--UM). Skeletal elements like vertebrae, femora, and pelvises are relatively poorly represented, and these elements come from the meatier parts of the skeleton. To us, this looks like material that was lying around on the site and eventually incorporated into a trash deposit. The same is true for the material from the rooms. The fact that we have a lot of tooth fragments (TFRAG) indicates that the material was not rapidly buried. If we were looking for feasting, we would expect a much higher number of upper limb elements, pelvis, femur, scapula, and vertebrae. Instead, we found lower limb elements, like the tibia, that tend to survive well due to their shape and robust character, and lots of teeth and tooth fragments.

MNI by Species	Trash	Room 1	Room 2	Total	%
Cattle	2	1	2	5	12.5
Sheep/goat	12	3	7	22	55.0
Pig	2	2	2	6	15.0
Dog	2	0	1	3	7.5
Equid (*Equus* sp.)	1	0	0	1	2.5
Red Deer	0	0	1	1	2.5
Fox	0	0	1	1	2.5
Hare	0	1	0	1	2.5
Total	19	7	13	40	

Table 5a.8a Square J5 Architectural levels 2/3 Building (MNI).

Figure 5a.7. Bone remains from Square J5.

---

278   Rothman 2011.
279   Palumbi et al. 2017.

We would also expect lots of vertebrae and meaty upper limb elements, and more exotic meats. The patterns of representation that we see in the MNIs are very similar to those we see in the NISP (fragment count) percentages. Most of these bones come from sheep and goats, with smaller numbers of cattle and pigs, and a few odd bits of equids and local wild animals. These deposits do not differ from what we see in the rest of the site. The rituals conducted there must have had other than feasting as their core (see Chapter 6a), or, if there were feasting, the trash from feasting was not deposited separately from other faunal remains.

Species/loci	Room 1	Trash	Room 2	Total	%
Sheep/goat	75	273	193	541	57
Domestic cattle	8	62	34	104	11
Large ungulate	4	31	17	52	5
Pig	0	18	9	27	2.8
Equid	0	8	0	8	0.8
Large artiodactyl	0	0	0	0	0
Small artiodactyl[1]	22	76	94	192	20
Dog	1	8	5	14	1.4
Hare	1	2	0	3	0.3
Red deer	0	1	1	2	0.2
Fish	1	5	0	6	0.6
Total	112	502	353	949	100

Table 5a.8b Square J5 Architectural levels 2/3 Building (Counts). Artiodactyls are any member of the mammalian order Artiodactyla, or even-toed ungulates, which includes pigs, peccaries, deer, giraffes, pronghorn, antelopes, sheep, goats, and cattle.

Comparisons to Other Kura-Araxes Sites

Several other Kura-Araxes sites have yielded faunal assemblages that are broadly contemporary with the faunal material from Shengavit. One of the most extensively excavated and published is the Kura-Araxes assemblage from Sos Höyük in eastern Turkey.[280] Like Shengavit, the Sos assemblage is dominated by the remains of caprines and cattle. Pigs and equids are quite rare. The Sos sheep-to-goat ratio of 2.6 to 1 is quite close to the ratio seen at Shengavit. The Sos assemblage included a wide range of wild animals, most of which are represented by small numbers of specimens. These wild species were obtained from a variety of different environments at both sites. At both Shengavit and Sos, red deer and hare were among the most common of the wild species.

The age profiles for sheep and goats based on dental eruption and wear show broad similarities as well. Neither the Sos nor the Shengavit assemblages produced evidence for sheep under the age of 6 months. Substantial numbers of sheep and goats were culled during the second half of the first and during the second year of life. Fewer sub-adults were culled; and the rest of the sheep and goat were culled after 48 months of age. While Howell-Meurs suggests that the sheep and goats were raised primarily for meat, she notes that the older animals would also have yielded milk and wool as well.[281] The overall similarities between the Shengavit and the Sos assemblages are somewhat surprising, given that Shengavit is a larger, permanent settlement, and Sos has been identified as a temporary camp for herders.[282] However, re-examination of Howell-Meurs' data suggests that Sos was not a temporary camp. The presence of nearly all age categories suggests that Sos was occupied year-round.[283]

There are, however, significant differences between the Sos and the Shengavit assemblages. The most significant is the difference in the equid remains. The Shengavit 2009-12 assemblage yielded small numbers of donkey and onager bones, but no evidence for domestic horses. Sos, on the other hand, yielded a small number of domestic horse bones and some equid remains that may represent either donkeys or onagers. A recently published study based on ancient

---

280   Howell-Meurs 2001.
281   Howell-Meurs 2001, 34.
282   Howell-Meurs 2001.
283   Piro and Crabtree 2017, 278.

DNA shows that domestic horses were introduced to the South Caucasus and Anatolia during the Bronze Age. They were not domesticated in Anatolia or the South Caucasus.[284]

More recent archaeological excavations have been carried out at the Early Bronze Age site of Gegharot, which sits on top of an outcrop at the southeastern edge of the Tsaghkahovit Plain in northwestern Armenia, 75 kilometers from Shengavit, but at a much higher elevation. The site was excavated as part of the ArAGATS project, co-directed by Adam Smith and Ruben Badalyan. Like Shengavit, the site appears to have been occupied during the KA2 period (2900-2500 BC), but also during the KA1.[285] The initial studies of the fauna from Gegharot focused on the question of whether the occupants of the site were pastoral nomads or whether they were farmer-herders.[286] This is a very different question than the ones that we have asked of the fauna from Shengavit. In the case of Shengavit, we have clear evidence for permanent settlement at a site that appears to be a larger site in a settlement system with sites of different size and functions. Our question is whether the inhabitants of Shengavit may have been supplied with meat and other animal products by pastoral specialists. Nevertheless, the faunal data recovered from Gegharot provide a useful comparison to the Shengavit faunal material.

As is the case at Shengavit, the vast majority of the faunal remains were unidentified fragments of animal bones. Less than 10% of the original Gegharot assemblage could be identified to genus.[287] The Gegharot faunal assemblage is dominated by cattle and caprines, but cattle are slightly more numerous than sheep and goats in the original faunal assemblage. This is typical of more high elevation versus lower elevation sites even today. The high number of cattle would suggest that the site was a sedentary village rather than a mobile herders' camp.[288] Pigs, equids, and other wild mammals were poorly represented.

The patterns of caprine husbandry seen at Gegharot differ markedly from those seen at Shengavit. First, the vast majority of the caprine remains recovered from Gegharot were sheep rather than goats. The Gegharot sheep-to-goat ratio was 7.7-to-1, far higher than that seen at either Sos or Shengavit.[289] In addition, the caprine kill patterns indicate that the majority of the sheep and goats lived to adulthood, while at both Sos and Shengavit, we see a substantial kill-off in the later first and second years of life. Monahan notes that the Gegharot kill-pattern would not be self-sustaining in the long-term.[290] The Sos and Shengavit patterns, on the other hand, are sustainable. They appear to represent herds that were raised for meat and herd security, with the older animals also supplying secondary products including milk, wool, and hair.

Excavations at Gegharot also yielded a very small number of horse bones,[291] and the 2008-11 excavations also yielded one bone that could be attributed to an onager.[292]

Another KA2 site from Armenia that has yielded a well-studied faunal assemblage from Armenia is Mokhrablur level V, which is dated to the first half of the third millennium and was analyzed by Piro.[293] Mokhrablur is a four-hectare site down in the Ararat Plain a couple of hundred meters above sea level below Shengavit on the Koytak

---

284 Guimares et al. 2020.
285 Monahan 2007, 382.
286 Monahan 2007.
287 Monahan 2007, 384: Table 15.1.
288 Piro and Crabtree 2017, 279.
289 Monahan 2007, 92.
290 Monahan 2008, 93.
291 Monahan 2008.
292 Badalyan 2015, 163.
293 see Piro and Crabtree 2017.

Plateau. Mokhrablur also yielded relatively equal numbers of cattle and caprines, suggesting broadly based, rather than a specialized animal management strategy. Pigs were quite rare, but there is evidence for the hunting of wild sheep and red deer as a supplement to animal husbandry.[294] Mokhrablur has been identified on the basis of both archaeological and zooarchaeological data as "an extremely stable, agro-pastoral village in the Early Bronze Age."[295]

Preliminary quantitative data are also available from the Kura-Araxes site of Köhne Shahar (Ravaz) in Iranian Azerbaijan.[296] The general composition of the assemblage is quite similar to the Shengavit assemblage. The faunal collection from Köhne Shahar is dominated by caprines, and sheep outnumber goats, although not to the extent it was at Shengavit. Cattle make up much of the rest of the collection, with only small numbers of pigs and equids. The most common wild animals are large deer that are likely to be red deer (*Cervus elaphus*). Red deer are also among the most numerous wild animals at Shengavit. The site of Köhne Shahar covers 15 hectares and included a fortification wall around its central, production area. Alizadeh suggests that this site "may have been socially and economically more complex than other known Kura-Araxes settlements in the region," although that is perhaps too broad a statement.[297] It was also founded in the late KA1 and abandoned at the end of the KA2, while Shengavit was founded in the KA2 and continued until the very end of the Kura-Araxes.

Davoudi[298] provides a summary of the animal bone data from six Kura-Araxes sites in northwestern Iran and Naxçivan (Tepe Hasanlu, Kul Tepe, Haftavan Tepe, Kohne Tepesi, Köhne Pasgah Tepesi, and Ovçular Tepesi). Their data paint a similar picture of Kura-Araxes animal economy. All these assemblages are dominated by the remains of caprines, although the ratios of sheep-to-goats are variable. Cattle are second in importance, and pigs and equids are quite rare. Hunting played a minor role at these sites, but as is the case for Shengavit, the hunted animals are drawn from a mosaic of different environments, from forest to steppe.

The zooarchaeological data from Godin IV in Iran present a somewhat different picture. While Shengavit, Sos, Mokhrablur, and Gegharot included substantial numbers of both cattle and caprines, the faunal remains from Godin IV were dominated by the remains of sheep and goats.[299] Cattle make up less than 11% of the identified faunal remains. Some of the cattle show traction pathologies, suggesting that they may have been used primarily to pull carts and plows.[300] The Godin assemblage also produced small numbers of pigs and equids, and there is evidence for hunting of red deer, roe deer, hare, and badger.

The age profile for the Godin caprines includes a much larger number of adult animals than are seen at the other Kura-Araxes sites. The peak of mortality is in the 4 to 6 year age class, and a number of animals survived to even older ages. Fewer animals were culled during the first two years of life than was the case at Shengavit. This pattern might suggest that the caprines were kept for secondary products, such as milk, wool, and hair. However, the kill-pattern is not a particularly good match for the meat- milk- or wool-kill-patterns identified by Payne.[301] The ratio of sheep-to-goats at Godin IV is about 2.5-to-1, quite like the ratios seen at Shengavit, pointing to a more generalized use of both sheep and goats for meat and secondary products. The paucity of younger sheep and goats at

---

294 Piro and Crabtree 2107, Table 19.2.
295 Piro and Crabtree 2017, 280.
296 Alizadeh et al. 2015.
297 Alizadeh et al. 2015, 49.
298 Davoudi et al. in press.
299 Piro and Crabtree 2017, 280: Table 19.3.
300 Crabtree 2011.
301 Payne 1973.

Godin suggests that some of the animals may have been kept away from the site, possibly using some form of vertical transhumance.[302] It is also possible that local pastoral groups provisioned Godin. This could be true for Shengavit as well, but it is not likely.

There is at least one other Kura-Araxes site that has a well-studied faunal assemblage, and the excavators argue it was occupied by mobile pastoralists on a seasonal basis, although this interpretation has been challenged.[303] Frangipane[304] notes that the site of Arslantepe in eastern Turkey underwent substantial changes around 3200 BC toward the end of the KA1. A monumental complex of public architecture was destroyed, and it was replaced by wattle and daub huts that appear to have been occupied on a seasonal basis by groups that had links to the Kura-Araxes culture.[305] Compared to the earlier occupations at Arslantepe, the Kura-Araxes horizon had a very high proportion of sheep and goats in relation to cattle and very few pig bones. The species ratios seen at early third millennium Arslantepe include a higher percentage of caprines (over 85%) than are seen at Shengavit, although, there is evidence for a waste disposal area that appears to be associated with ritual feasting,[306] which would skew the patterns. This area has no obvious parallel at Shengavit. The biggest difference between the Shengavit and the Arslantepe faunal assemblages is seen in the kill patterns for the sheep and goats. The Arslantepe assemblages include a substantial number of very young sheep and goats that were killed before the age of 6 months and very few caprines that were killed between the ages of six and twelve months. In contrast, many of the Shengavit animals were culled between the ages of six and twelve months. These probably represent surplus animals that were chosen for slaughter before the winter. The Shengavit kill-pattern is consistent with the use of these animals for meat, milk, and/or herd security. Siracusano and Bartosiewicz[307] suggest that the inhabitants of Early Bronze Age Arslantepe may have feasted on young lambs and kids in the late spring/summer. They further suggest that Arslantepe may have been occupied on a seasonal basis or that there may have been a core of permanent inhabitants and that the population was enlarged on a seasonal basis by the presence of mobile pastoralists during the spring and summer.

We have noted elsewhere that models of the Kura-Araxes cultural tradition that are based entirely on highly mobile forms of pastoralism are simply not supported by the zooarchaeological data.[308] Both the faunal and the archaeological data point to a diversity of settlement forms.

Conclusions

The rich and well excavated faunal assemblage at Shengavit provide important new information on the animal economy of the site. Our research indicates that caprines (primarily sheep) were the most common animals at Shengavit, but cattle would have produced the bulk of the edible meat based on their larger size. These results closely mirror the conclusions drawn by the Uerpmanns' based on the faunal remains that were recovered in 2000. Pigs, dogs, and donkeys were the other domestic animals that we recovered from the 2009-12 excavations.

The excavations over time also provided evidence for a diverse range of wild animals including red and roe deer, small numbers of wild sheep and cattle, onagers, and a range of carnivore species including brown bear, European

---

302 Piro and Crabtree 2017, 281.
303 Batiuk et al. 2022.
304 Frangipane 2014.
305 Fragipane 2014, 172.
306 Siracusano and Bartosiewicz 2012, 119; Samei in Batiuk et al. 2022.
307 Siracusano and Bartosiewicz 2012, 120.
308 Piro and Crabtree 2017.

badger, and otter. Foxes and hares, although wild, are commonly found in and around cultivated fields. Simonyan identified one figurine as a lion (Chapter 6c), although excavators recovered no lion bones.

Shengavit, at six hectares, is a larger site for the early third millennium BC in the South Caucasus. Some smaller sites are recorded nearby, but being in the heart of modern Yerevan, they were neither properly surveyed nor excavated before they were destroyed. This is a great shame. If we had access to the faunal data from these smaller sites, we might be able to determine how many of the animals were raised locally and how many were raised by mobile pastoral populations.

Acknowledgements

The authors would like to thank Siavash Samei for giving us access to his preliminary faunal data from Köhne Shahar (Ravaz). We also want to thank Rémi Berthon for sharing his zooarchaeological data with us. We also want to thank Mitchell Rothman and Hakob Simonyan for their support and hospitality. Crabtree's travel in Shengavit in 2013 was supported, in part, by a University Research Challenge Fund grant from New York University.

References

Alizadeh, K., Eghbal, H., and Samei, S. 2015 Approaches to social complexity in Kura-Araxes culture: a view from Köhne Shahar (Ravaz) in Chaldran, Iranian Azerbaijan. *Paléorient* 41(1): 37–54.

Badalyan, R., Smith, A. T., Lindsay, I., Harutyunyan, A., Greene, A., Marshall, M., Monahan, B., and Hovsepyan R. 2014 A preliminary report on the 2008, 2010, and 2011 investigations of Project ArAGATS on the Tsaghkahovit Plain, Republic of Armenia. *Archäologische Mitteilungen aus Iran und Turan* 46: 149-222.

Bartosiewicz, L., Van Neer, W., and Lentacker, A. 1997 *Draught Cattle: Their Osteological Identification and History*. Tervuren: Musée Royale de l'Afrique Centrale.

Bartosiewicz, L. 2008 Bone structure and function in draft cattle. in Limping together through the ages: Joint afflictions and bone infections, edited by G. Grupe, J.P. McLynn. *Documenta Archaeobiologiae* 6, 153-164.

Batiuk, S., Rothman, M. S, Samei, S., Hovsepyan, R. 2022 Unraveling the Kura-Araxes Cultural Tradition across Space and Time. *Ancient Near Eastern Studies* 59: 235-325.

Boessneck, J. A., Müller, H.-H., and Teichert, M. 1964 Osteologische Unterschneidsmerkmale zwischen Schaf (*Ovis aries* Linné) und Ziege (*Capra hircus* Linné). *Kühn-Archiv* 78: 1-129.

Bökönyi S. 1995 Problems with using osteological materials of wild animals for comparisons in archaeozoology. *Anthropológiai Közlemények* 37: 3-11.

Campana, D. 2010 FAUNA: Database and Analysis Software for Faunal Analysis. Poster presented at the meeting of the International Council for Archaeozoology, Paris, August 23rd-26th, 2010.

Crabtree, P.J. 1990 *West Stow: Early Anglo-Saxon Animal Husbandry*. East Anglian Archaeology 47. Ipswich: Suffolk County Planning Department.

Crabtree, P. J. 2011 The animal remains from Godin Period IV. in *On the High Road: the history of Godin Tepe, Iran*, edited by H. Gopnik and M. S Rothman, 178. Costa Mesa, CA: Mazda Pubications.

Crabtree, P. J., and Piro, J. J. 2021 Animal bones from the 2009-12 excavations at the Early Bronze Age site of Shengavit, Yerevan, Armenia: A First Look. in *Archaeozoology of Southwest Asia and Adjacent Areas XIII: Proceedings of the Thirteenth International Symposium, University of Cyprus, Nicosia, Cyprus, June 7–10, 2017*, edited by J. Daujat, A. Hadjikoumis, R. Berthon, J. Chahoud, V. Kassianidou, and J.-D. Vigne, 177-183. Archaeobiology 3. Atlanta: Lockwood Press.

Davis, S. J. M., Gonçalves, M. J., Gabriel, S. 2008 Animal remains from a Moslem period (12th/13th century AD) Lixeira (garbage dump) in Silves algarve, Portugal. *Revista Portuguesa de Arqueologia* 11, 183-258.

Davoudi, H., Berthon, R., Mohaseb, A., Sheikhi, S., Abedi, A., and Mashkour, M., in press. Kura-Araxes Exploitation of Animal Resources in Northwestern Iran and Nakhchivan.

Dimirbaş, Y. 2015 Density of European Hare and Red Fox in Different Habitats of Kırıkkale Province (Central Anatolia), with a Low Level in Hare Number and an Expected Correlation in Spring. *Acta Zoologica Bulgarica* 67 (4): 515-520.

Eisenmann, V. 1986 Comparative Osteology of Modern and Fossil Horses, Half-asses and Asses. in *Equids in the Ancient World*, edited by R.H. Meadow, and H.-P. Uerpmann, 67-98. Wiesbaden: Reichert.

Frangipane, M. 2014 After collapse: Continuity and disruption in the settlement by Kura-Araxes-linked pastoral groups at Arslantepe-Malatya (Turkey). New Data. *Paléorient* 40 (2), 169-182.

Grant, A. 1982 The use of tooth wear as a guide to the age of domestic ungulates. in *Ageing and Sexing Animal Bones from Archaeological Sites*, edited by B. Wilson, C. Grigson, and S. Payne, 91-108. Oxford: British Archaeological Reports. British Series 109.

Guimares, S., Arbuckle, B., Adcock, S., Buitenhuis, H., Chazan, H., Manaseryan, N., Uerpmann, H-P., Grange, T., Geigl, E-M. 2020 Ancient DNA Shows Domestic Horses Were Introduced in the Southern Caucasus and Anatolia During the Bronze Age. *Science Advances* 6(38): eabb0030.

Halstead, P., Collins, P., Isaakidou, V. 2002 Sorting the Sheep from the Goats: Morphological Distinctions between the Mandibles and Mandibular Teeth of Adult *Ovis* and *Capra*. *Journal of Archaeological Science* 29: 545-553.

Hite, E. 2008 *Morphological and molecular approaches to species identification in equid cheek teeth from Godin: Terminology, taxonomy and further implications*, Unpublished MA thesis, Department of Anthropology, New York University.

Højte, J. K. 2005 The Archaeological Evidence for Fish Processing in the Black Sea Region, in *Ancient Fishing and Fish Processing*, edited by T. Bekker-Nielsen, 133-160. Aarhus: Aarhus University Press.

Howell-Meurs, S. 2001 *Early Bronze and Iron Age Animal Exploitation in Eastern Anatolia: the faunal remains from Sos Höyük and Büyüktepe Höyük*. British Archaeological Reports, S 945. Oxford: Archaeopress.

Kimura, B., Marshall, F., Beja-Pereira, and Mulligan, C. 2013 Donkey domestication. *African Archaeological Review* 30: 83-95.

Lernau, O., Shapiro, J., Paz, S., and Greenberg, R. 2021 Fishing, fish consumption, urbanism, and migrants at Tel Bet Yerah, 3200-2700 BC. *Antiquity* 95(382): 885-899.

Librado, P., Khan, N., Fages, A. 2021 The origins and spread of domestic horses from the Western Eurasian steppes. *Nature* 598, 634–640 (2021). https://doi.org/10.1038/s41586-021-04018-9.

Lyman, R.L. 2008 *Quantitative Paleozoology*. Cambridge: Cambridge University Press.

Manaseryan, N. 2018 Archaeological Investigation of the Site of Shengavit, Armenia (Based on the archaeological excavations of 1965-80; 2003-2007)., 2018. *Proceedings of the 12th ASWA Conference, Groningen, Netherlands.* 73-78. Groningen : Barkhuis Publishing & University of Groningen.

Monahan, B. H. 2007 Nomadism in the Early Bronze Age southern Transcaucasia: the faunal perspective. in *Social Orders and Social Landscapes: Second University of Chicago Conference on Eurasian Archaeology*, edited by L. M. Popova, C. Hartley & A. T. Smith, 379–392. Chicago: Cambridge Scholars Publishing, Chicago.

Monahan, B. 2008 Appendix I: the faunal remains, pp. 90-97. in Village, fortress, and town in Bronze and Iron Age Southern Caucasia: A preliminary report on the 2003–2006 investigations of Project ArAGATS on the Tsaghkahovit Plain, Republic of Armenia, by R. Badalyan, A. T. Smith, I. Lindsay, L. Katchadourian, and P. Avetsyan, *Archäologische Mitteilungen aus Iran und Turan* 40: 45-105.

O'Connor, T. 2010 Livestock and deadstock in early medieval Europe from the North Sea to the Baltic. *Environmental Archaeology* 15: 1-15.

Palumbi, G., Alvaro, C., Grifoni, C. and Frangipane, M. 2017 A 'communal' building of the beginning of the Early Bronze Age at Arslantepe-Malatya (Turkey): Spatio-functional analysis and interpretation of the archaeological context. *Paléorient* 43(1): 89-123.

Payne, S. 1973 Kill-off patterns in sheep and goats: the mandibles from Aşvan Kale. *Anatolian Studies* 23: 281-303.

Payne, S. 1985 Morphological distinctions between the mandibular teeth of young sheep, *Ovis*, and Goats, *Capra*. *Journal of Archaeological Science* 12: 139–147.

Piro, J., and Crabtree, P. 2017 Zooarchaeological evidence for pastoralism in the Early Transcaucasian Culture. in *Archaeozoology of the Nears East 9: In Honour of Hans-Peter Uerpmann and François Poplin*, edited by M. Mashkour and M. Beech, 273-283. Oxford: Oxbow.

Redding, R. 1984 Theoretical Determinants of a Herder's Decisions: Modeling Variations in the Sheep/Goat Ratio. in *Animals and Archaeology 3: Herders and Their Flocks*, edited by J. Clutton-Brock and C. Grigson, 161–170. BAR International Series 227. Oxford: British Archaeological Reports.

Rothman, M. S 2011 Migration and Resettlement: Godin IV Period. in *On the High Road: the History of Godin Tepe, Iran,* edited by H. Gopnick and M. Rothman, 139-208. Toronto: Royal Ontario Museum/ Mazda Press.

Russel, S., Marshall, F., Peters, J., Pilgrim, T., Adams, Matthew D., and O'Connor, D. 2008 Domestication of the Donkey: timing, Processes, Indicators. *Proceedings of the National Academy of Sciences* 105 (10): 3715-3720.

Silver, I. A. 1969. The ageing of the domestic mammals. In *Science in Archaeology*, edited by D. Brothwell and E. S. Higgs, 283-302. London: Thames and Hudson.

Siracusano, G. and Bartosiewicz, L. 2012 Meat consumption and sheep/goat exploitation in centralized and non-centralized economies at Arslantepe, Anatolia. *Origini* 34: 111-123.

Uerpmann, M. 2006 Von Adler bis Zahnbrassen - Der Beitrag der Archäozoologie zu Erforschung Troias. in *Troia - Archäologie eines Siedlungshügels*, edited by M. Korfmann, 283-296. Mainz: Philipp von Zabern.

Uerpmann, M. and Uerpmann, H.-P. 2010 Zug- und Lasttiere zwischen Majkop und Trialeti. in *Von Majkop bis Trialeti - Gewinnung und Verbreitung von Metallen und Obsidian in Kaukasien im 4.-2. Jt. vor Chr*. Kolloquien zur Vor- und Frühgeschichte Band 13, edited by S. Hansen, A. Hauptmann, I. Motzenbäcker, and E. Pernicka, 237-252. Bonn: Rudolf Habelt Gmbh.

Vila, E. 2006 Data on Equids from late fourth and third millennium sites in northern Syria. in *Equids in Time and Space: Papers in Honour of Véra Eisenmann*, edited by M. Mashkour, 101-123. Oxford: Oxbow.

von den Driesch, A. 1976 *A Guide to the Measurement of Animal Bones from Archaeological Sites*. Cambridge: Peabody Museum (Bulletin 1), Harvard University.

Wright, H.T. 2001 Cultural Action in the Uruk World. in *Uruk Mesopotamia and Its Neighbors*, edited by M.S Rothman, 123-148. Santa Fe: SAR Press.

Zeder, M. A. 1986 The equid remains from Tal-y-Malyan, Iran. in *Equids in the Ancient World*, edited by R. H. Meadow and H.-P. Uerpmann, 366-412. Wiesbaden: Ludwig Reichert Verlag.

Zeder, M. And Lapham, H. A. 2010 Assessing the reliability of criteria used to identify postcranial bones in sheep, *Ovis*, and goats, *Capra*. *Journal of Archaeological Science* 37: 2887-2905.

Zeder, M., Pilaar, S. 2010 Assessing the reliability of criteria used to identify mandibles and mandibular teeth in sheep, *Ovis*, and goats, *Capra*. *Journal of Archaeological Science* 37, 225-242.

5b | Production, Foraging and Use of Plants at Shengavit

Roman Hovsepyan

Introduction

In order to understand the organization and adaptation of homeland zone Kura-Araxes culture populations, it is critical also to understand their agriculture and food culture. Remains of food— these include seeds, fruits, tubers, and other nutrient rich and edible parts of plants— preserved in archaeological deposits are the best and most direct evidence for food, agriculture and foraging. These organs and parts of plants collectively named carpological materials are the subject of archaeobotany or, more particular, archaeocarpology. They also help reconstruct vegetation cover and environment of the close surroundings of the investigated sites. This is unlike palynology (see Chapter 2), which usually provides information about general/regional vegetation cover and environment as pollen and spores can travel very long distances.

The goals of this study are to determine the taxonomic composition of archaeobotanical material, including cultivated plants, weeds, and wild plants. Using those identifications, the patterns of crop use are detailed overall and in specific architectural levels and in buildings and open spaces.[309] This is done in the context of the taphonomic conditions (preservation) that affected the composition of the crop remains recovered from the site.[310] In conclusion, we will propose the role for crop plants in the Shengavit economy and society.

M.G. Tumanyan studied the archaeobotanical materials from Shengavit for the first time in the 1940s.[311] The results of his study, published in 1948, was a paper entitled "The Main Stages of the Barley Evolution in Armenia," wherein the author provides valuable information on the varieties of barley with awnless,[312] multi-row, and elongated elliptical seeds (these varieties M. Tumanyan conditionally named *Hordeum antiquorum sphaerococcum* and *Hordeum Urartu*).

Figure 5b.1. Hoard of charred cereals from earlier excavations at Shengavit. From a bowl at the National History Museum excavated by Sardarian.

Materials Studied and Methodology [313]

Macroscopic (visible to the naked eye) remains of carpological materials, i.e. seeds, fruits and other plant diaspores, preserved in cultural deposits of the Shengavit archaeological site are the objects of current study (Fig 5b.1).

---

309   The full database will be available on the Shengavit web-archive.
310   Weide et al. 2017.
311   Tumanyan 1948.
312   Awns are bristlelike or hairlike appendages on the flowering parts of some cereals and grasses.
313   The initial stages of these investigations of the Shengavit archaeobotanical materials were conducted in the Institute of Archeology and Ethnography in Armenia, then continued in the Anthropology Department of the Ohio University Fulbright Visiting Scholar Fellowship of the author (2011-2012).

I used current archaeobotanical methodology to conduct the study.[314] The work was conducted in the following steps:

1) Sampling of archaeological sediments from particular contexts of the site. Excavators collected sediments during the excavations of 2005, 2009, 2010, and 2012. They selected samples which probably had plant remains from floors, pits, fireplaces, contents of vessels, etc. yielding 140 samples with total volume of 538 liters (Table 5b.1).

2) Recovery and separation of plant macro-remains from archaeological deposits. I used flotation (with use of 0.25 mm mesh size sieves) and wet-sieving (with use of 1 mm mesh size sieves) methods. Steps 3 to 9 of the work I carried out under laboratory conditions.

3) Cleaning and sorting of identifiable plant remains. After drying of "concentrates", I separated and cleaned useful (identifiable) plant remains from the dirt, then sorted and grouped them according to their organic ascription (seed, fruit, wood, etc.), morphology, anatomy, biometric features, preservation type (charred, mineralized, uncharred, imprints, etc.) and degree.

4) Packing and storing of the findings (I used Eppendorph tubes and other plastic containers of various sizes).

5) Identifying the findings to their taxonomical ascription (plant groups by Family, *Genus* and *species*). I identified plant remains according to their morphological, anatomical, and biometric features. I used a stereoscopic microscope. Identification of plant remains is the most difficult step of the archaeobotanical studies, requiring corresponding education and experience. I used several scientific publications for the identification work,[315] then consulted modern reference collections of fruits and seeds to verify identifications and for comparative analyses, when necessary.

6) Counting of the findings group by group and statistical analyses. I studied more than 17 thousand seeds and associated organs (Table 5b.2 & 5b.3). The average abundance of recovered carpological material is comparably high; the average concentration of carpological materials (unit/liter) is 31.7 (Table 5b.2).

7) Documentation /photography of the most representative findings. I photographed the most representative findings with 4800 dpi resolution using a scanner. I used the Adobe Photoshop computer program for the final processing and preparation of the figures.

Square	Number of Samples	Strata
I14	6	I
J5	34	O-III
J6	8	O-III
K/L 3/4	7	IV-VI?
K5	1	II
K6	61	I-VI
L6	2	IV?
M5	18	I

Table 5b.1 Archaeobotanical samples from Shengavit 2009-2012.

8) Interpretations of the retrieved archaeobotanical data in relation to the archaeological contexts.

9) Description of the past plant economy and vegetation cover of the site and surroundings.

I then assigned the samples to their proveniences and grouped them in the following strata: MBA (Early Kurgan), KA2 (Early Bronze Age II or II and III, depending on which chronological scheme one uses;[316] see Chapters 1 and 3). At Shengavit the Strata were I, II, II/III, III, III/IV, IV, V, VI and "unknown/mixed." The number of the archaeobotanical findings are different from sample to sample and from stratum to stratum;

---

314   cf. Hovsepyan 2017.
315   Maysuryan and Atabekova 1931; Dobrokhotov 1961; Takhtadzhyan and Fedorov 1972; Lukyanova et al. 1990; Terrell and Peterson 1993; Zohary et al. 2012; Takhtajyan 1954-2009; Jacomet, 2006; etc.
316   Batiuk et al. 2022.

the higher the numbers from a provenience, the more valid the statistical data are. We found valid data for MBA, Shengavit Strata I, II, III, III/IV, and IV. Data for the "unknown/mixed" group I list just for comparisons. There is not enough data for Shengavit Strata I/III, V, and VI (Table 5b.2)

I recovered more than 17,000 units of carpological material (seeds, fruits, and other seeds-associated parts of plants) from the excavated soil samples of Shengavit site. The quantity and density/concentration of the carpological remains for separate stratigraphic units and archaeological proveniences of the site are of major importance in order to establish a sample size large enough for statistical analyses. The data on the density/concentration of plant remains in particular loci enabled quantitative comparisons of the archaeobotanical material uncovered from separate layers, contexts, and samples. For each of the investigated sediment samples, which represent the provenience from strata and architectural level where it was sampled, I adjusted densities/concentration of all plant remains, and especially remains of cultivated plants based on 1 liter of fill. These values for the Shengavit settlement are respectively ca. 32 units/liter and 20 units/liter. Both of these values are mostly high in comparison to other sites excavated in Armenia (often ranging between 1-10 units/liter on average). Shengavit presents an excellent case for studying plant production and utilization and environmental conditions in the past.

Archaeobotanical materials from earlier excavations at Shengavit; for example, samples studied by Tumanyan were discovered as an accumulation of charred grains, which were visible to the naked eye and were not mixed with other deposits (e.g. cereal grains in a bowl from Sardarian's excavations (Fig. 5b.1)).[317] However, for our study, the plant remains were spread in a relatively diffuse way and mixed with other deposits, forming significant concentrations only in certain archaeological contexts (e.g. fireplaces, storage pits, pots, or rooms). We recovered a comparably small amount of charcoal from the site. It is not certain whether the predominant fuel was wood or dung, but the amount of charcoal found suggests that dung was probably used. On the other hand, the lack of soot in the ritual hearths suggests that they used charcoal (Chapter 6a). If it were mostly dung fuel, as Miller suggests,[318] the seeds and other indigestible parts of plants may be somewhat randomly deposited. This means that in general areas like floors, the comparisons of seeds are somewhat less reliable, as they may be coming from different practices and different times. Remains from grain pits are more reliable, as they usually represent deposits over a relatively short span of time.

Chrono-cultural ascription / Stratum		Total / Average	MBA	Shen-I	Shen-II	Shen-II/III	Shen-III	Shen-III/IV	Shen-IV	Shen-VI	unknown/ mixed
Number of samples		140	4	35	34	1	31	7	5	2	21
Soil sample Volume (liter)		538	14	115	153	7	109	33	23	3	81
Concentration of carpological materials (unit/liter)	Total	31.7	17.6	20.0	36.8	2.9	31.9	82.0	47.7	10.0	18.8
	Non-cultivated plants	11.5	5.4	7.0	13.8	1.1	13.5	24.1	17.2	4.2	6.6
	Cultivated plants	20.1	12.1	13.0	23.0	1.7	18.4	57.8	30.5	5.8	12.2
Findings		17,031	246	2,300	5,628	20	3,470	2,705	1,117	31	1,515

Table 5b.2 Samples numbers and volumes as well as recovered plant remains according cultural ascription at the archaeological site of Shengavit.

---

317   Tumanyan 1948.
318   Miller 1984.

In general, the plant remains in archaeological contexts are preserved in five main ways: carbonized/charred, mineralized, waterlogged, desiccated, and as impressions in clay (like mudbricks, plaster floors, pottery, etc.). The plant remains in the case of Shengavit are mainly carbonized (cereal grains, most of the weed and wild plants remains), sometimes mineralized (e.g. Boraginaceous weeds) and a few times preserved as imprints (e.g. cereals straw and chaff in building clay).

The plant remains underwent significant changes in the process of carbonization. The seeds and carpels carbonized at high temperatures within a short period of time bear several characteristic morphological and metrical alterations typical for the burnt or cooked plant remains. In particular, they can: a) be swollen, which results in shortening and widening of the seeds and fruits;[319] b) cracked, which results in fissures on the surfaces of the seeds and fruits, and the inner contents can be partially leaked out and suffer other deformations. Sometimes, the surface of the breaks can be smoothed or even swollen, which means that they were fractured prior to carbonization.[320]

In the charred and not completely mineralized plant remains the initial matter is preserved, although it is altered. Among the finds there are plant remains in very diverse states of preservation, depending on complex impact of several internal and external taphonomic (depositional) factors. All of the observed cases the plant remains underwent fragmentation in the course of deposition. The chaff remains were charred (Fig 5b.2 to 5b.4), except awns, which were bio-mineralized.

Archaeobotanical Data

The identification of recovered 17,031 units of carpological materials resulted in 71 taxa of Angiosperms (Flowering Plants). Fourteen of the abovementioned 71 taxa are cultivated plants: cereals (11), a pulse, an oil-plant, and grapes (Table 5b.3). Two of the recorded 57 wild plant taxa are arboreal plants, the rest are herbaceous ones (Table 5b.4 below).

Almost all of the cultivated plants' remains recovered from the Shengavit archaeological site were cereals (Gramineae/Triticeae). Unidentified remains of cereals (Triticeae gen. spp.) are listed when grain or chaff remains are not well enough preserved for identification at least to *genus*, yet represent essential part of cereals findings. Wheat (*Triticum*) and barley (*Hordeum*) are recorded amongst the identifiable remains of cereals. Both are represented with grains and chaff remains.

Remains of tetra- and/or hexaploid wheats (*Triticum aestivum/turgidum*) are the most common among cereal remains. Most of those remains are free-threshing (naked) wheats (*Triticum aestivum/durum*) among which common bread wheat (*Triticum aestivum* subsp. *aestivum* (*vulgare*)) is most common. Factoring in some ambiguity in their identification, emmer (*Triticum dicoccum*) and club wheat (*Triticum* cf. *aestivum* ssp. *compactum*; Fig. 5b.2) came next, while durum wheat (*Triticum durum*; Fig. 5b.3) and einkorn (*Triticum monococcum*) are barely present in our sample representation in the studied samples.

The presence of both hexaploid (bread wheat - *Triticum aestivum* s.l.) and tetraploid (hard wheat - *Triticum turgidum*) species of wheat are

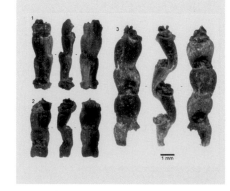

Figure 5b.2. Charred rachis fragments of club wheat (*Triticum aestivum* subsp. *compactum*) from Shengavit site (1,2 - J6B, L18012, B18328; 3 - L6, L4010, B4011).

---

319   Zohary et al. 2012.
320   Willcox, 2002; Riehl, 1999.

confirmed by findings of rachis fragments and individual internodes. The recovered remains of rachis allowed us to identify several varieties of bread wheat different in the density of spikelets in spikes and hardness (thickness) of the rachises of spikes.

Plant Taxa	Finding/Organ	Preservation	Counts
All remains			17,031
Cereals (Gramineae)			
Unidentified cereals			
cf. Triticeae gen. spp.	cf. grain unidentifiable fragments	charred	26
Triticeae gen. spp.	grain unidentifiable fragments	charred	4,149
	internode remains	charred	181
	glumes bases	charred	23
	spike awns	mineralized	+
	straw nodes	charred	155
Wheats			
Wheat grains			
cf. Triticum aestivum/turgidum	grains	charred	378
Triticum aestivum/turgidum	grains	charred	1,933
Triticum aestivum/durum	grains	charred	283
	grains	charred	218
Triticum cf. aestivum ssp. vulgare	grains	charred	206
Triticum cf. aestivum ssp. compactum	grains	charred	101
Triticum turgidum/dicoccum	grains	charred	3
Triticum cf. turgidum/dicoccum	grains, smaller and narrow egg-shaped	charred	59
Emmer			
Triticum cf. dicoccum	grains	charred	144
Triticum dicoccum (=T. turgidum ssp. dicoccum)	grains	charred	40
Triticum cf. monococcum	grains	charred	2
Wheat chaff			
Triticum spp.	internodes	charred	72
	glumes bases & glumes	charred	27
Triticum aestivum/durum (naked)	internodes	charred	310
Triticum cf. aestivum	internode	charred	84
	rachis fragments	charred	6
Triticum aestivum s.l.	incomplete internodes	charred	79
Triticum aestivum ssp. aestivum [=T. vulgare] var. 1	internodes	charred	252
	rachis fragments	charred	23
Triticum aestivum ssp. aestivum [=T. vulgare] var. 2	internodes	charred	76
	rachis fragments	charred	21
Triticum aestivum ssp. aestivum [=T. vulgare] var. 3	internodes	charred	124
	rachis fragments	charred	4

Plant Taxa	Finding/Organ	Preservation	Counts
Triticum aestivum ssp. compactum [=T. compactum]	internodes	charred	12
	rachis fragments	charred	10
Triticum cf. durum	internodes	charred	31
	rachis fragments	charred	12
Triticum durum (=T. turgidum ssp. durum)	internodes	charred	15
	rachis fragments	charred	5
Triticum cf. dicoccum	spikelet base	charred	2
Barleys			
Barley grains			
cf. Hordeum sp. (cf. Hordeum vulgare)	unidentifiable grains	charred	325
Hordeum vulgare	unidentifiable grains	charred	744
	middle grains	charred	6
Hordeum vulgare ssp. vulgare	triplet left grains	charred	2
	triplet right grains	charred	2
Hulled barleys			
Hordeum vulgare (cf. hulled)	triplet position unidentifiable hulled grains	charred	46
Hordeum vulgare (hulled)	triplet position unidentifiable hulled grains	charred	167
	triplet middle hulled grains	charred	31
		mineralized	1
Hordeum vulgare ssp. vulgare convar. vulgare	triplet left hulled grains	charred	25
	triplet right hulled grains	charred	17
Naked barleys			
Hordeum vulgare cf. var. nudum	triplet position unidentifiable naked grains	charred	72
Hordeum vulgare var. nudum	triplet position unidentifiable naked grains	charred	32
	triplet middle naked grains	charred	12
Hordeum vulgare ssp. vulgare convar. coeleste	triplet left naked grains	charred	8
	triplet right naked grains	charred	2
Barley chaff			
Hordeum vulgare	internodes	charred	210
Hordeum vulgare var.1 (lax-eared) [=?H. tetrastichum]	internodes	charred	28
	rachis fragments	charred	4
Hordeum vulgare var.2 (compactum)	rachis fragments	charred	9
Pulses (Fabaceae)			
cf. Pisum sp.	seeds	charred	3
Oil-Crop Linaceae			
cf. Linum sp.	seeds	charred	1
Linum cf. usitatissimum	seeds	charred	5
	seeds	calcified	4
	capsule sections/fragments	charred	1
Grape (Vitaceae)			
Vitis vinifera	pip	mineralized	1
	berry peduncle	charred	1

Table 5b.3 Carpological materials recovered from the Shengavit site, their preservation, and identifications (excavations of 2005, 2009, 2010, 2012; processed sediments volume – 538L).

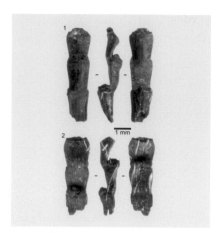

Figure 5b.3. Charred rachis fragments of durum wheat (*Triticum turgidum* var. *durum*) from Shengavit site (1 - J6B, L18012, B18328; 2 - L6, L4010, B4011).

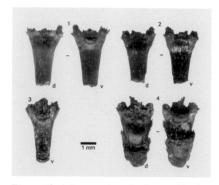

Figure 5b.4. Internodes of cultivated barley (*Hordeum vulgare*) from the Shengavit site. 1 – (J6B, L18012, B18328); 2 – (L6, L4010, B4011); 3 – Lax-eared form (K6, L1014, B1150); 4 – Compact-eared form (K6, L1014, B1140-1).

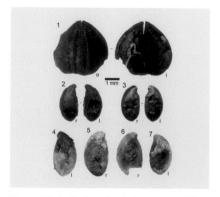

Figure 5b.5. Archaeological remains of flax from Shengavit site. 1 – charred fragment of pod (J6, L18043, B18999), 2-3 – charred seeds (J5, L2087; 2 - B2936, 3 - B2935), 4-7 - biomineralized seeds (K6, L1014; 4-6 - B1150-1, 7 - B1150-2).

The combination of barley taxonomy suggested by Lukyanova et al. and Zohary et al.[321] is used here to ascribe barley findings to subspecies, co-varieties and varieties of barley species (*Hordeum vulgare*). The presence of six-rowed barley (*Hordeum vulgare* ssp. *vulgare*) was confirmed by lateral asymmetric grains of triplets (Fig 5b.4).

Meanwhile, the essential prevalence of triplet middle grains suggests the presence of two-rowed subspecies as well. Both hulled and naked varieties are recorded and both of them may come from six-rowed and two-rowed subspecies. At least for the six-rowed subspecies, the presence of hulled and naked varieties of barley were confirmed by hulled and naked lateral grains of triplets: hulled six-rowed barley (*Hordeum vulgare* ssp. *vulgare* convar. *vulgare*) and free-threshing six-rowed barley (*Hordeum vulgare* ssp. *vulgare* convar. *coeleste*). As was the case for wheat, the remains of chaff, more particularly the rachis, helped to identify at least two varieties or possibly better to say forms of barley – lax-eared and compact-eared. The lax-eared one may be the four-sided ear form of barley (Fig. 5b.4).

Cultivated pulses and oil-crops are mostly absent in the archaeobotanical record of the Shengavit site so far. There are only 3 large seeds or cotyledons of fabaceous plants (Fabaceae) that may be coming from cultivated pea (cf. *Pisum* sp.). Regarding oil-plants, ten seeds of flax (*Linum* cf. *usitatissimum* L.), five charred and five mineralized, and one charred fragment of capsule existed (Fig. 5b.5). Another rare but notable find is the record of grape (*Vitis vinifera*): a mineralized grape pip (Fig. 5b.6), and a charred peduncle that we recovered so far.

Here are the key results regarding archaeobotanical statistical data for archaeological strata of Shengavit (Table 5b.4):

• Cultivated plants comprise roughly 60-70% of all carpological findings and the values are more or less similar for all strata of the site.

• Cultivated plants are exclusively or almost exclusively represented with cereals: 99.7% to100% of all cultivated plants.

• Chaff remains are up to one quarter of cereal remains. The portion of cereal remains as chaff is roughly 13 to 16% in four of five strata with trustworthy statistical data from Shengavit Strata I, II, III, III/IV (i.e. in the strata where we have thousands of archaeobotanical findings). Thus, 13 to16% may be considered as an average value for the cereal chaff portion at the site. In the fifth most trustworthy stratum, Shengavit IV, chaff portion is especially high, almost 26%, which may indicate that threshing and winnowing of cereals took place in or near to the excavated part of the site during formation of Stratum IV. Because the remains of

321   Lukyanova et al. 1990; Zohary et al. 2012.

Stratum IV were from a fire, the data may just be skewed from there.

• Wheat remains, both grains and chaff, comprise from 62% to 76% of all genus of identifiable cereal remains. Seeds of wild and weedy plants are less than the cultivated ones, and they are sometimes mineralized, while cereal remains were mostly charred. This difference in preservation is a sign that charred and mineralized seeds recovered from these contexts have different origins and were not contemporaneous. In all probability, first charred seeds appeared in particular proveniences, or they were charred there. Then fresh seeds found their way into this context and were mineralized over time until we excavated and recovered them. Observations in the field show that ants dug nests and collected seeds of certain plants there. These nests usually are not too deep, often several tens of centimeters maximally. Sometimes, ants may abandon these nests (e.g. because of flood) with the seed hoards still in them, or the nests may collapse and or be covered with additional sediments. Some of these seeds in hoards have thick covers primarily rich in minerals, usually carbonates and silicates. These seeds survive erosion in the soil better than the others. They are recovered and classified as bio-mineralized findings (i.e. mineralized still when they were alive). Mineralization may occur also secondarily, when seeds are in a mineral rich (e.g. calcium/lime) and humid (water is necessary for minerals to dissolve and transport in seeds covers) environment for a long time. These plants could have been collected by insects right after the creation of these loci or sometime later. In any case, it had to be long enough in the past in order for the seeds to get mineralized. Usually, that takes centuries. Thus, the recovered mineralized seeds of capers, chenopod, bristle grass (Fig. 5b.7), caryophyllaceous, and other plants in all probability are seeds from ancient ant hoards. If there are charred remains in this context, they may have another origin and should be considered separately.

Chrono-cultural ascription / Strata	Total	MBA	Shen-I	Shen-II	Shen-II/III	Shen-III	Shen-III/IV	Shen-IV	Shen-VI	Unknown / mixed
Number of samples	140	4	35	34	1	31	7	5	2	21
Soil sample Volume (liter)	538	14	115	153	7	109	33	23	3	81
Number of findings	17,031	246	2,300	5,628	20	3,470	2,705	1,117	31	1,515
Cultivated plants / ALL =	64%	69%	65%	63%	60%	58%	71%	64%	58%	65%
Cereals / Cultivated plants =	99.9%	100.0%	99.9%	99.9%	100.0%	99.7%	99.9%	100.0%	100.0%	99.6%
Cereals chaff / Cereals =	15.0%	3.5%	14.3%	16.3%	0.0%	12.7%	14.9%	25.9%	5.6%	10.5%
Unid. Cereals / Cereals =	42%	48%	38%	38%	8%	43%	46%	48%	44%	46%
Wheat all | Wheat / (Wheat+Barley) =	72%	63%	68%	76%	100%	76%	62%	74%	20%	77%
Wheat grains | Wheat / (Wheat+Barley) =	69%	62%	66%	72%	100%	76%	55%	73%	22%	75%
Emmer / Wheat =	4%	5%	0%	4%	0%	4%	11%	2%	0%	4%
Wheat chaff | Wheat chaff / Wheat all =	26%	7%	23%	28%	0%	20%	33%	37%	0%	19%
Wheat chaff | Wheat / (Wheat+Barley) =	82%	80%	78%	89%	-	77%	80%	78%	0%	83%
Barley all | Barley / (Wheat+Barley) =	28%	37%	32%	24%	0%	24%	38%	26%	80%	23%
Barley grains | Barley / (Wheat+Barley) =	31%	38%	34%	28%	0%	24%	45%	27%	78%	25%
Barley grains hulled / (hulled+naked) =	69%	50%	47%	75%	-	23%	98%	0%	100%	54%
Barley grains naked / (hulled+naked) =	31%	50%	53%	25%	-	77%	2%	100%	0%	46%
Barley chaff | barley chaff / barley all =	14%	3%	14%	11%	-	19%	13%	31%	13%	12%
Pulses / Cultivated plants =	0.03%	0%	0%	0%	0%	0%	0.10%	0%	0%	0.10%
Oil-crops / Cultivated plants =	0.10%	0%	0.13%	0.06%	0%	0.20%	0%	0%	0%	0.30%
Grape / Cultivated plants =	0.01%	0%	0%	0%	0%	0.08%	0%	0%	0%	0%
Unidentified / ALL =	3%	4%	5%	2%	5%	4%	2%	2%	23%	3%
Wild Arboreal plants / Wild plants =	0.10%	0%	0%	0.19%	0%	0%	0.19%	0.25%	0%	0%
Wild Herbs / Wild plants =	36%	31%	35%	37%	40%	42%	29%	36%	42%	35%

Table 5b.4 The most important summarizing numbers and proportions of archaeobotanical data according to their chrono-cultural and stratigraphic ascriptions.

Discussion and Interpretation of the Archaeobotanical Data

FOOD CROPS

Of special interest for this volume are the food crops. The organization of production of these crops in large measure defines this KA2 society. We believe that the people of Shengavit were producing surpluses of grain as part of their role as the small center of a local polity. This goes along with a regime in which cereals dominated over pulses.[322]

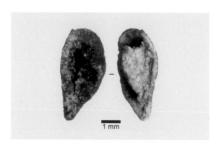

Figure 5b.6. Biomineralized fragment of grape pip (*Vitis vinifera*) from Shengavit site (K6, L1014, B1150).

Figure 5b.7. Biomineralized hulled grains of *Setaria* cf. *viridis* (K6, L1014, B1150-1).

All of the recorded cereals species and subspecies were known to be extant in the region since the appearance of agriculture in the Neolithic period about 8 thousand years ago. In addition, emmer (*Triticum dicoccum*), einkorn wheat (*T. monococcum*), and barley (*Hordeum vulgare*) are included among the Near Eastern Neolithic earliest domesticated crops.

Wheats (*Triticum*)

The presence of hexaploid wheats (*Triticum aestivum*), largely used for breads, is clearly recorded in the South Caucasus without breaks from the Neolithic period.[323] The most common was always the sub-species of common (*Triticum. aestivum* subsp. *aestivum* (*vulgare*)) and club wheat (*T. aestivum* ssp. *compactum*). In the Bronze Age, farmers possibly cultivated small quantities of soft, round-grained wheat (*T. aestivum* ssp. *sphaerococcum*), which, however, later dropped out of cultivation and is no longer grown. Tetraploid, hard wheats (*T. turgidum, T. durum*) were of less economic importance. In Shengavit, people also grew one of the best known, traditional crops of Armenia, emmer (*Triticum dicoccum*), from the beginning of the Neolithic period. Its economic significance makes it an essential ingredient of the local population's grain resources. Einkorn wheat (*Triticum monococcum*) possibly emerged on the territory of Armenia in the Neolithic period, but unlike emmer wheat, it didn't have significant economic importance. However, the naked wheats, particularly the hexaploid bread wheats cultivated since the Neolithic era were important to local people. Particularly in areas with difficult growing conditions,[324] their importance did not diminish.

Barley (*Hordeum vulgare*)

Barley in its various subspecies and forms have had an important place in the nutrition of the local population since the Neolithic period. Ancient peoples used them as grains in making breads and pasta and for brewing beer. Farmers in the South Caucasus cultivated all the main varieties of cultivated barley: hulled two-rowed barley, hulled six-rowed barley, naked two-rowed barley, and naked six-rowed barley. The presence of hulled and naked six-rowed barleys is confirmed for the Shengavit site by the presence of triplet lateral grains, while two-rowed subspecies with hulled and naked varieties are, considering the prevalence of triplet middle grains in archaeobotanical record, likely. Barley is a hardier plant than wheats especially in dry or saline environments. In the Early Bronze Age, especially in the mountainous areas, barley cultivation increased; 80-90 percent of the cereal analyzed from sites at the higher

---

322 Hovsepyan 2010, 2011, 2015.
323 Hovsepyan 2012.
324 Alabushev et al. 2019.

elevations consisted of barley. The ratio between wheat and barley cultivation in the lower elevations like the Ararat Valley favored wheat over barley.

Plants like wheat and barley could be important also for foddering animals, especially cattle, which do not tend to be moved to pastures of different elevations. The stalks of wheat are useful for this purpose; however, they cannot be fed to the cows exclusively, as too high a percentage of wheat stalks will cause bloat in a cow, even leading to its death.

Pulses

Pulses, rich in protein, were largely absent in the Kura-Araxes culture sites. They represent a very small sample size from Shengavit as well. However, according to Riehl in her summary of archaeobotanical data from the Early and Middle Bronze sites of Near East, cultivation of pulses and oil-producing crops dropped considerably in the Bronze Age overall, but farmers still cultivated lentil, bitter vetch, pea, grass pea, chickpea, and linseed there. Probably, the absence of pulses is characteristic for the Kura-Araxes population and/or for the region under study. [325]

Cultivated oil-plants

Flax (*Linum usitatissimum*) was one of the ancient Near East's primary oil-producing plants. As described in the pollen study (Chapter 2), this species of flax occurred at Shengavit, although apparently for cloth, not for oil producing.

Grape

The grape was another crop of importance to the local Kura-Araxes communities. Evidence from Areni-1 Cave in Armenia includes all the stages of wine production from the late fifth millennium BC.[326] The use of the grape for wine continued into the Kura-Araxes. Batiuk[327] proposes that expertise in wine production was one of the skills that made the settlement of Kura-Araxes groups in the diaspora both possible and peaceful, filling an economic niche that provided a desired good to the indigenous inhabitants. Since grapes were common throughout the Middle East,[328] local peoples were familiar with its fruit and its possible products. Like metallurgy, the important element may have been technical skill in the technique of growing and processing the right grapes for a good product. This kind of expertise is rarely passed from mouth to mouth; it requires the physical presence of experts to teach people these sorts of skills.

Weeds and Wild Plants

Wild and weedy plants probably appeared in the sites with harvested crop or may have originated in dung fuel,[329] but some of them can be also utilized as food. The most common and abundant weeds in the Shengavit settlement are the Boraginaceae (non-edible) and Poaceae (conventionally edible or non-edible) family plants, which together are around two thirds of all wild and weedy plants' findings (Table 5b.5). For boraginaceous plants the most abundant and representative species is the field gromwell (*Lithospermum arvense* [= *Buglossoides arvensis*]), thousands of nutlets of which are found at the site. However, in the case of boraginaceous plants this abundance doesn't mean that these plants were the most widely distributed weed at the site. Their quantitative dominance is due to selective preservation (the nutlets are biomineralized and preserve better) and/or the activity of ants. The boraginaceous plants appear in

---

325   Hovsepyan 2015.
326   Wilkinson et al. 2012; Batiuk 2013; Smith et al. 2014.
327   Batiuk 2013.
328   Miller 2008.
329   Miller 1984.

almost all of the archaeological sites of Armenia, even the ones with the least favorable preservation conditions. Poaceous plants, especially *Bromus* and *Lolium*, are among the most common weeds of cereals' cultivation.[330] Other taxonomic groups or individual taxa of wild and weedy plants are less than 10% of archaeobotanical material from Shengavit (Table 5b.5).

Plants with edible herbs

Most of these and other species from the mentioned genera have supposedly been gathered and used for food, since they have edible herbs or other parts, and nowadays they are being gathered and used in food by the local population of the region: *Rumex* spp., *Polygonum aviculare*, *Chenopodium spp.*, *Astrodaucus sp.*, *Urtica spp.*, malvaceous plant, etc. In addition, comparably large seeds of fabaceous, poaceous, polygonaceous, cyperaceous and other plants also might have been gathered and used in food.

Chrono-cultural ascription / Stratum	Total / Average	MBA	Shen-I	Shen-II	Shen-II/III	Shen-III	Shen-III/IV	Shen-IV	Shen-VI	unknown/mixed
Plant Taxa	17,031	246	2,300	5,628	20	3,470	2,705	1,117	31	1,515
Wild Arboreal plants	0.10%	0%	0%	0.19%	0%	0%	0.19%	0.25%	0%	0%
Wild Herbal plants	36%	31%	35%	37%	45%	42%	29%	36%	45%	35%
Boraginaceae: *Buglossoides arvensis*, etc.	33%	12%	31%	29%	43%	32%	28%	48%	17%	52%
Poaceae: *Bromus* sp., *Lolium* sp., *Setaria* cf. *viridis*, Poaceae gen. sp. MB etc.	31%	38%	45%	32%	29%	35%	18%	25%	50%	22%
Capparidaceae: *Capparis spinosa*	8%	2%	3%	16%	0%	4%	2%	0%	0%	4%
Polygonaceae: *Polygonum* spp., etc.	5%	12%	4%	7%	0%	5%	4%	6%	0%	1%
Chenopodiaceae: *Chenopodium* sp., etc.	5%	3%	3%	0%	0%	6%	19%	0%	0%	5%
Rubiaceae: *Galium* cf. *spurium*, *Galium* cf. *aparine*, etc.	4%	25%	3%	1%	0%	4%	5%	2%	0%	7%
Brassicaceae: *Euclidium syriacum*, *Camelina* sp., etc.	4%	0%	1%	1%	0%	7%	9%	10%	17%	2%
Thymeleaceae: *Thymelaea passerine*	3%	0%	1%	8%	0%	0%	0%	1%	0%	1%
Cyperaceae: *Carex* sp., *Scirpus* sp., etc.	3%	8%	6%	3%	0%	2%	5%	5%	17%	2%
Caryophyllaceae: *Vaccaria* sp., *Silene/Stachys* spp., etc.	2%	0%	0%	0%	0%	3%	7%	0%	0%	1%
Fabaceae: *Viceae* gen. spp., Fabaceae gen. spp. 2 (small seeded), etc.	1%	0%	2%	1%	29%	1%	2%	2%	0%	1%

Table 5b.5 The most abundant taxa of wild and weedy plants in the Shengavit site.

Plants with edible fruits and nuts

Fruits of hip rose (*Rosa* spp.) berries, capers (*Capparis spinosa*), and hackberry (*Celtis* spp.) are known amongst locals for their taste and nutritional value. Traditionally people have gathered and used them for food in fresh (hip rose, capers, hackberry), dried (hip rose, hackberry), or pickled (capers) state.

Environmental Remarks

If we try to group the recorded plants according to their environmental requirements/adaptation, we get the following: The following plants are typically found in dry environments:

- **Semidesertic plants:** *Tribulus terrestris, Salsola, Capparis spinosa, Celtis* sp.
- **Steppe plants:** *Thymelaea passerina, Hyoscyamus* sp., boraginaceous, poaceous, fabaceous, malvaceous, brassicaceous, rubiaceous, chenopodiaceous, papaveraceous, apiaceous, lamiaceous, caryophyllaceous, polygonaceous plants, *Celtis* sp. Many of these taxa may grow also in comparably dry environments.

The following plants may indicate more humid environment:

- **Meadow plants:** *Cephalaria* sp. (Fig. 5b.8), *Hyoscyamus* sp., fabaceous, brassicaceous, rubiaceous malvaceous, lamiaceous, papaveraceous, apiaceous, ranunculaceous, caryophyllaceous, polygonaceous plants.
- **Hygrophylous plants:** *Calystegia sepium, Urtica* sp., ranunculaceous, polygonaceous plants.
- **Wetland plants:** *Potamogeton* sp., cyperaceous plants, *Phragmites australis.*

The majority of the recorded taxa are common elements of steppe vegetation, but there are also other plants

---

330   Mkrtchyan 2003

indicating the presence of drier (semidesert) and more humid (meadows) environments as well as the presence of humid eco-niches (water basin, flowing water, and humid banks along river, lakes, or canals). We know that in the arid environment of the Ararat Plain hydrophilic wild plants grew among irrigated fields. According to Lisitsina and Prishchepenko, the Ararat Plain belongs to the type of irrigated land cultivation with regular irrigation cultivation.[331] Three percent of the wild and weed plants at Shengavit are in the Cyperaceae family, which are good indicators of water related eco-niches, possibly canals. Direct evidence of irrigation canals came from Elar, Mokhra Blur, and Metsamor. Were such canals present at Shengavit, they would likely be at the northern foot of the mound on the open river plain north of the original bed of the Hrazdan River (Fig. 5b.9). Unfortunately, that land is now under the artificial Lake Yerevan.

Figure 5b.8. Charred seeds of *Cephalaria sp.* from Shengavit site (J5, L2072, B2776).

Turning to the floatation samples from the 2005, 2009-2012, Tables 5b.3 and 5b.4 show that the overall count of plant remains was dominated by varieties of wheat. We did recover pulses (peas), flax oil crops (*Linum*), and grape pips, but in very small numbers compared to the cereal grains. Perhaps this is because animals would be fed or would eat wild grasses, and their dung would find itself in many places in the settlement. We also recovered stored, clean grain. Grape and oil-plants generally would be represented at the site by the final products, wine and oil; we did not find the processing sites or grape berries and seeds of oil-plants that were directly consumed, although a possible vat did emerge from earlier seasons. The small number of recoverable seeds or vegetal parts of grape or oil producing plants does not necessarily mean that they were not being grown or used to produce secondary products at Shengavit.

The percentage of the cereal crop that consisted of wheat varieties constitutes 77% averaging grains and chaff counts (Table 5b.3 & 5b.4). Barley is on average 23% of cereals. The free-threshing wheats are by far the most common among cereals. Free-threshing wheat appears to be a popular Kura-Araxes culture crop. In the Southern Levant its introduction comes at the same time the Kura-Araxes— they are locally called Khirbet Kerak— people arrived in the Galilee.[332]

When looked at over time, no great difference is apparent from stratum to stratum, period to period. These numbers are a bit deceiving, as the sources and numbers of samples varied quite a lot. Stratum I contained three different buildings, Squares I14, K6, and M5. Stratum II is found clearly only in Squares K6, K5 and a corner of J5. It was a working floor, perhaps for, among other things, threshing and winnowing, with a number of pits. Stratum III contained two buildings in Square K6 and one level of the Square J5 ritual room. Stratum IV had the earlier J5 building and a burned and not fully excavated building in K6. Under Stratum IV is

Figure 5b.9. The fields beyond the Hrazdan River at the foot of Shengavit when Lake Yerevan was drained.

---

331   Lisitsina, and Prishchepenko 1977.
332   Paz 2009.

a small area inside the wall of Square K6 Building 3, Strata V, VI, VII, and VIII. So, not all are completely comparable. However, there were no radical changes evident, showing that free-threshing wheat was already established by the beginning of the occupation of Shengavit, as were the ratios of wheat to barley.

Going into detail of the individual samples in relation to the context from which we collected them adds some detail, although many of the samples have too few remains to give definitive answers.

One issue that we raised because of the large number of stone lined grain pits was whether the farmers at Shengavit intensified their production of grain. This excess grain would be useful not only for the long-term food security of its residents, but potentially as rations to attract laborers from other settlements for public tasks like building the settlement wall (Chapter 4b), farm work, or perhaps even defensive activities. One possible indicator of irrigation is the hydrophilic Cyperaceae family plants. We recovered remains of cyperaceous plants from an ashy pit into which a large storage jar (*karas*) was sunk under the floor of Architectural Level 2, Stratum III, Building 2 in Square K6 (Locus 1014). Other places where we found cyperaceous plants were in a grain pit from Stratum 0 (Early Kurgan) in Square J5, a floor in Square L6, probably Strata III or IV, the round building earlier than Stratum IV (see Chapter 3) in Squares K/L 3/4, a large storage jar under the floor of Building 3, Stratum III in Square K6, the bottom of the pit dug to trash burned remains of Stratum IV in Square K6, and in the hearth of the ritual room in Square M5 from Stratum I. This would suggest, but not prove, that irrigation was practiced from fairly early in the history of Shengavit.

The same locus (1014) where we found the Cyperaceae family plants yielded a significant number of both grain and chaff remains of difference species of wheat. Also, we recovered it from the Early Kurgan Period pit in Square J5 mentioned above. Other occurrences include a grain pit in the southwest corner of Square K6 (Locus 1032, Stratum III), the pit into which the ruins of Stratum IV were dumped (Loci 1065, 1067), a pit under the center pole of Building 2, Square K6 (Locus 1079), the bottom floor of Building 3, Square K6, by the bench (Loci 1099 and 1101), an ash pit inside the round wall of Building 3, Square K6 (Locus 1117), the top of the burned Stratum IV under Building 3 in Square K6 (Locus 1102), the area around the ceramic hearth in the secondary room of Stratum IV (Locus 1125), an ash pit by wall 5 pit 2 in Room 1 of the building in Square M5 (Locus 24020). All yielded significant numbers of wheat and a few barley grains. Especially rich in grains and chaff, especially *Triticum aestivum/turgidum* grains, and bread wheat internodes and rachis, were a number of surfaces and a pit in square J5, Room 2 next to the Room 1 ritual space of the Stratum III/IV (Loci 2071-2073). This suggests that food was being processed and probably cooked there, perhaps for rituals in the adjoining room. We recovered burned remains of the same range of grains and chaff from a pit in the "back yard" (the northern half of Square J5) at Stratum III. More such finds came from other deposits in J5, Strata III and IV.

There is little evidence of great variation in the plant varieties found in the various loci of Shengavit excavated from 2009-2012. The same pattern for the overall plant remains was mostly true for the various loci from which samples came.

Most of the cultivated plants species and varieties we know from the Kura-Araxes culture, especially in this case from the KA2 mound of Shengavit, are recorded in the Caucasus starting from the Late Neolithic Aratashen-Shulavi-Shomutepe cultural tradition at the beginning of the sixth millennium BC. The plants cultivated at the Neolithic period represented a broad spectrum of cereals, pulses, oil-producing plants and grape.[333] The agriculture of the Kura-

---

[333]   Hovsepyan and Willcox 2008; Decaix et al. 2016; Kadowaki et al. 2015; Nishiaki et al. 2015; Flannery 1969; Lisitsina and Prishchepenko 1977, etc.

Araxes cultural tradition narrowed that diversity, no longer growing significant amounts of pulses and oil-producing plants. The proteins and fats previously derived from plants may have come from animals instead.[334] This agricultural/ pastoral regime was less risk averse than the earlier ones. Ethnobotanists recovered a similar agricultural regime in the highland of Armenia.[335]

Environmental and climatic conditions determined how the farmers mixed different proportions of wheat and barley. At Gegharot, a mere 75 kilometers from Shengavit but 1100 meters higher in elevation, cereal production often consisted of up to 90% hulled barley. At Shengavit, as shown above, various identifiable wheat remains constitute up to 77% of the recovered cereals remains, and barley represents the remainder.

As populations grew in the homeland zone during the KA2, evidence exists of intensification of agricultural production. This is documented by the construction of irrigation canals on the Aragats Mountains, Geghama Mountains, and a dam on the Kasakh River near Mokhra Blur.[336] The use of plows powered by draft animals and terraced farming systems also testify to an intensification of agriculture.[337] Plows were mostly made of deer antler.[338] Archaeologists found a few of these in the Kura-Araxes culture sites. Digging stick weights indicate other techniques of planting as well.[339] At Shengavit large, stone-lined grain pits suggest the production and storage of surpluses. These developments indicate a greater coordination of effort in supplying food to the growing Kura-Araxes population, and the possibility that surpluses of grain were being used by emerging people of influence to recruit labor and establish new social statuses.[340] "The use of free threshing wheat may, of course, shed light on food preferences for the Kura-Araxes. Similar to modern bread wheat, the hexaploidy, free threshing wheat is more ideally suited for leavened bread" (as opposed to a *lavash*-like flat bread).[341] This conclusion is also supported by the preponderance of grinding stones and pestles in the lithic assemblages, with the seeds being ground or pounded into a flour within each household for bread production. Paz has noted that the ceramic assemblage of the Kura-Araxes is dominated by larger serving and small individual consumption vessels and suggested that they may reflect a diet with more liquid foods like stews or gruels.[342] A leavened bread may have been an ideal companion to add carbohydrates and sop up the liquid contents of the vessels.

> "Free threshing wheat involves a greater level of risk as it is more vulnerable to animal and insect predation as well as fungal attack (Hilman 1984), and is perhaps better stored in smaller domestic batches where they can be more easily cared for. Additionally, as all the processing is done at harvest, the stored grain is cleaner, resulting in less work processing the grains for consumption in a domestic setting."[343]

"This focus on the domestic sphere could be seen as a form of "social storage within Kura-Araxes communities,"[344] or simply more evidence of the importance of domestic production in Kura-Araxes economies." [345]

---

334   Hovsepyan 2015.
335   Stoletova 1930, Melkonyan and Hovsepyan 2018.
336   Simonyan 2013.
337   Javakhishvili and Glonti. 1962; Kushnareva 1997; Lisitsina and Prishchepenko 1977.
338   Kushnareva 1997.
339   Kushnareva 1997.
340   Rothman 2015.
341   Longford 2015, p. 143.
342   Paz 2009.
343   Alonso et al. 2013.
344   Longford 2015, p. 166.
345   Batiuk et al. 2022.

The Early Bronze Age crop assemblage is practically the same from site to site. This raises the question of why people from lowlands started to follow the agricultural, household, and dietary traditions of high mountainous populations starting from the end of the Chalcolithic period. Perhaps, during a time of climate aridification, the higher rainfall and increasing forest[346] in the upland regions permitted those people to have a better quality of life, and more chances to survive more drought-like conditions. People living in lowlands would have periodically lost their crops to droughts and later obtained seed material from highlands neighbors via trade and barter and may have adapted the more resilient highland agricultural regime accordingly[347]. Additionally, as Longford notes:

> "The cultivation of hexaploid cold-adapted free threshing wheats may possibly have eased the Kura-Araxes agricultural expansion into new regions. Modern studies have shown that cold tolerant hexaploid wheats planted as summer crops at high altitudes in Eastern Anatolia can produce higher yields when sown at lower altitudes [...] Whether this applied to the wheat varieties grown by the Kura-Araxes in the fourth and third millennium is unknown, but it is an intriguing possibility that may also have contributed to the Kura-Araxes preference for free threshing wheat."[348]

Roughly the same proportions of wheat and barley existed in each of the contexts the excavation team sampled, whether they be from simple households to ritual emplacements. This conservatism is apparent in many other spheres of food and craft productions at Shengavit and other Kura-Araxes sites. The possibility that intensification of grain production happened is minorly evident in the wild and weedy plants, but more so in the large number of stone-lined grain storage pits and in contemporary evidence of irrigation works in the Lower Province. There is no way for certain to tell from the plant remains themselves whether the production was controlled or simply domestic production.

Conclusions

• Cereals, possibly in a form of porridge and stew-like dishes, were the main vegetal food of the Early Bronze Age populations of Shengavit.

• The cereal crop was preliminarily processed (roasted, threshed, sieved, winnowed) and stored at the site.

• The agriculture of the Bronze Age community of the Shengavit settlement were cereal-based and the lands in the vicinity of the settlement were cultivated.

• A notable diversity of cereals was cultivated and consumed by the Kura-Araxes culture people (namely, seven varieties of wheat and four varieties of barley in Shengavit): naked common bread wheat with at least three varieties, club wheat, macaroni wheat, emmer, einkorn, hulled and naked varieties of two-rowed and six-rowed barleys amongst which lax-eared and compact-eared forms existed.

• Wheat "always" was a more important component of food and agriculture than barley in Shengavit and consisted of from 2/3 to 3/4 of the cereals (wheat and barley). Free-threshing bread wheat definitely was the main vegetal food product for the Kura-Araxes culture communities of Shengavit.

• Pulses and vegetal oil, in all probability, were not an important component of diet and were rarely cultivated, or they were not cultivated at all.

• People ate some edible plants, i.e. fruits (capers, rosehip, hackberry) and herbs (mostly weedy species).

---

346 Connor and Kvavadze 2014.
347 Hovsepyan 2015
348 Longford 2015, 169.

- Grape, possibly, was cultivated as the natural environment around the site is not especially suited for the wild grape's growth.

- The climate and environment of the site was not much different from what Yerevan is today: the environment of the site was covered with steppe and semidesert vegetation common for warm and dry arable areas of the region (see also Chapter 2a).

- Water ecosystems or at least permanently working artificial canals probably existed at the site.

Acknowledgements

The author expresses his gratitude to the editor of the book, Dr. Mitchell Rothman, for his persistence, patience and participation in the preparation of this chapter.

References

Alabusheev, A., Ivanisov, M., Ionova, E., Marchenko, D., Nekrasov, E. 2019 Resistance of winter soft wheat varieties to low negative temperatures. *Earth and Environmental Science* 403: 1-8.

Alonso, N., Cantero, F., Niella, R., López, D., Moya, E.M., Prats, G. and Valenzuela-Lamas, S. 2013 Milling wheat and barley with rotary querns: The Ouarten women (Dahmani, Kef, Tunisia). in *Seen through a millstone. Geology and archaeology of quarries and mills*, 11–30. Bergen (Norway): Museum of Archaeology. University of Stavanger.

Batiuk, S. 2013 The Fruits of Migration: Understanding the 'longue duree' and the socio-economic relations of the Early Transcaucasian Culture. *Journal of Anthropological Archaeology* 32: 447–477.

Batiuk, S., Rothman, M. S, Samei, S., Hovsepyan, R. 2022 Unraveling the Kura-Araxes Cultural Tradition across Space and Time. *Ancient Near Eastern Studies* 59: 235-325.

Connor, S.E. and Kvavadze, E. 2014 Environmental context of the Kura-Araxes culture. *Paléorient* 40(2): 11–22.

Decaix, A., Messager, E., Tengberg, M., Neef R., Lyonnet B. and Guliyev F. 2016 Vegetation and plant exploitation at Mentesh Tepe (Azerbaijan), 6th–3rd millennium BC initial results of the archaeobotanical study. *Quaternary International* 395: 19–30.

Dobrochotov V.N. 1961 *Seeds of weeds*. Moscow. (in Russian).

Flannery, K. 1969 Origins and Ecological Effects of Early Domestication in Iran and the Near East. in *The Domestication and Exploitation of Plants and Animals*, edited by P. Ucko and GW. Dimbleby, 73–100. Chicago: Aldine Publishing Co.

Hillman, G. 1984 Interpretation of archaeological plant remains: The application of ethnographic models from Turkey. In *Plants and ancient man*, edited by W. van Zeist and W. A. Casparie, 1-41. Rotterdam: Balkema.

Hovsepyan, R. 2010 New data on agriculture of Aparan-III Early Bronze Age settlement (Armenia). *Biological Journal of Armenia* 4(62): 31–37.

Hovsepyan, R. 2011 Palaeoethnobotanical data from the high mountainous Early Bronze Age settlement of Tsaghkasar-1 (Mt. Aragats, Armenia). *Ethnobiology Letters* 2: 58-62.

Hovsepyan, R. 2012 Spread of hexaploid wheats in the Southern Caucasus (6th millennium BC). *Quaternary International* 279–280: 207–208.

Hovsepyan, R. 2015 On the Agriculture and Vegetal Food Economy of the Kura-Araxes Culture in the South Caucasus. *Paléorient* 41(1): 69–83.

Hovsepyan, R. 2017 Archaeobotanical sampling: Instructions for fieldwork. *Proceedings of the Institute of Archaeology and Ethnography*, vol. 2: Habitus: Studies in Anthropology and Archaeology - 2, 212-216. Yerevan, «Gitutyun».

Hovsepyan, R. and Willcox, G. 2008 The earliest finds of cultivated plants in Armenia: evidence from charred remains and crop processing residues in pisé from the Neolithic settlements of Aratashen and Aknashen. *Vegetation History and Archaeobotany* 17(1): 63–71.

Hovsepyan, R., Stepanyan-Gandilyan, N., Melkumyan, H., and Harutyunyan, L. 2016 Food as a Marker for Economy and Part of Identity: traditional vegetal foods of Yezidis and Kurds in Armenia. *Journal of Ethnic Foods* 3: 32–41.

Jacomet S. 2006 Identification of cereal remains from archaeological sites. 2nd ed., Basel University (http://pages.unibas.ch/arch/archbot/pdf/index.html)

Javkhishvili, A.I. and Glonti L.I. 1962 *Urbnisi I: Archaeological Excavations Carried Out in 1954-1961 at the Site of Kvatskhelebi*. Tblisi. (in Russian).

Kadowaki, S., Maher, L., Portillo, M., Albert, R. M., Akashi, C., Guliyev, F., and Nishiaki, Y. 2015 Geoarchaeological and Palaeobotanical Evidence for Prehistoric Cereal Storage in the Southern Caucasus: he Neolithic Settlement of Göytepe (Mid 8th Millennium BP). *Journal of Archaeological Science* 53: 408–25.

Kushnareva K. 1997 *The Southern Caucasus in Prehistory. Stages of cultural and socioeconomic development from the 8th to the 2nd millennium BC*. Philadelphia: University of Pennsylvania Museum Press. (translated by Michel H.).

Lisitsina, G. N. and Prishchepenko, L. V. 1977 *Palaeoethnobotanical finds of Caucasus and Near East*. Moscow: Nauka. (in Russian)

Longford C. 2015 *Plant Economy of the Kura-Araxes: A Comparative analysis of agriculture in the Near East from the Chalcolithic to the Middle Bronze Age*. Unpublished PhD diss, University of Sheffield.

Lukyanova M. V., Trofimovskaya A. Ya., Gudkova G. N., Terenteva I. A., Yarosh N. P. 1990. *Cultural flora of USSR*, vol. 2, part 2: *Barley*. Leningrad, "Agropromizdat" (in Russian)

Maysuryan N. A., Atabekova A. I. 1931 *Identifier of seeds and fruits of weeds*. Moscow-Leningrad, 406 p. (in Russian).

Melkomyan H., Hovsepyan R. 2018 Economic transitions and land ownership: challenging traditions among rural Yezidis in post-Soviet Armenia. *Anthropology of the Middle East* 13(1): 121–129.

Nishiaki, Y., F. Guliyev, S. Kadowaki, Alakbarov, V., Miki, T., Salimbayov, Sh., Akashi, Ch., and Arai, S. 2015 Investigating cultural and socioeconomic change at the beginning of the Pottery Neolithic in the Southern Caucasus – The 2013 Excavations at Hacı Elamxanlı Tepe, Azerbaijan. *Bulletin of the American Schools of Oriental Research* 374: 1–28.

Miller, N. 2008 Sweeter than Wine? The Use of the Grape in early West Asia. *Antiquity* 82: 937–946.

Miller, N. 1984 The Use of Dung as Fuel: An Ethnographic Model and an Archaeological Example. *Paléorient* 10(2): 71–79.

Mkrtchyan, A. L. 2003 *Flora and vegetation of the weeds of Ararat valley*. Yerevan: Zangak Publishing. (in Armenian).

Paz, S. 2009 A Home Away from Home? The Settlement of Early Transcaucasian Migrants at Tel Bet Yerah. *Tel Aviv* 36: 196–216.

Riehl, S. 2008 Climate and agriculture in the ancient Near East: a synthesis of the archaeobotanical and stable carbon isotope evidence. *Vegetation History and Archaeobotany* 17(1): 43-51.

Riehl, S. 1999 Archäobotanik in der Troas. *Studia Troica* 9: 367– 409.

Rothman, M. S 2015 The Changing Organization of Kura-Araxes Culture. in *International Symposium on East Anatolia South Caucasus Cultures, Vol. 1.*, edited by M. Isikliand and C. Barol, 121–131. Cambridge: Cambridge Scholars Publishing.

Smith, A., Bagoyan, T., Gabrielyan, I., Pinhasi, R., and Gasparyan, B. 2014 Late Chalcolithic and Medieval Archaeobotanical Remains from Areni-1 (Birds' Cave)," in *Armenia. Stone Age of Armenia, A Guide-book to the Stone Age Archaeology in the Republic of Armenia*, edited by B. Gasparyan and M. Arimura, 233–260. Kanazawa: Kanazawa University.

Stoletova, E.A. 1930 Field and garden cultigens of Armenia. B*ulletin of applied botany, of genetics and plant-breeding* 4: 23. (in Russian)

Takhtajyan A.L. (Ed.), 1954 (v.1), 1956 (v.2), 1958 (v.3), 1962 (v.4), 1966 (v.5), 1973 (v.6), 1980 (v.7), 1987 (v.8), 1995 (v.9), 2001 (v.10), 2009 (v.11). *Flora of Armenia*, vols. 1–11. Gitutyun (vols. 1-8), Koeltz Scientific Books (vol. 9), A.R.G. Gantner Verlag KG (vols. 10-11), Yerevan (vols. 1-8), Hrnčířská (vol. 9), Ruggell (vols. 10-11) (in Russian).

Takhtajyan A.L., Fedorov An.A. 1972 *Flora of Yerevan*. Identifier of wild plants of Ararat valley. Leningrad, "Nauka", 396 p. (in Russian) 164. Terrell E.E., Peterson P.M. 1993 Caryopsis Morphology and Classification in the Triticeae (Pooideae: Poaceae). Smithsonian Contributions in Botany, N83, Washington, D.C., Smithsonian Institution Press.

Tumanyan, M. G. 1948 The main steps of barleys' evolution in Armenia. *Journal of AS of Arm. SSR, Biol. & Agr. Sciences* 1(1): 73–85. (in Russian).

Weide, A., Riehl, S., Zeidi, M., Conard, N. 2017 Reconstructing subsistence practices: Taphonomic constraints and interpretation of wild plant remains at aceramic Neolithic Choga Golan, Iran. *Vegetal History Archaeobotany* DOI 10.1007/s00334-017-0607-1.

Wilkinson, K., Gasparyan, B., Pinhasi, R., Avetisyan, A., Hovsepyan, R., Zardaryan, D., Areshian, G. E., Bar-Oz, G. and Smith, A. 2012 Areni-1 Cave, Armenia: a Chalcolithic–Early Bronze Age settlement and ritual site in the southern Caucasus," *Journal of World Prehistory* 37: 20–33.

Willcox, G. 2002 Charred plant remains from a late tenth millennium kitchen at Jerf el Ahmar (Syria). *Vegetation history and archaeobotany* 11: 55-60.

Willcox, G. 1999 Geographical variation in major cereal components and evidence for independent domestication events in the Western Asia. In *The dawn of farming in the Near East. Studies in Near Eastern production, subsistence and environment*, edited by R. T. J. Cappers and S. Bottema, 133-140. Berlin: Ex oriente.

Zohary, D., Hopf, M. and Weiss, E. 2012 *Domestication of Plants in the Old World*. New York: Oxford University Press.

5c | Lithics

Dan Rahimi

Introduction

Kura-Araxes artifact studies have focused on its impressive array of ceramics, whose traditions of form, fabrication and finishes were cultural markers. Less attention has been given to lithic assemblages from sites of the period, due, in part, to the paucity of diagnostic types. Discussions mainly center on projectile points and sickle elements. In addition, many Kura-Araxes lithic assemblages from Sos Höyük in the west[349] to Kohne Tepesi in the east have been appropriately characterized as informal flake industries.[350] As such, comprehensively describing and comparing Shengavit's corpus of lithics is made difficult by lack of comparable reports, with some notable exceptions.

The recent excavations at Shengavit under the direction of Simonyan and Rothman from 2009-2012 provide data that broaden the lithic picture. Some 12,000 pieces of Kura-Araxes chipped stone recovered from secure excavated contexts reveal a lithic craft that was based less on formal techniques and more on *ad hoc* fabrication for domestic use. Ancient flintknappers made most of the tools from locally sourced obsidian by quick, simple reduction techniques, often requiring little planning or refined methods. These techniques can be termed expedient, opportunistic, or *ad hoc* in their production. The tools that were made using a more formal, consistent technique consist of sickle elements[351] in both flint and obsidian, and obsidian projectile points. So, the Shengavit lithic picture is bifurcated: simple domestic tools are casually made; essential agricultural tools and projectile points are given more attention.

The study presented here illustrates the scope of the Shengavit chipped stone craft. The projectile points and sickles are of particular interest, as they relate to the broader Kura-Araxes cultural landscape across the homeland and migrant diaspora and are adequately discussed in the literature. Obsidian points are attested in form and technology across the region and may have carried symbolic weight in some communities, as has been suggested for the concentration of obsidian arrowheads at Arslantepe in this period (see Chapter 6a).[352] Flint and obsidian sickle elements of the type found at Shengavit— all these were bifacially worked— are much more limited geographically. They were dramatically different in their production techniques than the blade-based, unifacially retouched sickles that are more prevalent across the region and throughout the Near East. The expedient, informal obsidian industry that comprises most of Shengavit's lithic assemblage was domestically produced. Flintknappers used edge modification that is functional but not technologically or morphologically consistent or prescribed. The largest group of tools, about 34 percent of all tools, are retouched flakes, and about eight percent are unretouched flakes whose edge damage indicates use. At a time when metal tools had already been introduced, Shengavit's lithic assemblage is particularly illuminating in

---

349 Sagona et al. 1997.
350 Jayez et al. 2017.
351 Chipped stone pieces that were set into a handle, mostly likely made of wood.
352 Fornaseri et al. 1975-77; Mouralis et al. 2016.

identifying which stone tools exhibit careful investment based on regularity of production and maintenance—the sickle elements are primary among these— and which have important domestic functions and are more simply made. The sickles and projectile points were not replaced by metal versions until later in the Bronze and early Iron Ages. The assemblage speaks to relative levels of investment in different tool types within a community and to the sourcing of raw materials. It also reflects the time depth of its elements, some of which are found in Chalcolithic horizons and others that continue into the Iron Age of Armenia.

Materials

The chipped stone assemblage excavated at Shengavit in the 2009-2012 seasons comprises 11,647 pieces of obsidian and flint from all stages of production (Table 5c.1). Excavated materials were sieved through six millimeters mesh screens and lithic materials of all sizes were meticulously collected. Nearly all the lithic material is obsidian, some 97% of the total, and the remainder is flint or related stone. The obsidian pieces derive primarily from river-rolled pebbles whose fragments are abundant throughout the mound, with some very limited evidence of blades from larger prismatic cores. The flint, unlike the obsidian, is not local to the immediate area of Shengavit, but Gasparyan identified a nearby source in an area called Mushakan. There he identified outcrops of both flint and obsidian[353] (see below). The obsidian and flint have not been subjected to mineralogical study in the laboratory, and I base identifications on assessments in the field.

The mound of Shengavit rises above the Hrazdan River, an important source of materials for its inhabitants. Obsidian pebbles with finely abraded gray surfaces, ranging in length from approximately 30 mm to 80 mm, rolled down the river. These pebbles were the primary source material for Shengavit's flake-rich assemblage (Table 5c.2). The principal elements of the obsidian tool set at Shengavit, which includes projectile points, notches and gravers, splintered pieces (wedges, or *pièces esquillées*), retouched flakes and blades, fall within the size range and reduction technologies compatible with small obsidian pebbles used as cores.

	n	*n* obsidian	% obsidian	*n* flint	% flint
Debris	9015	8863	98.31	152	1.69
Debitage	1990	1767	88.79	223	11.21
Tools	642	611	95.17	31	4.83
Total	**11647**	**11241**	**96.51**	**406**	**3.49**

Table 5c.1 Lithic assemblage by material.

Type	number	no. obsidian	% obsidian	no. flint	% flint
flakes	1642	1434	87.33	208	12.67
blades	44	41	93.18	3	6.82
cores	273	263	96.34	10	3.66
core trimming elements	31	29	93.55	2	6.45
cortical debris	2982	2952	98.99	30	1.01
non-cortical debris	6033	5911	97.98	122	2.02
total	11005	10630	96.59	375	3.41

Table 5c.2 Debitage and debris by material.

While we refer to a number of tools and associated debitage and debris in the assemblage as flint, mineralogically, these materials fall into several related groups including jasper, chalcedony, agate, and chert. In addition, I counted other volcanic rocks in the flint category to distinguish them materially from the dominant obsidian corpus. The flint materials are variable in color from white to brown, red, and black and in texture from coarse volcanic rock to fine-grained agate. While used primarily for sickle elements, flint is also used to make other tools.

353 Boris Gasparyan took Rothman and Simonyan to Mushakan, where they discussed the flint sources in 2010.

It is found as debitage throughout the site in small clusters (see table 5c.2 here and 5c.3 below).

Flint and similar siliceous rocks are not found in the immediate surroundings of Shengavit, but a source for these rocks has been identified by Boris Gasparyan of the Institute of Archaeology and Ethnography of the National Academy of Sciences of the Republic of Armenia in an exposure at Mushakan[354] on the outskirts of Yerevan, about eight kilometers from Shengavit. In the valley of the Shoraghbyur River, a tributary of the Hrazdan, Gasparyan describes Mushakan as a small hill with an exposure of siliceous pebbles. The surface deposits at Mushakan include evidence of material sourcing and

Figure 5c.1. Hill with blocks of obsidian on Yerevan-Sevan road.

tool production from many prehistoric periods dating back to the Lower Palaeolithic, as well as the Bronze and Iron Ages. Gasparyan has established that the Bronze Age sickle elements of the Ararat Depression, including those of Shengavit, were prepared from Mushakan flints.[355]

Archaeologists found no flint cores large enough for sickle element production in the Shengavit excavations, although they did find roughouts for sickle elements. Diggers recovered flint debris, mostly non-cortical, consistent with sickle element manufacture and resharpening. It is possible that lithic material from Mushakan came to Shengavit as pebbles, even though we recovered no pebble cores or quantities of cortical debris. But it seems more

likely that they were brought as large flakes or reduced pebbles and were worked on-site. Archaeologists did recover two blocks of black obsidian in Squares M5 and J6, probably from the obsidian hill (Fig 5c.1).

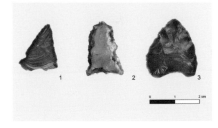

Figure 5c.2. Unfinished projectile points: 1. triangular, 2. notched base and barbed, 3. notched base.

Categories of Tools

PROJECTILE POINTS

Excavators found projectile points throughout the excavation of Shengavit. Of the 40 points analyzed, two were made of flint and the remainder of obsidian. Only a handful of the points were complete, finished artifacts. Some 60% of the points were broken, often at sensitive points of production. Breaks at barbs formed by deep notching are an example with some breakage likely during the life of the object or after its deposition. Broken tips or damaged edges are common. Many of the points were unfinished, either due to breakage during production or abandonment of the incomplete forms for other reasons (Fig 5c.2). The obsidian points are made of a colorful variety of material: black, red, translucent, and banded obsidian. One point was made of buff-colored flint (Fig 5c.3, 5).

Shengavit's projectile points fall into two groups based on form: points with stems (or tangs), and those without. The largest group comprises

Figure 5c.3. Stemless points with straight bases. 1-2 wide; 3-4 lanceolate; 5 triangular.

354 Sardarian 2004, 88 also identified Mushakan as a source of flint some years ago.
355 Gasparyan 2010.

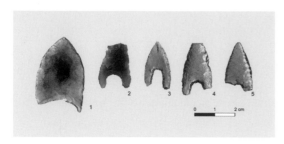

Figure 5c.4. Notched-base points. 1 shallow notch; 2 notched with incurved barbs; 3 deep- notched; 4-5 diagonal pressure flaked.

Figure 5c.5. Stemmed points. 1-3 with pointed barbs; 4-5 with straight barbs; 6 with pointed stem.

Figure 5c.6. Sickle elements. 1 flint (resharpened); 2 obsidian (resharpened); 3 volcanic rock.

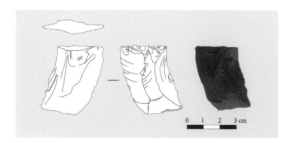

Figure 5c.7. Blade blank for sickle production.

points without stems whose bases are either straight, notched, or convex. The second group of points have stems and barbs, some of which are pointed, and some of which are straight. All the Shengavit points, except triangular points, have convex edges.

The stemless, straight-based points fall into three subgroups. In the first, the convex edges meet the straight base in a tight curve, and the length is about the same as the width (Fig 5c.3, 1& 2). The second group is more elongated, with a more incurved bottom corner, lanceolate in form (Fig 5c.3, 3& 4). The third group represents triangular points, with straighter edges and sharper corners (Fig 5c.3, 5).

Shengavit's notched-base points vary in the arc of the notch. Some have a shallow notch spanning most of the base and producing two small barbs (Fig 5c.4, 1). More invasive notching produces longer, wider barbs which curve inward (Fig 5c.4, 2). The most invasive, deepest notching is narrow, creating long, slightly incurved barbs (Fig 5c.4, 3). Although many of the points were broken during manufacturing, a number have fine diagonal pressure flaking scars on their surfaces, representing the final stage of production (Fig 5c.4, 4 & 5).

Points with stems (or tangs) at Shengavit fall into two subgroups, those with pointed barbs (Fig 5c.5., 1-3) and those with straight barbs (Fig. 5c. 5., 4-5). Both types have rectangular or sub- rectangular stems. Both types have convex edges. All edges are finely bifacially retouched, but none exhibit the diagonal pressure flaking of some of the notched points. There is one example of a point with pointed stem (Fig. 5c.5, 6).

From the number of points found in different stages of production and those apparently abandoned due to breakage during production, it is clear that a variety of points were produced at Shengavit. The design of the points and the skill applied in their production suggest that making points required an experienced tool maker and careful planning of the steps of fabrication. There is no evidence, however, for organized workshop production of projectile points at Shengavit nor for a tradition with one model of what an arrowhead should be. They appear at multiple loci throughout the site, and there is no evidence of specialized production areas. Nor is there evidence of organized debitage production for point manufacturing. The points seem to be made of locally available obsidian pebbles from which flakes were struck to produce individual points by skilled, competent flintknappers.

SICKLE ELEMENTS

One category of chipped stone used primarily in agricultural activities at Shengavit is the sickle blade. With great regularity in production, bifacially worked, denticulated pieces of flint and obsidian were inserted into curved hafts using bitumen as an adhesive. Of the sickle elements in the assemblage, 66% are flint (and related rocks) and the remainder obsidian. Ranging in length from 30 to 95 millimeters, most of the sickle elements are unbroken. Many have dulled teeth, and there is extensive evidence of re-sharpening; some 20% of the examined pieces were re-sharpened and, absent fresh gloss or dulling, they were not put back into service. Flint was the preferred material for sickle elements. One third of the sickle elements at Shengavit were made of obsidian and include pieces that were re-sharpened (Fig 5c.6, 1-2).

Shengavit's sickle elements were fully bifacially retouched. Roughouts for sickle elements originated as flakes or blades struck from cores (Fig 5c.7), or as thick flakes struck from pebbles (Fig 5c.8, 1). Further bifacial retouch formed the working edge and the hafted edge (Fig 5c.8, 2). Each of the edges describes an angle that is more obtuse on the working edge and more acute on the hafted edge. The hafted edges are not backed, or vertically retouched. The angle of the working edge was often modified when the edge was re-sharpened; thus, it became more obtuse. Nearly all of Shengavit's sickle elements were denticulated, some more finely than others.

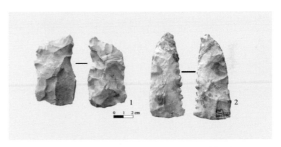

Figure 5c.8. Flint roughout and finished sickle element: 1, flint roughout; 2, flint sickle element.

Nearly 70% of the sickle elements at Shengavit had gloss (sickle sheen) on at least part of their denticulated edges and one or both adjacent faces. Resharpening removed the gloss from the dull sickle selectively, sometimes entirely. Remains of gloss help identify resharpened elements (Fig 5c.9). Three general shapes appear among the sickle elements: rectangular, curved, and tapered (Fig 5c.10). Shapes of sickle elements were likely informed by the size and shapes of hafts and their positions along the haft.   Tapered elements were most likely set at the end of curved hafts, mirrored by the bitumen remains on tool pictured in Figure 5c.10, 6.

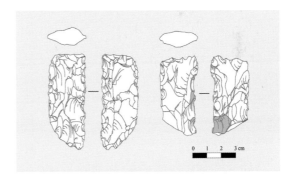

Figure 5c.9. Resharpened sickle elements with remains of gloss.

The regularity in production and the care taken in resharpening reinforce the central importance of the sickle as an agricultural tool at Shengavit. There is good evidence for the manufacture of sickle elements on-site. In one locus (Square J5, locus 2017), a domestic courtyard, we recovered 202 chips and small flakes of flint and one flint sickle element. Notably, all the debris was non-cortical. The flakes were consistent in size and technology with the bifacial reduction process of Shengavit's sickle elements. A similar deposit was found by E. A. Bayburtian in an outdoor area of Building 1 during the 1936/37 excavation at Shengavit and published in his dissertation (Fig.

Figure 5c.10. Flint sickle elements. 1-3 rectangular; 4-5 curved; 6-7 tapered.

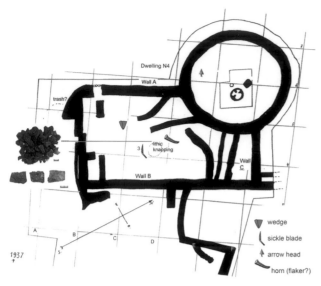

Figure 5c.11. Sickle elements and production debris in courtyard outside Bayburtian Building 1.

5c.11).[356] Given the absence of large flint blade cores and quantities of cortical debris, it seems probable that flint sickle elements were made on prepared blanks, most likely thick blades or flakes struck from pebbles at Mushakan and brought to Shengavit.

The presence of resharpened, but not yet re-used sickle elements reinforces their economic significance at the site. Essential harvesting tools are carefully maintained in order to ensure an efficient and successful harvest. Sickle elements are found in domestic contexts where they were being resharpened by household members who likely also used them in the field. The skills required to resharpen them were basic pressure flaking and knapping skills at a level sustainable by household members. Much as today's farmers sharpen their tools in preparation for (and during) harvest time, Shengavit's ancient farmers fabricated and maintained their tools at home.

Flake Tools and Pebble Cores

Most stone tools at Shengavit were produced on obsidian flakes. Prominent among these were retouched flakes and, to a much lesser extent, retouched blades, gravers (scraping tools associated with notches), splintered pieces (wedges, or *pièces esquillées*), utilized pieces (unretouched, but showing signs of use), projectile points, denticulates, scrapers, and borers (Table 5c.3).

tool	n	% of tools	n obsidian	% obsidian	n flint	% flint
retouched flake	210	33	205	98	5	2
graver	170	27	167	98	3	2
splintered piece	53	8	53	100	0	0
utilized piece	53	8	53	100	0	0
point	41	6	39	95	2	5
retouched blade	30	5	30	100	0	0
retouched piece	29	5	27	93	2	7
sickle	24	4	8	33	16	67
notch	14	2	13	93	1	7
denticulate	6	1	6	100	0	0
borer	6	1	5	83	1	17
scraper	4	1	3	75	1	25
burin	1	0	1	100	0	0
TOTAL	**641**	**100**	**610**	**95**	**31**	**5**

Table 5c.3. Correlation of tool types and material for their manufacture.

356   Bayburtian 2011.

Shengavit's obsidian pebble cores were reduced by multi-directional flaking or by bipolar percussion. Multi-directional cores (Fig 5c.12, 1) yielded flakes of varying sizes and do not exhibit regularity in technology.

This fits the picture of an expedient industry, where tools are casually made to suit domestic needs. Some of the obsidian pebbles (Fig 5c.12, 2) were placed on a hard anvil for knapping, producing flakes with signs of percussion from both proximal and distal ends. Bipolar technology is common in lithic industries where the cores are small and would be difficult to hold and strike accurately without stable footing.[357] Flakes struck from these cores by either method were often unretouched or modified for immediate use.

As is common with bipolar fracture, splintered pieces appear as byproducts and, in the case of Shengavit, are frequently further modified on the site. Often called wedges (particularly in North America[358]) or chisels (as in the Chalcolithic of Armenia[359]), these tools were first described in the European Palaeolithic as *pièces esquillées*, or, literally, splintered pieces, which avoids a functional attribution. These small obsidian tools often exhibit end retouch and end damage, where one end is beveled like a wedge or chisel and often shows use wear, and its opposite end has crushing fracture or signs of battering. Functionally, these may have been used as wedges, where the beveled end is used to split bone or antler or wood or ivory, struck with a hammer or billet from the opposite end. In the example shown in Figure 5c.13, flintknappers struck a burin spall off one edge, perhaps to provide a safe surface for gripping.

Very few unretouched blades and bladelets are found in the assemblage. They amount to 2% of the debitage, while unretouched flakes account for 82%. Blades and bladelets derive almost exclusively from local obsidian pebbles, although there is limited evidence for wider blades, struck from prismatic cores of non-local material (Fig 5c.14, 2 & 3). However, we found no large prismatic cores at Shengavit.

Gravers make up a significant portion of the obsidian repertoire, some 26% of the tool total. Often flintknappers formed them on the corners of thick flakes by notching adjacent edges. Gravers are very narrow-nosed scrapers, used to scrape or incise (Fig 5c.15). Gravers often appear as multiple tools

Figure 5c.12. Obsidian pebble cores. 1 multidirectional; 2 bipolar.

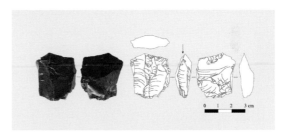

Figure 5c.13. Burin spall struck off one edge.

Figure 5c.14. Retouched blades: 1 irregular; 2 trapezoidal; 3 triangular.

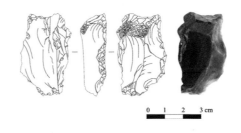

Figure 5c.15. Graver on flake with retouched edges.

357   Shott 1999.
358   LeBlanc 1992.
359   Arimura et al. 2014.

on one flake, where strategic notching isolates the working edges (Fig 5c.16). The precise function of these pointed scraping tools at Shengavit is unknown. They could have been used to cut a groove in wood, bone, ivory, or antler. Given the prominence of incised decoration in the ceramics produced at the site and their common appearance across the site, it is possible that gravers were used to incise ceramics in their leather-hard state.

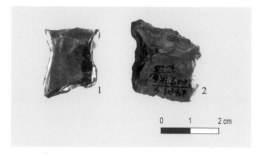

Figure 5c.16. Multiple gravers: 1 obsidian; 2 flint.

Production Techniques, Organization, and Tools

As I suggested already, most of the tools produced at Shengavit were simple modifications to or direct use of obsidian flakes. This suggests that the organization of production on the site was domestic and on an as-needed basis. There was no evidence of a workshop production for use by the broader Shengavit community or for exchange.

One should draw a distinction between expertise and workshop production in the context of stone tools at Shengavit. Expertise in stone tool making was widely held and employed at the household level; workshop production, turning out quantities of consistently formed tools and distributing them widely, is absent at the site. To resharpen a sickle element by pressure flaking, performed at the household level, is an essential activity for agricultural production.

Discussion

Most of the obsidian tools at Shengavit were made on flakes and show little regularity in production technology or morphology. Two interesting exceptions, splintered pieces and gravers, have more consistent features. Splintered pieces, products of the bipolar technology common in Shengavit's use of small pebbles, often have beveled ends and were used as splitting tools. These tools are rarely included in publications of Kura-Araxes excavations, as many site reports tend not to emphasize their lithic components beyond projectile points and, in some cases, sickle elements. In the Chalcolithic of Armenia a number of examples of splintered pieces identified as chisels have been published from cave and burial sites.[360] They came from the Late Chalcolithic site of Ovçular Tepesi in Naxçivan,[361] and were published in quantity at the Eastern Anatolian site of Norşuntepe, where the excavator, Klaus Schmidt, refers to them as splintered pieces (*ausgesplitterten Stücke*).[362] He suggests that they were used to split caprid metapodia and confirms that they appear in the Chalcolithic as well as the Early Bronze Age levels of the site.

Flintkappers made gravers, often in multiples, on thick flakes by strategic notching. They are a common tool in the Shengavit assemblage. Often grouped with notches, as at Norşuntepe[363] and at Sos Höyük,[364] they are not published as common tools in reports on the Early Bronze Age of the South Caucasus.

The exceptional tools of Shengavit are its projectile points and sickle elements, which are more commonly published– particularly the projectile points – as hallmarks of the Kura-Araxes lithic artifact repertoire. Obsidian projectile points at Shengavit appear across the Kura-Araxes landscape. All Shengavit's projectile points have parallels at Norşuntepe: stemmed points with straight barbs and with pointed barbs, unstemmed points with flat bases, and

---

360   Arimura et al. 2014.
361   Marro et al. 2011.
362   Schmidt 1996, 45-46.
363   Schmidt 1996, 45-46.
364   Sagona et al. 1996, 49.

points with notched bases ranging from minimal, concave notches to deep notches with incurved barbs and diagonal pressure flaking.[365] Stemmed and barbed points appear in Chalcolithic burials in the Armavir province of Armenia and at Karnut in Shirak province in Kura-Araxes levels.

The sickle elements tell a different story. The general Near Eastern picture from the Neolithic to the Early Bronze Age traces a long tradition of blade technology that provides debitage for simple, unifacially worked sickle elements. For example, eastern Anatolian sickles are products of prismatic blade core technology,[366] typically long, narrow blades, unifacially retouched. By contrast, this blade technology is conspicuously rare in the Kura Araxes horizon of Shengavit. Sickles are robustly bifacial, made on heavy flakes and irregular blades, mostly of flint.

Within Shengavit's two diagnostic groups of projectile points and sickle elements there is an interesting division. The obsidian points fit well within the greater Kura-Araxes complex. Stylistic differences appear at different sites, but the same general forms are found across the region. In contrast, bifacial flint and obsidian sickle elements are the norm at Shengavit, reported from only a few other sites in its horizon, principally at Karnut and at Kohne Tepesi. The preference for flint as a working material for sickles may be based on its resilience, in contrast to brittle obsidian. This, and the proximity of a secure source of raw flint pebbles, may have helped determine the nature of Shengavit sickles. The sickle elements of Shengavit are extremely well crafted and well maintained. Their consistent quality reinforces a view of their importance in the agricultural life of Shengavit.

In sum, the lithic production at Shengavit represents one that was decentralized, meant for household use and not for the larger community or for trade. It was mostly *ad hoc*, except for sickle elements and arrowheads. Even then, the technology was not highly sophisticated and often could be done by people who were not trained specialists. The materials used came from nodules that tumbled down the Hrazdan River or from outcrops within a 10-kilometer radius from the site. The techniques were different in many ways from other regions of the contemporaneous Middle East, but they generally represent a shared cultural tradition with the other homeland and diaspora Kura-Araxes sites from which we have sufficient information.

Acknowledgements

The author would like to thank the Royal Ontario Museum for its support of his participation in the Shengavit project through the offices of Mark Engstrom and Chen Shen. Thanks also to Tiziana Gallo, Department of Anthropology, University of Toronto, for lithic illustration. I would also like to thank Boris Gasparyan in particular for his support of the Shengavit field project, for taking me to see the site of Mushakan, and for sharing his encyclopedic knowledge of Armenian prehistory.

References

Arimura M, Gasparyan, B., Nahapetyan, S., and Pinhasi, R. 2014 Forest Exploitation During the Holocene in the Aghstev Valley, Northeast Armenia. in *Stone Age of Armenia*, edited by Boris Gasparyan and Makato Arimura, 261-82. Kanazawa University: Center for Cultural Resource Studies.

Badalyan, R. S. and Avetisyan, P.S. 2007 *Bronze and Early Iron Age Archaeological Sites in Armenia. I. Mt. Aragats and its Surrounding Region.* Oxford: BAR International Series 1697.

Bayburtian, Y. E. 2011 *Sequence of Ancient Cultures of Armenia on the Basis of Archaeological Material.* Yerevan: Armenian Museum of History. (in Russian).

---

365 Schmidt 1996.
366 These involve a prepared core in which pressure flaking is a common way to remove blades.

Fornaseri, M., Malpieri, L., Taddeucci, A. and Palmieri, A. 1975-77 Analyses of Obsidians from the Late Chalcolithic Levels of Arslantepe (Malatya). *Paléorient* (3): 231-246.

Gasparyan, B. 2010 Landscape Organization and Resource Management in the Lower Palaeolithic of Armenia. *TÜBA-AR* 13: 159-87.

Jayez, M., Kazemnejad, A., Zalaghi, A. 2017 Dichotomous Early Bronze Age Chipped Stone Industry: Statistical Assessment of Congruence among Chert and Obsidian Chipped Stone Assemblages from Kohne Tepesi, East Azerbaijan, Iran. *International Journal of the Society of Iranian Archaeologists* 3(5): 45-54.

LeBlanc, R. 1992 Wedges, *Pièces Esquillées*, Bipolar Cores, and Other Things: An Alternative to Shott's View of Bipolar Industries. *North American Archaeologist* 13(1): 1-14.

Marro, C, Bakhshaliyev, V. and Ashurov, S. 2011 Excavations at Ovçular Tepesi (Nakhchivan, Azerbaijan) Second Preliminary Report. The 2009-2010 Seasons. *Anatolia Antiqua* 19: 53-100.

Mouralis, D., Massussi, M., Palumbi, G., Akköpru, E., Restelli, Balossi F., Brunstein, D., Frangipane, M., Gratuze, B., Mokadem, F., Robin, A-K. 2018 The procurement of obsidian at Arslantepe (Eastern Anatolia) during the Chalcolithic and Early Bronze Age: Connections with Anatolia and Caucasus. *Quaternary International* 467: 342-359.

Sagona, A., Erkmen, M., Sagona, C. and Thomas, I. 1996 Excavations at Sos Höyük, 1995: Second Preliminary Report. *Anatolian Studies* 46: 27-52.

Sagona, A., Erkmen, M., Sagona, C., McNiven, I. and Havel, S. Excavations at Sos Höyük, 1997: Fourth Preliminary Report. *Anatolica* 24: 31-64.

Shott, M. 1999 On Bipolar Reduction and Splintered Pieces. *North American Archaeologist* 46: 217-38.

Schmidt, K. 1996 *Norşuntepe Kleinfunde 1 Die Lithische Industrie*, Mainz am Rhein: Verlag Phillip von Zabern.

5d | Metal Artifacts from Shengavit in the Context of Kura-Araxes Metallurgy

Khachatur Meliksetian and Ernst Pernicka

Metallurgy has long been considered as one of the great achievements of human ingenuity. This is so because of metal's ability to provide tools that enable the development of new technologies. Historically, these new technologies catalyzed economic in conjunction with societal evolution. Metal objects also have had symbolic meaning that could signify developing social status and establish new economic orders.[367]

This chapter discusses recent analyses of metal artifacts excavated at Shengavit to reveal the provenance of the metal used and some metalworking techniques and processes. Metallurgy may be one kind of expertise that fueled the pull of migrations from the Southern Caucasus after 3200 BC.[368] The Kura-Araxes was characterized by the use of a wide range of metals comprising primarily copper, gold, and silver and local metallurgical technological traditions, especially the production of arsenical copper in the period between 3500 and 2500 BC. Numerous metal artifacts and a long record of metalworking techniques coupled with the absence of regional copper ores within a distance of less than 100 km makes Shengavit particularly important for understanding the regional metallurgical techniques, early mining of copper ores, and exchange networks that were part of the economic organization of the Kura-Araxes culture.

The metal finds unearthed in archaeological excavations in Armenia cover all of the early stages of metallurgy.[369] These stages include Neolithic use of native copper, the transition to extractive metallurgy in the Chalcolithic, the extensive use of copper, arsenical copper, the first appearance of tin bronze in the Early Bronze Age (Kura-Araxes), and the more advanced metallurgy and alloying techniques of the Middle and Late Bronze Ages. The Early Bronze Age metallurgy of the entire region associated with the Kura-Araxes cultural tradition is of particular importance, because it marks the transition to extensive use of metal for the production of decorative objects and some weapons and tools, as well as the use of advanced alloying and smelting techniques, such as the production of arsenic-rich bronze for jewelry. Its value may have resulted in re-melting worn-out metal tools to make new ones, possibly leading to an underestimation of the number of tools in circulation. In addition, in the KA2 the number of settlements and the density of their distribution grew in Georgia around gold mines and in Armenia around copper mines.[370]

This study is based on geochemical and isotope characteristics of metal artifacts excavated at Shengavit and analyzed in the Curt-Engelhorn Zentrum Archaeometrie, Mannheim, Germany, in 2015 with the aim of investigating the technology of metal production and the possible provenance of the metal.[371] In addition, we will compare these Shengavit objects with other copper-based artifacts of the Kura-Araxes culture in Armenia (including several Shengavit

---

367   Renfrew 1986.
368   Batiuk et al. 2022.
369   Meliksetian et al. 2011a, Bobokyan et al. 2014.
370   Batiuk et al. 2022.
371   We thank the White-Levy Foundation for funds to complete this work.

artifacts from earlier excavations) as well as with analyses of metal objects from other parts of the Kura-Araxes culture in Anatolia and the South Caucasus studied earlier by Meliksetian & Pernicka.[372]

Overview of Kura-Araxes Metallurgy

Considering the wide regional distribution of the Kura-Araxes cultural tradition over geologically and metallogenetically diverse regions during the Early Bronze Age, copper-based artifacts exhibit a wide range of chemical and trace element characteristics providing evidence of utilization of different types of copper and polymetallic ore deposits.

Archaeologists have recovered metalworking remains such as furnaces, crucibles with copper globules (Fig 5d.1), casting molds (Fig 5d.2) and finally, numerous metal artifacts (Fig 5d.3) at many Kura-Araxes sites in the South Caucasus.[373] Numerous finds of copper-based artifacts, some gold objects, and metalworking tools like casting molds and crucibles signify that metallurgy played an important role in Shengavit during the Kura-Araxes. One casting mold recovered during the 2009-2012 campaigns, and another one is listed in the catalogue of Shengavit artifacts in the National History Museum (Fig 5d.2).[374] In addition, archaeologists found various metal objects (Fig 5d.3).

Many earlier studies by researchers, such as Chernykh, Selimkhanov, Abesadze, and Gevorgyan applied optical emission spectrometry, often called spectral analysis, to study the chemical compositions of Kura-Araxes artifacts.[375] More recent investigations of Kura-Araxes metallurgy include the application of X-Ray fluorescence (XRF), instrumental neutron activation analysis (INAA), and lead isotope analysis applied for the first time in the Southern Caucasus region by Meliksetian and Pernicka.[376] Courcier provides several XRF analyses of metal artifacts from Azerbaijan as well as an overview of regional prehistoric metallurgy.[377]

Figure 5d.1 Ceramic crucible from Shengavit for metal smelting.

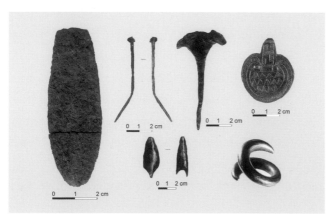

Figure 5d.2 Molds for a flat axe and pins from Shengavit.

Figure 5d.3 Metal artifacts from Shengavit.

---

372   Meliksetian & Pernicka 2010.

373   Chubinishvili, 1971, Khanzadjan, 1975, Gadzhiev et al., 2000, Peterson, 2003, Gevorgyan, 1980, Courcier, 2014 and others.

374   Badalyan et al. 2015.

375   Chernykh 1966, 1992; Selimkhanov 1962; Abesadze 1969; Gevorgyan 1980.

376   Meliksetian et al. 2003; Meliksetian and Pernicka 2010.

377   Courcier 2014.

Analysts classified XRF and INAA analyses of 87 metal objects from Armenia into five main groups according to their chemical compositions, namely, unalloyed copper, arsenical copper, copper-arsenic-tin alloys, copper-arsenic-lead alloys, and tin bronze. In addition to the five main groups the trace element concentrations of the artifacts also pointed to a group characterized by relatively high nickel and silver contents.[378]

The set of samples analyzed by a combination of XRF and INAA also included five artifacts from the Shengavit museum, namely a bracelet, two pins, and two fragments of copper-based artifacts. We also analyzed specimens of oxidized copper from crucibles.

In past publications, analysts noted that the high concentration of arsenic is a specific feature for most of the Kura-Araxes copper-based artifacts.[379] Some objects, such as a necklace from Gegharot,[380] contain up to 20 percent of arsenic by weight This feature is not limited to the Armenian Kura-Araxes metallurgy; it also occurred at some levels of the North Caucasus (Maikop and Derbent), Georgia, Azerbaijan, and Arslantepe in Anatolia. Specialists of archaeometallurgy have long debated whether the high arsenic concentrations are due to the composition of the ores smelted and are thus a kind of natural alloy, or if arsenic were intentionally added by ancient metalworkers. In fact, in the Armenian Middle and Late Bronze Ages high arsenic contents are not typical and tin (or rarely antimony) replaced arsenic as a principal alloying component.[381] Nevertheless, the smelting technique used to produce high arsenic alloys and achieve significant color changes of copper-based artifacts occurred in the late phase of the Late Bronze Age as well. Some unique Late Bronze Age bi-metallic decorative objects from Lori Berd consisted of tin bronze (yellow) and high-arsenic bronze. The latter is a dark gray to black, shiny metal containing up to 24 percent arsenic.[382] Based on their statistical distribution, high arsenic contents are typical for decorative objects and jewelry, rather than for tools and weapons. Chernykh reached a similar conclusion much earlier for the Early Bronze Age metallurgy of the North Caucasus.[383] This feature is associated with high brittleness of copper if it contains more than five percent of arsenic. Below five percent arsenical copper was mostly used for tools and primarily for weapons due to the good mechanical properties, particularly hardness, compared with pure copper.[384] For decorative objects and jewelry variable concentrations of arsenic permit the metalsmith to achieve different colors of bronze and surface appearance.[385] For a detailed description of the processes of working metal in this region in antiquity, see Tedesco.[386]

Samples and Analytical Techniques

We sampled twenty-four metal artifacts from Shengavit for this study (Table 5d.1, Fig 5d.4). The majority of the artifacts were copper-based alloys. In addition, we found some gold and silver alloys. The samples belong to the KA2 period. The contexts of some objects are unclear, and a few are from Middle Bronze Age pits or graves that may date in the Kura-Araxes/Early Kurgan transitional period. The descriptions of the analyzed artifacts with their suggested dates are summarized in the Table 5d 1.

We sampled all twenty-four metal artifacts from Shengavit and one EBA arrowhead from Berqaber (northeastern

---

378   Meliksetian and Pernicka 2010.
379   Meliksetian et al. 2011a; Courcier 2014.
380   Meliksetian et al. 2007.
381   Meliksetian et al. 2011a.
382   Meliksetian et al. 2011a.
383   Chernykh 1966.
384   Northover 1989; Lechtman 1996.
385   Giumlia-Mair 2008; Meliksetian et al. 2011a.
386   see Tedesco 2006.

Armenia) by drilling them with a one mm titanium nitride covered drill. We collected metal shavings of 30 to 50 mg in small plastic vials and numbered them. We then carefully filled the drill holes with specially colored waxes, mixed to achieve a color that exactly matches the color of each artifact and to leave no visible changes. We weighed all samples and inserted them into polyethene containers for the analysis with energy dispersive X-ray fluorescence (EDXRF) to determine the concentrations of the major and some trace elements using the analytical procedure described in detail by Lutz & Pernicka.[387]

We subjected a selection of samples to lead isotope analysis in order to compare them with Armenian Kura-Araxes artifacts and with copper ores analyzed earlier. The determination of the lead isotope ratios was performed with a

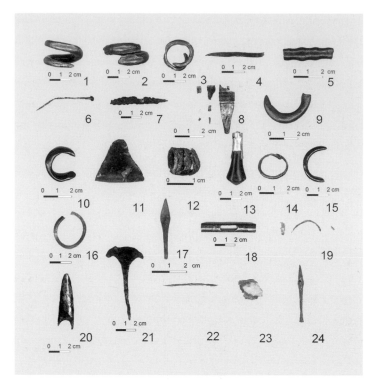

Figure 5d.4. Shengavit metal artifacts analyzed.

multiple-collector, inductively-coupled, plasma mass spectrometer (MC–ICP–MS) at the Curt–Engelhorn Center for Archaeometry (CEZA) in Mannheim, Germany. The instrument used was a Thermo Scientific Neptune Plus mass spectrometer. Sample preparation followed the protocol described by Niederschlag et al.[388] and modified by Nørgaard et al.[389] We used international analytical reference materials during all analytical work.

The detailed results of major and trace element concentrations of the artifacts determined by EDXRF appear in Table 5d.2, while the results of lead isotope analysis appear in Table 5d.3.

Results and Discussion

Chemical compositions

The artifacts from Shengavit belong to seven compositional groups, namely pure copper (two objects), copper-arsenic alloy (eleven objects), tin bronze (three objects), copper-arsenic-tin alloy (one object), copper-nickel-zinc alloy (one object of unclear period), copper-zinc-tin alloy (one object), and gold-silver alloy (one object). In addition, as mentioned above, we analyzed five artifacts and three copper samples from crucibles recovered at Shengavit earlier. All consisted of copper-arsenic alloys, including the arrowhead from Berqaber in northeastern Armenia. These groups are listed in the sample list (Table 5d.1). Thus, the metallurgy of Shengavit is dominated by copper-arsenic over all other types of alloys (20 samples out of 31, including one tertiary copper-arsenic-tin alloy). This holds particularly true for the Kura-Araxes period of occupation at Shengavit, because some of the other alloys belong to late phases of KA2 or the Early Kurgan Period (2500-2000 BC) or to objects whose dating is unclear. We observed exceptionally

---

387 Lutz and Pernicka 1996.
388 Niederschlag et al. 2003.
389 Nørgaard, et al 2019.

No	Site	Location	Description	Excavation date	Alloy type	Date (KA2 is 3000-2450 BC)
1.	Shengavit	Locus III	Spiral ring	2005	Cu+As	KA2
2.	Shengavit	Locus III	Spiral ring	2005	Cu+As+Sn	KA2
3.	Shengavit	Chance find	Spiral ring	8.10.05	Cu+As	KA2?
4.	Shengavit	Locus III T4	pin	26.10.05	Cu	KA2
5.	Shengavit	Chance find	Cylindrical item-?	15.10.05	Cu+As	KA2?
6.	Shengavit	Chance find	Awl	2005	Cu+As	KA2?
7.	Shengavit	Chance find	Awl	2005	Cu	KA2?
8.	Shengavit	Locus IX	Unknown object-?	2005	Cu+Ni+Zn	???
9.	Shengavit	Locus IV	Fragment of ring	2008	Cu+Sn	KA2
10.	Shengavit	Sq K6 Locus 1002	Fragment of ring	13.7. 09	Cu+Sn+Zn	Late KA2
11.	Shengavit	Sq K6, Locus 1007	Metal plate	14.6. 09	Cu+Zn	Late KA2
12.	Shengavit	K4/L4,Locus 5051	Spiral ring	25.07.09	Cu+As	KA2
13.	Shengavit	Sq J5, Locus 2002	Decorative object	17.07.09	Au+Ag+Cu	Early MBA-?
14.	Shengavit	Sq J5, Locus 2029	ring	02.07.10	Cu+As	KA2
15.	Shengavit	Locus 4	Fragment of ring	15.07.10	Cu+Sn	KA2
16.	Shengavit	Sq K6, Locus 1007	Ring	18.7.09	Cu	Later KA2
17.	Shengavit	Locus 4	Tetrahedral arrow-head	21.07.10	Cu+As	KA2?
18.	Shengavit	Sq L7, Locus 15007	cylindrical item,	30.07.10	Cu+Zn	Late KA2-MB
19.	Shengavit	Sq J5, Locus 2029	Fragment of ring	22.07.10	Cu+Sn	KA2?
20.	Shengavit	Sq K6, Locus 1128	Arrowhead?	10.7. 12	Cu+As	Middle KA2
21.	Shengavit	Sq J6, Locus 18024	Awl	6.7.12	Cu+As	Late KA2 or MB,
22.	Shengavit	Sq J6A Locus 18010	Awl	27.06.12	Cu+As	Late KA2/Early Kurgan
23.	Shengavit	K6, Locus 1099	Ingot?	20.6.12	Cu+As	KA2
24.	Berqaber	Tomb 1	arrow-head	?	Cu+As	KA2?

Table 5d.1 Shengavit metal artifacts, phase 2 of the Kura-Araxes culture (KA2).

high contents of arsenic of up to 20% only for previously analyzed artifacts from the small museum on the Shengavit mound studied earlier.[390] The concentrations of arsenic in the artifacts of this study range from 1.4 to 7.2%.

This corroborates the results of previous studies that the majority of the Kura-Araxes metal objects from Armenia and the South Caucasus consisted of arsenical copper. This is one of the most prominent features of this period, as noted by many scholars who studied prehistoric metallurgy of the region, namely, Chernykh, Selimkhanov, Abesadze, and Gevorgyan.[391] A recent summary of XRF analyses of 98 EBA artifacts reached similar conclusions.[392] Ancient metallurgists must have known that the addition of arsenic made copper harder at low concentrations but more brittle at high concentrations. They would, however, turn the color of the alloy to bright or a darker silver, or even black with a unique gloss at higher concentrations. Again, in Armenia the high level (seven percent or more arsenical content) is mostly found on Kura-Araxes decorative objects and jewelry, rather than in tools and weapons. This supports the idea that producers were attempting to create this distinctive appearance (gloss and color) during Kura-

---

390   Meliksetian & Pernicka 2010.
391   Chernykh 1966, 1992; Selimkhanov 1962; Abesadze 1969; Gevorgyan 1980.
392   Badalyan et al. 2016.

No	Orig No	Lab no. MA-	$^{208}Pb/^{206}Pb$	±2σ	$^{207}Pb/^{206}Pb$	±2σ	$^{208}Pb/^{204}Pb$	±2σ	$^{207}Pb/^{204}Pb$	±2σ	$^{206}Pb/^{204}Pb$	±2σ	Alloy type
1.	1	153035	2.0545	0.0001	0.82999	0.00002	18.865	0.001	38.757	0.008	15.658	0.001	Cu+As
2.	2	153036	2.0685	0.0001	0.83126	0.00002	18.871	0.001	39.035	0.003	15.686	0.001	Cu+As+Sn
3.	3	153037	2.0686	0.0001	0.83223	0.00003	18.753	0.002	38.791	0.014	15.606	0.002	Cu+As
4.	4	153038	2.0839	0.0003	0.84465	0.00006	18.489	0.002	38.528	0.026	15.616	0.003	Cu
5.	5	153039	2.0756	0.0001	0.83661	0.00003	18.648	0.001	38.705	0.015	15.601	0.002	Cu+As
6.	6	153040	2.0803	0.0001	0.84395	0.00001	18.549	0.001	38.587	0.004	15.654	0.001	Cu+As
7.	9	153043	2.0663	0.0001	0.83004	0.00002	18.906	0.001	39.065	0.007	15.693	0.001	Cu+Sn
8.	11	153045	2.1238	0.0001	0.87575	0.00001	17.763	0.001	37.726	0.004	15.556	0.001	Cu+Zn
9.	12	153046	2.0579	0.0001	0.82767	0.00001	18.909	0.001	38.913	0.002	15.650	0.001	Cu+As
10.	14	153048	2.0787	0.0001	0.83768	0.00002	18.710	0.001	38.892	0.006	15.673	0.001	Cu+As
11.	15	153049	2.0671	0.0001	0.83006	0.00001	18.917	0.001	39.104	0.005	15.703	0.001	Cu+Sn
12.	16	153050	2.1045	0.0001	0.86143	0.00002	18.095	0.001	38.081	0.002	15.588	0.001	Cu
13.	17	153051	2.0696	0.0001	0.83201	0.00002	18.839	0.001	38.989	0.005	15.674	0.001	Cu+As
14.	18	153052	2.0781	0.0002	0.84645	0.00004	18.438	0.002	38.315	0.019	15.606	0.002	Cu+Zn
15.	21	153055	2.0550	0.0002	0.82383	0.00003	18.943	0.001	38.927	0.014	15.605	0.002	Cu+As
16.	22	153056	2.0772	0.0001	0.84133	0.00001	18.595	0.001	38.626	0.004	15.644	0.001	Cu+As

Table 5d.2 Artifacts determined by EDXRF (All concentrations are given in weight percent.)

	Lab no. MA-	Cu, %	Mn, %	Fe, %	Co, %	Ni, %	Zn, %	As %	Se,%	Ag, %	Cd,%	Sn,%	Sb,%	Te,%	Au,%	Pb,%	Bi,%	Alloy type
1	153035	95.7	<0.01	<0.05	<0.01	<0.01	<0.1	4.1	<0.01	0.027	<0.005	0.024	<0.005	<0.005	<0.01	<0.01	0.02	Cu+As
2	153036	93.7	<0.01	<0.05	<0.01	0.06	<0.1	4.0	<0.01	0.041	<0.005	1.9	0.045	<0.005	<0.01	0.14	0.03	Cu+As+Sn
3	153037	98.1	<0.01	<0.05	<0.01	0.01	<0.1	1.44	<0.01	0.025	<0.005	0.069	0.014	<0.005	<0.01	0.29	<0.01	Cu+As
4	153038	98.5	<0.01	<0.05	<0.01	<0.01	<0.1	0.62	<0.01	0.019	<0.005	0.076	0.55	<0.005	<0.01	0.17	<0.01	Cu
5	153039	94.9	<0.01	<0.05	<0.01	<0.01	<0.1	4.2	<0.01	0.024	<0.005	0.082	0.024	<0.005	<0.01	0.69	0.02	Cu+As
6	153040	97.7	<0.01	0.16	<0.01	0.03	<0.1	1.43	<0.01	0.028	<0.005	0.6	0.025	<0.005	<0.01	<0.01	<0.01	Cu+As
7	153041	99.4	<0.01	0.10	<0.01	<0.01	<0.1	0.33	<0.01	0.166	<0.005	<0.005	<0.005	<0.005	<0.01	<0.01	<0.01	Cu
8	153042	80.9	0.02	0.09	0.14	11.0	7.8	<0.01	<0.01	0.008	<0.005	0.006	<0.005	<0.005	<0.01	0.03	<0.01	Cu+Ni+Zn
9	153043	91.4	<0.01	0.87	0.01	0.32	0.1	0.43	0.04	0.056	<0.005	6.6	0.058	<0.005	<0.01	0.11	<0.01	Cu+Sn
10	153044	93.0	<0.01	0.11	0.01	0.18	2.7	1.02	0.03	0.010	<0.005	2.6	0.024	<0.005	<0.01	0.25	<0.01	Cu+Sn+Zn
11	153045	71.4	<0.01	<0.05	0.02	<0.01	28.6	<0.01	<0.01	<0.002	<0.005	0.022	<0.005	<0.005	<0.01	<0.01	<0.01	Cu+Zn
12	153046	97.0	<0.01	0.20	0.01	0.02	<0.1	2.62	<0.01	0.024	<0.005	0.010	<0.005	<0.005	<0.01	0.06	0.02	Cu+As
13	153047	2.9	n.d.	n.d.	n.d.	n.d.	n.d.	n.d.	n.d.	39.000	n.d.	n.d.	n.d.	n.d.	58	n.d.	n.d.	Au+Ag+Cu
14	153048	97.2	<0.01	0.40	<0.01	0.05	<0.1	1.50	<0.01	0.016	<0.005	0.012	0.633	<0.005	<0.01	0.18	<0.01	Cu+As
15	153049	92.6	<0.01	0.10	<0.01	0.68	<0.1	0.11	0.06	0.006	<0.005	6.4	0.011	<0.005	<0.01	0.02	<0.01	Cu+Sn
16	153050	99.8	<0.01	<0.05	<0.01	0.06	<0.1	0.01	<0.01	<0.002	<0.005	0.033	0.015	<0.005	<0.01	0.02	<0.01	Cu
17	153051	96.3	0.02	<0.05	<0.01	0.05	<0.1	3.3	<0.01	0.034	<0.005	0.030	0.043	<0.005	<0.01	0.25	0.05	Cu+As
18	153052	59.9	<0.01	0.26	0.02	0.02	39	<0.01	<0.01	0.004	0.018	0.067	<0.005	<0.005	<0.01	1.16	<0.01	Cu+Zn
19	153053	55.7	0.01	0.38	0.04	0.06	0.3	0.13	<0.01	0.011	0.027	43	0.088	<0.005	<0.01	0.04	<0.01	Cu+Sn
20	153054	92.7	<0.01	<0.05	<0.01	0.00	<0.1	7.2	<0.01	0.016	<0.005	0.053	0.052	<0.005	<0.01	<0.01	<0.01	Cu+As
21	153055	96.0	<0.01	<0.05	<0.01	0.01	<0.1	2.76	<0.01	0.026	<0.005	0.125	0.039	<0.005	<0.01	0.90	0.02	Cu+As
22	153056	98.1	<0.01	<0.05	0.01	<0.01	<0.1	1.69	<0.01	0.050	<0.005	0.041	0.017	<0.005	<0.01	<0.01	<0.01	Cu+As
23	153057	97.5	<0.01	0.44	<0.01	<0.01	<0.1	1.66	<0.01	<0.002	<0.005	0.004	0.079	<0.005	<0.01	0.28	<0.01	Cu+As
24	153058	98.2	<0.01	0.06	<0.01	<0.01	<0.1	0.99	<0.01	0.077	<0.005	0.050	<0.005	<0.005	<0.01	<0.01	<0.01	Cu+As

Table 5d.3 Lead isotope abundance ratios of analyzed artifacts.

Araxes culture and even much later in the Late Bronze Age.[393] Only one object in our sample is not from a decorative object, namely, an arrowhead with 3.4 percent arsenic (sample 17). Figure 5d.5 shows the statistical distribution of different copper-based alloy types of Kura-Araxes culture of the South Caucasus analyzed in last decade using state of the art analytical methods.

Regarding the ore sources (Fig 5d.6), the concentrations of nickel may be important for identifying the origin of the copper. High nickel contents are typical for copper and polymetallic ores formed within ultrabasic rocks, usually associated with regional ophiolites (a section of the Earth's oceanic crust and the underlying upper mantle that has been uplifted and exposed above sea level and is often typical of continental crustal rocks). In Armenia only the Sotk epithermal gold deposit in the Akera ophiolite in the region of Sevan has copper and polymetallic ores.[394] Other deposits within ophiolites are known from Anatolia and northwest and western Iran. Other Armenian ores that belong to volcanogenic-massive sulfide and porphyry types usually do not exhibit high nickel contents. Archaeologists found a group of Early Bronze Age artifacts with high nickel and silver contents by chance at Gyumri, and another from the Kura-Araxes tombs at Talin.[395] As for the analyzed objects from Shengavit, some of them do exhibit relatively high nickel (Ni) contents, as indicated in Fig. 5d.6, where the nickel concentrations are plotted against silver in comparison with the local ores (normalized to copper) and Kura-Araxes artifacts analyzed earlier. A single copper-nickel-zinc alloy (sample 8) of unclear date is not shown on the diagram. This type of alloy is unusual for the regional Early Bronze Age metal artifacts, and most likely belongs to later periods.

In spite of the use of several types of alloys during the Kura-Araxes period, three objects

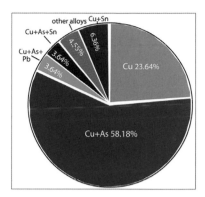

Figure 5d.5 Statistical distribution of copper-based alloys in the South Caucasus used to produce metal objects during Kura-Araxes times, based on a total of 110 artifacts analysed in the last decade by EDXRF. The majority of the artifacts are copper (Cu)-arsenic (As) alloys (58%), some of the other groups are triple alloys with arsenic, i.e. copper-arsenic-tin (Sn) (3.6%), copper-arsenic-lead (Pb) (3.6%), so that more than 65% of the artifacts consist of copper alloys with arsenic. Other alloys shown in the diagram include: Cu+Ni+Zn (zinc) (1 artifact), Cu+Pb+Sn (1 artifact), Cu+Sn+Zn (1 artifact), Cu+Zn (2 artifacts).

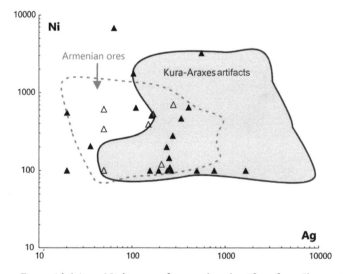

Figure 5d.6 Ag vs Ni diagram of copper-based artifacts from Shengavit. Filled triangles are artifacts analyzed in this study, while open triangles are artifacts and copper samples from crucibles found at Shengavit and analyzed earlier (Meliksetian & Pernicka, 2010). The compositional fields of Armenian ores and Kura-Araxes copper-based artifacts are also shown for comparison. A single copper-nickel-zinc alloy (MA-153042) with unclear dating is not shown in the diagram.

393   Meliksetian et al. 2011b; Badalyan et al. 2016.
394   Wolf et al. 2013.
395   Meliksetian and Pernicka, 2010.

belong to this group with 6.4, 6.6 and 43 percent tin. Pure (or unalloyed) copper was also used. Other chemical groups of metal used at Shengavit are represented by five objects made of copper-tin alloys: three tin-bronzes, one copper-arsenic-tin alloy (1.9% Sn), and one copper-zinc-tin alloy (2.6% Sn). In general, few tin bronzes from the Kura-Araxes period are known in Armenia, and with the exception of a tin bronze from Talin of the KA1 period of the Early Bronze Age,[396] most are related to the later KA2 phases. They mark a period when tin began to replace arsenic as the major alloying component. It was presumably used as an alternative to alloying with arsenic for some period of time. Tin alloys permitted metalsmiths to make a harder and more durable product. The fact that the yellow color resembled gold may also have been an important factor.

The metal casing of an obsidian pendant consisted of a gold-silver alloy with 58% gold, 39% silver and about 2.9% copper. It is unclear if the gold was alloyed with silver to make the metal frame, or if craft persons used electrum, a natural alloy of native gold and silver that occurs in nature. This object very likely derives from a grave or pit of the post-Kura-Araxes period.

Lead isotope ratios

Lead isotope analysis of copper artifacts and ores was introduced to archaeometallurgy by Gale and Stos-Gale[397] and has been successfully applied in many regions of the Old World to relate archaeological alloys to parent ore sources.[398] Natural lead occurs in nature as a mixture of ^{204}Pb (lead) and three radiogenic isotopes ^{206}Pb, ^{207}Pb, ^{208}Pb, which are products of the radioactive decay of ^{238}U, ^{235}U (uranium) and ^{232}Th (thorium) respectively. In most rocks lead, uranium, and thorium occur together, and the freshly produced lead from radioactive decay is constantly mixed with the lead that is already present. This mixing is particularly fast and thorough during magmatic processes that usually form various ore-magmatic systems. However, during the formation of copper or polymetallic ore deposits, lead is separated from uranium and thorium, and from this moment the lead isotope ratios do not change anymore. Thus, the lead isotopes ratios are important geochemical signatures of ore deposits and are related to their ages and types of ore-magmatic system and the compositions of parental magmas. For archaeometallurgy it is important to note that during smelting lead tends to concentrate in the metal rather than in the slag. Furthermore, metallurgical processes and chemical reactions do not affect the lead isotope signature. Thus, it can be applied as important geochemical fingerprinting tool to reveal a possible relationship of copper artifacts to their parent ore sources.

Studies of lead isotope signatures of Armenian copper ores demonstrate that that a large variation of lead isotope ratios is typical for Armenian copper ore deposits.[399] Presumably, the complex geological structure of the territory of Armenia with different tectonic units and complex volcanic magmatism, yielding to formation of ore deposits that mix ores of different ages and different types, affect the lead isotope signature of the ores of each region. It is also possible that some copper deposits also contain uranium minerals, since in many cases intrusive rocks rich in uranium bearing minerals host deposits like the Kadjaran copper-molybdenum porphyry deposit in the southern part of the current Republic of Armenia. In this case the model's assumption is not met, so no changes must have taken place in the isotopic composition since the formation of the ores. Thus, a large variety of lead isotope ratios develops within one deposit even on the microscale, depending on the U/Pb ratios within

---

396   Meliksetian et al. 2010.
397   Gale and Stos-Gale 1982.
398   See Pernicka et al. 1993; Begemann et al. 1992; Stos-Gale et al. 1994; Kohl et al., 2002; Meliksetian and Pernicka 2010; etc
399   Meliksetian and Pernicka, 2010.

single minerals. Of course, this makes the interpretation of lead isotope ratios of artifacts and their comparison with ores more complicated and precludes definitive statements about the sources of copper in the Early Bronze Age. Nevertheless, we observed some relationship between the isotope compositions of Armenian ores and some artifacts.[400]

Three groups of ores are defined based on their lead isotope ratios: "radiogenic, "ordinary," and "old" lead. This grouping is somewhat arbitrary and does not characterize single ore deposits or metallogenic provinces, because samples from some of the investigated ore deposits can be found in all three groups. The "ordinary" lead overlaps with the Anatolian lead isotope field, generally matching the isotope composition of the ores of the Pontides (the northernmost tectonic zone in modern Turkey). Parts of the "radiogenic" and "old" lead groups are located outside the "Anatolian" field suggesting larger variations of lead isotope compositions in Armenian ores.

Earlier we demonstrated that a comparison of artifacts and ores suggests a significant probability that northern Armenian copper ores and/or isotopically similar ores from the territory of present-day eastern Turkey could be related to some of the artifacts analyzed from the Early Bronze Age settlements in the Ararat Plain, the Shirak plateau, and northern Armenia. This conclusion was based on isotope composition of artifacts matching the "ordinary" and "radiogenic" lead groups of Armenian ores, as well as on the trace element patterns that generally fit Armenian ores. These artifacts match the "ordinary," "radiogenic," and "Anatolian" compositional fields, and it can be assumed that they were produced from local copper ores.

In this study we determined the lead isotope ratios of 16 artifacts from Shengavit (Table 5d.3.), and additionally five artifacts from the museum at the site and earlier three copper samples from crucibles.[401]

Fig 5d.7 shows the $^{207}Pb/^{206}Pb$ vs. $^{208}Pb/^{206}Pb$ isotope abundance ratios in all metal artifacts from Shengavit so far analyzed. Objects and copper samples from crucibles discussed earlier are grouped in the "ordinary" lead field of Armenian ores and are mostly believed to originate from the volcanogenic massive sulphide (VMS) Alaverdi-Kapan metallogenic provinces such as the deposits at Alaverdi, Shamlug, Akhtala, and Kapan (Fig 5.7). Close to those and overlapping with them are also four samples of an arsenical copper- analysed in this study, particularly a cylindrical item, a ring and two awls (samples MA-153039, MA-153048, MA-153040, MA-153056 respectively), as well as one pure copper object (MA-153038) and one of two analysed brass objects (copper and zinc, MA-153052). Another pure copper object (MA-153050) and a brass one (MA-153045) have

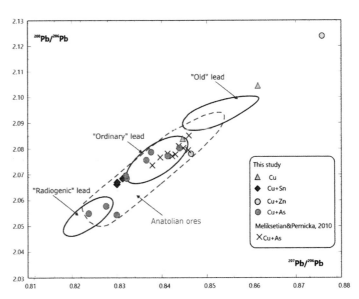

Figure 5d.7 Diagram of the 207Pb/206Pb vs. 208Pb/206Pb ratios in copper-based artifacts (this study and those from Meliksetian and Pernicka, 2010) from Shengavit combined with isotope compositional fields of Armenian ores: 1. "radiogenic" lead group, 2. "ordinary" lead group, 3. "old" lead group (after Meliksetian and Pernicka, 2010). Dotted lines outline lead isotope compositional fields of Anatolian ores after Begemann et al. (1992). Artifacts that belong to different chemical groups and those analyzed earlier are shown by different symbols.

400   Meliksetian and Pernicka 2010.
401   Meliksetian and Pernicka 2010.

high ^{207}Pb/^{206}Pb and ^{208}Pb/^{206}Pb ratios that are unknown in Armenian ore deposits. All three tin-containing objects: two tin bronzes (MA-153043, MA-153049) and a single copper-arsenic-tin alloy (MA-153036) are grouped in the middle part of the Anatolian lead isotope field, close to the "ordinary" lead field of Armenian ores. Close to them are also two copper-arsenic alloys (samples MA-153037 and MA-153051). Considering the provenance of objects consisting of alloys with tin, one should note that in the entire region the rare Early Bronze Age I-II tin-bronzes, particularly in Armenia (Talin EBA I tombs[402]), at Troy,[403] in the Gulf,[404] and in Dagestan[405] exhibit high ^{207}Pb/^{206}Pb and ^{208}Pb/^{206}Pb isotope signatures not typical for Armenia and Anatolian ores that have so far been characterized. This suggests that their origin should be sought somewhere else, possibly from central Asian, Proterozoic or Paleozoic copper deposits. In the case of alloying, lead isotopes inherit the signatures of copper ores, rather than tin ores, because tin ores are very poor in lead. This point of view is in good agreement with the fact that any usable tin deposits that were able to cover the tin needs of the region are unknown in the South Caucasus and eastern Anatolia. However, such unusually high ^{207}Pb/^{206}Pb and ^{208}Pb/^{206}Pb isotope ratios demonstrated by rare Early Bronze Age tin bronzes are not typical for more abundant Middle Bronze Age tin bronzes of Armenia.[406] This suggests that with the extensive use of tin for alloying of copper since the beginning of the Middle Bronze Age, imported and rare tin was smelted with locally produced copper, while in the Early Bronze Age tin bronzes were imported from unknown source, probably as metal ingots for casting or in form of polymetallic ore concentrates (for example, stannite copper and tin ores). Therefore, going back to the three tin containing objects from Shengavit, it is noteworthy that their isotope signatures are typical for local ores. Accordingly, these objects probably belong to the Early Kurgan Period or the late phases of the KA2, when presumably local copper was alloyed with imported tin.

Three objects made of copper-arsenic alloys (MA-153035, MA-153046, MA-153055) exhibit radiogenic lead isotope signatures that are typical for some deposits in northern and central Armenia and in the copper-molybdenum porphyry deposits of the current south of the Republic of Armenia, such as Kadjaran.

Conclusions

Metallurgical production has long been considered as one of the major technological advances of the Kura-Araxes culture. It was based on the use of specific copper-arsenic alloys and a wide range of metals such as copper, gold, silver, as well as the early appearance, although rare, of tin bronze. Shengavit has one of the more extensive and well-studied samples of metals from the Kura-Araxes cultural tradition with the presence of numerous metal artifacts and a long record of metalworking techniques. Most of the metal objects presented in this study are copper-based decorative objects, such as awls, rings, hair decoration, as well as a few weapons like spikes and arrowheads. Excavators also found molds for axes and spikes. One of the decorative objects likely from the Kura-Araxes/ Early Kurgan transition is a unique polished translucent obsidian pendant encapsulated in a foil of a gold-silver alloy that represents one the unique cases when obsidian was used as gemstone. It is not clear if gold was alloyed with silver, or this foil was made of a natural silver-gold alloy called electrum. Electrum is common both in primary epithermal gold deposits, as well as in alluvial places that are particularly abundant in the Masrik River basin in east Armenia.[407]

---

402   Meliksetian and Pernicka 2010.
403   Pernicka et al. 1990.
404   Weeks 1999.
405   Kohl et al. 2002.
406   Meliksetian et al. 2011.
407   Wolf et al. 2013.

Copper alloys analyzed in this study exhibited a wide range of compositions. Most (58%) are copper (Cu)-arsenic (As) alloys, some of other alloy groups are triple alloys of copper-arsenic-tin (Sn) (3.6%), or copper-arsenic-lead (Pb) (3.6%). Two thirds of the artifacts consist of copper alloys with arsenic. Other alloys include Cu+Ni+Zn (zinc) (one artifact), Cu+Pb+Sn (one artifact), Cu+Sn+Zn (one artifact), Cu+Zn (two artifacts). These artifacts with high content of zinc most probably belong to later periods. Thus, the majority of copper-based artifacts recovered from Shengavit, including those analyzed earlier, were made by alloying with arsenic. This was typical for decorative objects from other Kura-Araxes sites in Armenia and in neighboring regions. The presence of artifacts rich in nickel suggests that some objects originated from deposits located within a regional ophiolite belt such as Sotk in Armenia or Ergani Maden, Siirt-Madenköy, and others in southeastern Turkey.[408] Lead isotope analyses of selected objects confirm the conclusion, based on their trace element patterns, that multiple ore sources were used for the metal production at Shengavit. These sources included Armenian VMS Alaverdi, Shamlug, Akhtala or Kapan deposits, copper-molybdenum porphyry deposits such as Kadjaran in Armenia, and sources of copper located within regional ophiolite belts with relatively high contents of nickel.

Some objects turned out to consist of tin bronze, one of them containing 43 percent by weight of tin (Sn). Copper-tin alloys are linked to sources of copper rather than tin reveal that copper in these objects is of local origin, as were objects alloyed with imported tin.

The skill of the Armenian metalsmiths suggest that Kura-Araxes migrants perhaps were accepted by local populations outside the homeland of metallurgy. Sources of metal ores existed in the Zagros and in the Taurus Mountains to which they migrated, but they were welcomed to local societies because of their technical knowledge of metallurgy. Passing on technical skill is usually done face-to-face. It also suggests that although some small percentage of ores used in smelting were exotic to the South Caucasus, most were available in the so-called Lower Province of the Kura-Araxes homeland, mostly Armenia and a small section of far northwest Iran and northeastern Turkey.[409] This area was a kind of local interaction network, distinct from the Upper Province, whose midpoint was the Kura River, and from the Kura-Araxes diaspora.

References

Abesadze, C. 1969 *Metal production in Transcaucasia in III Mil. BC*. Tbilisi. (in Russian).

Akinci, Ö. T. 2009 Ophiolite-hosted Copper and Gold Deposits of Southeastern Turkey: Formation and Relationship with Seafloor Hydrothermal Processes. *Turkish Journal of Earth Sciences* 18: 475–509. doi:10.3906/yer-0803-8.

Badalyan, R., Smith, A.T., Lindsay I., Harutyunyan A., Greene A., Marshall M., Monahan, B., Hovsepyan, R., Meliksetian, Kh., Pernicka, E., Haroutunian, S. 2016 A Preliminary Report on the 2008, 2010, and 2011 Investigations of Project ArAGATS on the Tsaghkahovit Plain, Republic of Armenia. *Archäologische Mitteilungen aus Iran und Turan* 46: 123–222.

Badalyan, R., Hovsepyan, S., Khachatryan, L. 2015 *Shengavit. Catalogue of archaeological materials from the collections of the History Museum of Armenia. Yerevan*. History Museum of Armenia. (in Russian).

Batiuk, S., Rothman, M. S, Samei, S., Hovsepyan, R. 2022 Unraveling the Kura-Araxes Cultural Tradition across Space and Time. *Ancient Near Eastern Studies* 59: 235-325.

Begemann, F., Schmitt-Strecker, S., and Pernicka, E. 1992 The metal finds from Thermi III-V: a chemical and lead isotope study. *Studia Troica* 2: 219-39.

Bobokhyan, A., Meliksetian, K., Gasparyan, B., Avetisyan, P., Chataigner, C., and Pernicka, E. 2014. Transition to Extractive Metallurgy and Social Transformation in Armenia at the End of the Stone Age. in *Stone Age of Armenia*, edited by B. Gasparyan and M. Arimura. 283-314. Kanazawa Japan: Center for Cultural Resources, Kanazawa University.

Chernykh, E. 1966 *The history of oldest metallurgy of Eastern Europe*. Moscow: Nauka. (in Russian).

Chernykh, E. 1992. *Ancient Mining and Metallurgy in the USSR. The Early Metal Age*. Cambridge: Cambridge University Press.

Chubinishvili, T.N. 1971 *Toward the ancient history of Southern Caucasia*. Tbilisi: Metsniereba. (in Russian).

---

408   Akinci 2009.
409   Batiuk et al. 2022.

Courcier, A. 2014 Ancient Metallurgy in the Caucasus From the Sixth to the Third Millennium BC. in *Archaeometallurgy in Global Perspective*, edited by B. Roberts and C. Thornton. 579–664. New York, NY: Springer.

Gadzhiev, M. G., Kohl, P. L., Magomedov, W. R. G., Stronach, D., Gadzhiev, B., and Gadzhiev S. M. 2000 Dagestan-American Archaeological Investigations in Dagestan Russia, 1997–1999. *Eurasia Antiqua* 6: 47–121.

Gale, N.H. and Stos-Gale, Z.A. 1982. Bronze Age copper sources in the Mediterranean. *Science* 216: 11-19.

Gevorgyan, A.C. 1980 *A History of Ancient Metallurgy of Armenian Highland*. Yerevan. (in Russian)

Giumlia-Mair, A. 2008 The metal of the moon goddess. *Surface Engineering* 24(2): 110-117.

Khanzadjan, E. V. 1975 Jrahovit site. *Archaeological Studies of 1974*: 475–478. (in Russian).

Kohl, P. 2002 Bronze production and utilization in south-eastern Dagestan, Russia: c 3600-1900BC., L. Weeks, Appendix: Summary of Velikent compositional and lead isotope analyses. in *The Beginnings of Metallurgy in the Old World*, edited by M. Bartelheim, E. Pernicka and R. Krause, 161-183. Freiberg: TU Bergakademie.

Lechtman, H. 1996 Arsenic bronze: dirty copper or chosen alloy? A view from the Americas. *Journal of Field Archaeology* 23: 477- 513.

Lutz, J. and Pernicka, E. 1996 Energy Dispersive X-Ray Fluorescence Analysis of Ancient Copper Alloys: Empirical Values for Precision and Accuracy. *Archaeometry* 38(2): 313-323.

Meliksetian, Kh., Pernicka, E. 2010 Geochemical characterisation of Armenian Early Bronze Age metal artifacts and their relation to copper ores. in *Von Majkop bis Trialeti. Gewinnung und Verbreitung von Metallen und Obsidian in Kaukasien im 4. - 2. Jt.*, edited by S. Hansen, A. Hauptmann, I. Motzenbacker, E. Pernicka, 41-58. Bonn: Rudolf Habelt Gmbh.

Meliksetian, Kh., Pernicka, E., Badalyan, R. 2007 Compositions and some considerations on the provenance of Armenian Early Bronze Age copper artifacts. *Proceedings, Selected papers, Second International Conference Archaeometallurgy in Europe 2007, June 17-21*, 125-134. Italy: Aquiliea.

Meliksetian, Kh., Krauss, S., Pernicka, E., Avetissyan, P., Devejian, S., Petrosyan, L. 2011a Metallurgy of Prehistoric Armenia, Anatolian Metal V. *Der Anschnitt* 24: 201-210.

Meliksetian, Kh., Schwab, R. Kraus, S. Pernicka, E., Brauns, M. 2011b Chemical, lead isotope and metallographic analysis of extraordinary arsenic-rich alloys used for jewelry. in Bronze Age Armenia. *Metalla. Proceedings, International conference Archaeomtelalurgy in Europe III*, 211-212. Germany: Bochum.

Meliksetian, K., Pernicka, E., Badalyan, R. and Avetisyan, P. 2003 Geochemical Characterisation of Early Bronze Age Metal Artifacts and their Relation to Copper Ores. in *Proceedings International conference Archaeometallurgy in Europe*. 24-26 September 2003, Vol. I: 597-606. Milan, Italy: Associazione Italiana di Metallurgia.

Niederschlag, E., Pernicka, E., Seifert, Th., Bartelheim, M. 2003 Determination of Lead Isotope Ratios by Multiple Collector ICP-MS: A Case Study of Early Bronze Age Artefacts and their possible relation with ore deposits of the Erzgebirge. *Archaeometry* 45: 61-100.

Nørgaard, H.W., Pernicka, E., Vandkilde, H. 2019 On the trail of Scandinavia's early metallurgy: Provenance, transfer and mixing. *PLoS ONE* 14(7): e0219574. https://doi.org/10.1371/journal.pone.0219574

Northover, P. 1989 Properties and use of arsenic-copper alloys, in *Archäometallurgie der Alten Welt / Old world archaeometallurgy*, edited by A. Hauptmann, E. Pernicka and G.A. Wagner. *Der Anschnitt* 7: 111-118.

Pernicka, E., Begemann, F., Schmitt-Strecker, S. Grimanis, A.P. 1990 On the composition and provenance of metal objects from Poliochni and Lemnos. *Oxford Journal of Archaeology* 9(3): 263-298.

Pernicka, E., Begemann, F., Schmitt-Strecker, S.G. Wagner, A. 1993 Eneolithic and Early Bronze Age copper artifacts from Balkans and their relation to Serbian copper ores. *Praehistorische Zeitschrift* 68: 1-54.

Peterson, D. L. 2003 Ancient Metallurgy in the Mountain Kingdom: The Technology and Value of Early Bronze Age Metalwork from Velikent, Daghestan. in *Archaeology in the Borderlands: Investigations in Caucasia and Beyond*, edited by A. T. Smith and K. Rubinson, 22–37. Los Angeles: Cotsen Institute of Archaeology.

Renfrew, C. 1986 Varna and the emergence of Wealth in Prehistoric Europe. in *The Social Life of Things*, edited by A. Appaduri, 141-168. Cambridge: Cambridge University Press.

Selimkhanov, I. 1960 *Historical-Chemical and Analytic Research of Ancient Objects made of Copper Alloys*. Baku: Publications of the Academy of Sciences of Azerbaijan SSR. (in Russian).

Stos-Gale, Z.A., Gale, N. H., Gilmore G.R. 1984 Early Bronze Age Trojan metal sources and Anatolians in the Cyclades. *Oxford Journal of Archaeology* 11(2): 155-77.

Tedesco, L.A. 2006 Refining the definition of technology in the southern zone of the Circumpontic Metallurgical Province: copper alloy in Armenia during the early and middle Bronze Age. in *Beyond the Steppe and the sown: Proceedings of the 2002 University of Chicago Conference on Eurasian Archaeology*, edited by D.L. Peterson, L.M. Popova, and A.T. Smith, 310-321. Leiden: Brill.

Weeks, L. 1999 United Arab Emirates: new data regarding the 'tin problem' in Western Asia. *Antiquity* 73: 49-64.

Wolf, D., Borg, G., Meliksetian, Kh., Allenberg, A., Pernicka, E., Hovanissyan, A., Kunze R. 2013 Neue Quellen für altes Gold? in *Archäologie in Armenien II Veröffentlichungen des Landesamtes für Denkmalpflege und Archäologie Sachsen-Anhalt-Landesmuseum für Vorgeschichte*, edited by H. Meller and P. Avetisyan. Band 67. 27-44. Halle: Verlag Beier and Beran.

5e | Pottery

Mitchell Rothman

Introduction

Pottery, as described in the Chapter 1, has been a focus of Kura-Araxes research from its beginning. Certainly, its style is distinct from the pottery traditions of surrounding cultures, and in the migrant diaspora it is the clearest marker of those who associate themselves with the Kura-Araxes cultural tradition (Fig 5e.1).

In this chapter we concentrate on the pottery of the KA2 in the Lower Province, (the area associated with the Araxes River and its tributaries in the South Caucasian homeland); that is, the pottery of Shengavit. However, for the Kura-Araxes as a whole, one of the most salient cultural changes that marked the transition from the KA1 to KA2 was in the style and complexity of the pottery corpus.[410] As Burney[411] noted over a half century ago, the pottery of the KA1 is very homogeneous. There are only a few shapes. Most are mottled pink-brown or gray-brown with a thick paste.[412] The earliest burnished, black- brown mottled wares appeared in this phase. The shapes include round-sided bowls, carinated-jars with rounded handles, jars with collar rims, and rounded jars with tall, slightly flaring rims.[413] Potters added flat lids to this repertoire. They also added a few designs to the surface. These are rare in the KA1 compared to the KA2. Many more shapes and forms were added in the KA2, and these forms varied from region to region. The pottery of the KA2 therefore provides a particularly rich corpus for analysis.

In general, the information that can be gleaned from pottery contains many different clues to the societies in which it was made. One type of evidence relates to identity.[414] Kura-Araxes pottery style encodes this.[415] Style is that factor that potters add after the

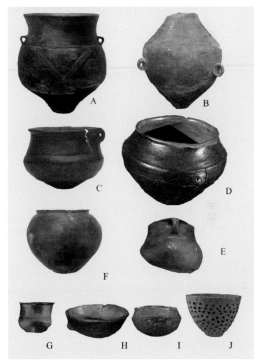

Figure 5e.1 Varieties of Shengavit Kura-Araxes pottery: A. intermediate vessel with inscribed design, B. Closed storage vessel from under K6 Building 3 floor, C. intermediate vessel, D. large intermediate storage vessel, E. small intermediate eating/ serving pot, F. Cooking pot, G. small intermediate eating pot, H. open vessel, I. intermediate eating pot, J. open vessel, strainer.

---

410   Batiuk et al. 2022 Fig. 2; Badalyan 2014; Smith 2015.
411   Burney 1958.
412   Sagona 2018, 253-256.
413   Sagona 2018, Fig. 5-9; for Armenia, see Badalyan 2014.
414   Rothman 2014.
415   Abramov et al. 2006.

requirements of function and manufacturing technology are accounted for. It reflects how members of one cultural group perceive the normal and desirable in pottery. They include the design, surface treatment, elements of rim or body shape, and color, among other factors. Of these surface design may be the most telling in terms of identity. The range of style can be regional or in some cases very local. In part this depends where the pottery is made. The more local the production the more likely that greater regional variation exists. The less interaction communities have, the more probable that their pottery styles will be different.[416]

Pottery style changes over time and place. As such, time is another factor pottery encodes. It can aid modern researchers in constructing a relative chronology.

Identity is also represented in the *châine opératoire* or the process of manufacture.[417] Potters teach the next generation the traditions of manufacture of their culture. Post-processualists (practice theorists) refer to this as "communities of practice." The skills or proclivities of potters are honed during their training in one or another tradition. The physical movements that a potter uses are programmed into them at an early stage of learning to make pottery. In addition to the more general characteristics, potters teach the next generation the symbols of their groups, reflected in the language of pottery style. In a society with professional potters, this may reflect the fashion of their place and time.

The *châine opératoire* reflects not only cultural traditions of pottery-making, but also its technology. How are the clays collected and prepared for pottery, how are they shaped—be it by hand, slow or fast wheel—, how are they finished and decorated, and how and where are they fired? Rarely is pottery-making the enterprise of a single individual.[418] Was pottery made by domestic units? Those units could be individual households or more likely small sets of kin or neighbors. Was it made by pottery specialists? Were those specialists independent and serving a narrow customer base, or were they specialists mass-producing pottery? The economic organization of a society is reflected in the answers to these questions.

The organization of pottery distribution further reflects the social and potentially political structures of ancient societies. How was distribution handled? Was distribution person-to-person gifting or exchange within the community, was it done in market places where makers exchanged their wares for other goods or favors? Did middlemen acquire and distribute their wares to consumers? The last system represents commodities trade.[419] Each variation implies a different overall societal organization. Were there high-level controls over the distribution and production? In fact, all these factors are critical in painting a multi-dimensional picture of the societies of the ancient world.

Another factor, often ignored or too little discussed, is pottery function. This element indicates a range of diet, food preparation, and serving traditions.[420] Modern studies have proposed that food preferences, including ways of preparing dishes, are one of the longest-lasting cultural traditions among migrant populations. Because good relative chronology compares changes within each functional category separately, studies that ignore function[421] reduce the accuracy of schemes for dating. Further, they limit the ability of the researcher to discover the choices made by potters. At the same time, we must be aware of the nature of potters' work. Imposing a multivariable model of difference without understanding how potters actually conducted their craft often produces an elegant but inaccurate

---

416   Rothman 2014; Deetz 1965; Sackett 1977.
417   Iserlis et al. 2010; Batiuk et al. 2022.
418   Crown 2007.
419   Rothman 2000.
420   Wilkinson 2014.
421   Palumbi 2008.

picture that reflects the analyst's viewpoint over that of the ancient potter.

Much of what follows are analyses and photographs of 1430 potsherds measured in detail by M. Rothman, with help from A. Hayrapetyan and N. Manoukian, counts of non-diagnostic sherds by Rothman and the staff of Simonyan's laboratory in Yerevan, drawings of pottery from Simonyan's 2000-2008 excavations, and observations from publication of Shengavit pots at the National History Museum of Armenia.[422] A major help in the discussion of the process of production and residue analysis is the petrographic work of Nyree Manoukian[423] and Stephen Batiuk.[424] The detailed matrix of variables for the 1430 potsherds, as well as drawings and photographs of pots are available at the Shengavit web archive site.

KA2 Process of Production

As discussed above, the process of production can give us clues to the traditions (communities of practice) and technology of pottery making at Shengavit, as well as to the economic, social, and political relationships in a society. Iserlis, cited above, has shown that there were some basic traditions in preparation of the paste of pottery through choice of clay sources, tempering, and firing across the Kura-Araxes landscape.

Probably as critical, however, for the study of the KA2 homeland is whether there was specialization in the production process. Domestic production will produce more variation in the various steps of production than centralized workshops, whether run by part- or full-time potters.[425] The best measurement to determine specialization is standardization. Specialized production will tend to be more standardized, since the efficiency of producing larger quantities is critical for success. Specialization can be measured in (a) the preparation of the clay body involving the choice of sources, including tempering, (b) the means of forming the vessel, (c) treatment of the interior and exterior surfaces: designs, color, and various surface treatments from burnishing to engraving or otherwise producing designs, (d) firing the pot, and (e) the regularity of the same form, including similarity in features such as rim shape and measurements such as the thickness of the clay body, circumference, etc. Simonyan sees potters as specialized ("professional") potters, because the technical sophistication of the pottery increased from the KA1 to the KA2.[426] In this conclusion Rothman believes Simonyan fails to note two important factors. First, potters in kinship societies like the Mesopotamian Halaf have produced some of the most beautifully made and decorated pots known. They clearly had no professional potters. Second, the existence of a class of workshop potters is commonly associated with a societal complexity unlikely to have existed at Shengavit or anywhere else in the Kura-Araxes landscape (see Chapter 1). Van der Leeuw sees a variety of organizations from household production for their own use to "household industry" to "village industry" to "large-scale industry."[427] How the potters' production process is organized first depends on who will consume the pots made. If it is just for the use of the makers, standardization is unlikely. If it is for the use of the wider community, some specialization and some elements of workshop production are possible. In large-scale industry the consumers are widespread and the mechanisms for distribution are critical. This last is very likely to be very standardized and "professional." Such a system also permits the control (or interference) by centralized leadership. Most analysts agree that Kura-Araxes pottery is locally made, and therefore is for the use of

---

422   Badalyan et al. 2015.
423   Manoukian 2015.
424   Batiuk 2005.
425   Roux 2003.
426   Simonyan 2002.
427   Van der Leeuw 1977.

its makers or the community.[428] Ethnographically, village potters in rural Rajasthan constitute village industries.[429] They are not full-time specialists, but they have separate physical workshops. They are also part of a network of shops and transport specialists who sell their goods for money. Pots become commodities, which is defined as there being a step between the maker and the consumer who profits off the sale of that commodity.[430] Nothing in the Kura-Araxes appears to follow such a pattern, and all the materials analysis points to household production, as the reader will learn about below.

CLAY SOURCING AND PREPARATION

The clays that were used for Kura-Araxes pottery making in this area are often the clayey soils on sites, as is the case with Tsaghkasar.[431] Two geological zones intersect at the Yerevan basin where Shengavit is located: (1) those from sandstone, shale, and conglomerates worn by water, such as the Hrazdan suite of reddish clays, sandstones, alevrites, and conglomerates, and (2) lake or river deposited pebbly sands, clays, glacifluvial, slope and flood block-pebbles and breccia formations (broken-angular rocks at the edges of alluvial deposits).[432] At Shengavit the soil is clayey, and it would make a good matrix for the pottery found. As the geological descriptions imply, the deposits by the Hrazdan River are also clayey and pre-mixed with ground sands and other grit or pebbles. Fine calcite was one of the fine particles in the matrix already in the raw clay.[433]

To make these clayey soils ready for use, they need to be cleaned, possibly by dissolving them in water (levigation), and then kneading them. Some traditional potters screen the clay before kneading, but the irregularity of many of the Kura-Araxes clay bodies suggest that Shengavit potters did not. The levigation of clays for pottery at KA1 sites was often incomplete, showing a lack of regular production standards.[434] This was the case with KA2 pottery in Armenia, at Sos Höyük near Erzurum,[435] and at Godin Tepe.[436] At Gegharot, 75 km from Shengavit in the higher elevation on the border of the Tsaghkahovit Plain and the Pambak Range, its fabric seems so similar that it could have all come from the same source. The fabric of the pots was also the same there whatever the vessels' function.[437] The same was the case in the Amuq region of the Levant.[438] At Bet Yerah in the Southern Levant diaspora the Kura-Araxes potters used clays from a variety of sources for pots of different functions.[439] At Shengavit the same pattern appears likely. However, we were not able to test the actual sources, so we do not know their chemical characteristics.

Part of the manipulating of clays is achieved by tempering, which means adding in other materials to give the clay particular characteristics. These are the materials that constitute the skeleton of the pot. They "correct stickiness, increase porosity, reduce shrinkage, reduce deformation in drying, and improve firing characteristics."[440] They also help create the characteristics needed for pots of different function. For the purposes of investigation, we divided

428   Hayrapetyan 2008; Sagona 2018, 1984; I. Hovsepyan and Mnatsakanyan 2011; Manoukian 2015.
429   Kramer 1997.
430   Rothman 2000.
431   Iserlis et al. 2015.
432   Geological Society in London UK map.
433   Manoukian 2015, 42.
434   I. Hovsepyan and Mnatsakanyan 2011.
435   Kibaroğlu et al. 2011; Kibaroğlu 2015, 223.
436   Rothman 2011.
437   Hayrapetyan 2008.
438   Batiuk 2005.
439   Iserlis 2009.
440   Rice 1987, 74.

Shengavit pots into three groups: fine wares, cooking pot wares, and utilitarian wares. They were readily identified macroscopically based on the size of pots, thickness of the clay body, fineness, elements of tempering used, the treatment of the surfaces, and the stylistic elements that related to these functional categories (see below).

Across the Kura-Araxes landscape, cooking pot wares (Fig. 5e.1, F, Fig 5e.2) were often distinguishable by their tempering or clay source (Fig 5e.3). At Shengavit cooking wares are quite obvious macroscopically. The paste is brittle, there are signs of burning, and larger, dense white chunks of temper dominate. Other tempers in smaller amounts included grog (crushed pottery),[441] obsidian,[442] ground grit (basalt, sand), tufa, mica, and volcanic ash. In her petrography study, Manoukian identified the white chunks microscopically as second-generation grog with "quartz, biotite mica, plagioclase feldspar, pyroxenes, and micaceous inclusions."[443] We identified them macroscopically as quartz or calcite in the database. Volcanic ash was added to many of the fabrics. These larger tempering pieces are "weakly aligned and randomly oriented."[444] To Manoukian, this indicates a lack of standardization typical of workshop-produced ceramics.

Fine wares (Fig. 5e.1, E, G, and I; Fig 5e.4) we defined based on the thinness of their fabric and the predominantly fine grit, sometimes with calcite, obsidian, and smaller bits of grog. Fine wares also tended to be smaller vessels, although not exclusively. Manoukian analyzed these wares as having "silt-sized fine-grained quartz, weathered feldspars and pyroxene-olivine-rich basaltic inclusions" (Fig 5e.5).[445] She notes that "the clay matrix is relatively homogeneous, and inclusions are well-to moderately-sorted." If any of the classes would require a potter with more experience—this does not necessarily mean a formal workshop— it would be the fine wares.

The third category of utility wares is somewhat broad. In many ways it is defined in the negative: vessels that are neither fine nor cooking wares. On the other hand, utility wares clearly are different based on the size, thickness, and tempering of vessels, as well as their probable function. It was our belief that larger, utilitarian vessels would require different tempering to hold the vessel together and prevent cracking. Among the functional categories included are larger (mixing?) bowls,

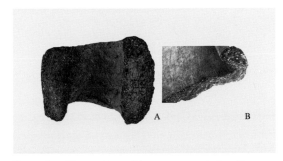

Figure 5e.2 Temper in cooking pot ware: A. handle of cooking pot, B. temper of late Shengavit greenish collared cooking pot.

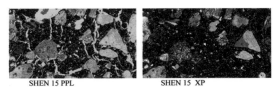

Figure 5e.3 Photomicrographs of interior of Shengavit Fabric Group 15, cooking pot wares.

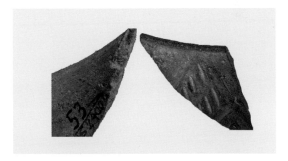

Figure 5e.4 Fine ware temper.

Figure 5e.5 Photomicrographs of interior of Shengavit Fabric Group 12, fine ware pots.

---

441   Mason and Cooper 1993.
442   Palumbi et al. 2014.
443   Manoukian 2015, 41.
444   Manoukian 2015, 52.
445   Manoukian 2015, 46.

closed pots (jars), storage pots (*karas*), larger serving vessels, and those with special functions like strainers (see below) (in Fig. 5e.1, A, B, C, D, H, J).

Figure 5e.6 Temper in utility wares.

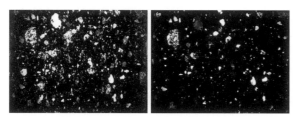

Figure 5e.7 Photomicrographs of interior of Shengavit Fabric Group 22, utility pot wares.

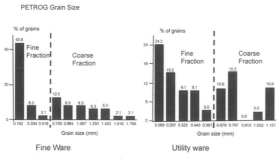

Figure 5e.8 Grain size of two classes of pottery.

Figure 5e.9 Slab construction.

Unlike the cooking pot ware, the temper of this class macroscopically has small pieces and few if any of the larger quartz or calcite chunks (Fig 5e.6). Macroscopically, we saw the temper as dominated by small to medium sized basalt grit. Mixed into it are small pieces of grog, calcite, and obsidian. Manoukian's microscopic/petrographic analysis found pumice and rhyolite tufa with shapes that are rounded or angular (Fig 5e.7).[446] We defined them in the database macroscopically as basalt.

So, the basic clay sources of the Shengavit ceramic repertoire is very similar. The base appears to be clayey soils from the site or perhaps, material from the bank of the Hrazdan and the nearby bluffs. The skeleton, consisting of the tempering, is what differs most. What we classified as cooking, fine, and utility wares have many of the same tempering materials, but they have differing proportions, and differing sizes (Fig. 5e 8).[447] The quartz or calcite, or secondary grog containing those elements in profusion, were used for cooking pots. Fine wares had the smallest, most consistently distributed tempers. Pumice was a common tempering element. Utility wares had small and medium basalt as the dominant tempering element.

What does this practice say about process of production and those who did the production? "Changes effected in later Kura-Araxes industries, such as at Karnut, seem to include a gradual decrease in raw material variability—i.e., more consistent acquisition of preferred raw materials, usually off-site—and clear improvements in technique (e.g., thinner slips, high degree of control over firing). These can be interpreted as signaling the emergence of more specialized workshops [...]. It is tempting to suggest that the early, 'slow' phase of production that utilized ready-to-hand materials would have been largely the province of household potters [...], whereas the introduction of specialization could have been a response to more sophisticated demands."[448] The

---

446   Manoukian 2015, 56-57.
447   Manoukian 2015, 66.
448   Iserlis et al. 2015, 21.

period at Karnut they are describing is the same period, KA2, as was Shengavit. The 'slow' period (Aparan III) was KA1. Certainly, the KA2 is a more complex society than KA1 (see Chapter 1). However, as we discussed above, positive evidence for specialized, workshop production is lacking. A number of analysts from Sos Höyük, nearby Gegharot, cited above, and other KA2 sites still describe the pottery as purely local and household-produced. The Tsaghkasar petrographic study also indicates, as other studies do, that the same fabric was used for all functions. This confirms the idea that "ceramics in sedentary, non-industrial societies were made at or close to the exploited sources of raw materials."[449] The "presence of plastic inclusions in the clay matrix, such as clay pellets, indicates poor clay mixing."[450] In addition to many of the minerals present already in the clay, potters at Shengavit added a variety of tempering materials. These appear to correlate generally to three classes of pots: fine, cooking, and utility. Still, based on tempering alone, we cannot conclude that the potters were specialized. We will look at other aspects of the production process below to see if they indicate true specialization, even within the limits of Shengavit society.

Forming the Vessels

Once the appropriate fabric was created, the next step is to form the pots. The forming starts with either a single lump of clay or builds the form through adding pieces.[451] The six possible ways to go from these initial forms are pinching, slab modeling, molding, casting, coiling, and throwing.

Throwing with a potter's wheel is definitely not a technique used in the Kura-Araxes world. For producing large numbers of standardized vessels throwing would have been the most efficient. In the diaspora Kura-Araxes populations certainly lived among potters who used this technique,[452] as did some Chalcolithic potters at Leilatepe and Boyuk Kesik.[453] Nonetheless, Kura-Araxes potters did not adopt it, perhaps until the very end of its time, and then to a small degree.[454] As they did everywhere, they maintained the same conservative traditions.

The primary technique used among Kura-Araxes potters, certainly at Shengavit, was slab construction. In this technique the potter takes a lump of clay and flattens it by rolling. This is then formed into the final shape. Most often at Shengavit smaller slabs were joined. The end of one of the slabs was pinched into a tongue. One slab is then added onto the next slab. Each is folded into the previous tongue, as illustrated in Figure 5e.9. In this method, sometimes called morsel building,[455] the interior and exterior are smoothed with a stone (Fig 5e.10) or with a kind of paddle and anvil technique (see Chapter 5f.). Badalyan observed this in large storage jars (*karas*) at Gegharot and other sites.[456] Potters built the body, and then using the same slab technique built the neck and rim separately. These two parts were then glued together with bitumen.[457]

Another technique that potters at Shengavit used less frequently

Figure 5e.10 Smoothing interior.

---

449   Manoukian 2015, 83.
450   Manoukian 2015, 83.
451   Rice 2015, 124.
452   Iserlis 2009.
453   Sagona 2014
454   Hayrapetyan 2008.
455   Rice 2015, 125.
456   Badalyan et al. 2014.
457   Badalyan et al. 2014, footnote 16.

was coiling. In this technique clay is rolled into a long coil. That coil is placed on top of the previous coil and the then smoothed in. This coiling technique is mostly used in larger utility vessels during the Kura-Araxes in the homeland, but not frequently even then. Potters used coiling more frequently in the Southern Levant Khirbet Kerak variant of the Kura-Araxes cultural tradition.

Heinsch and Vandiver[458] analyzed a series of pots from Serkertepe near Baku and Velikent using xeroradiography. They found some evidence of woven material, which they suggest was used for molding. Elements of the cultural tradition existed in the area like the high burnishing and a few storage jar shapes. However, the Velikent pottery had chaff tempering, which is unusual in Kura-Araxes pottery. Some are wheel turned, their tempering is different, and many are fired in kilns, all unlike the Kura-Araxes traditions. A recent analysis suggests that these sites are not really a Kura-Araxes cultural tradition, but "Kura-Araxes related."[459] In addition to this probably inapposite comparison, the fabric has to be well levigated and elastic enough to be smoothed evenly over the form for molding, often another pot of the intended product. Little evidence of this kind of forming for whole pots is present at Shengavit, macro- or microscopically. Also, the carinated and angular forms common at Shengavit would not be the most practical shapes for molding.

Treatment of the Interior and Exterior

Kura-Araxes pottery is famous for the treatment of the exterior and interior surfaces. One kind of that treatment of KA2 pottery corpus is burnishing.[460] Burnishing is common for the vast majority of Shengavit pottery of all types. Some of the burnishing gives pots a very bright burnish (Fig. 5e.1., C, D, E, G); others are less bright. Burnishing is accomplished by rubbing a smooth surfaced object like a stone or a potsherd ground into a rounded disk vigorously over the surface. Burnishing compresses and re-orients elements of the surface of the pot. Most of the time analysts speak of burnishing as a stylistic design element. While it might be that, Wallace points out that burnishing strengthens the surface of the pot, which shrinks and cracks less than the bulky interior during firing.[461] Potters might have used burnishing as a design technique or equally for its practical benefits.

Many of the fabrics of Shengavit pottery are very rough. Burnishing requires a surface that can be smoothed. For Shengavit, this most often means applying a slip (see Fig. 5e.11.), a wet clay solution poured over the surface of the vessel and dried before firing. Hayrpetyan felt that some of the finer wares were wet smoothed, rather than slipped. This is possible, but most often potters used slips. Slips, especially burnished ones, have a second practical advantage in reducing the permeability (water-proofing) of a pot's surface. Interiors of serving and storage pots are virtually all slipped probably for that reason.

This thinned clay slip can be applied at a number of stages in the production process. Iserlis proposes that Khirbet Kerak (Kura-Araxes diaspora) potters in the Southern Levant first

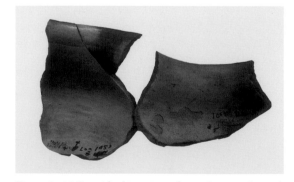

Figure 5e.11 Burnished interiors of pots showing slip and burnishing.

---

458   Heinsch and Vandiver 2006.
459   Batiuk et al 2022.
460   Ionescu and Hoeck 2020.
461   Wallace 1989.

did a bisque firing before the slips were added.[462] A second firing would be necessary to finish the pot. It is equally possible that the slip was applied when the pot's shape was formed and permitted to dry leather hard. Another element commonly painted onto the surface when pots are leather hard is graphite (Fig 5e.12).[463] Tests have shown that the graphite would not adhere to an already fired fabric, so it must have been done when the pot was leather hard, unless it was bisque fired wet with a weak acid like vinegar.

Slips are also part of the Shengavit potters' procedure for adding design to the pot. They added a thick layer of slip and removed enough material to leave a raised design (Fig 5e.1, E; Fig 5e.13). An alternate method in the diaspora was to add a thick slip and hollow out wide lines to make the design. Then potters filled the design with white lime.[464] This decoration was common east of Lake Urmia in pottery style group known as Yanik Ware in the

diaspora, but it was a very rare part of the Shengavit tradition. The third way, the most common, is to incise a design with pointed lithic tools, called gravers (see Fig. 5e.1, A, Chapter 5c.). Since the lines appear to be covered over, this probably was done in the leather hard stage as well. In one case, a pot from square M5 at the end of the Kura-Araxes had combed design with high burnish under the rim (Fig 5e.14). This is a common form in the post-Kura-Araxes Bedeni tradition. One pot, also from the very end of the Kura-Araxes in Square K6 locus 1005, had painted line design. The use of painted designs is evident at Norşuntepe[465] in the Taurus diaspora and at Kvatskhelebi phase B in the Upper (Kura River) Province of the homeland,[466] both from very late in the Kura-Araxes or early in the Early Kurgan Period.

Potters did not put any decoration on the majority of pots they made. Of the 1430 sherds we analyzed, 267 had incised or raised decoration. Potters decorated only five pots classified as cooking pot ware. The percentage of pots with designs is higher in the Shengavit collections at the National History and the Erebuni Museums. As a guard who had worked with Sardarian at the small Shengavit Museum on site told us, Sardarian only saved the prettiest or largest sherds. Our sample is probably more like the actual corpus of pots used by the ancient population of Shengavit. This highlights a general problem with most pottery reported for the Kura-Araxes. These reports are based on a purely typological sample that represents a minority of the total pottery excavated.

Figure 5e.12 Graphite finish.

Figure 5e.13 Thick slip for making a design.

Figure 5e.14 Combed Bedeni ware.

462   Iserlis 2009.
463   Martino 2017.
464   Rothman 2011.
465   Hauptmann 1982, Plate 50.
466   Sagona 1984, 39.

FIRING

As mentioned above, analysts believe the colors of the exterior and interior surfaces was a focus of ancient potters. These colors were created by the chemical characteristics of the clay and, more importantly, the firing. The chemical characteristics of different clay slabs tested from Gegharot appear to be different, even though there only appears to have been one source of clay for potting.[467] The potters therefore created fabrics with different percentages of iron oxide chemical constituencies and other elements, which tend to fire red or alternatively, gray to brown.

At the same time, pots at Shengavit exhibited a wide variety of shades of color. Mottling of colors on one surface was common. We took this to mean that potters did not have precise control over the firing process. So, we believe, as mentioned above, coding every possible color variation of every potsherd would not reflect the decisions of the potters. We therefore choose basic colors according to Table 5e.1 of color names and their Munsell numbers.[468]

Analysts take special note of pots with black exterior and red interior.[469] At Gegharot 40% of the KA2 pots were black and red.[470] However, although the majority of vessels (930 out of 1430) potsherds from Shengavit we analyzed had black exteriors, only 128 have red, light red, or red-brown internal colors. Still, there must have been some feeling that the colors were important, because, especially in large vessels whose firing is difficult to control, potters at times painted the inside red with some kind of ferric oxide paint. Potters used this same technique even for fine wares in the Taurus diaspora.[471] The numbers and percentages of different exterior and interior colors is summarized in Table 5e.2.

The distribution of these patterns of internal colors with different exterior colors is summarized in Table 5e.3. The black surface most often is paired with brown, gray, red, or buff interiors. Most pots with gray, brown, red, and yellow exteriors have the same color interior. Presumably, the black exterior was originally made of the same color clay as the internal color.

There was a conscious effort to produce a black exterior.

The question is, how did potters produce what was clearly their favorite black color? They must have accomplished this in the firing and the treatment during the firing process.

Generic color	Munsell color	Generic color	Munsell color
black	N3	red	7.5R 4/8
gray	7.5YR 6/1	light red	7.5R 7/6
gray black	7.5YR 4/1	yellow buff	2.5Y 8/4
brown	7.5YR 4/4	green gray	10YR 6/1
red brown	2.5YR 5/8	dark buff	2.5YR 6/2
buff	10YR 8/2	yellow red	7.5R 8.4
yellow	10 YR 10/4		

Table 5e.1. Munsell designations of Kura-Araxes pottery colors at Shengavit

Color*	Exterior	Percent	Interior	Percent
black	930	67.00	106	7.70
brown	117	9.00	236	17.20
buff	51	3.70	254	18.50
gray	66	4.70	234	16.80
dark buff	6	0.04	34	2.50
gray black	35	2.50	90	6.60
green gray	11	0.08	51	3.70
light red	21	0.02	49	1.40
red	39	2.80	108	7.90
red brown	59	4.20	99	7.20
yellow	28	2.00	55	4.00
yellow buff	23	1.60	40	3.00
yellow red	2	0.0014	13	0.09
Total	1388		1369	

*Some colors not identifiable because of thick patina or burned surface

Table 5e.2. Number and percent of colors on the exterior and interior.

467   Hayrapetyan 2008.
468   Globe Soil Color Book 2012.
469   Palumbi 2008.
470   Hayrapetyan 2008.
471   Rothman 2014.

Interior*						Exterior							
	black	brown	buff	dark buff	gray	gray black	green gray	light red	red	red brown	yellow	yellow buff	yellow red
black	88	4	3	0	2	1	0	2	3	1	2	1	1
brown	152	42	2	0	10	0	0	0	4	9	2	3	0
buff	154	19	33	0	9	5	0	3	9	7	4	0	0
dark buff	17	4	1	3	3	3	0	1	0	2	0	1	0
gray	187	11	1	0	20	1	0	1	1	2	1	0	0
gray black	74	3	0	0	2	9	0	1	2	1	0	0	0
green gray	37	3	1	0	2	1	0	0	0	0	0	0	0
light red	24	4	4	0	3	1	8	5	3	0	0	0	0
red	128	7	2	0	3	2	1	1	15	0	1	0	0
red brown	70	7	2	0	3	0	0	0	0	0	0	0	0
yellow	23	3	2	0	2	2	0	0	0	0	17	0	0
yellow buff	18	3	1	0	2	0	0	1	2	2	0	11	0
yellow red	4	4	0	0	2	0	0	1	0	0	0	0	1

*38 not possible to tell color because of patina or burning

Table 5e.3. Coordinating exterior with interior colors of Shengavit pots.

All Kura-Araxes pots were fired at relatively low temperature, a maximum of 850°C.[472] Many were fired at temperatures as low as 600°C.[473] This is good for the type of cooking they did, in which they put pots directly on the flame of the hearth. Higher fired ceramics would crack more easily under such conditions. Although excavators found pottery kilns at Velikent, and Simonyan reports an unpublished kiln at Mokhrablur,[474] "In terms of firing temperatures, there is no distinct standardised temperature among ETC [Kura-Araxes] ware for pottery production, supporting the contention that ETC wares were most likely pit-fired."[475] These pits can be small, as is the one shown in Figure 5e.15, or quite large. For the latter, firing can be done in a bonfire, which permits many more pots to be fired at one time. Ethnographers have documented this bon fire technique in many parts of the modern Middle East.[476]

Creating colors seems to follow a regular procedure. All clays have some iron elements in them. Commonly, in clay with 1% iron the clay will turn yellow, with1.5-3% light brown or orange (red brown), and with 3% red.[477] Letting in oxygen gives most clays a red, yellow, or brown color. However, adding a slip changes this formula somewhat, as does the temperature and the organic content of the fabric.[478] Temperatures in the lower part of the range will tend to give a mottled color, as we already observed for Shengavit pottery. One way to get a black surface is through reducing the amount of oxygen in the burn in the final stage of firing. This can be achieved in a pit firing by covering the fire with sand.[479] This sounds very straightforward, but there are many factors involved. If

Figure 5e.15 Pit firing.

472 Manoukian 2015.
473 Hayrapetyan 2008.
474 Simonyan, personal communication.
475 Manoukian 2015, 86.
476 Rice 1987, Fig. 5.17 and 5.18.
477 Rice 1987, 333.
478 Batiuk, personal communication.
479 Iserlis 2009.

there is organic material, the core will burn black and remain so until enough oxygen can permeate the body. The surface color depends on some of the factors mentioned above.

Another possibility is the stages of firing and the treatment of the pot in each stage. Shengavit pots commonly show the color of the interior color on the outside by the rim (Fig 5e.16). A common technique to achieve this could be to remove the pot when it is red hot and dip it into a bath of a greasy substance, one with silicone,[480] grease, or a bath of plants that will color the surface of the pot. This technique is documented ethnographically and archaeologically. To keep the interior separate from the exterior, the pot must have been held on the exterior, leaving some of the exterior the same color as the inside. An alternative way is literally to paint the grease or other substance on the outside, and, in the case of the pot shown in Figure 5e.17, on the rim and top of the interior. Presumably, the pot was then re-fired, making the exterior black, allowing carbon to seep in and react with the clay fabric in a reducing fire. A last possible technique entails the fuel used.[481] Modern potters produce

Figure 5e.16 Color overflow from interior to exterior.

Figure 5e.17 Interior of pot showing the painted- or dribbled- on grease that made the exterior and rim black.

pit-fired black, gun-metal black, and brown using hardwood sawdust and grass-fed cow dung, oranges and yellows using salt, and reds and yellows using ferric chloride. At the moment, we cannot say that one particular method was used exclusively at Shengavit. More likely, individual potting production units used different techniques over time. Still, as we examine the characteristics of individual types, more patterns in the production process emerged.

Characteristics of pots

The sum of evidence so far does not indicate specialization at the village industry level. Most analysts suggest that production of pottery in the homeland occurred at every site. There is little indication of standard practice in choosing clay sources. At Shengavit, we see a difference in the tempering of three classes of pottery: cooking, fine, and utility ware. This indicates some increasing sophistication in production, but that is not the same as standardization. The pottery appears to have been pit-fired at relatively low temperatures, and the frequent mottling gives little impression of the inability of potters to control the temperature of the firing. A number of different techniques appear to have been used to produce the black color, indicating multiple production sites. We do not have direct evidence of a workshop or a kiln at Shengavit, although we clearly cannot say there was not one. Negative evidence in this case is not sufficient to draw a conclusion. The last factor, one related to the nature of the cultural tradition, is the characteristics of production of different types. That will require details of the different pottery types.

---

480   Wallace 1989, 34.
481   Lazlo 2016.

Typology of Shengavit Pottery

Typology can be done in many ways. It depends on the questions being asked, the criteria used, and the order of importance of each criterion. We constructed our typology based on a number of characteristics. Like ground stone (see Chapter 5f.), we believe that the same shapes were used for different functions (see below). Rather than use culturally defined terms like bowls and jars, Simonyan suggested that we use generalized descriptive terms. We, therefore, used as a first criterion whether a vessel was open(i.e., the opening is the widest part, as in bowls), closed (i.e., the opening is narrower than the body, as in jars, especially with storage jars (*karas*)), or intermediate (i.e., the opening is often the same width as the body). This last category includes what we think are eating pots, as well as cooking pots, serving jars, etc. The line between some of the intermediate and open forms is somewhat arbitrary. Sometimes, the difference is in size, although most types occur in many sizes (see below). We began with Sagona's classification for the pot forms he attributed to Shengavit,[482] and then added (and sometimes subtracted) types as we observed actual pots.

Within the open, closed, and intermediate groupings, our description of the types below is very much directed toward four elements. First is the work of ancient potters. What technical choices did they make to create the forms we classified into types? These represent the potters' traditions (*habitus*). Second is whether the characteristics other than color and tempering, discussed above, indicate household production or village industry type of production. Third is whether these types changed over the 400 or so years that Shengavit was occupied. Fourth is what commonalities in style with other local and more distant sites says about the networks of interaction in which Shengavit's residents were involved. A fifth element, function, we will discuss in a section below.

OPEN FORMS

Characteristics of the open types relate to the height, the rims and bases, shape, and features like handles (Fig 5e.18). Type I vessels are variations of the same vessel, open, relatively low with pinched rims, flat bases, and small handles on one side (H4 and H9, Fig 5e.19, see Fig 5e.1, H). Its sides are straight or slightly flaring. Type II vessels are generally the same shape, but the rims are folded. Most pots of Types I and II are black on the outside, but with various colors on the inside. Type III vessels are the same shape, but the pinched rim is in-turned with a ridge on the inside. In these the both the exterior and interior colors vary. Type IV open forms have an 's'-shaped profile. That stylistic feature is a common Kura-Araxes trait, especially In the Karnut-Shengavit group.[483] It occurs in both open and intermediate types as well, as some of the closed types. All have pinched rims, but there is the more variation in this type than

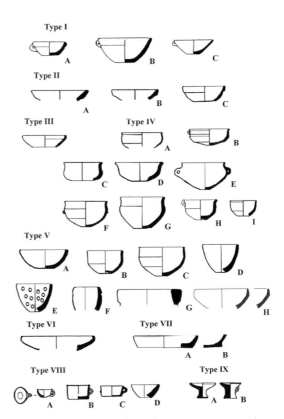

Figure 5e.18 Open vessels in Shengavit pottery typology.

---

482   Sagona 1984.
483   Badalyan 2014.

bases

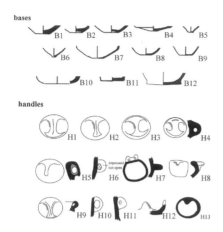

handles

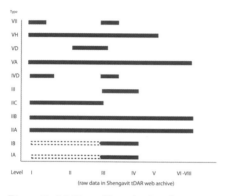

Figure 5e.19 Bases and handle shapes.

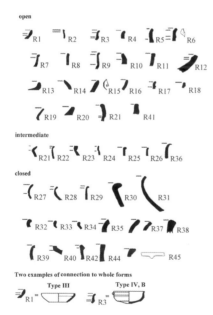

(raw data in Shengavit tDAR web archive)

Figure 5e.20 Open Types by Level.

open

intermediate

closed

Two examples of connection to whole forms

Figure 5e.21 Rims of uncertain types.

any other. Bases go from flat to ones with a raised bump in the middle to pointed ones (see Fig 5e.19). Types IVB and F have small, rounded handles on one side like Type I. The sample we measured of type IVF had an H8 handle (see Fig 5e.19), whereas Type IVE has two H6 (and probably an H10) handles. Types IVB, F, and I have a typical stylistic feature of Karnut-Shengavit pots, a double carination (see Fig 5e.1, A, B, C, and D). The exterior of most of these are black, with a contrasting color inside. Type V is a rounded, 'u'-shaped, open form. Type VA has a flat rim, whereas a square, "rail" rim characterizes Type VG. Type VH is similar to III, but more rounded with a tapered or pinched rim. The only one of the Type V open shapes with a handle is VF; the one we observed had a lug (H8). Type VD and E are the same type; VE potters made into a sieve by poking holes in its sides (Fig 5e.1, J). It is unusual in having no outside slip. Most pieces we recorded have black exteriors and black or brown interiors. Type VI and VII are wide open vessels with pinched rims and flat bases. Type VI pots are mostly black on the outside and inside. The fabric of Type VII is that of cooking pot. At about 30 cm in circumference we saw it as a husking or grilling tray, or perhaps for making flat bread. Potters did not bother to make them black; most are buff or brown on the exterior and buff on the interior. The last two open categories are small forms, the equivalent to cups with H9 handles, rounded or squared sides, and in some cases with no handle at all. These Type VIII vessels are small; most are buff or brown on the outside and buff on the inside. The last type, IXA and B, are small pedestalled cups or braziers.[484] The illustrated one from the National History Museum with tripod feet is brown.

These types are distributed differently over time. Figure 5e.20 illustrates this.[485] In order to get this pattern, we used only the identifiable types. Some of the rims (Fig 5e. 21) can be correlated with types, but not with complete certainty. The area and therefore the size of the sample declined significantly under level V, as most of them were from Square K6, which was the only square to reach bedrock. I thus combined levels VI-VIII. Relating levels between squares is difficult at times (see Chapter 3), because the mound is sloped, and absolute depth alone is not sufficient to accomplish this. In addition, some types had too few cases to be representative. Once incomplete profiles with just rims or bases were removed from the sample, 464 sherds remained.

---

484   See Badalyan et al. 2015, 773.
485   Types IA and IB did not appear in the residential sample from Strata II and I, but excavators did recover them from graves contemporaneous to Stratum I.

In Figure 5e.20, Type I open vessels did not appear in the latest occupation architectural levels of our sample. They were most common in the Buildings 2 and 3 of K6 and the building in J5/J6A. However, this type did appear commonly in tombs of the transition of the late Kura-Araxes to Early Kurgan Period. Type III pots were also open vessels with a limited span in the occupational levels. Archaeologists recovered many fewer of this type in tombs.[486] The most common open vessel is the round bowl with a flattened rim. It existed throughout the life of Shengavit. Type VA is the easiest shape to mold. It may be the most frequently produced open form, and if there had been workshops, it was the most likely one made in them. Rim type 16, a possible rim of Type VA, is the most common form as well, especially in period I. This evidence indicates that some forms continued unchanged, and others were limited in time, suggesting that these vessels were household-made. They lack the kind of standardization one would expect from specialized production. The circumference of 34 examples of Type VA varies from 6 to 48 centimeters, with an average of 21.6 cm. and a median of 20 cm. All but 6 are utilitarian wares; none are cooking pot wares. The thickness of the body varies from 7.1-18 cm.; their average is 10.66 cm. No particular difference is noticeable from level to level. So, again, these Type VA pots do not seem to be standardized. Other open forms are not numerous enough to use for this kind of analysis.

CLOSED VESSELS

The second category includes vessels with a circumference at the rim much smaller than the circumference of the vessel's body (Fig 5e.22). The overall shape of Types X to XVI of these vessels is fairly similar (see Fig 5e.1, B, a Type XVIB vessel, whose rim is cut off when it was buried under the floor of K6, Building 3). Most have pinched, out-flaring rims. The most numerous ones in our sample are Type XIA with a squared rim, and XXXA/B. The bases of these forms are either flat or pointed. The most common handle is H4 (see Fig 5e.19). These vessels tend to be among

the larger, certainly taller than other types. Except for Type XII, which I classified as fine and a couple of cooking pot wares, all the examples we measured from Types X to XVI we classified as utility wares. Types X to XIV had mostly black exteriors with a contrasting brown to red, buff or light red interior. Types XVI had various colors outside and inside. XVII was mostly black on the outside and buff on the inside.

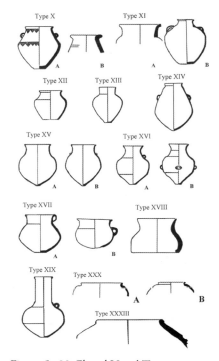

Different from those above Type XVII is a shape common in the KA1. We found few of them in our sample. Globular bodied Types XXX and XXXIII with rounded bodies are, however, common. Most of Type XXX pots are cooking pot wares, with no fine wares and some utility wares. Types XXX and XXXIII have various colors inside and out. Potters did not seem to take as much care with their design or surface treatment as with other forms. We found no Type XIX vessels in our sample, but we did find a toy version of it in architectural level 2 of Square K6. Type XVIII is recorded from earlier excavations,[487] but we did not find one from 2009-2012.

In terms of dating and standardization, Type XIA was most common in Levels II to IV; Types XXX and XXXIII were most common in Level I. Both types existed from the beginning of Shengavit but in smaller numbers

Figure 5e.22 Closed Vessel Types.

486   Badalyan et al. 2015, 145-217.
487   Sagona 1984, Fig 94, form 204.

than they did later. Within our sample, standardization again is not indicated. Among Type XIA pots the average circumference was 19.33 cm.[488] They varied from 11 to 30 cm. The thickness of their rims averages 9.2 mm, with a range from 6.7 to 11 mm. Their body thickness average 12 mm., with a range of 8.3 to 18.3 mm. The ratios of circumference to rim thickness to body thickness are not consistent either. The same applies to Type XXXA/B. The average circumference is 14.68 cm., and the range is from 8 to 34 cm. The thickness of the rim on average is 6.7 mm., and its range is 6.4 to 13.9 mm. (see Table 5e.4 below). Body thickness on average is 7.45 mm., and its range is 5.6 to 13.4 mm. Again, the ratio of circumference to rim thickness to body thickness is not consistent. Even if one limits the sample to only those from Level I the results are the same, although the average size is smaller than examples of this type from other levels. Type XXXIII is large than Type XXXA/B on average. The average circumference is 26.94 cm., the average thickness of the rim is 9.5 mm., and the average thickness of the body is 10.85 mm. The range is 16 to 50 cm. (excluding one fine one), 6.4 to 12 mm in rim thickness, and 8.2 to 16.20 m in body thickness. So, again in this class of vessels, we see no standardization in key measures. We also see the great variability in size in most of the types.

INTERMEDIATE VESSELS

The final category of vessels in our typology is intermediate vessels (Fig 5e.23). Types XX-XXIII are mostly vessels I classified as fine wares. They are smaller than most of the closed types. They are also some of the most frequently recorded (see Fig 5e.1, C, D, G, I). Rim Types 22 to 26 and 36, which we felt were originally on Intermediate 1 vessels in the XX to XXIV range are even more numerous. They were particularly frequent in Level I, but also in the remaining levels of Shengavit.

Typically, they have pinched slightly out-turned rims and a sinuous profile, at times close to an 's', shape. Type XX vessels all have the double-carinated profile of many Shengavit types. Their bases are flat, but at times quite narrow. Some have handle types H3, H9, H10, or H11 on the upper body Type XXH had its handle as an extension of the rim. Type XXI is on average larger and did not have the second carination. The position of handles varied in position from coming off the rim (Type XX, H, common in graves), on the neck, and on the body (handle types 8, 9, 10). Types XXII to XXIV have slight variations with slightly different shapes. Type XXIII has more angled sides, and Type XXXIV has sharply outturned rims or mid-body ridges. Type XXVI include smallish forms with type H10 handles. Most of these vessels had black exteriors, but they exhibit a wide variety of interior colors. Type XXVI have mostly gray interiors.

Intermediate 2 Types XXVII, XXVIII, and XXIX (Fig 5e.24) are

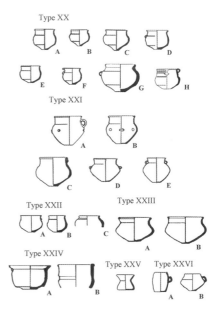

Figure 5e.23 Intermediate vessels 1.

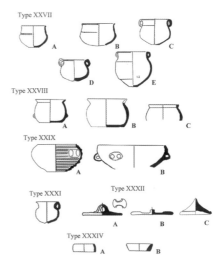

Figure 5e.24 Intermediate vessels 2.

---

488   See web archive for the raw data for these calculations.

more often utilitarian or cooking pots than fine wares. Types XXVIIA and B have pinched rims and ridges at the junction of the shoulder and body. Types XXVII C, D, and E have H9 and H10 handles. Type XXVIII pots are large, squat utility vessels and cooking ware vessels. Their rims are flared out and pinched or squared. These variations do not appear to be related to time. XXIX types are hole-mouth vessels with H4 handles. XXIXA has a grooved design. Type XXIXB is a hodgepodge with cooking wares, fine ware, and mostly utility wares. Type XXXII are lids. They are of three basic shapes. Type XXXIIA lids are flat disks with a central handle. Type XXXIIB lids have a thicker outside part of the disk than the thinner inner part of the disk. Type XXXIIC is a cone. We observed no Type XXXIIC in our sample, but one is illustrated in the catalog of the National History Museum of Armenia.[489] Frequently, the grip is a simple loop or an H4 handle, but idiosyncratic shapes like a dome with three vertical stands[490] also existed at Shengavit. The lids in our sample fit on pots with openings of 9, 14, 16, 17, 19, 20, 22, 24, 26, 28, 29, 32, and 40 cm. We recorded only one example of Type XXXIV, which may be used as a pot stand, 18 cm. in circumference, and two examples of Type XXXI, both of which are from the lowest levels of the site. Given that the form is often associated with KA1,[491] this is not surprising. No noticeable color scheme is used for these types. Type XXIX tends to be brown inside and out. Most of the rest have various colors on the exterior and interior.

In terms of standardization, the Intermediate types follow the same pattern as the closed and open forms (Table 5e.4). The variation in size within one type is quite large, and there is little correlation within any type among the characteristics of rim and body thickness. In short, I see little evidence of specialized workshop or village industry production of pots at Shengavit.

POTTERY DESIGN

Type	Circum-ference avg. cm.	Circum-ference range cm.	Circum-ference median cm.	Rim thickness avg. mm.	Rim thickness range mm.	Rim thickness median mm.	Body thickness avg. mm.	Body thickness range mm.	Body thickness median mm.	N
XX	9.39	3.6-9.37	10	6.2	3.1-9.37	4.9	7.9	3.9-12	8	38
XXI	11.95	7-24	12	5.79	4.9-9.36	5.4	8.25	5.2-14.6	7.4	21
XXII	7.8	4-43	12	4.33	3.2-11.5	8.3	6.3	4.2-19.6	8.3	46
XXIII	13	6-20	14	6.82	6.5-8.7	7.6	9.1	7.7.-12	8.4	12
XXIV	16.17	7-24	13	7.95	4.8-11.9	13	10.1	6-14.1	10	6
XXVI	12.75	5-34	9	6.5	3.7-12.4	7.2	8.6	5.3-14.1	8.9	9
XXVII	15.54	4.5-32	17	6.8	4.4-12.2	5.8	9.43	4.8-17.6	12.2	22
XXVIII	28.38	8-46	26	12.29	8.2-24	10.5	13.05	8.2-22	11.9	9
XXIX	16.29	9-26	22	6.81	5-11.9	8.3	7.81	5.4-14.4	8.2	15
XXXII	19.75	9-40	20	7.65	5.9-12.2	8.7	13.12	7.7-19.8	12.2	22

Table 5e.4. Variation in Intermediate Vessel 1 Types.

As discussed above, one of the characteristics of Shengavit, and other KA2 pottery is the increase in the numbers and complexity of designs added to pottery surfaces. These designs are either cut into the clay or made by adding a thick slip and removing some of it to create a raised design (see Fig 5e.13). For details about their variation and possible meanings see Chapter 6a.

---

489 Badalyan et al. 2015, Plate 12, 129.
490 Badalyan et al. 2015, Plate 13.
491 Sagona 1984.

Type Comparisons

The various analyses of Kura-Araxes pottery in the homeland and diaspora suggest that pottery was made close to home. Proof of this is, in part, the local sources of tempering materials. The functional repertoire of Kura-Araxes pottery is actually somewhat limited and quite similar throughout the homeland as well as in parts of the diaspora (see below).

However, defining which traditions (communities of practice) Shengavit shared with whom is best determined by pottery style. The variability in style is visible in the details of the open, closed, and intermediate types of pots. The profiles, rim shape, and base forms are the key variables. Sometimes, the variability was limited; for example, whether the curve of the profile was smooth or sharp. Still, these details may well represent local traditions. Shengavit has a great variety of stylistic types, certainly compared with small upland sites like Gegharot only 75 km away. At Gegharot, for example, all the rims were pinched.[492] Shengavit had numerous variations in rim form (see above). As the discussed below (see summary Table 5e.5), Shengavit was a node in networks of sharing the stylistic similarities. Like dialects in language, these similarities represent the degree of interaction among locations; they define a geographical realm of cultural meaning to the ancients.[493] At the same time, Shengavit had stylistic characteristics within its repertoire like open vessel Type II with folded rims that appear to be unique to the practices of its potters.

Areas	Types
Lower Province	IA, IB, IC, VII, VIIIA, VIIIB/C, IXA, IXB, XVI, XXA, XXB, XVIIA, XXD, XXE, XXF, XXXIA/B, XXIC, XXIVA, XXVIIB, XXVIIC
Upper Province	IA, IB, IC, IVA, IVB, IVD, VII, IXB, XVI, XVIIB, XXVIB, XVIIC, XXVIIE, XXXI, XXXIIB
Zagros	IC, VII, VIIID, XIA, XII, XVI, XXC, XXD, XXF, XXIIA, XXIVB XXVIB, XXXI, XXXIIA/B
Taurus	IB, IC, IVC, IVD, IVG, VA, VB, VC, VD, VH, IXB, X, XIA, XII, XVI, XXIE, XXIIA, XXIII, XXIVB, XXVIIIA/B, XXXIIA/B
Unique to Shengavit	II, III, IVE, IVF, VB, VE, VF, VG, VI, VIIIA, IXA, XIB, XIII, XIV, XV, XVIII, XIX, XXXA/B, XXG, XXID, XXIIB, XXVIIB, XXIX, XXV, XXVIA, XXVIID, XXVIIIC, XXIXA/B, XXXIV, XXXIV

Table 5e.5. Shengavit types shared in other culture areas of the Kura-Araxes and unique to Shengavit.

Within Armenia, Badalyan defined four style groupings. Presumably this means four distinct communities of practice. They include Elar-Aragats, Shresh-Mokhrablur, Karnut Shengavit, and Ayrum-Teghut.[494] The first grouping is mostly associate with the KA1. Nonetheless, there are a few parallels at Shengavit. A square cup[495] matches Type VIIIC. An open form[496] matches Shengavit Type IVE. One closed and one intermediate forms with handles[497] appeared as Shengavit Type XVIIA and XXIAB. The remaining style areas are considered KA2. Few Ayrum-Teghut forms from the area north of Lake Sevan into the Upper Province have parallels at Shengavit. Most parallels are with the Shresh-Mokrablur and Karnut-Shengavit areas that cover the Ararat Plain and the Koytak Plateau. Most prominent are the intermediate pots with two carinations in profile.[498] Other parallels with the Shresh-Mokhrablur

---

492   Haroutunian 2014.
493   Rothman 2014.
494   Badalyan 2014.
495   Smith et al. 2009, Fig 3, A.
496   Smith et al. 2009, Fig 5, U.
497   Smith et al. 2009, Fig 3, T.
498   Smith et al. 2009, Fig 6, 8.

style grouping from the Ararat Plain at Shengavit include a deep intermediate form with a flaring rim[499] to Shengavit Type XXIV, a footed bowl (a brazier)[500] to Shengavit Type IXA, a large intermediate pot with two handles at the rim[501] to Shengavit Type XXVIIC, and a rounded cup with a handle[502] to Shengavit Type VIIIA.

Looking more broadly at the Kura-Araxes landscape, among the open types, similarities with Shengavit exist in the Lower[503] and Upper Provinces of the homeland, the Yanik Ware area of the Zagros, and the Taurus highlands. Little similarity exists with lands beyond in lowland Malatya and the Levant. Type I is marked by the presence of a handle on one side. Types IA and B are rounded, IC has straight, flaring sides. Archaeologists have found Type IA (Sagona's forms 113 and 121[504]) pots at Shresh Blur in the Lower Province[505] and Didube in the Upper Province. Sagona forms 122 and 124 (Variant C) are the same as Type IB. Archaeologists recovered these types from Van and Kültepe II in Naxçivan of the Lower Province. A similar form came from Khizanaant Gora in the Upper Province.[506] Type IC (Sagona form 124) without a handle was also used at Yanik Tepe, Godin Tepe in the Zagros, Gegharot, and Kilisetepe in the Taurus. Open vessel Type II with folded rims and Type III with in-turned rims do not have any parallels that we could find. Open Type IVA (Sagona form 115) occurred at Dangreulis Gora, while nearby Khizanaant Gora had matches to Form IVB (Sagona form 19) in the Upper Province. Types IVC, IVD, IVG (Sagona form 55D), and IVI (Sagona form 53) all occurred in the Taurus at Pulur Sakyol,[507] Aşvan Kale,[508] and Korucutepe. Type IVD with a handle occurred in Kvatskhelebi cemetery.[509] Type VA (Sagona form 111), a rounded bowl with a flattened rim is a very common form. Examples came from Norşuntepe, Aşvan Tepe,[510] and Pulur Sakyol.[511] Type VB (Sagona form 53) is very much the shape of Type IVI, but with a dimpled base. It has parallels at Geoy Tepe west of Lake Urmia. Archaeologists recovered Type VC (Sagona form 16) from Korucutepe. They found slightly wider examples of Type VD (Sagona 109) at Korucutepe, Norşuntepe,[512] and Aşvan Tepe.[513] Type VH is paralleled at Aşvan Kale (its Type 4).[514] Type VII (Sagona form 121, 143) is a tray made of cooking pot ware. With slight variation it existed at Godin,[515] Ozni, and Gegharot.[516] Type VIII is a class of what we would call cups. Cups is a category absent from nearby Gegharot, while Mokhrablur did have some.[517] Excavators found the more squared versions of cups (Sagona form 131) at Osman Bozu in Naxçivan. A last cup without a handle, Type VIIID (Sagona form 237),

---

499   Smith et al. 2009, Fig 5, 24, 6, J.

500   Smith et al. 2009, Fig 5, 28; 6, O.

501   Smith et al. 2009, Fig 6,S.

502   Smith et al. 2009,Fig 6, Q.

503   See Badalyan 2014 for lists of Lower Province (specifically Armenian) sites.

504   Sagona 1984, Part iii.

505   Batiuk et al. 2022.

506   Rova 2014.

507   Koşay 1976, Plate 75, 179 and 184.

508   Sagona 1994, Fig. 37, 12.

509   Rova 2014, Fig. 5, 5.

510   Sagona 1994, Fig. 73, 8.

511   Koşay 1976, Plate 75, 144.

512   Hauptmann 1982, Plate 46,9.

513   Sagona 1994, Fig. 74, 14.

514   Sagona 1994, Fig. 78, 11; Fig. 16.

515   Rothman 2011, Fig. 5.59, trays, b.

516   Haroutunian 2014, Bowls 1, 17.

517   Badalyan 2014, Fig. 5, 21.

occurred at Yanik Tepe. The last open form are probable braziers. Type IXA examples came from Mokhrablur.[518] Type IXB (Sagona form 228) archaeologists found at Mokhrablur, Korucutepe, and Kvatskhelebi.

Closed vessels at Shengavit tend to be larger storage vessels (Fig. 5e.22). They vary stylistically by where on the body the widest circumference is, the shape of the rim, the shape of the base, and placement of handles, if there are any. Type X (Sagona form 178) is paralleled by vessels at Pulur Sakyol with a similar profile, rim, and base, but without handles. We did not have a complete profile for Type XB or XIA. Their shape fit elements of Types X and XI and had distinctive rims. Type XB matches Type 13 at Taşkun Mevkii.[519] Type XIA (Sagona form 182C) occurred at Godin and Kilisetepe. We found no match to Types XIB, XIII, or XIV. Type XII (Sagona form 193) excavators found at Norşuntepe and at Godin Tepe.[520] Type XV (Sagona form 40) surveyors recovered from Cinis Höyük in the Taurus. Storage jar Type XVI (Sagona form 159) was common at Norşuntepe, Gegharot, Yanik Tepe, Ozni, and Kvatskhelebi cemetery.[521] Type XVIIA (Sagona form 156) occurred at Kültepe I, and Type XVIIB (Sagona form 32) had parallels at Kiketi. For Types XVIII (Sagona form 204), XIX, and XXX we found no parallels. Type XXXIII had a comparable type at Kilisetepe.[522]

Intermediate 1 pottery types include many smaller pots that we have interpreted as eating pots (see below), as well as cooking and utility vessels and lids (Fig. 5e.23). Type XXA (Sagona form 9c) also occurred at Mokhrablur, Shresh Blur in the Lower Province, and also in Aradetis Or Gora.[523] Type XXB excavators recovered from Gegharot,[524] and Type XXC from Godin Tepe.[525] Archaeologists found Type XXD from Jrahovit,[526] Type XXE from Godin,[527] and Type XXXF (Sagona form 182) from Godin, Jrahovit,[528] and Agarak.[529] For Type XXXG (Sagona form 45) we found no exact match. Type XXI is still mostly fine wares with a few utility and cooking pots. Type XXIA/B (Sagona form 6D) also comes from Sadakhlo in the Lower Province, and Type XXIC (Sagona form 10B) comes from Kamo near Lake Sevan. We found no clear match to Type XXID, but Type XXIE (Sagona form 21F) had a parallel at Geoy Tepe. The next set, Type XII, is on average smaller than Type XXI. Type XXIIA parallels types from Kızıluşağı,[530] Godin Tepe,[531] and Norşuntepe.[532] Type XVIIB (Sagona form 10A) is rare. One of the few we recovered was by the inside of the settlement wall and had a lime filled design (Fig 5e.25). This technique resembles that of the Yanik Ware tradition. Type XVIIC (Sagona 102C)

Figure 5e.25 Vessel from near the base of the settlement wall, presumably Stratum III or IV.

518   Badalyan 2014, Fig. 5, 28/29.
519   Sagona 1994, Fig. 17.
520   Rothman 2011, Fig. 5.58 Storage Jars b.
521   Rova 2014, Fig. 3.
522   Rothman 2014, Fig. 8, v.
523   Rova 2014, Fig. 5, 11.
524   Badalyan 2014 Fig, 7, 16.
525   Rothman 2011, Fig. 5.59, Narrow mouth, a.
526   Badalyan 2014, Fig. 5, 8.
527   Rothman 2011, Fig. 5.59, Open mouth, g.
528   Badalyan 2014, Fig. 5,7.
529   Badalyan 2014, Fig. 5, 9.
530   Rothman 2014, Fig. 8, y.
531   Rothman 2011, Fig. 5.58, Cooking pot e.
532   Hauptmann 1982, Plate 45, 9.

excavators unearthed at Van. Type XXIII (Sagona form 18A) parallels a type at Güzelova in the Taurus. Archaeologists recovered a parallel to Type XXIVA at Mokhrablur,[533] and to Type XXIVB at Godin[534] and Muş.[535] A similar but not identical type to Type XXV (Sagona form 119) excavators found at Elar, but perhaps closer to Sagona form 118A from Shresh Blur. We found no similar examples to Type XXVIA. Type XXVIB (Sagona form 37B) has matches at Samshvilde and Godin.

Intermediate 2 types include more cooking and utility than fine wares (Fig. 5e. 24). We found no clear matches to Type XXVIIA. Type XXVIIB (Sagona form 6E) had parallels with Franganots in the Lower Province, and Type XXVIIC (Sagona form 186B) had them with Kvatskhelebi and Gegharot.[536] Type XXVIID is a minor variation of XXVIIC for which we found no exact parallel. Type XXVIIE (Sagona form 171) has matches at Dangreulis Gora in the Upper Province. Types XXVIIIA and B (Sagona form 118C) excavators recovered from Güzelova. We could not find exact matches for XXVIIIC. Similarly, we could find no parallels for Type XXIXA (Sagona form 105) or Type XXIXB. Type XXXIV is what we thought could be pot stands. The typical pot stand from Pulur Sakyol west into the Southern Levant (Sagona form 215) is absent at Shengavit. A few stone pot stands (see Chapter 5f) may have fulfilled its function. This small stand in ceramic and ground stone appears to be unique to Shengavit. A small handled pot, Type XXXI, existed at Godin[537] and Kvatskhelebi.[538] The last type, a series of lids existed in many forms with varying shapes and handles over the whole extent of the Kura-Araxes. One Type XXXIIC conical lid (Sagona form 219) is housed in the National Museum collection,[539] which is unusual as most of the parallels are in the Levant from Tell al-Judaidah, Beth Shean, Tabara el-Akrad, and Bet Yerah.[540] Type XXXIIA (Sagona form 221B) excavators recovered from Korucutepe, Pulur Sakyol,[541] and Godin Tepe.[542] Type XXXIIB (Sagona form 224A) is paralleled at Kvatskhelebi and Pulur Sakyol.[543]

This discussion of the parallels to Shengavit's typology results in a number of conclusions. First, the networks of interaction (the communities of practice) are much more geographically extensive than we originally thought. Second, there are nonetheless more types that are unique to Shengavit than are shared with any of the other areas. Third, there does not appear to be any pattern of only fine, utility, or cooking wares being shared with any one culture area (sub-region). In fact, many of the types have examples of two or three of the categories: fine, utility, and cooking ware. Altogether the picture these data paint for us is one of a series of options in the profile, the rim, and base shape, as well as the width to height ratio and other measures, that potters had in their repertoire. There was a clear concept among potters of what Kura-Araxes pots should look like, but not set types of the exact same size and function. There were so many variations that, again, the idea of specialization is questionable.

As discussed in Chapter 6b, while most of the pottery at Shengavit fits comfortably within the Kura-Araxes cultural tradition, in the graves of the transitional Kura-Araxes/ Early Kurgan period, and from infrequent finds

533   Badalyan 2014, Fig. 5, 10.
534   Rothman 2011, Fig. 5.59, Type 1b.
535   Rothman and Kozbe 1997, Fig. 10b.
536   Badalyan 2014, Fig. 7, 20.
537   Rothman 2011, Fig. 5.60, IIId.
538   Rova 2014, Fig. 5, 2.
539   Badalyan et al. 2015, Plate 12, 129.
540   Greenberg et al. 2006, Fig 3.27, 1.
541   Koşay 1976, Plate 80, 284.
542   Rothman 2011, Fig. 5.61, Lid a.
543   Koşay 1976, Plate 80, 285.

on the residential mound we found some other types. Some of the wares and designs we include in Figure 5e.26

Figure 5e.26 Post-Kura-Araxes pottery.

Pottery Function

The function of Shengavit pottery types is another critical, but often ignored variable. Function, as discussed in the Introduction above describes a number of activities. The first of them is cooking and serving. The cooking wares are most prominent in Types XXVIIA/B/C/D, XXXA/B, XXXIII, VII, XXIA and D, and VF. Lids, Type XXXII, were made of cooking, utility and fine wares. These fit Wilkinson's assemblages as "characterized by lids [...], suggesting boiling, stewing, or steaming of foods."[544] Cooking consisted of making a porridge or stew. Palynology evidence (Chapter 2b) suggests that groats of goosefoot were stored in pots in K6, M5, and in a grave in the necropolis. Wheat noodles were strained through sieves. Cooks put pots on andirons, like the pieces of a circular ring from M5 (Fig 5e.27C), over the fire. Evidence of charcoal and charred wood in a wheat porridge, detected by our palynologists in another ceramic vessel, confirm this. Simonyan's crew recovered a vessel in the necropolis with porridge cooked in grape juice (Chapter 2b). Goosefoot leaves were often added to porridges. Shells of walnuts and hazelnuts occurred in the fire.

Andiron pieces A and B are more like corners that hold up a pot. However, we discovered flat pieces that would fit into these verticals. That and the probable trays Type VII suggest that the ancient also grilled. Perhaps they were grilling meats. This makes some sense in terms of the griddle hearth at Godin.[545] They could have been charring seeds. Alternatively, they could be making a flat bread like modern Armenian *lavash*. Kvavadze and Atoyants (Chapter 2b) discovered pollens of the starch from flour. The s-shaped smaller vessels like Type XXA-G are likely the eating vessels for the stew-like meals or porridges. These are fine ware vessels. This fits ethnographic examples.[546] Another possibility is that Types XXXA-G, XXIVA/B, and VIII may be part of a "wine kit."[547] The slightly out-turned rims are good for drinking. The open vessels, Types I-VC, are often utilitarian wares, but they are the right size for single or small family serving and eating more solid foods. Types I, II, and III

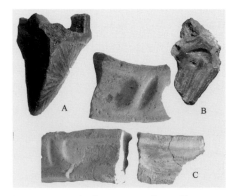

Figure 5e.27 Andiron pieces from Shengavit.

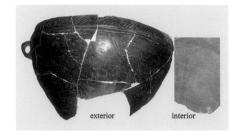

Figure 5e.28 Shengavit Vat.

544   Wilkinson 2014, 213.
545   Rothman 2011, Fig. 5.29.
546   Henrickson and McDonald 1983.
547   Batiuk 2013.

would not work for drinking. Type IV vessels could have been used for drinking, although they are on average larger than Type XX vessels. Serving vessels could include Types XVIIA/B, XVIII, XXVI, XXXI. Simonyan's team unearthed a very large Type IB vessel in their work from 2000 (Fig 5e.28). We suggest that it might be a wine vat. Another piece of the wine kit is liquid storing jars, the equivalent of amphorae. Closed Types XB, XIA/B, XIII, XIV, XVIA/B, XIX, and, with a lid, Types XVA/B would serve this function. We recovered three Type XVI jars (Fig. 5e.1B) under the floors of Buildings 2 and 3 with their rims cut off and a flat stone covering their mouths. Patrick McGovern of the Penn Museum analyzed scrapings from the interior of one of those, and found evidence of a resonated substance, perhaps a wine, but not the tannic acid typical of grape wine. Ethnographically, storage of dry goods requires an opening big enough for a scoop. Types XA, XII, and XXI have that characteristic. Type VD, especially the version with holes punched through are good for making cheese as well as noodles. Many of the utilitarian types would be good for mixing. Any number of activities from melting bitumen to processing salt, mixing chemicals for tanning, soaking etc., etc. would require such types.

Some of these functions can be verified by analyzing the inside surfaces of the vessels for residues, work begun but not yet ready for publication by Manoukian.

Conclusion

This chapter, then, paints a picture of a complex of probably locally made vessels, reflecting a common cultural ideology of design. That commonality stretches over much of the Kura-Araxes homeland, as well as the Zagros and Taurus highland diaspora. Yet, there are so many typological variations within Shengavit that are not shared elsewhere that local production is most likely. Variations in the size of each type and measurements of wall thickness indicate that the idea of industrial manufacture or village industry does not apply to the KA2 at Shengavit. Molding, the technique most appropriate for mass production other than the fast wheel, for which we have very few examples at Shengavit, does not fit the shapes of most of the pottery types. The functional differences suggest a liquid, stew type of cooking, served in individual eating bowls. The archaeobotanical remains (see Chapter 5b) suggests that the ancients grew bread wheat. Breads would have been appropriate with a diet of stews.

References

Abramov, I., Farkas, A., and Ochsenschlager, E. 2006 A Study in Classification: Style and Visual Perception. *Visual Anthropology* 19:255-274

Badalyan, R. 2014 New data on the periodization and chronology of the Kura-Araxes culture in Armenia. *Paléorient* 40 (2): 71-92.

Badalyan, R., Smith, A. T., Lindsay, I., Harutyunyan, A., Greene, A., Marshall, M., Monahan, B., Hovsepyan, R., Meliksetian, Kh., Pernicka, E. and Haroutunian, S. 2014 A Preliminary Report on the 2008, 2010, and 2011 Investigations of Project ArAGATS on the Tsaghkahovit Plain, Republic of Armenia," *Archäologische Mitteilungen aus Iran und Turan* 46: 123–222.

Badalyan, R., Hovsepyan, S., Khachatryan, L. 2015 *Shengavit: Catalog of archaeological materials from the collections of the Museum of History of Armenia.* Yerevan: Museum of History of Armenia. (in Russian).

Batiuk, S. 2013 The Fruits of Migration: Understanding the 'longue dureé and the Socio-economic Relations of Early Transcaucasian Culture. *Journal of Anthropological Archaeology* 32: 449-477.

Batiuk, S. 2005 *Migration Theory and the Distribution of the Early Transcaucasian Culture.* Unpublished Doctoral dissertation, University of Toronto.

Batiuk, S., Rothman, M., Samei, S., Hovsepyan, R. 2022 Unraveling the Kura-Araxes Cultural Tradition Across Space and Time. *Ancient Near Eastern Studies* 59: 235-325.

Burney, C. 1958 Eastern Anatolia in the Chalcolithic and Early Bronze Age. *Anatolian Studies* VIII: 159-209.

Crown, P. 2007 Life Histories of pots and potters: situating the individual in archaeology. *American Antiquity* 72 (4): 677-690.

Deetz, J. 1965 The Dynamics of Stylistic Change in Arikara Ceramics. *Illinois Studies in Anthropology*, No. 4. Urbana, Il: University of Illinois Press.

Globe, 2012 *The Globe Soil Color Book.* 2nd edition. Visual Color Systems.

Haroutunian, S. 2010 Appendix 2 The Early Bronze Age Pottery from Gegharot. in Badalyan, R., Smith, A., Lindsay, I., Harutyunyan, A., Greene, A., Marshall, M., Monahan, B., and R. Hovsepyan. A Preliminary Report on the 2008, 2010, and 2011 Investigations of Project

ArAGATS on the Tsaghkahovit Plain, Republic of Armenia. *Archäologische Mitteilungen aus Iran und Turan* 46:149-222.

Hauptmann, H. 1982 Die Grabungen auf dem Norşuntepe, 1974. In *Keban Project 1974-75 Activities*, edited by Pekman S. Ankara: Middle East Technical University. 41-70.

Hayrapetyan, A. 2008 Some Technical Aspects of the Pottery of the Early Bronze Age Site of Gegharot (Armenia). in *Ceramics in Transitions: Chalcolithic Through Iron Age in the Highlands of the Southern Caucasus and Anatolia*, edited by K. Rubinson, and A. Sagona, 71-86. Leuven: Peeters.

Heinsch, M. and Vandiver, P. 2006 Recent Radiographic Analysis of Kura-Araxes Ceramics. In *Beyond the Steppe and the Sown*, edited by A. Peterson, L. Popova, A. Smith, 382-394. Leiden: Brill.

Henrickson, E. and McDonald, M. 1983 Ceramic Form and Function: An Ethnographic Search and an Archaeological Application. *American Anthropologist* 85 (3): 630-643.

Hovsepyan, I. and Mnatsakanyan, A. 2011 The Technical Specifics of Early Bronze Age Ceramics in Armenia: Tsaghkasar-1 and Talin Cemetery. *Aramazd* VII(2): 24-54.

Ionescu, C. and Hoeck, V. 2020 Ceramic Technology: How to investigate Surface Finishing. Archaeological and Anthropological Sciences. Springer: http://doi.org/10.107/s12520-020-011 44-9.

Iserlis, M., Goren, Y., Hovsepyan, I., Greenberg, R. 2015 Kura-Araxes Ceramic Technology in the Fourth Millennium BCE site of Tsaghkasar, Armenia. *Paléorient* 41 (1): 9-23.

Iserlis. M., Greenberg. R., Badalyan. R., and Goren, Y. 2010 Beth Yerah, Aparan III, and Karnut I: Preliminary comments on Kura Araxes homeland and diaspora ceramic technology. *TÜBA-AR* 13: 245–26.

Kibaroğlu M., Sagona, A., and Satır, M. 2011 Petrographic and Geochemical Investigations of the Late Prehistoric Ceramics from Sos Höyük, Erzurum (Eastern Anatolia). *Journal of Archaeological Science* 38: 3072-3084.

Kibaroğlu M. 2015 Archaeometric Investigations of Kura-Araxes Ware: A Review. in *Proceedings of the International Symposium on East Anatolia— South Caucasus Cultures*, edited by M. Işıklı, and C. Birol, 221-30. Newcastle: Cambridge Scholars Publishing.

Koşay, H. 1976. *Keban Project Pulur Excavations 1968-1970*. Ankara: Middle East Technical University.

Kramer, C. 1997 *Pottery in Rajasthan: Ethnoarchaeology in Two Indian Cities*. Washington, DC: Smithsonian Institute Press.

Lazlo, E. 2016 In the Studio: A Pit Firing Color Palette. *Pottery Making Illustrated*. Nov/Dec. https://ceramicartsnetwork.org/pottery-making-illustrated.

Manoukian, N. 2015 *The Kura-Araxes Culture: Technological and Compositional Characterization of Early Transcaucasian Ware Pottery from Shengavit, Armenia*. Unpublished Masters thesis. University College London, Institute of Archaeology.

Martino, S. 2017 Graphite-Treated Pottery in the Northeastern Mediterranean from the Chalcolithic to the Bronze Age. *Near Eastern Archaeology* 80 (1): 3-13.

Mason, R., and Cooper, L. 1999 Grog, Petrography, and Early Transcaucasians at Godin Tepe. *Iran* 37: 25-31.

Palumbi, G. 2008 *The Red and Black. Social and Cultural Interaction between the Upper Euphrates and Southern Caucasus Communities in the Fourth and Third Millennium BC*. Roma: Università di Roma Sapienza.

Palumbi, G., Gratuze, B., Harutunyan, A., Chaitinger, C. 2014 Obsidian-tempered pottery in the Southern Caucasus: a new approach to obsidian as a ceramic-temper. *Journal of Archaeological Science* 40: 43-54.

Rice, P. 1987 *Pottery Analysis: A Source Book*. Chicago: University of Chicago Press.

Rice, P. 2015 *Pottery Analysis: A Source Book*. Second edition. Chicago: University of Chicago Press.

Rothman, M. S 2000 The Commoditization of Goods and the Rise of the State Mesopotamia. in *Commodities and Globalization*, edited by A. Haugerud, P. Stone, P. Little, 163-178. Society of Economic Anthropology Publications. Lanham: Rowman and Littlefield Publishers.

Rothman, M. S 2011 Migration and Resettlement: Godin IV Period. in *On the High Road: the History of Godin Tepe, Iran*, edited by H. Gopnik, and M. Rothman, 139-208. Toronto: Royal Ontario Museum/ Mazda Press.

Rothman, M. S 2014 Kura Araxes Culture Areas and the Late 4th and Early 3rd Millennia BC Pottery from Veli Sevin's Surveys in Malatya and Elaziğ, Turkey. *Origini* XXXVI: 37-91.

Roux, V. 2003 Ceramic Standardization and the Intensity of Production: Quantifying Degrees of Specialization. *American Antiquity* 68 (4): 768-782.

Rova, E. 2014 The Kura-Araxes in the Shida Kartli Region of Georgia: An Overview. *Paléorient* 40 (2): 47-69

Sagona, A. 2018 *The Archaeology of the Caucasus from the Earliest Settlements to the Iron Age*. Cambridge: Cambridge University Press.

Sagona, A. 2014 Rethinking the Kura-Araxes Genesis. *Paléorient* 40(2): 23-46.

Sagona, A. 1994 *The Aşvan Sites 3: Keban Rescue Excavations, Eastern Anatolia, The Early Bronze Age*. London and Ankara: British Institute of Archaeology at Ankara.

Sagona, A. 1984 *The Caucasian Region in the Early Bronze Age*. 3 vols. Oxford: B.A.R. International Series 214.

Sackett, J. R. 1977 The Meaning of Style in Archaeology: A General Model. *American Antiquity* 42(3): 369–380.

Smith, A. T. 2015 *The Political Machine: Assembling sovereignty in the Bronze Age Caucasus*. Princeton: Princeton University Press.

Van der Leeuw, S. 1977 Towards a Study of the Economics of Pottery Making. in *Ex. Horreo Cingula IV*, edited by B. Beek, R. Brandt, W. Groeninen-van Waateringe, 68-76. Amsterdam: University of Amsterdam.

Wallace, D. 1989 Functional Factors of Mica and Ceramic Burnishing. in *Pottery Technology: Ideas and Approaches*, edited by G. Bronitsky, 33-40. Boulder, CO: Westview Press.

Wilkinson, T. C. 2014 The Early Transcaucasian Phenomenon in Structural Systemic Perspective: Cuisine, Craft and Economy the Early Transcaucasian Phenomenon in Structural Systemic Perspective: Cuisine, Craft and Economy. *Paléorient* 40(2): 203-229.

5f | Ground Stone Tools

Mitchell Rothman

Introduction

A large percentage, at least by weight, of artifacts excavated from Shengavit fall into the category of ground stone tools. These tools are largely ignored in final reports from Armenian and other South Caucasian sites. Often excavators report only the presence of saddle querns, the odd macehead, or hammer.[548] The catalog[549] of material from Shengavit at the National Museum of History, on the other hand, illustrates saddle querns, maceheads, hammers, possible digging stick weights, harrows, pecking (or drilling) stones, anvils, grinders, shaft straighteners, spindle whorls, measuring, and fishing (or loom) weights. The excavations of Simonyan prior to 2009 and Simonyan and Rothman 2009-2012 produced many more samples with other functional types as well.

The importance of these tools should not be minimized. They represent good indicators of many productive activities. Among these activities are the processing of foods (especially grains), preparing fields (harrowing, digging stick weights), clearing land and household construction (axes and celts), processing salt, fishing, chipped and ground stone knapping, bead making, bone tool making, processing of pigments, weaving (spindle whorls and loom weights), working leather and wood, burnishing pottery (in later times pottery wheels were made of ground stone as well), weapons (maceheads), polishing and straightening arrow shafts, applying wall and floor plaster, and no doubt other activities as well. Documenting these activities and understanding how they fit in various productive processes, where they were found and who used them remain important tasks of interpretation.

In addition, ground stone tools are made of a number of different kinds of stone (see below). Each material had characteristics like malleability and hardness that defined their uses. These stone types were exchanged over some distance.[550] At Shengavit material used in ground stone included sandstone, basalt (rough or "sluda" and refined basalt [part of a class with rhyolite and andesite]), tufa, pumice (also called perlite), limestone, marble, granite, and diorite. All are available fairly near Shengavit, some washed down by the Hrazdan River from the Tsaghkunyats massif.[551]

Manufacturing Ground Stone Tools

The manufacture of every ground stone tool requires the creator to go through a series of decisions: (1) selection of the stone for a particular purpose, (2) shaping the stone to best accomplish its functions (this can be done by the end user or at the source), (3) the actual use, and (4) refinishing or re-using sometimes for a different secondary function.[552]

Typically, the process is comparable to chipped stone manufacture. At the source, a block is removed.[553] Like

---

548   Rutter and Philip 2008.
549   Badalyan et al. 2015.
550   Rutter and Philip 2008
551   Boris Gasparyan, Ruben Badalyan, personal communication.
552   Adams 2014.
553   Abadi-Reiss and Rosen 2008

larger flint or obsidian blocks, transporting the raw block is inefficient. So, the first reductions are often done at the resource extraction site.[554] Sandstone, which doubles in use for construction, might be on the site already to be modified into tools. The block is then knapped, removing flakes with a harder stone to get the basic shape. We recovered some debitage from our 2009-2012 excavations at Shengavit, and similar debitage is illustrated in the National History Museum catalogue,[555] so we know that residents did some of the manufacturing or re-purposing on site.

The final stage is to grind and polish the surface smooth. Evidence of this last stage is harder to recover. Often, an archaeologist can differentiate a ground stone tool from chunks of ground stone used as a building material, because they have been modified to fit into a human hand (Fig 5f:1). Others, like saddle querns have a rather obvious function. I observed this pattern at Shengavit and more recently at Tel Yaqush in the southern Levant.

point retoucher   edge tool   bottom grinder   top saddle quern

Figure 5f.1 Adaptation of different working surfaces to their handling.

Typology

The first major step in analyzing an assemblage of ground stone is to create a typology.[556] This is much more difficult than it might seem.[557] Our tendency would be to use function: what the tool was used for. However, the same tool was often used for various purposes. A grinding stone can be used with a quern for grinding seed (a *mano*), but it can be used for scraping fur off leather,[558] or for preparing a temper for pottery, or for polishing other ground stone, bone, or wood. Ultimately, a detailed microscopic study of wear patterns may distinguish them,[559] but in this current study time constraints and equipment prevented a microscopic view of the surface of the stones.

Analysts must first define the criteria used in order of their importance to create a typology. Wright, for example, suggests a classification system based first on general functional categories and then shape. [560]

Some examples of her types include:[561]

A. Grinding slabs/querns	B. Mortars	C. Handstones
1. block quern	15. pebble mortar	24. bifacial discoidal/oval
2. block grinding slab	16. bowl mortar	25. bifacial discoidal/lens
3. boulder quern	17. boulder mortar	26. bifacial discoidal/tapered
4. saddle-shaped quern		32. bifacial ovate/oval
5. saddle-shaped grinding slab		33. bifacial ovate/lens
6-14. other		57. bell-shaped muller

554   Rosenberg and Garfinkel 2014, 16.
555   Badalyan et al. 2015, 43, Fig 148.
556   Peterson 2008.
557   Adams 2014; Wright 1992.
558   Adams 1988.
559   Stemp et al 2015.
560   Wright 2002.
561   Wright 2002: 61-62.

<table>
<tr><td colspan="2">D. Pestles</td><td colspan="2">F. Polishing pebbles</td><td colspan="2">H. Axes and celts</td></tr>
<tr><td>65.</td><td>bipolar cylindrical</td><td>80.</td><td>unifacial</td><td>89.</td><td>trapezoidal axc</td></tr>
<tr><td>66.</td><td>unipolar cylindrical</td><td>81.</td><td>bifacial</td><td>90.</td><td>trapezoidal celt</td></tr>
<tr><td colspan="2">E. Pounders</td><td colspan="2">G. Worked pebbles</td><td>92.</td><td>chisel</td></tr>
<tr><td>75.</td><td>irregular core pounder</td><td>83.</td><td>ground pebble</td><td></td><td></td></tr>
<tr><td>76.</td><td>spherical irregular</td><td>84.</td><td>ground sphere</td><td></td><td></td></tr>
<tr><td></td><td></td><td>85.</td><td>pecked cobble</td><td></td><td></td></tr>
</table>

The logic here is to focus on the production of the tool: the tool maker would have chosen a stone chunk and shaped it through scraping, hammering, cutting, flaking, grinding, etc. to create a tool of the proper shape for a particular range of functions. Horsfall believes that this process is best understood using design theory; that is, the theory used by architects and engineers to create buildings.[562] Design (shape) would have function as its end point, but a variety of factors would affect the final form. Among those factors are knowledge of technology, constraints in availability of materials, and cultural traditions (practices). If the ground stone technology at Shengavit was like its chipped stone industry, then one would expect a fairly unrefined tool making process, as the chipped stone seems to be based on taking flakes from whatever stone (mostly obsidian) was at hand, rather than preparing a formal core and removing blades (see Chapter 5c, this volume).

In some ways Wright's classification does not fully address the problem of multiple functions. I would suggest a different scheme that takes as the first criterion the nature of the working surface. The second criterion would be shape, then size, then material. This classification system emphasizes the possibility that tools of the same type had multiple functions. A tool for grinding grain would have a flat, rough bottom surface, but so would a tool to process tempers. Leather-working tools would have similar characteristics (see below). Such a tool could even have been used as a polisher for bone tools (see Chapter 5g).

Our sample is 806 pieces from 2000 to 2012, plus material from Sardarian and Bayburtian's excavations now stored in the National History Museum. At the moment, we have enough data to analyze pieces from 2009-2012 and the Natural History collection, a sum of 359 objects. This is a sufficiently large sample for statistical and pattern recognition. It is at the moment the most controlled in terms of provenience. Statistics are therefore best limited to the later samples at the moment (see our web archive for the statistical database, edited to capture larger groupings, the original database with more finely detailed data, and images of ground stone tools from 2000-2008 examples (see below)).

Working Surface and Function

The heart of the typology proposed here is the primacy of the working surface. The multiple functions of tools begin with this surface, and are then further defined by their size, shape, and material. The worked surfaces fall generally into one of six parts of the tool: whole, top, edge, end, bottom, and point. Statistically, Chi square statistics run comparing the likelihood that the pattern of working surface versus putative function, size versus function, and material versus working surface all showed that they were non-randomly distributed (according to Pearson's correlate in SPSS). What are these patterns and what do they mean?

Our typology yielded the following:

---

562   Horsfall 1987.

Working surface	Possible functions
Whole:	burnisher, digging stick weight, macehead, pot stand, sinker/loom weight, spindle whorl, weight
Top:	querns (*metates*), pecking (drilling) stones, shaft straightener, platform, anvil.
Edge:	cutter (axe), grinder, celt.
Bottom:	grain grinder (*mano*), abrader, scraper, polisher, whetstone
End:	hammer, pestle, harrow, pounder, retoucher
Point:	small hammer, retoucher, hole grinder.

Table 5f.1. Working surfaces and putative functions within each category

WHOLE

This category represents a wide variety of tools and of activities (Fig 5f.2). Maceheads are theoretically weapons of war. Crafts persons overwhelmingly made them out of the hardest stone, marble (except for a couple made of limestone). Most marble, in fact, is only used for maceheads (see Table 5f.2. below). As weapons this makes sense. Two Widener University students of forensic anthropology, Emily Loucks and Jennifer Parisi, conducted an unpublished study of the skulls of those killed at the Iron Age battle on the citadel of Hasanlu IV.[563] The vast majority were killed by a strike against the occipital bone at the back of the head with a small heavy object, most likely a macehead. Certainly, these objects represent warfare, but their presence does not necessarily mean active war. Such objects often are markers of status because of their finer material and their symbol of control.

A second category is the digging stick weight. Kushnareva writes that agricultural tools fall into a number of categories.[564] The first of these are tools to break up lumps of soil. The second is to plow or dig holes to plant the seed and to direct water when there was irrigation. Evidence does not verify that Kura-Araxes people, for the most part, plowed the soil. The materials for tilling she cites are mostly made of bone. Most of what she illustrates are from Mesopotamia or from a time before or after the Kura-Araxes. Archaeologists have not recovered those sorts of materials at Shengavit, despite the fact that preservation of bone was extraordinarily good (see Chapter 5g and below). The one possible exception is a red deer horn with a square notch carved out in M5. Little wear is evident on the point of that horn, so it may be a symbolic representation of agriculture in a ritual space (see Chapter 6a). The shoulder bones of cattle at Shengavit do not show signs of wear typical of ones that pulled plows, although figurines of pairs of oxen on a single yoke may contradict that conclusion (see Chapters 5a and 6c).

The alternatives to bone and horn plows are a digging stick and a ground stone harrow. The stick is made more efficient by adding a donut-shaped weight to it. Excavators did recover a few of these possible digging stick weights. Ground

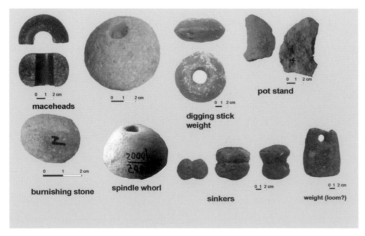

Figure 5f.2 Ground Stone Tools with the whole as the working surface.

---

563   Medvedskaya 1988.
564   Kushnareva 1997, 166f.

Figure 5f.3 Modern burnishing tools.

Figure 5f. 4 Spinning yarn.

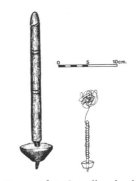

Figure 5f. 5 Spindle whorl.

stone harrows, heavy wide ended hammers for breaking up the soil, were common at Shengavit (see below).

The bottoms of many pots at Shengavit are round (see Chapter 5e). Ceramic pot stands were common there, but there were also ground stone pot stands.

The vast majority of pots produced at Shengavit were burnished. Burnishing is a technique used to bring up a shine by rubbing the surface of a pot at the leather hard clay stage (see Chapter 5e). In modern times potters use a small polished stone or a metal spoon (Fig 5f.3). Potters in ancient times used small polished ground stones. We recovered a significant number of these at the site, reflecting the wide distribution of pottery making activity.

Another craft represented in ground stone is weaving (Figs 5f.4, 5f.5). The first step is making the yarn. Stone, bone, and ceramic spindle whorls are used in this process. As some suggest, the wool of the highland sheep is the best for weaving, because they have long strands. Making yarn for woolen fabrics begins with the twisting done on a stick with a spindle whorl weight at the bottom.

After the yarn is made, the weaving process begins. Ethnographically, weavers use a variety of looms.[565] A common feature of all known looms are weights to hold the warp strings. Certainly, the clay one from Shengavit in Figure 5f.6 (3) would fall into that category. The stone weights illustrated in 5f.2 could easily be loom weighs as well.

A number of these ground stone objects, especially the tufa pieces synched in the middle have been identified as fishing sinkers. Certainly, the fish bones recovered in the screens demonstrate that locals at Shengavit did fish in the Hrazdan River (see Chapter 5a above). Whether these were loom weights or sinkers will require more study of Kura-Araxes fishing technology. We need to determine if they were fishing with nets, with lines and hooks (no unambiguous examples recovered at Shengavit), spears, with baskets, or in weirs. A start in this inquiry would be to learn ethnographically what sinkers' requirements were in size and weight for each of these possible technologies.

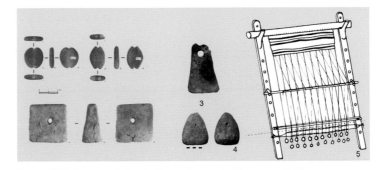

Figure 5f.6 Loom weights 1. Ground stone 2. Terracotta 3. Terracotta weight from Shengavit, 4. Anatolian clay, 5. Horizontal loom.

A last category is that of weights. Simonyan et al. claim that a number of weights were necessary in the metallurgical processes at Shengavit.[566]

---

565   see Wulff 1966 for a description of various traditional Persian looms.
566   Simonyan et al. 2019.

Top

The category of top working surfaces is divided into three categories. First are querns on which mostly grains were processed into flour. Other querns, such as the bowl-shaped one illustrated in Figure 5f.7 are for processing other materials. This one is a softer stone, so it would be inappropriate for use with something as gritty as grains. Second are stones used as a base for making something. Variously called a working platform, pecking stone, drilling stone, or small anvil they are used for some process in which the maker needs to have a base for striking, drilling, or grinding (Fig 5f.8). Pecking stones, what Rosenberg and Garfinkel call drilling boards,[567] are examples of this (Fig 5f.10).

Figure 5f.7 Top surface ground stone tools.

A variety of objects could be ground by these: nuts, chipped stone, objects for bead making, or other craft activities we just do not know much about. Alternatively, the making of pottery forms is at times done with a wooden paddle and an anvil.[568] The anvil with a convex side is worked on the inside opposed by a flat wooden anvil on the outside. Given what we know about pottery techniques at Shengavit this and the small anvils illustrated in Figure 5f. 7 would be the right size and shape for the task.

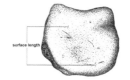

Figure 5f. 8 Lithic working stone.

Another tool type is the shaft straightener. In addition to wooden shafts, polishing bone tools (Fig 5f.9), or a drilling platform might be other top forms (Fig 5f.10).

Edge

A third category of working surfaces is edges. I suspect these are underrepresented in our sample. They are heavy and have a sharper edge. With evidence of increased forest cover, one would expect that a lot of clearing needed to be done. Axes would be the best tool. It is surprising that we do not have evidence of handles on all of these, but there is one with a hand-hold in Figure 5f.11. Perhaps, these were not finished tools.

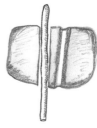

Figure 5f.9 Shaft straightener.

Bottom

Tools with bottom working surfaces are quite common (Fig 5f.12). Locals usually made the complimentary piece (*manos*) to saddle querns (*metataes*) of rough basalt (*sluda*) or sandstone. However, within the category of bottom working surfaces, many appear to have been used for grinding other materials: tempers for pottery, other ground stone tools, wood, plaster, etc. Images of *manos* and *metates* from ancient and ethnographic Mesoamerica, Egypt, and Mesopotamia all confirm, that a *mano* needs to be about as wide as a *metate*. Otherwise, grain will simply slide around the side, making grinding harder. Querns (*metates*) at Shengavit ranged from 13 to 20 centimeters wide, most in the upper part of that range. Any grinding stone less than 13 cm., therefore, I considered as not a *mano*, but for one of the other uses.

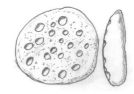

Figure 5f.10 Drilling stone.

Pumice scrapers are too soft for grinding rough materials like seeds or tempering. Ethnographically, Wulff in

---

567   Rosenberg and Garfinkel 2014: 191-2.
568   Adams 2014, 160f.; Rice 1987, 136.

Figure 5f. 11 Shengavit edge tools.

Figure 5f.12 Ground Stone Tools with bottom working surface.

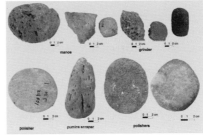

Figure 5f. 13 Polisher.

describing leather tanning specifically mentions the use of a pumice grinder.[569] The steps in tanning include soaking, liming, swelling, salting, tanning, grinding, and burnishing. Grinding happens "when the tanning is completed, the hides are dried in the sun, and then placed on a polishing board [...]. With the flesh side up the hide is ground smooth with a pumice stone. Burnishing involves placing the dyed hide on the polishing board and burnished with a highly polished stone with heavy pressure." Most of the earlier processes are done in a ditch, although large ceramic basins were sometimes used. We had identified a vat as being for wine making. That still seems its most likely use, but it is possible that leathermaking was another possible use.

Polishing is another task for the bottom working surface tools (Fig 5.13). In Iran I watched villagers put plaster on their walls. They used a flat stone that fit in their hands to apply and smooth it. Two polishers on the bottom row of Figure 5f. 12 fit this tool. Many other polishing tasks from finishing bone wood, ground stone tools required small, rough-edged polishing or grinding tools. Pounding tools for the burnishing of leather would also fit these types of surfaces.

END

The working edge category of end includes a number of kinds of tools (Fig 5f.14). One is a hammer (Fig 5f.15). Makers drilled many hammers through to accommodate a handle or thinned them on one end, so they could be hafted (fig 5f.16). Of particular interest are hammers used for processing salt. Hammers would also have been important in construction. Another functional type in this category are hoes or harrows. Pestles are a third type (Fig 5f.17). Most are tubular, although some were more rounded, coming close to the final pointed category, although the tips show less pecking or breakage and more smooth surfaces. A last type are handheld hammers for lighter hammering activity than hammers or harrows.

POINTS

Points are the final working surface. Here their size and material are critical (Fig 5f.18). Pointed tools made of a heavy,

Figure 5f. 14 End working surface tools.

Figure 5f.15 Hammers from salt mine.

Figure 5f.16 Hafted hammer or ax.

Figure 5f.17 Pestle use.

---

569 Wulff 1966, 230f.

hard stone are used to grind the holes in other ground stone (Fig 5f.19). Experimental work with ground stone shows that artisans used another large pointed tool with sand or other abrasive material to grind a hole or make a concave stone bowl, like the grinding stone illustrated in 5f.7. above.[570] At times this procedure grinds the point flat, as in one of the tools in Figure 5f.12 above. Other activities require tools of this type. Breaking nodules of obsidian would take some force. In one location in K6 a series of talc nodules lay on a floor of layer VI with a collection of ground stone tools. A small hammer, pressure flaker, and two small stones, these stones are traditionally used to rough the edge of a lithic flake before pressure flaking, so make up a flint knapping tool kit, as we found, illustrated above. These are the working surfaces. Again, it is not always easy to say what any given tool was used for exactly.

Figure 5f.18 Point work surface tools.

Figure 5f.19 Making a hole in ground stone.

Size

After working surface, the next variable is size. As discussed above, size is one way to distinguish a grinder that is used with a quern for grinding grain, a *mano,* versus a grinder used for other materials. Trying to refine what size categories were relevant proved difficult. A distribution map of square centimeters showed that although there were peaks and valleys, the chart was relatively continuous. The valleys in the chart I marked as breaks. There were 7. So, I ran a sample with 8 divisions. These were less than 10 cm² (1), 10-20 cm² (2), 20-40 cm² (3), 40-90 cm² (4), 90-170 cm² (5), 170-265 cm² (6), 265-500 cm² (7), 500-1300 cm² (8). There were almost none in category (1).

Table 5f. Table 2 below maps the likely functions occurring in each size category. In this way it was possible to define and calibrate the functions better. I adjusted the final data matrix based on this table. As the table demonstrates, burnishers are in the two smallest size categories, as are spindle whorls, maceheads, and most lithic retouchers. Querns are most common in size categories (6), (7), and (8), as are most matching grinders of the *mano* type. The category of hammers is widely distributed in size, and probably consist of two sub-types, smaller (3) and (4) and larger (mostly 5 and 6).

Size index/ Function	2	3	4	5	6	7	8
anvil	0	0	1/1%	0	0	0	0
axe	0	0	1/1%	7/12%	1	0	0
burnisher	7/26%	15/12%	0	0	0	0	0
celt	0	2/2%	1/1%	0	0	0	0
cutter	0	0	0	2/4%	0	0	0
dig weight	0	5/4%	1/1%	0	0	0	0
grinder	3/11%	9/7%	7/8%	9/16%	2/10%	0	0
hammer	2/7%	22/17%	46/49%	11/19%	1/5%	0	0
harrow	0	0	0	0	2/10%	0	0
loom weight	0	0	0	1/2%	0	0	0
macehead	1/7%	10/8%	0	0	0	0	0
mano	0	0	5/5%	16/28%	8/40%	1/7%	1/7%
pecking stone	0	5/4%	4/4%	0	0	0	1/7%
pestle	0	5/4%	6/6%	0	0	0	0
polisher	3/11%	10/8%	11/12%	3/5%	1/5%	0	0
pot stand	0	1/.7%	1/1%	0	0	0	0
pounder	0	0	2/1%	1/2%	0	1/7%	0
quern	0	0	1/1%	6/11%	5/25%	12/86%	12/80%
retoucher	8/30%	26/20%	2/2%	0	0	0	0
scraper	0	2/2%	0	0	0	0	1/7%
sinker/loom weight	0	6/5%	6/6%	0	0	0	0
spindle whorl	3/11%	2/2%	0	0	0	0	0
straightener	0	0	1/1%	0	0	0	0
wedge	0	1/.7%	1/1%	1/2%	0	0	0
weight	0	2/2%	0	0	0	0	0
whetstone	0	0	1/1%	0	0	0	0
total	**27**	**130**	**93**	**57**	**20**	**14**	**15**

Table 5f.2. Function versus Size

---

570   Moorey 1999, 71; Squitieri and Eitam 2016.

Material

The residents of Shengavit had seven basic stone types for making ground stone tools: varieties of basalt, sandstone, diorite, marble, tufa, pumice, and limestone (Fig 5f.20). A few other materials are minor contributors, such as conglomerate. Basalt and sandstone are the most common. The density of rocks will to some degree determine its function. The denser a rock is, in effect, the "harder" it is, the more it can be used to break, drill or polish other rocks, such as opening pebbles of obsidian.[571] Diorite is denser than basalt, which is denser than marble, which in turn is denser than sandstone. Tufa varies in density by how deep it is in volcanic laid sediments. Marble is a denser limestone, formed by heat and pressure. Andesite is a different flow of the same type as basalt, but it is essentially a basalt. Sandstone, marble, and limestone are all sedimentary rocks.

Figure 5f. 20 Stone types.

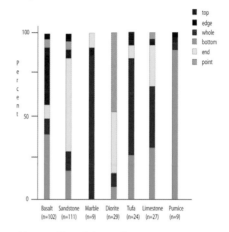

Figure 5f.21 Material versus Working Surface.

No./% worked surface	Top	Edge	Whole	Bottom	End	Point	Total
Basalt	35/34%	2/2%	10/7%	37/37%	15/15%	3/3%	103
Sandstone	2/1.5%	6/5%	12/10%	20/17%	68/58%	10/8%	118
Marble	1/9%	0	8/89%	0	2/18%	0	11
Diorite	1/4%	0	1/4%	2/8%	13/50%	11/42%	26
Tufa	2/7%	0	16/57%	7/25%	2/7%	1/4%	28
Pumice	1/7%	1/7%	1/7%	10/77%	0	0	13
Limestone	0	0	12/31%	13/33%	12/31%	1/5%	39

Table 5f. 3. Material and Working Surface (number/percentage of stone type)

Table 5f.3. and Figure 5f.21 show the variation in materials used for various working surfaces. The artisans making these tools clearly show that they have the design elements discussed above in mind when they make a ground stone tool.

Variation Over Time

Patterns are good for understanding typology. The importance, once that is established, is what they tell us about the adaptations and activities of the people of the time. We can do that along two axes: place and time. The first variation, place, tells us where the activities represented by the ground stone tools occurred (see Chapter 7). The second, time, tells us whether these activities changed over time. The two variables of time and place intersect in the artifacts' findspots. This is the closest to the ancient reality. It describes the activity along with other artifact types in a moment in time.

As such, throughout our analysis we have measured only artifacts from primary and secondary contexts. Artifacts from tertiary proveniences were not included in the data matrix. This can reduce our sample size, but we believe it provides the best picture of the past.

Table 5f.4 summarizes the frequency of tool function by square. The data from the National History Museum are included as a contrast only, since we have no reliable indication of where Sardarian found those artifacts.

Our 2009-2012 excavations recovered more of the later phases of the site's history than the earlier ones. Square I14, which was located with georadar (see Chapter 4c), appears to be contemporaneous with Building 1in Square

---

571   Rafferty 201, Figure 12.

K6, the remains of the pebble floor in Square J5, and the Square M5 shrine, also located by georadar. L7 is part of the Square K6 Building 1. The second stratum (see Chapter 3) is unique to squares K6, K5 and the southeast corner of J5. Stratum III is well documented in K6 and J5. All of the remaining strata are evident in K6, some in the earlier excavation of K5, K/L 3/ 4, and the 2000 excavations. Before seeing what conclusions are possible to gather from the distribution, Table 5f.4 below summarizes the functions by stratum and square.

Missing from the ground stone objects recovered from 2009-2012 were a number of important functions; among them maceheads, cutters, digging stick weights, straighteners, and weights. Burnishers, which we suggest indicated pottery production, were present in all squares but Square L7, the annex of Square K6 Building 1. Square K6 appears to have the greatest number, but when one breaks down the numbers into the different levels, the average number appears the same. The shrine room in Square M5[572] had that average number. Grinders are very common in Square M5, and again, although the number seems similar to Square K6, when one looks at them over time, each phase of Square K6 had a lower number than Square M5, which appears by stratigraphy and carbon-dating to be from the latest Stratum I. Square I14 had only one grinder. Most of the grinders from Square J5 came from pits, one 2017 carbon dated to 2200 BC, although it is unclear whether they were from levels cut into by the pitting. The most common functional type associated with end working surfaces was hammers. This is a broad category mostly in the 3-6 size categories. Presumably, the larger hammers would be for a different purpose than the small ones. As Table 5f.5. shows, the distribution of hammer sizes is quite different. In Square I14 and Square K6, most are in size 4. Square J5, accounting for the displacement through pitting, had as many of size 3 as of 4, but together with Squares J6/J5 (part of the stratum III building mostly in Square J5) type 3 constituted the largest number. Square M5 had more harrows or pounders than contemporaneous Square K6, where the three recovered were from earlier strata. All had significant numbers of *manos* and querns, showing that processing of grains was a common feature of all excavated buildings. Polishers were very common in Squares M5 and J5, but less in contemporaneous Square K6. Pestles were mostly recovered from Square J5. Retouchers, small-

Phase/tool type	I14	K6	J5	J6 (J5)	M5	L7	Nat Hist
anvil							1/ 1
axe	1/ 2.5	1/ 0.8					5/ 6
burnisher	3/ 7.5	11/ 10	2/ 3.6	1/ 2	2/ 5		4/ 5
celt		2/ 1.7					1/ 1
cutter				1/ 2			
dig stick weight							7/ 9
grinder	1/ 2.5	13/ 11.6	8/ 14.5	2/ 4.4	6/ 15		1/ 1
hammer	14/ 35	34/ 30	14/ 25	34/ 75.5	7/ 17.5	17/ 89	4/ 5
Harrow/pounder		3/ 2.6			1/ 2.5		1/ 1
loom weight							2/ 2.5
macehead							12/ 15
mano	8/ 20	11/ 10	7/ 13	2/ 4.4	5/ 12.5		
pecking stone		1/ .08			1/ 2.5		7/ 9
pestle	2/ 5		5/ 9				2/ 2.5
polisher	2/ 5	7/ 6	6/ 11	3/ 6.6	7/ 17.5	2/ 11	
pot stand		1/ 0.8	1/ 1.8		1/ 2.5		
quern	8/ 20	4/ 3.6		1/ 2	6/ 15		15/ 19
retoucher	1/ 2.5	19/ 17	11/ 20	1/ 2	3/ 7.5		
scraper		1/ 0.8	2/ 3.6				
sinker		2/ 1.7					9/ 11.5
spindle whorl			1/ 1.8				4/ 5
straightener							1/ 1
wedge		1/ 0.8			1/ 2.5		
weight							2/ 2.5
whetstone		1/ 0.8					
Total	40	112	55	45	40	19	78

Table 5f.4 Frequency of Tools by Square (number/*percent in square*).

Square /Size	3	4	5/6
I14	2	9	3
J5	6	6	2
J6/J5	5	3	1
K6	9	23	2
M5	1	3	3

Table 5f.5. Hammer size categories by square.

---

572   Simonyan and Rothman 2015, and Chapter 6a.

pointed hammers of a size and shape good for knapping lithics, were most common throughout the strata of K6. The only ground stone spindle whorl came from Square J5. The only sinkers (loom weights?) came from Square K6.

Conclusion

Again, the reality of this category of artifact shows how varied it was, and how critical it is for understanding the lifeways of the ancient residents of Shengavit. Many different activities are represented using the new typology suggested here. Odds are most of materials used for ground stone were locally available. Certainly, the craft of ground stone tool making is as critical as that of chipped stone, metal, cloth, or pottery.

References

Adams, J. 2014 *Ground Stone Analysis*. Second edition. Salt Lake City: University of Utah Press.

Adams, J. 1989 Experimental Replication of the Use of Ground Stone Tools. *Kiva* 54 (3): 261-271.

Adams, J. 1988 Use-Wear Analyses on Manos and Hide-Processing Stones. *Journal of Field Archaeology* 15 (3): 307-315.

Badalyan, R., Hovsepyan, S., Khachatryan, L. 2015 *Shengavit: Catalog of Artifacts in the National History Museum*. Yerevan: National History Museum (in Russian)

Horsfal, G. A. 1987 Design Theory and Grinding Stones. in *Lithic Studies Among the Contemporary Highland Maya*, edited by B. Hayden, 332-377. Tucson: University of Arizona Press.

Kramer, C. 1982 *Village Ethnoarchaeology*. New York: Academic Press.

Kushnareva, K. 1997 *The Southern Caucasus in Prehistory*. translated by H.N. Michael. Philadelphia: The University Museum Press.

Medvedskaya, I. 1988 Who Destroyed Hasanlu IV. *Iran* 26: 1-15.

Moorey, P. R. S. 1994 *Ancient Mesopotamian Material and Industries: The Archaeological Evidence*. Winona Lake, Indiana: Eisenbrauns.

Peterson, Jane 2008 New Insights from Old Stones: A Survey of Ground Stone Studies. in *New Approaches to Old Stones: Recent Studies of Ground Stone Artifacts*, edited by Y. Rowan and J. Ebeling, 361-370. London: Equinox.

Peterson, J. How to Burnish Pottery *https://www.thesprucecrafts.com/how-to-burnish-pottery-2746229*

Rafferty, J. 2011 *Rocks*. New York: Britannica Educational Publishing (ebook).

Rosenberg, D., Rowan, Y., and Gluhak, T. 2016 Introduction: Leave No Stone Unturned: Perspectives on Ground Stone Artefact Research. *Journal of Lithic Studies* 3(3): 1-15.

Rosenberg, D. and Garfinkel, Y. 2014. *Sha'ar HaGolan Volume 4: The Ground Stone Industry*. Jerusalem: Israel Exploration Society.

Rutter, G., and Philip, G. 2008 Beyond Provenance Analysis: The Movement of Basaltic Artefacts. In *New Approaches to Old Stones: Recent Studies of Ground Stone Artifacts*, edited by Y. Rowan and J. Ebeling, 343-359. London: Equinox.

Schoop, U. 2014 Weaving Society in Late Chalcolithic Anatolia: Textile Production and Social Strategies in the 4th Millennium BS. in *Western Anatolia Before Troy: Proto-Urbanization in the 4th Millennium BC?*, edited by B. Horejs and M. Mehofer, 421-446. Vienna: Austrian Academy of Sciences Press.

Simonyan, H., Gevorgyan, A., and Bobokhyan, A. 2019 Cognitive Links Between Mountains and Lowlands: Balance Weights from the Early Bronze Age Site Shengavit, Armenia in Context. *Aramazd* XIII (2): 34-52.

Squitieri, A. and Eitem, D. 2016 An Experimental Approach to Ground Stone Tool Manufacture. *Journal of Lithic Studies* 3 (3): 565-587.

Stapleton, L., Margaryan, L., Arshian, G., Pinhasi,G., and Gasparyan, B. 2014 Weaving the Ancient Past: Chalcolithic Basket and Textile Technology at Areni-1 Cave, Armenia. in *Stone Age Armenia*, edited by B. Gasparyan and M. Arimura, 219-232. Kanazawa University, Japan: Center for Cultural Resource Studies.

Watson, P. J. 1979 *Archaeological Ethnography in Western Iran*. Tucson: University of Arizona Press.

Wulff, H. 1966 *The Traditional Crafts of Persia*. Cambridge: M.I.T. Press.

Wright, K. 1992 A Classification System for Ground Stone Tools from the Prehistoric Levant. *Paléorient* 18 (2): 51-81.

5g | Bone Tools

Mitchell Rothman

Another material used for tools is bone. Animals were clearly a key resource for Kura-Araxes populations. Meat and milk products provided key nutrients (Chap 5a). The hair of mammals was used for cloth. Their skin was processed into leather for making clothes, possibly armor, thongs, and straps. Their bone was also used for making tools. The last is the topic of this chapter (Fig 5g.1).

The numbers of bone tools recovered at Shengavit is small compared with that of lithics, pottery, or ground stone. The total is 59, 16 from the 2000-2008 seasons, 18 at the National History Museum, and 25 from 2009-2012 (see tDAR web archive for catalog and details). Statistical analysis is therefore not possible. We have little or no evidence where they were produced or by whom. The only piece in the process of being made we recovered from a mixed context in J6. Nonetheless, this category adds information on activities at the site.

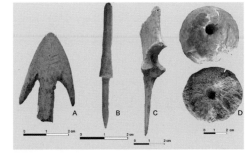

Figure 5g.1 Sample of bone tools.

Manufacture

Making bone tools begins with the selection of the bone source. Long straight bones are typically the best source.[573] At Shengavit this means mostly the ulna of caprids or femur of cows (long bones of the leg). Makers used other bones like cow or deer ribs, or caprid (sheep/goat) knucklebones and metacarpals, and caprid horns. The animals from whom bone was extracted tended to be large and older.[574] The second step is to cut it into a blank. Sometimes, the bone is split or shortened. In the case of sheep ulnas, this step is often unnecessary. Artisans used the whole bone; they only modified the tip (Fig 5g.1. C; Fig 5g.2., B, C, F). A third step is finishing. This includes polishing and thinning the bone to the desired final shape, probably with a ground stone abrader (see Chapter 5f). The bone can be cut with chipped stone knives or stone wedges to create features like tangs or to add designs. Bone tools are almost always polished in the production process.

Functions

Archaeologists have recovered many bone tool types that reflect the same functions from the Mesolithic to the Iron Age. Amazingly similar tools emerged from across the ancient Old and New Worlds.

These I classified by their shape and probable function.

---

573   Vinayak 2016.
574   Maeir et al. 2012.

Most common were the first category, the awls (Fig 5g.2). They constituted 35 out of the 59 tools, including five broken tips. The average length of these tools was 8.28 cm. The awl is a general category of longer pointed tools. However, as Figure 5g.2 illustrates, this category is actually quite varied. Their producers mostly used a whole ulna of a sheep or goat (B, C and F). The one exception is illustrated in Fig 5g.2., E, which producers carved from the rib of an ox. Sometimes, makers split a long bone with a chipped stone wedge and a ground stone hammer (Fig 5g.2., D).[575] Watson calls these "flake awls" at Jarmo.[576] Artisans cut down a smaller portion or flattened a piece, and then sharpened one end into a point (D and E). Awl type A was smaller, and they carefully sculpted into a wider and narrower point. Excavators recovered quite a few points that were probably from awls, as the end above the point appears broken and not finished at the break.

These different awls must have been used for different purposes. Types C and D have sharp points. These are most often used ethnographically and archaeologically in making leather goods or weaving basketry.[577] We recovered impressions of basketry in Square K6 as a base for construction. No actual baskets survived. Pairs of long awls were also used for knitting (Fig 5g.3).[578] Type E looks very much like a spacer used in weaving.[579] The spacer lifts the warp to allow easier transit of the shuttle cock carrying the weft. Atisans mostly made shuttle cocks from wood, which disintegrated in the ground. Excavators found a bone shuttle cock at Sos Höyük (Type H). The heavier Types B, F, and G awls are too crude for making basketry or piercing leather. However, similar bone awls are utilized in ethnographic cases to de-flesh animals and remove their hair in the leather-making process.[580] Awl A is a finished tool, but it is very generalized. It could have been used for basketmaking, leatherwork, or a number of other tasks. Microscopic analysis of the working point might have given us a more precise idea of the material they were made to manipulate,[581] but we did not have the time or tools necessary to conduct this analysis.

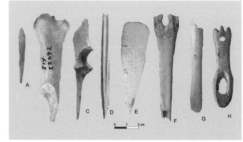

Figure 5g.2 Bone tools in the general category of awls.

Figure 5g.3 Basketry and knitting from Sos Höyük.

The best published sample of Kura-Araxes bone tools I found is from Pulur Sakyol.[582] Most bone tools illustrated from there fit in the types of Awls C or D with long narrow points. The second most common were of Type B or F, but there were a few of types A and E. This implies that leather-making and basketry were very likely important activities throughout the Kura-Araxes world, even though we have very few products of either activity.

A second category of bone tools is arrowheads. Hardening arrowheads can be achieved by soaking, covering with substances like beeswax, burning, and rolling. [583]

---

575   https://www.primitiveways.com/bone_awl.html.
576   Watson 1983.
577   Keddie 2012; Stone 2011, Fig 4.
578   C. Sagona 2018.
579   McCafferty and McCafferty 2008.
580   Steinbring 1966
581   Buc 2011.
582   Koşay 1976, 104-109.
583   Vinayak 2016.

There are two basic shapes that archaeologists recovered from Shengavit and other sites like Pulur Sakyol and Kvatskhelebi.[584] These average 4.5 centimeters in length. One form is narrow and round with a straight tang that would have been hafted into the arrow shaft (Fig 5g, 3, A, B, and C). A variation of that is a more pointed arrowhead with a barb on one side only (Fig 5g.3. D). A few had barbs on both sides and a flattened tang for hafting (Fig 5g.3., E and F; Fig 5g.4.). Types E and F are closest to the obsidian arrowheads in shape (see Chapter 5c).

These variations raise the question of how effective these bone arrowheads could be, and whether they were primarily for hunting or military use. Surprisingly, bone arrows can be quite deadly.[585] They can pierce the hide of a deer or the leather tunic of a person from some distance. Experimental tests with bone-tipped arrows show that they have an advantage over chipped stone arrowheads.[586] Since they are more flexible, they do not break as easily or come off the shaft of the arrow (Fig 5g.5). This makes them good for hunting, as they can be retrieved and used again. At the same time, they can be used as weapons against other human beings. Most of the time, the arrow does not kill its animal prey or human opponent immediately. The idea is to slow them down or make them bleed to death. The more cylindrical ones are best at a greater distance. The barbed ones are more dangerous to the animal or human, because in trying to remove them or in moving while they are still stuck in the body the likelihood of death increases. Looked at from a different angle, larger arrowheads are better for hunting birds. They are used to knock down the bird in flight. Cylindrical points, on the other hand, penetrate the flesh of larger deer, boars, or fish better. Metal arrows are no better at this, except that they can penetrate bone, which bone arrows usually cannot. Most analysts favor the idea that bone arrowheads were for hunting animals,[587] although the military option cannot be ignored.

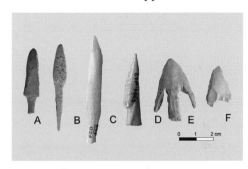

Figure 5g.4 Arrow points.

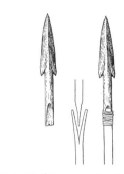

Figure 5g.5 Hafting arrowheads.

There remain a few bone objects of other functions at Shengavit (Fig 5g.6). Type A is needle-like, although ethnographically attested needles for cloth work had to have either a hole or a ridge to hold the thread.[588] This appears more likely to be a straight pin to hold clothing together. The relatively short rod (type B) and the spindle whorl (type F) appear in cloth-making contexts, the former for use with a loom and the latter to create yarn for weaving. Type C is the horn of a sheep or goat. In Chapter 5f, the tools used for flint knapping appear to have been ground stone. In the New World, the favorite tool of flintknappers for retouching is a deer antler. Those, however, are harder and more pointed. Type C therefore could be used for retouching lithics. Excavators found similar horn implements at Pulur Sakyol.[589] Horns of this type were cut down to function as hammers. Their exact use here, however, is unclear. The polished bone wafer, type D, is also a bit of a mystery in terms of what it was used for. Polishers and abraders are larger.

584   Koşay 1976, 106; Kushnareva 1997, Fig 23.
585   https://www.youtube.com/watch?v=Pl7fb6wBdYY
586   Luik 2006.
587   Luik 2006
588   McCafferty and McCafferty 2008; Stone 2008, Fig 1.
589   Koşay 1976, 109.

The knucklebone (*astragalus*), type E, on the other hand has a long history from the Neolithic to the present day as a gaming piece.[590] In modern Iran, the game is called *Bojul,* in Egypt *Senet.*[591]. Because the knuckle bone is roughly squared, the odds of it landing on a given face is roughly equal. Flattening different edges, which is the case with the one illustrated in Fig 5g.6 enhances its usefulness for this purpose. They can be thought of as a kind of dice. In addition, these knuckle bones are used as a tool for divination.[592] Lastly, and perhaps related to the latter function, these bones were buried in mortuary contexts from Early Bronze to Hellenistic times.[593] Where they are found in numbers, they are isolated from other animal bones in domestic or funerary contexts.

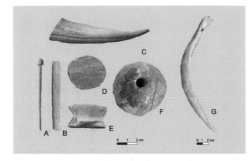

Figure 5g.6 Miscellaneous bone tools.

The last bone object is a red deer horn polished with a square hole drilled away from the pointed end. At 21.2 cm it is the longest of the bone artifacts. Archaeologists at Pulur Sakyol discovered an almost identical object in level VI.[594] That is a group of four small Kura-Araxes rooms. This is not the two room apartments in the semi-circle with andirons and altars. Koşay believes the square hole was for hafting as a light pick. The Shengavit example came from the bottom of the steps in Square M5, the room with the ceramic hearth and altar. It could be part of the symbolic suite of objects associated with the hearth. However, we also found a bone arrowhead, ground stone tools, and a normal set of domestic animal bones in the same general context (see Chapter 5a). It might be an agricultural tool for weeding or to make a hole for seeding, or a way to pierce an animal's body to release blood onto the altar, although this one had few signs of wear on the tip.

Conclusion

This analysis illustrates how varied and important bone tools were. Aside from rather expected function, they indicate that activities like basket- and leather-making, which are rarely discussed. Information on where these artifacts were discovered are discussed in Chapter 7 below.

590   Sabori et al. 2016
591   Greenfield et al. 2018, 115.
592   Minniti and Peyronel 2005.
593   Minniti and Peyronel 2005; De Grossi Mazzorin and Minniti 2003, Gilmour 1997.
594   Koşay 1976, 106.

References

Badalyan, R., Hovsepyan, S.G. Khachatryan L.E. 2015 *Shengavit: Catalog of archaeological materials from the collections of the Museum of History of Armenia*. Yerevan: Museum of History of Armenia. (in Russian).

Buc, N. 2011 Experimental series and use-wear in bone tools. *Journal of Archaeological Science* 38: 546-557.

De Grossi Mazzorin, J. and Minniti, C. 2013 Ancient Use of Knuckle-bone for Rituals and Gaming Piece. *Anthropozoologica* (December): 371-380.

Gilmour, G. 1997 The Nature and Function of Astragalus Bones from Archaeological Contexts in the Levant and Eastern Mediterranean. *Oxford Journal of Archaeology* 16(2): 167-175.

Greenfield, H., Brown, A., Shai, I., and Macir, A. 2008 Unravelling the Meaning of Faunal Assemblages in an Early Urban Domestic Neighborhood: worked bone frequencies from the Early Bronze Age III neighborhood at es-Sâfi/Gath, Israel. in *Archaeozoology of the Near East XII*, edited by C. Çaktlar, J. Chahoud, R. Berthon, S.P. and Birch, 109-121. Eelde, Netherlands: Barkhuis.

Keddie, G. Bone 2012 Awls: Bridging the gap between Archaeology and Ethnography. *The Midden* 44(1): 10-12.

Koşay, H. 1976. *Keban Projesi Pulur Kazisi 1968–70*. METU, Ankara.

Kushnareva, K. Kh. 1997 *The Southern Caucasus in Prehistory*. Philadelphia: University Museum Publications.

Luik, H. 2006 For Hunting or for Warfare? Bone Arrows from the Late Bronze Fortified Settlements in Eastern Baltic. *Estonian Journal of Archaeology* 10(2): 132-149.

Maier, A., Greenfield, H., Lev-Tov, J., and Horwitz, L.K. 2012 Macro- and Microscopic Aspects of Bone Tool Manufacture and Technology in the Levantine Iron Age: a 9th Century BCE Workshop from Tel-es-Safi/Gath, Israel. in *Techniques and People*, edited by S. Rosen and V. Roux, 41-68. Paris: De Boccard.

McCafferty, S. and McCafferty, G. 2008 Spinning and Weaving Tools from Santa Isabel, Nicaragua. *Ancient Mesoamerica* 19 (1): 143-156.

Minniti, C. and Peyronel, L. 2005 Symbolic or functional Astragali from Tell Mardikh-Ebla (Syria). *Archaeofauna* 14: 7-26.

Sabori, H., Basafa, H., Hejininezhad, E., Bolandi, R., and Khorasani, M.N. 2016 Game Pieces of Knucklebones: Evidence about the Continuation of Local Games in Khorasan, Iran. *The Silk Road* 14: 209-212.

Sagona, C. 2018 Two-Needle Knitting and Cross-Knit looping: Early Bronze Age Pottery Imprints from Anatolia and the Caucasus. *Oxford Journal of Archaeology* 37 (3): 283-297.

Steinbring, J. 1966 The Manufacturing and Use of Bone Defleshing Tools. *American Antiquity* 31(4): 575-581.

Stone, E. 2011 The Role of Ethnographic Museum Collections in Understanding Bone Tool Use. in *Written in Bones: Studies on Technological and Social Contexts of Past Skeletal Remains*, edited by J. Baron and B. Kufel-Diakowska, 25-40. Warsaw: Uniwersytet Wroclawski Institute of Archaeology.

Vinayak, V. 2016 *An Archaeological Study of Bone and Antler Arrowheads from the Upper Ganga Plains (circa 1100-200 B.C.)*. unpublished Doctoral thesis. Jawaharlal Nehru University.

Watson, P.J. 1983 Jarmo Worked Bone. in *Prehistoric Archaeology Along the Zagros Flanks*, edited by L. Braidwood and R. Braidwood, B. Howe, C. Reed, and P.J. Watson, 347-368. Chicago: Oriental Institute Publications 105.

5h | Items of Personal Adornment

Hakob Simonyan and Mitchell Rothman

Adornment as Social Communication

"Jewelry. or personal adornment is generally defined as small decorative items intended to be worn on the body or attached to clothing."[595] Forms of personal adornment, especially what we perceive as jewelry, are often more than mere display. They represent ways of expressing identity in terms of gender, social group, and culture. Potentially, jewelry is also an art form that signals one's status in society. This relationship is a complex one. It assumes that we have some idea of how the value system of ancient societies worked.[596] Most likely, value was established based on the interactions of groups in their exchange networks through which goods moved, and value was determined.

As we will show, such changes are clearest in the transition from the Kura-Araxes to the Early Kurgan period. Some associate jewelry with the idea of wealth,[597] the idea that some in society are able to emass more culturally valued items, be they houses, metals, jewelry, or other objects, than others. This wealth is a way to mark oneself as better than less wealthy individuals or families. If, as Rothman proposes, the society of the Kura-Araxes Lower Province were egalitarian, wealth and a status it portrays to others in society would present problems with getting cooperation among other kin folk.[598] If as Simonyan proposes, the society of the Kura-Araxes Lower Province were already more complex than a tribal society, the concept of wealth be among its likely characteristics. Both agree that the organization of Early Kurgan societies would include the concept of wealth.

This does not mean that value is universal. Gold, which has clear value for modern societies, may not have the same value in ancient time. Its value is not necessarily intrinsic to the raw material and its rarity, as it is to us. Just as was the case for the chiefdoms of Panama,[599] the ability of artisans to manipulate and decorate golden objects may have been as important as its possible rarity.

These social elements can be recorded in adornments' shape, decoration, and material. They had meaning in everyday life. Jewelry was found in the houses of Shengavit. The ancients also deposited them in burials as part of the rite of passage to death (see Chapter 6b).

Types of Adornments

BEADS

The simplest form of adornment were beads (Fig 5h.1).[600] They were mostly round and flat, although some were

---

595   Golani 2022, 171.
596   Renfrew 1986.
597   Renfrew 1986, 163f.
598   Sahlins 1968.
599   Helms 1976.
600   Carminati 2014, 170.

cylindrical. Fig 5h.1., 45 is an anchor shape that is very typical of the Kur-Araxes cultural tradition.[601] A few have special functions like the spacer (Fig 5h.1., 10 and 42), which must have been part of a necklace. The materials of these relatively simple beads varied significantly. Number 1 and 2 had a silica base like glass. We recovered no other glass products. Because the color is a kind of blue green, perhaps sand got into a copper smelt, which would produce this material accidently. Other kinds of stone, some came from local sources like limestone, some like carnelian came from northern Armenia or the borderland between Armenia and Iran.[602] In addition, craftsmen made beads of agate, jasper, crystal, black amber, tufa, feldspar, and copper. Artisans also used obsidian (Fig 5h.1., 45). At Shengavit only 43 and 44 consisted of metal (arsenical bronze).

Beads were widely dispersed in the settlement. Some like Fig 5h, 45 were recovered from what were most likely burials. We recovered no actual necklaces or bracelets intact.

Pins

A second category of adornment consisted of pins.[603] The use of these could be for clothing, especially Fig 5h.2., 4, which might be part of a fibula. At the Ur Royal tombs, the pins, which were somewhat thicker, lay by the shoulder of the deceased, as if closing a tunic.[604] It is perhaps more likely that these were used in long hair. Certainly, that is the use hypothesized for the so-called Tsalka pin (Fig 5h.2., 5). Most of these metal objects archaeologists found in burials.

Spiral-Shaped Ornaments

Objects in the next category are all made of metal. They

Figure 5h.1   Beads from Shengavit (not to scale). By square and locus: 1) K4/L4 5051, 2) K4/L4 5051, 3) L7 15009, 4) K6 1018, 5) J5 2024, 6) J5 2058, 7) J5 2039, 8) K6 1171, 9) 2008, 10) I14 22014, 11) M5 24008, 12) J5 2038, 13) M5. -, 14) J6 18038, 15) K4/L4 5051, 16) K6 1099, 17) J5 2029, 18) 2008. 19) J5 2045, 20) K6 1165, 21) B5 11000, 22) K6 1078, 23) J5 2015, 24) IV 2025, 25) K6 1043, 26) J5 2024, 27) J6 185010, 28) K3 9000, 29) K6 1141, 30) L4 8000, 31) K6 1110, 32) C15 051, 33) J5) 2029, 34) M3 19002, 35) 2008, 36) O10 019, 37) L4 7048, 38) O10 53, 39) O10 56, 40) J5 2011, 41) J5 2010, 42) J5 -, 43) O15 -, 44) L7 15007, 45) J5 2002.

share the same spiral shape.[605] Their functions are not absolutely clear. Figure 5h.3., 2 is a bracelet. The remaining ones have been called earrings. Again, looking at Ur, the earrings there[606] have very thin wires where they pierce the ear. None of the Shengavit artifacts do. Woolley suggested that they might be for braiding hair, as the image in Fig

---

601   Carminati 2014, 169.
602   Brunet 2009.
603   Carminati 2014, 165.
604   Pittman 1998.
605   Carminati 2014, 168.
606   Pittman 1998, Fig 37.

5h.3. illustrates. This makes sense for the Kura-Araxes. Most are from graves. Fig 5h.3, 9 is from Square K6 Stratum V, Fig 5h.3, 6 is from the pebble floor of Building 1 in Square K6, and 7 is from the turf at the top of Square K6. The material used for these ornaments are mostly bronze, but also silver.

PENDANTS AND RINGS

The final among the groups of ornaments are those in the category of pendants and rings. We recovered few of these. Figure 5h.4.,1 was made of a soft stone. Its design with double circles is the same as small spools and boxes of the same sort of material made at Köhne Shahar in the workshop district.[607]

Among the best known of this category is a pendant in gold from Burial 1 at Shengavit (Fig 5h.4., 2). Archaeologists recovered a very similar item from the contemporary kurgan at Ananauri in Georgia near the site of Martkopi (Fig 5h.4., 3).[608] The triangular design that is common on transitional Kura-Araxes/ Early Kurgan (Bedeni) pottery appears on these pendants. Pendants or earrings made from obsidian with gold foil (Fig 5h.4., 4) as well as the soft stone pendant came from the bottom of a pit above the pebble floor of Stratum I in Square J5. Both probably came from a deteriorated burial pit.

The final part of this category is a golden ring from Burial 2.[609] Rings are not common in the Kura-Araxes, although people may have worn some small coiled metal objects on their fingers.

An item found at Kvatskhelebi and Arslantepe— the latter may have been from a post-Kura-Araxes phase— are diadems.[610] Excavators recovered three of these from Kvatskhelebi in a grave contemporaneous with Shengavit, and two they found buried under the floor of a house in Gudabertka, both in Georgia. No such item came from Shengavit. The Kvatekhelebi diadem was made of beaten copper. On it appeared a series of animals, including one

Figure 5h.2 Pins from Shengavit (not to scale). By square and locus: 1) M5 24001, 2) Burial 17 022, 3) 1967, 4) Burial 1, 5) Burial 15, 6) Tsalka pin.

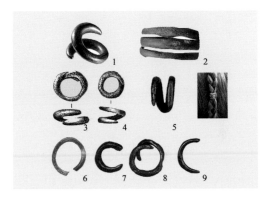

Figure 5h.3 Spiral-Shaped Ornaments (not to scale). 1/2) Burial 1, 3/4) Burial 17, 5) 2005 burial area III, 6)K6 1007, 7) K6 1002, 8) 2005 burial area, 9) K6 1126.

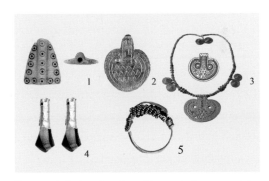

Figure 5h.4 Amulets from Shengavit (not to scale). 1) J5 2002, 2) Burial 1, 3) from Ananauri kurgan 2, 4) J5 2002, 5) Burial 2, 6) Necropolis area III.

that appeared on the painted pot from Shengavit (Fig 6b.7). The presumption has been that this represents a kind of crown, and therefore the person who wore it had a political role. In this case it could fulfill such a symbolic meaning, or a number of others, such as a religious role, or a senior member of a clan.

Sourcing the metal, especially the gold, would help us understand the network through which the material

---

607   Alizadeh et al. 2018.
608   Miron and Orthman (eds.) 1995.
609   Badalyan et al. 2015 claim that this ring is Hellenistic in date, but the simple technology and gold's composition, in our opinion, indicate a much earlier date.
610   Carminati 2014, 171.

traveled, and therefore the way its value was set. The bronze in the Gegharot necklace from a grave (Fig 5h.5), for example, comes from sources outside the area where the site is located. Crafts persons outside this area must have produced parts of it and residents imported it as part of a larger network of exchange. For the most part, analysts have not sourced many Kura-Araxes or Early Kurgan metal items.

Figure 5h.5 Gegharot necklace.

Symbolism

As stated at the onset, jewelry is more than mere ornament. It carries a host of cultural symbols. For example, analysts have many opinions on the symbolism of the gold pendant from Burial 1 (Fig 5h.4., 2). The front side of the gold plate is decorated with deep-line designs typical of the Kura-Araxes cultural tradition. On the hook one could see 90 degree turns in the cross-hatched lines with slant lines. These are often interpreted as thunder and lightning. This motif is contained in a delicate rectangular box. On the lower part of this are two small balls, which, according to Emma Khanzadyan, symbolize a woman's breasts. Underneath, on both sides, by the engraving technique, are triangles with tops upward and filled with slant lines. Again, this is similar to pottery designs, especially those of the Kura-Araxes/Bedeni transition. A ribbon-like fringe belt decorated with slant lines encircles the central image with its ends resting on the small balls.

The previous researchers considered the pendant-amulet to be a stylized female body where the hook was the head, the oval part of the amulet represented the body with breasts and female attributes on it. Simonyan believes that other explanations are possible. In many cases, female attributes were represented by triangles with the sharp points down, while triangles with the sharp points upward have been interpreted as mountains, which in turn represented a male phallus (*lingam*) and further than that, the gods creative beginning.

In Simonyan's opinion, what is portrayed on the amulet from Shengavit is not a woman's body, but the narrative of a myth. The geometrical figures represent the ritual environment, the vertical and horizontal structure of the space. The triangles with their sharp points upward denoted mountains or mountainous landscape. The ribbon-like circle surrounding (around) the central motif with the ends resting on two small balls, in his opinion denotes the two-headed global snake (in Greek *amphisbaena*), its heads threateningly hanging over the highland. In its iconography, it is quite close to dragons portrayed on the helmet of Sarduri II of the later first millennium BC.[611]

Another look at the pendant suggests that the pendants are an elaborated double volute, as is clearer in the Ananauri pendant (Fig 5h.4, 3).

In ancient Armenia, the motif of two-headed snake (dragon) is represented on the black-polished storage jars from rooms of the temple complexes in Metsamor and Dvin with relief figurines of the dragon-snake. The front side of the gold plate is decorated with deep-line ornaments typical of the Kura-Araxes cultural tradition.

Judging by the finds in the grave, we can conclude that the whole necklace was intricate like the one from Ananauri. Unfortunately, the information about the excavations is rather scarce and we are unable to restore its former image. However, it is quite certain the necklace was luxurious and impressive. This burial was in the transitional phase between the Kura-Araxes and Early Kurgan periods.

---

611   Barnett and Watson 1952, Fig 15.

Conclusions

Jewelry in the Kura-Araxes served to express cultural messages about identity and reflected the perception of the local Kura-Araxes people in the worlds of myth and in the exchange network through which value on the ornaments produced and worn was negotiated. Evidence of jewelry at Shengavit emerged from the houses and from burials.

Most common jewels were beads. Artisans made them from a variety of stone, as well as some metal, gold, copper, and bronze. In the broader Kura-Araxes, pins were common. Their use by analogy was either to close garments, or, in the case of the thinner ones, for use in styling long hair. Analysts sometimes attribute spiral-shaped ornaments to use as earrings. Give their thickness and size, hair ornaments appear a more likely function. Most pendants and rings were metal, either copper or gold. A clay one emerged from the disturbed area III of the Necropolis. The bottom of a small pit in Square J5 that was probably a deteriorated burial pit yielded obsidian and gold foil earrings or pendants and a small pendant of soft stone with a design reminiscent of designs from the workshop at Köhne Shahar.

"The manufacture of jewelry in the Kura-Araxes was highly standardized and conventional."[612] Artisans added few new techniques in the following Early Kurgan period, although it was less standardized than that of the Kura-Araxes.

What clearly changed in the transitional phase near the end of the Kura-Araxes, marked particularly by Burials 1 and 2, was an increase in gold and in ornaments with artistic detail. Similarities between Shengavit and Ananauri indicate that a connection, perhaps a network, existed among sites in Georgia and the Ararat Plain/Koytak Plateau areas. Artifacts like the finely wrought gold pendants from the two sites represent this transition. We see it as evidence of a new kind of leadership, part of whose status was signified by these special goods. At the same time, Burials 1 and 2 were not individual graves. They contained a variety of male and female skeletons. Does this indicate the ascendance of one clan, or some broader change in the importance of wealth and political control? We cannot say with any assurance.

References

Alizadeh, K., Samei, S., Mohammadkhani, K., Heidari, R. and Tykot, R. 2018 Craft production at Köhne Shahar, a Kura-Araxes settlement in Iranian Azerbaijan. *Journal of Anthropological Archaeology* 51: 127–143.

Badalyan, R., Brunet, O. 2009 Bronze and Iron Age carnelian bead production in the UAE and Armenia: new perspectives, *Proceedings of the Seminar for Arabian Studies* 39, 57–68.

Barnet, R. D. and Watson, W. 1952 Russian Excavations in Armenia. *Iraq* 14(2): 132-147.

Carminati, E. 2014 Jewelry manufacture in the Kura-Araxes and Bedeni cultures of the southern Caucasus: Analogies and distinctions for the reconstruction of a cultural changeover. *Polish Archaeology in the Mediterranean* 23(2): 161-186.

Golani, A. 2020 Beyond Ornamentation: Contextualizing Research of Personal Adornment in the Ancient Near East. in *Proceedings of the 11th International Congress on the Archaeology of the Ancient Near East. Vol. 1. Images in Context.* edited by A. Otto. M. Herles. K. Kaniuth. 171-184. Wiesbaden: Harasowitz.

Helms, M. 1976 *Ancient Panama: Chiefs in Search of Power.* Austin: University of Texas Press.

Meliksetian. K., Kraus. K., Pernicka. E., Avetisyan, P. Devejian, S., and Petrosyan. L. 2011 Metallurgy of Prehistoric Armenia. in *Anatolian Metal V*, edited by Ü. Yalçın. 201-210. Bochum: Bergbau-Museum.

Miron, A., Orthmann, W. (eds) 1995 *Unterwegs zum Goldenen Vlies. Archäologische Funde aus Georgien,* Saarbrücken: Saarbrücken:Museum fur Vor- und Frühgeschichte.

Pittman, H. 1998 The Jewelry. in *Treasures from the Royal Tombs of Ur*, edited by R. Zettler and L. Horne. 87-125. Philadelphia: University of Pennsylvania Museum.

Renfrew. C. 1986 Varna and the emergence of wealth in prehistoric Europe. in *The Social Life of Things*, edited by A. Appaduri. 141-168. Cambridge: University of Cambridge Press.

Sahlins, M. 1968 *Tribemen.* Englewood Cliffs, NJ: Prentice-Hall.

---

612   Carminati 2014, 180.

6a | Symbols, Ritual, and Ideology[613]

Mitchell Rothman and Hakob Simonyan

Introduction

Chapter 5 explored the economics of Shengavit, both what its residents produced and how they organized that work. Economics is a key aspect of society, but so, too, are those mental aspects that define how people see their world. In this section, we explore those mental aspects of Kura-Araxes culture through symbolism and religious ritual. Chapter 6b covers the other aspect of ritual: mortuary practices. Chapter 6c describes and interprets the figurines that were such a common part of ancient cultures.

Studying the ideology of an ancient people is difficult at best. What we have are the symbols they used to reflect their divine entities, beliefs, views of nature and of themselves, including their social positions and statuses. Behind these are the stories or myths that were the psychological frames they used to interpret information on their world. Rarely can we really understand what these symbols meant to the ancients, even if there are written texts. Of course, for the Kura-Araxes there are no such documents. We can, however, see how they used symbols and constructed the ritual process. Behind them are real individuals and groups of people who used these symbols for a socially complex variety of purposes.[614] In practice, individuals create these symbols, and their meanings are negotiated and determined by their users based on their cultural traditions.

We believe the Kura-Araxes cultural package discussed in Chapter 1 is represented in the symbols we find at Shengavit. Those symbols signify shared identity among Kura-Araxes populations, but also significant variations within the homeland and within its various diaspora locales.[615]

Symbol and Ritual in a Cultural System

Ritual is a special form of communication within or between cultures.[616] Ritual is the re-enactment of and therefore the representation of social relationships. In Gell's analysis ritual is the agent of action.[617] Therefore, "artistic products," often discussed by art historians, put into action ideas about these social relationships, including those with the divine. Further, "artworks, in other words come in families, lineages, tribes, whole populations, just like people. They have relations with one another as well as with the people who create and circulate them as individual objects. They marry, so to speak, and beget offspring which bear the stamp of their antecedents.

---

613   Part of this chapter is taken directly from Simonyan and Rothman 2015.
614   Hodder 1986, 63f.
615   Rothman 2014, 2015a.
616   Sosis 2004.
617   Gell 1998.

Artworks are manifestations of 'culture' as a collective phenomenon; they are, like people, enculturated beings."[618]

In the broadest sense, ritual's symbolic systems therefore serve a role within a particular culture as it relates to other aspects of that culture. Ritual can itself be part of the economic and political adaptation of a culture.[619] In part this is because ritual "was the mechanism that integrated the individuals of the community across household and kin ties, and it provided long-term stability."[620] Ritual also models economic activities like hunting or agriculture, and certainly in ancient societies became the focus of pleas for fertility of the land and the people. If, as we will propose, the economic, social, and political organization of sites like Shengavit changed over the span of 400 or more years, we should see ritual change as well.

So, what is ritual and why should it be such an important factor in explaining the two interrelated problems cited above, content and comparison? Ritual is the physical acting out of a shared cognitive view of how the world works, often, but not exclusively, in relation to the divine (religion). In that ritual process aspects of culture are reflected, as are peoples' appropriate roles within a culture's organization. Ritual uses a variety of symbols as artwork, including the special place in which the ritual takes place. Eliade calls these ritual places "irruptions of the sacred in the secular world."[621] They can be specialized buildings like churches, synagogues, mosques, temples, or shrines, sacred spaces like meeting places in the woods for covens, or ritual areas within a home or other building whose primary function is otherwise not ritualistic. Chapels within modern institutions like hospitals or universities are an example. Even prayer rugs and ritual circles for individual worship are sacred spaces in this sense. Ritual can be practiced by an individual or by a congregation. We today are most familiar with congregational worship, yet a shrine or ritual space can be a central place for a larger population. In Armenia, an interesting case of ritual places are high mountain cultic locations where thousands of rock drawings were carved and where initiations were performed, vestiges of which have been preserved up to the present time in the national feast called *Vardavar*.[622] In Iran, small roadside *Imamsadeh*'s, or shrines of the saintly scholars, permit a few people to worship at the shrine of a respected, late religious leader. Armenian "churches" include basilicas where many people worship as a congregation and chapels or shrines where only a few people can be accommodated at a time. The hospital on top of the Shengavit mound built one of these chapels adjoining the Shengavit Museum in 2011. Therefore, spatially, religious ritual "imbues space with meaning, thus transforming it from mere locale to socially important space."[623] The same can be said about civic ritual spaces like city halls, the steps of Congress where presidents are inaugurated, tribal communal halls (in Iraq *mudhifs*), or Westminster Abbey where English kings are crowned, combining religious and civic ritual.

Ritual practice tends to reflect the population that shares it. The more specialized, formal religious buildings tend to occur in societies with greater occupational specialization and political centralization. Representing Great (as opposed to folk or Small) Tradition religions,[624] these more formal, centralized religions also tend to have specialized priesthoods. To fund and operate specialized religious buildings, presumably with formally trained priests, requires an ability to organize the community as a whole, to collect needed resources for building and

---

618   Gell 1998, 153.
619   Sosis 2004.
620   Gilman and Stone 2013, 609.
621   Eliade 1958.
622   Simonyan personal communication
623   Gilman and Stone 2013, 610.
624   Redfield 1971.

maintaining ritual spaces, and to train and provide for those full-time priests. Rarely is there ethnographic evidence of formal religious buildings and full-time priests in kinship-organized societies or simple chiefdoms. Shaman, sorcerers, or practitioners of an earlier Small Tradition religion were not considered to have a specialized occupation; they had to provide for their own subsistence like any other member of society. They acted as intermediaries to the divine world, on an individual basis or episodically for the group, by manipulating commonly understood symbols and rituals as mechanisms to gain mystical power.[625] Often they employed hallucinogenic substances to achieve this divine interaction.[626]

Sagona and Sagona suggest that the frame of the Kura-Araxes mind does not divide the world into secular and sacred spaces.[627] This would be a characteristic shared by many among so-called tribal populations. Alternatively, one can see what modern peoples see as secular to be part of the religious world. Even economic activities have a ritual meaning. As we pointed out in Chapter 5d above, the ritual hearth (see below) seems to have been fueled by charcoal, not raw logs or dung. This is the fuel necessary for metal smelting, so perhaps it relates to the social importance of metallurgy.

In ritual, participants carry out repeated sequences of different combinations of dance, song, verbal expressions, gestures, displays of symbols, or actions (including sacrifice). These acts often serve to call on supernatural entities or forces on behalf of the congregation, to bless them, and also to affirm the social order reflected in the ritual and its accompanying narratives (myths). Sometimes, it is for divination to predict the consequences of current actions. The rituals can be commemorative, as Christmas is, or they can be transformational, as in a rite of passage,[628] for example, the coronation of a king or puberty rituals.[629] The performance of the ritual on one level affirms the shared understanding of the participants and their loyalty to the group. "Certain fixed offices in tribal [and more complex] societies have many sacred attributes; indeed, every social position has some sacred characteristics. But this sacred component is acquired by the incumbents of positions during the *rite de passage,* through which they changed positions."[630] Think of leaders, who swear to fulfill their new secular role on a Bible, and then invoke the divine, ending every speech, "God Bless Our Country." Such use of religion and ritual to legitimize secular power is a common practice in state societies. Anthropologists call this "sanctification."[631] In less complex societies, positions tend to be less formally defined:

> "there are here two [...] 'models' for interrelatedness [...] The first is of society as a structured, differentiated, and often hierarchical system of politico-legal-economic positions [...] The second [...] is of society as an unstructured or rudimentarily and relatively undifferentiated *comitatus,* community, or even communion of equal individuals [...]."[632]

Most anthropologists would not call the latter "unstructured," but rather societies built on kinship or communal relationships of various kinds.

Rituals can also mediate the relations between human populations and the natural environment. Nature is

---

625   Romain 2009.
626   Sagona and Sagona 2009.
627   Sagona and Sagona 2009.
628   Van Gennep 1960.
629   Turner 1978.
630   Turner 1969, 96–97.
631   Webster 1976; Netting 1978.
632   Turner 1969, 96.

often invested with sacred characteristics, and the social and economic structures of a society are reflected in rituals concerning natural cycles.[633] Ritual's symbols often recall either elements of the natural world that are important to a group, or the divine character of natural forces; for example, the ancient Greeks saw their gods as reflections of the fickleness of the natural world, especially in regard to economic needs (agriculture and uses of the seas).

In general, therefore, as Victor Turner, an ethnographic interpreter of ritual and symbols, writes,

"I found that I could not analyze ritual symbols without studying them in a time series in relation to other "events," for the symbols are essentially involved in social processes. I came to see performances of ritual as distinct phases in the social processes whereby groups became adjusted to internal changes and adapted to their external environment."[634]

Symbol systems that are an inherent part of the ritual process are key actors; Geertz calls religion "a system of cultural symbols."[635] In many ways, "it is this ritual transformation of the material that empowers the image [symbol] to speak, or to see, or to act, through various culturally-subscribed channels, after which it may be said to exercise its own agency."[636] Agency here, based on Gell's theories,[637] is not so much human intention,[638] which many archaeologists now believe is a key to understanding human social structures and change; rather, it is an ability of "art" to generate action and define social relationships. Winter suggests that as important as the concept of "agency" is, that of "affect," the way the agent's action is received by the observer:[639] "Affect is located *in* and so comes *from* the work, the result of properties that then impact upon the viewer/user."[640]

Ritual, whether we classify it as secular or sacred (or both at the same time), is a key mental map or psychological frame for ancient populations. It integrates their societies, establishes the nature of social (and political) relations, mediates a group's economic adaptation to its natural environment, and confirms its common identity. Further, it is possible to study ritual using archaeological remains, even prehistoric ones.[641]

Symbol and Ritual at Shengavit and its Interpretation

Symbol and ritual can tell us about the cultural traditions of the Kura-Araxes at Shengavit. Certainly, the rituals and ritual spaces evidenced at Shengavit will tell us about the mental maps of its residents and cultural relationships with other homeland and diaspora sites based on other ritual spaces and symbols of the Kura-Araxes cultural tradition. As Gell argued (see above), symbols (art) and their use in ritual are interrelated like a family. One piece of art reaffirms the importance and meaning of other works of art in the same cultural context. They connect people to a social reality represented in a set of symbols through affect.

Another way of looking at the same idea is to see symbols as containing culturally relevant information.[642] The messages or meaning of symbols depend in part on the target group. Some target groups tend to have exclusive

---

633   Rappaport 1968; Moore 1957.
634   Turner 1967, 20.
635   Geertz 1973.
636   Winter 2007, 44.
637   Gell 1998.
638   Gardiner 2008.
639   Winter 2007, 44.
640   I. Winter, personal communication (e-mail).
641   Fogelin 2007.
642   Wobst 1977.

symbols. The love modern bureaucracies have for abbreviations that only insiders would understand is an example of a limited target group. Artifacts that are seen by more people have must carry simple and generally understood messages.

POTTERY DESIGN

One of the more widespread sets of symbols in the Kura-Araxes are the styles of pottery (see Chapter 5e). These styles have long been associated with the identity of Kura-Araxes populations wherever they lived.[643]

A second set of related symbols are the designs on pottery. While the increasing number of different pottery styles differentiates the KA1 from KA2, so does the appearance of many symbols incised, impressed, or raised on the pottery's exterior. The KA2 at Shengavit has many more designs than KA1 or anywhere in the diaspora, even in the KA2.

Having the database of over 1400

Figure 6a.1 Shengavit Pottery Designs.

potsherds permits us to explore patterns of their use. Below we divided the designs we found into categories A to F (Fig 6a.1). To be fair, we could have divided them any number of ways. In the realm of ancient meaning all classifications are theoretical; there is no independent way to verify them with certainty. Our hypothesis is based on two criteria: how they were made and the subject of the designs as *we* saw them. The latter hopefully represents some approximation of the ancient perception (see below). Group A designs are all cut with a graver and tend to represent triangles and diamonds in repeated strings. Category B are also engraved, although they are usually made in wide bands with interior lines and as with Category A tend to appear in running lines. Still, some like Design 25 may be a variant of Design 11. Category C often have a raised design and are typified by spirals associated with larger "v" shapes. Category D are both made by raising and incising, but most consist of animals. Category E consists of various designs, mostly incised, that we felt did not fit the other categories. Category F are decorative elements that we propose have no particular symbolic meaning at all. Among them are very common designs 12 and 14. Some have suggested that design 12 was used to create a copy of a metal container. Given its date, we wonder whether rather the metal forms copied this pottery form.

Some designs appear together on a single pot. For example, Design 4 appears with design 21, Design 5 with 15, 6 with 14, 18, 24, and 50, 7 with 13, 14, 8 with 1, 18, and 21, 9 with 15, 10 with 1, 6, 12, 13, 39, 40, and 54, 12 with 17 and 59, 14 with 9, 11, 24, 25, 39, 15 with 9, 18, 24, and 59, 16 with 39, 17 with 40, 24 with 32, and 39 with 40.

---

643   Rothman 2015a.

In terms of the kind of pots, potters applied the raised or impressed designs (12, 15, 23, 32, 40, and 58) more often to utility and cooking wares than to fine wares. Except for Design 12, which was applied to more open and intermediate 1 ware types. These raised designs potters most often put on closed forms like Types XA, XVIA, XVI. Design 10 was mostly applied to fine or intermediate 1 ware types, such as Types XX, XXI, and XXII, the proposed eating pots. Potters also applied Design 14, the design we propose as purely decorative, mostly to fine, intermediate 1 ware Types XX, XXI, and XXII, but also intermediate 2 ware Types XXVII, open Types IIA and IVD, and closed ware Type X. On the other hand, potters carved Designs 9, 11, 24 mostly onto open, utility wares.

In short, there does not appear to be any clear pattern where the same design is used in relation to the ware type of the pot, as one would expect in a workshop; that is, in a village industry process of production. Perhaps, it depends more on by whom and where the pot was used (see below). Sometimes, if Rothman is right about pottery being a domestic craft, they may represent in part the tastes of the potter or their associations within the community.

In terms of change through time, the stratum with the most pots with designs in raw numbers and as a percentage all potsherds measured is Stratum III (Table 6a.1). Although the size of the sample in Stratum VIII is perhaps too small for statistical validity, the pattern is one of increasing percentages until Stratum III and then a decline to Stratum I.

	I	II	III	IV	V	VI/VII	VIII
No w/designs	79	42	235	33	8	16	1
Total sherds	443	152	368	171	61	175	37
Percentage	18%	28%	64%	19%	13%	9%	3%

Table 6a.1. Number of designs on pots by Stratum

Specific designs appear in different strata (Table 6a.2). Design types 8, 10, 11, 12, 13, 18, 24, 40 appear over a long span. Most of these are in Design Categories A and B. Designs 1, 2, 3, 4, 5, 7, 9, 21, 22, 23, 25, 26, 28, 29, 32, 36, 38, 41, 44, 51, 58, and 59 appear in the latter half of the mound's occupation from Strata III to I.

The critical issue is whether we can reasonably attribute some cultural meaning to the designs of different types and our categories. One way to do so is to look at how these artistic images correlate with artifactual remains of ritual, specifically hearths and andirons; that is, what kind

Design no.	N	Strata	Design no.	N	Strata	Design no.	N	Strata
1	26	I, II, III*	19	5	I, III	40	11	I, III, IV, V,VI/VII
2	16	III*	21	6	I, II, III	41	3	III
3	19	I, II, III*	22	1	III	44	1	III
4	18	I, II, III*	23	2	II, III	46	1	IV
5	18	III*	24	16	I*, II, III, VI/VII	50	5	III, IV, VI/VII
6	21	I, III*, IV	25	3	I, II, III	51	2	I
7	13	I, III*	26	1	III	52	1	VI/VII
8	26	II, III*, IV, V*, VI/VII	27	4	II, III, VI/VII	53	1	IV
9	10	I, II, III*	28	1	III	54	4	II, IV
10	38	I*, II, III*, IV, V, VI/VII	29	2	I, III	56	1	V
11	23	I*, II, III*, VI/VII	31	1	III, V	58	3	III
12	17	I, II, III, IV, V,VI/VII	32	5	I, III	59	5	I, II
13	12	I, II, III*, IV,V	33	1	I			
14	30	I, II*, III, V	34	3	II			
15	17	I, II, III, IV, VI	35	4	III, IV			
16	7	II, III, IV	36	2	I, III			
17	10	II, III, IV	38	1	III			
18	21	I, II, III, IV, VI/VII	39	10	I, II, III, IV			

Table 6a.2. Specific Designs that appear in Different Strata.

of "family" of meaning they make. Design Category C appears to have a relationship with both (Fig 6a.2). Excavators at Pulur Sakyol in the rooms with a ritual emplacement that are almost identical to Shengavit M5 (see below) found a large serving jar and an andiron, both with images of what looks like a face (see Fig 6a.2). Designs 38, 60, and 61 at Shengavit mirror the images from Pulur Sakyol and other elements of Design Category C. Also, Sardarian found a classic type of Kura-Araxes open form (exact provenience unknown). The inside has a painting of a tri-lobed ceramic hearth circled by some kind of bird. That same bird is drawn in Design 60 with the design just like Design 38. This correlation suggests that our proposal of a face in relation to other aspects of ritual is plausible.

What is the face? Sagona and Sagona[644] suggest that a key part of the ritual is ingestion of a hallucinogenic mushroom, *haoma*. In documents of the Iron Age Medians, Magi are said to ingest this drug in order to experience a direct connection to the divine world and the ability to harness mystical powers to heal, curse, or predict the future. These are powers usually attributed to shaman, as opposed to a priest who leads the liturgy of Great Tradition religious ritual in a large space with a congregation. They see metal pins and images like Shengavit Design 59 as evidence of this hallucinogenic use. Symbol 59 exists in Square K6 Stratum II, in the mixed fill over the more secure proveniences in Square M5 and on a floor in the I14 buildings. We recovered another potsherd with it in Locus 2083, which Hayrapetyan writes in her notebook was a wall later than the Square J5 Stratum III/IV building with remains of ritual. Psychologists who have studied the visions of shaman under the influence of hallucinogens see similar shapes to some of the Kura-Araxes images. Spirals, star bursts, running sets of wavy lines, triangles, and diamond shapes are among them.[645] Proposing that these "faces" with spirals represent some kind of mystical spirits is not out of the realm of the possible. However, figurines of abstractly or naturalistically human form (Chapter 6c), some of which Simonyan says represent gods, have little association with these.

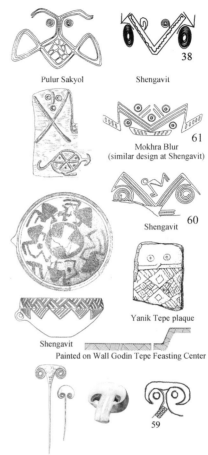

Figure 6a.2 Meaning of Designs.

Otherwise, many of the images appear abstract. Are they decorative or do they, too, have ritual meaning? Shengavit Design 11 and 6 appear on the outside of the same bowl with the hearth and circling bird. Parenthetically, the same designs on pots appeared in the Square M5 and J5 buildings (Fig 6a. 3). Design 11 also appeared as a painting on the wall of the feasting center (Building 3) at Kura-Araxes diaspora site

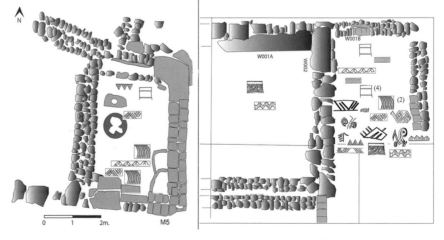

Figure 6a.3 Distribution of Pot Designs in Buildings with Ritual indications in Square M5 (left), J5 (right).

---

644   Sagona and Sagona 2009, 2011.
645   Sagona and Sagona 2011, Fig. 2.

Godin Tepe (Fig 6a.2).[646] Design 6 appeared in Building 3 of Square K6, although we did not find Design 11 in Square I14 or Buildings 2 or 3 from Square K6 (Fig 6a.4). At the same time, we recovered potsherds with Design 18, which appeared elsewhere with Design 6 on the same pot, in Square K6 Buildings 2 and 3, and I14. Design 6 also

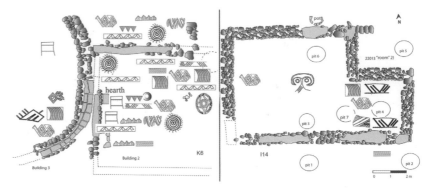

Figure 6a.4 Distribution of Pot Designs in Secular Buildings.

appeared with Design 24 in Square I14. With this relatively small sample Design 11 seems to be the most likely candidate for a mystical symbol. Alternatively, those symbols could represent social units like clans.

However, that the designs' meanings are not random is suggested by the percentages of potsherds with designs in particular buildings. The two buildings with a clear ritual element are in Squares J5 and M5 (Fig 6a.3). In Square M5 44 percent of all potsherds had designs, and in the J5 Building number was 40 percent. In Square I14 only .08 percent and in K6 Buildings 2 and 3 only 20 percent of the potsherds had designs. These designs seem then to have a ritual meaning.

Style Category D designs appear to be animals. Type 41 is one of the rare cases where a human form is present. It looks like a human and a dog. Birds are among them, as are quadrupeds. Design 48 looks like a caprid, Design 43 like an equid. Given the importance of sheep/goat and bovid figurines, especially those associated with ritual emplacements, we wonder why they do not appear more frequently in pottery design. The difficulty of making sense of the meaning of symbols to the ancients is re-affirmed by their heterogeneity.

Pots in the graves dug by Sardarian in 1958, 1962, 1964, and 1965 had no designs.[647] Tombs in second 1962 and 1965 seasons had some designs (see below). The designs on pots from those tombs include 2, 6, 11, 12, 18, 15, 19, and a complex variation on 11 that combines the features of Categories of A and B. The symbolism in graves may be more related to what was in the pot, rather than on its exterior surface. Unfortunately, we have no independent way of dating these tombs other than by the pottery itself, which creates a tautology.

Based on Sagona's catalog from 1984 and other sources, not many of the 61 designs at Shengavit are reproduced elsewhere. Among the comparisons that do exist are Design 1 at Norşuntepe in the Taurus[648] and Chkalovka and Hatagyugh in Armenia,[649] Design 2 at Pulur Sakyol and Godin,[650] Design 4 at Pulur Sakyol[651] and the Aragats tomb, Design 5 at Godin Tepe,[652] Design 6 at Pulur Sakyol and Dangeulis Gora,[653] Design 8 at Pulur Sakyol,[38] Design 10 at Tepecik,[40] Design 11 at Norşuntepe,[36] Design 22 at Dangeulis Gora,[654] Design 35 (with variations) at Godin,[40] Design 38 at Karnut, Shresh Blur, Aragats,[37] Mokhrablur,[38] and Güzelova,[38] Design

646   Rothman 2011.
647   Badalyan et al. 2015.
648   Hauptmann 1982, Plate 50.
649   Smith et al. 2009, Fig 5.
650   Sagona 1984.
651   Sagona 1984.
652   Rothman 2011, Fig 5.48.
653   Sagona 1984.
654   Sagona 1984.

40 at Norşuntepe[655] and Beth Shean,[41] Design 42 at Gegharot,[37] Design 40 at Sadakho (Design 60 with Design 40 in the middle instead of a bird),[41] Design 46 at Karnut,[37] Design 51 at Karnut,[37] Design 59 at Gaitmazi[42] and Yanik Tepe,[656] and Design 58 at Kohla.[42] No doubt there are some others, but these parallels suggest a limited ideological connection to the western Taurus, the Zagros front, the uplands of Armenia and Kvemo kartli in Georgia. However, again, the majority of designs are unique to Shengavit.

So, the designs on pots from Shengavit represent some kind of artistic symbols that communicated messages. The high percentage of decorated pots in the two ritual spaces of Squares M5 and J5 suggests that some of them reflected religious ideas that are part of the systems or family of religious artifactual symbols and were used in the rituals described below. Other symbols may represent social groupings. From the data we have we can only offer general suggestions of which are which. Given the wide variety of designs rather than limited and often repeated ones apparent in the post-Kura-Araxes Early Kurgan Period, it would make sense that groups within the site and maybe the polity made contributions for ritual performance in pots with designs meaningful in different households or communal groups, but this is pure speculation. This would make sense, if as we discuss below, a major function of ritual is consulting the spirits to predict the future of individuals or small groups. Certainly, the rich variety of symbols suggests increasing development of some societal complexity. That evolutionary change is also suggested by artifactual patterns (see Chapter 7).[657]

RITUAL BUILDINGS AND PRACTICE

Public buildings, that is, buildings in which larger groups gather for various rituals (including political meetings, which tend to have ritualistic elements), tend to have open areas and seating for those meeting as a community or congregation. The orientation of the building to cardinal points can be meaningful, although at Kvatskhelebi, where buildings with ritual were oriented to cardinal points, the direction of the doors may simply be intended to avoid the winds (Fig. 6a.5).[658] Within the building, the placement of symbols often directs the attention of participants to the front, as in a modern church, synagogue, mosque, or Buddhist temple, or a House of Parliament, or Congress. This arrangement reflects the hierarchical

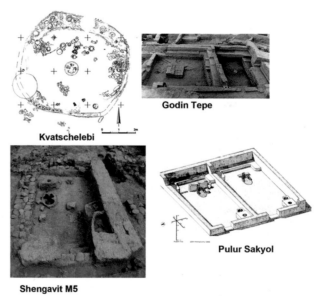

Figure 6a.5 Kura-Araxes ritual places.

nature of those at the front leading the ritual as opposed to the members of the community facing the front. In the Kura-Araxes cultural tradition the focus of public buildings is to the center of the room, theoretically reflecting a more egalitarian community. However, there are examples of cultures with the central, as opposed to the frontal, orientation of the ritual space that have a less egalitarian nature (Fig 6a.5).[659]

---

655   Hauptmann 1982, Plate 50.
656   Rothman 2014, Fig 5a.
657   Rothman 2015b; 2021.
658   Palumbi 2008.
659   Adler 1993; Waters 1963; Wills 2000.

In the Kura-Araxes cultural tradition the center of public or communal rooms was often bracketed by painted benches. At Godin Tepe IV, they are placed along three walls facing the doorway in the front, public room of what Rothman has interpreted as a feasting center (the back room, entered by steps down into the building, appears to have been a kitchen where the feast was prepared).[660] Residents painted the benches black and painted the proposed ritual pottery Design 11 on the wall (Fig 6a.2).[661] The central room at Godin had a hearth and an ash pit on both the entry wall and on the wall opposite the doorway in the corner. It also had a low platform in the center of the room (excavators did not recover whatever may have been placed on the platform). At Kvatskhelebi in level C1, which is parallel in time to the 3rd millennium BC KA2 deposits at Shengavit,[662] an unusual round house—most buildings were more squarely shaped with rounded corners—shared some of the same features. There was a red painted bench that encircled the back half of the building away from the doorway; other houses have back benches, but the excavator thought this one was special.[663] Residents placed 12 small bins filled with ash at the back of the benches. No stairways are apparent. By contrast, only a small bench sat by the entry steps in Shengavit Square M5, and as far as we can tell it was unpainted. At Pulur (Sakyol) and Norşuntepe there is evidence of ritual emplacements within otherwise domestic spaces. The pattern is particularly clear at Pulur Sakyol, as each of a set of adjoining two-room buildings seems to have had a similar ritual emplacement in the back room. One entered these rooms down a series of steps facing a hearth and a raised platform at Shengavit, Pulur, and Godin IV. Two bins filled with ash and burned pottery sat near the entrance by the steps at Shengavit and Pulur Sakyol, as did similar containers at Godin IV (see above). Filled with ash, these may be places where people lit fires during the ceremony, perhaps burning particular items. At Shengavit, Roman Hovsepyan found remains of wheat and barley in the ash. The layout of ritual emplacements at Pulur and Square M5 at Shengavit were strikingly similar, even to the presence of a narrow standing platform or altar behind the hearth. At Pulur Sakyol the hearth had three small channels carved in it, which Koşay suggests may have been "to drain away the blood of the animal sacrifices or the wine used in libations."[664] At Pulur Sakyol residents mounted a saddle quern on a clay basin by the corner. The same feature was built into the west wall of the room adjoining the Square M5 Room 2 where the ritual emplacements were, assuming the two rooms were part of the same construction. Simonyan argues that like Godin, the one room was for ritual and the other for household tasks including food preparation, but the bone remains do not indicate a feasting center (Chap 5a and below).

A different kind of public space may be represented at Mokhrablur at a period contemporaraneous with Shengavit. There builders constructed a stone tower on which stood a standing dressed stone.[665] This is not so much a building whose interior is the focus of ritual, but likely a focus for communal ritual outside in a plaza or open area. Simonyan believed that a similar open public ritual space existed south of the Square M5 building, but excavations in 2022 show that this was not the case. It is possible a building adjoined the Mokhrablur stela, but excavators did not excavate it. Excavations in 2022 rejected that conclusion. Sardarian excavated a similar dressed stone at Shengavit, shaped like a phallus, but we do not know in what context.

---

660   Rothman 2011.
661   Rothman 2011, Fig. 5.10.
662   Palumbi 2008, Table 5.1.
663   Sagona 1984, 37.
664   Koşay 1976, 136.
665   Areshian 2005.

Ritual, however, is not limited to congregational or communal meeting spaces. At Late Bronze Gegharot,[666] in the higher elevation country north of Shengavit, small, round, built-up pits with pottery and other artifacts, were certainly shrines. Smith and Lyon interpret them as divination centers for those in the region,[667] all contained within a walled fortress. They had a centralizing function, drawing people from the surrounding countryside, even if the ritual was carried out by an individual or very small groups of supplicants (see below).

Magic and healing rituals were certainly part of the ancient Kura-Araxes repertoire. One of the interesting finds was at the top of the pit into which they dumped the burned remains of Building 4 of Stratum IV: the whole skeleton of a turtle (Fig 6a.6). Fresh-water turtles have served a symbolic role in Mesopotamia, and likely beyond, as part of healing or other magical rituals.[668]

Figure 6a.6 Turtle in Square K6 Locus 1060 (Stratum IV) pit.

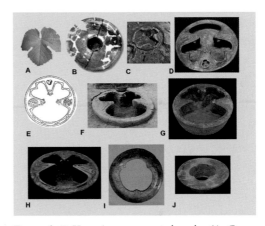

Figure 6a.7 Kura-Araxes ceramic hearths. (A. Grape leaf, Hearths from B. Sos Höyük, C. Norşuntepe, D -J. Shengavit).

Artifacts as Symbols in Shengavit and Kura-Araxes Ritual

If the spaces are the stage on which the mental maps of ritual are acted out and which define its target audience, the symbols are the agents that define the meaning of the ritual. They speak to the subjects that are of concern to the participants and initiate the ritual action. Often, they refer to shared myths and stories.

The Hearth

According to Bayburtian, Sagona, and others, the core of Kura-Araxes ritual is the hearth.[669] To say the "hearth" in reference to the Kura-Araxes cultural tradition is to refer to a number of quite different structures. They generally fall into two categories: built-in or freestanding. The built-in ones, called *ojakh* in Armenian, are ceramic and tend to have broad, raised lines and triangles on them. At Sos Höyük the hearth had a single hole (Fig. 6a.7, B). Elsewhere, a common shape is three lobes. Batiuk suggests that it looks like a grape leaf (Fig 6a.7, A).[670] Excavators found three-lobed hearths at Norşuntepe in the early third millennium BC/ EBI provenience K/ L19 XIX.[671] This date is as much a reflection of the Early Bronze Age Northern Mesopotamian Reserve Slip ware as the Kura-Araxes pottery. This form of hearth existed at Kvatskhelebi C and B,[672] and throughout the occupation of Shengavit, as well as at other sites within the Kura-Araxes cultural tradition.[673] Common features

666   Badalyan et al. 2014.
667   Smith and Lyon, 2014.
668   Berthon et al. 2016.
669   Sagona 1998; Smogorzewska 2004, Bayburtian 1938.
670   Batiuk 2013.
671   Hauptmann 1982.
672   Palumbi 2008.
673   Bayburtian 2011, 31, 32, 34.

include dimples between the short parts of the two smaller lobes, presumably to balance a round bottomed pot. In Square M5 we found a small beaker sitting on the dimple. Simonyan suggests that this was used for libations. It had Design 11 on it. The hearths often are placed near the center of the room where the roof support pole rises to an opening in roof (*yertik* in Armenian) structure where smoke from the fire can escape.

THE ANDIRON

A second artifact class is the andiron. At sites, particularly to the west of Shengavit, excavators found quite a variety of andirons (Fig 6a.8).[674] They do exist at Shengavit and elsewhere in the Kura-Araxes landscape. Thus, a cultural distinction is likely, even though the ritual may be similar. The most common andirons

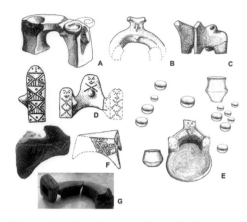

Figure 6a.8 Kura-Araxes andirons (A. Shengavit, B. Amiranis gora, C. Dzhraovit, D./E. Pulur Sakyol, F/G. Shengavit).

are horseshoe shaped (Fig 6a.8. A, B, D, E, G), although some are in the shape of bull's horns and the front of the torso of a ram (Fig. 6a.8. C). They are decorated with images of animals (Fig. 6a.8. A, C), or creatures that could be human or perhaps some mystical entity (Fig. 6a.8., B, D, E). However, many andirons are completely undecorated (Fig. 6a.8, G). In addition, most have a tab on top, to which many have attributed their ability to be moved. Some have assumed that this feature is representative of a nomadic life.[675] We disagree with this, but rather assert that the Kura-Araxes migrants were not primarily seasonal nomadic pastoralists, but rather agro-pastoral populations who settled long enough to generate mounded sites.[676] At the same time, in the round, perhaps ritual building in C1 at Khavskhelebi with its three-lobed hearth, the excavation team found an andiron on the red painted bench.[677] A third fireplace tool we would call a griddle was decorated with pottery Symbol 11 or the spirals of Symbol Category C (Fig. 6a.8, F and see Chapter 5e above). It is often drawn and photographed upside down. Functionally, this griddle probably was used like the griddles on top of Zagros horseshoe-shaped ovens at Godin.[678] We found flat, highly burned pieces of ceramic in K6 that clearly were the tops of these griddle type of andirons.

The assumption of scholars has been that andirons sat directly on the fireplace when there was no ceramic hearth. Ishoev and Greenberg[679] argue that it was where the cooking pot was placed after it was taken off the fire. Evidence from Shengavit suggests that sometimes that was true, and sometimes it was placed on the hearth, based on burning patterns. The hearths have small tabs inside presumably to hold a pot in place over the fire.

What is the ritual meaning of the hearth and andiron? If the hearth is the center of Kura-Araxes ritual, what is it an agent to convey? Fire is surely one element. Fire is one of the most universal symbols of ritual action, occurring in almost all cultures. The use of fire might be in the form of an eternal flame, candles or torches, or as a vehicle for sacrifice of burnt offerings.[680] In sacrifice, many peoples believe the soul of the animal or the

674   Smogorzewska 2004; Takaoğlu 2000.
675   Smogorzewska 2004.
676   Rothman 2017.
677   Sagona 1984, 37.
678   Rothman 2011, Fig. 5.29.
679   Ishoev and Greenberg 2019.
680   Child and Child 1993, 72f.

smoke enters the sacred realm and communicates the message of the supplicant to the divine.[681] Eliade writes, "Fire with its warmth and light, fulfills a vital requirement of human life. Yet the same element can wreak sheer destruction. Both the positive and negative functions are united in fire's role as an instrument of melting, refinement, and purification."[682] In other words, fire reminds people of the essential nature of life and also of a kind of transformation through rites of passage, including death. That the ceramic built-in hearth (*ojakh*) may have had a special ritual function is further suggested by the treatment of one example at Shengavit in square K6. The hearth was placed in the middle of one of the small ancillary rooms of burned Building 4. Presumably, after the main room went out of use, in this case through burning, the ancillary rooms were abandoned as well. The ancients scrupulously cleaned out the room, leaving the hearth in place, and then applied about six centimeters of clean, pure plaster on top of the hearth, as if to seal and, perhaps, to desacralize it.

OTHER OBJECTS

As Sagona suggests, however, the topic of ritual involving the hearth may be best understood at Sos Höyük. A common symbol was an animal important for agriculture. Those figurines include bovines, sheep, equids, and wild animals (Fig. 6a. 9). Excavators at Shengavit recovered carvings of phalluses, which relate to fertility. In addition, they found obsidian arrowheads, an antler from a red deer, and a human phalange in the room with the cult objects.[683] Some of these objects were intentionally buried around the hearth in Square M5. Simonyan suggests that this could be used in an initiation ceremony or as an offering to the gods. All these symbols theoretically represent fertility and the integration of human beings and the natural environment on which they depended. In Square M5 at Shengavit, ash from the hearth contained wheat and barley seeds,[684] supporting an interpretation of agricultural fertility as a key concern. Sagona reports no finds of buried seeds near the hearth at Sos Höyük. According to Sagona and Rothman, all the symbols discussed here reflect the concerns of a domestic economic unit. Even the obsidian points at Sos and Shengavit and the bone points relate to that world. Ironically, for a cultural tradition that is supposed to have specialized in metallurgy, archaeologists have found no metal objects associated with the hearth. Contrast this with the so-called royal tomb at Arslantepe with its many metal objects.[685] However, that tomb is now dated to Arslantepe VIB2, considered post-Kura-Araxes by its excavators. Some consider Arslantepe, despite having some Kura-Araxes-like pottery, to be in a very different culture area than that of societies farther east in the highlands.[686] Simonyan, believing that the whole Kura-Araxes

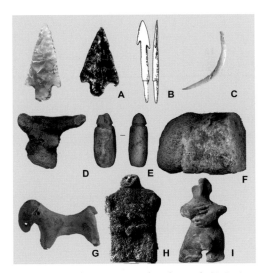

Figure 6a.9 Object associated with ritual. (A-B=Sos Höyük, C-I Shengavit).

681 Eliade 1958, 85.; Takaoğlu 2000
682 Eliade 1987, p. 340.
683 Sagona 1998.
684 Roman Hovsepyan, personal communication. This material was in a lower level within the hearth, showing it was there when the hearth was last used, not blown in later. The sample was, however, somewhat compromised, since these fills were first sieved through a fine metal screen.
685 Frangipane et al. 2001.
686 Batiuk et al. 2022.

cultural tradition was one culture, sees the black painted pottery over the temple-palace as an indication of a unity, while Frangipane and Palumbi argue that the Upper Euphrates black ware of the late fourth millennium BC is not Kura-Araxes at all.[687]

RITUAL EMPLACEMENTS IN SQUARES J5 AND M5.

Two buildings at Shengavit displayed clear evidence of ritual behavior in Squares J5 and M5. From our stratigraphic analysis (Chapter 3), the Square J5 building fits into Strata III/IV and the Square M5 one into Stratum I. In some ways they look incredibly alike (Fig 6a.10). Both have a room with the ritual emplacement and an adjoining room with evidence of food preparation and storage. We and the square supervisor, Armine Hayrapetyan, believe that J5 was cleaned out, like the annex room in Square K6 in Stratum IV with a ceramic hearth desacralized after it went out of use. The remains in Square J5 were few and were concentrated in Room 2. The altar appears to have been cut down (Fig 6a.11). Evidence of burned clay and the bottom of a larger ceramic vessel remained (Fig 6a.11) where the ceramic hearth was located in M5. The residents may well have removed the hearth, but they broke the bottom when they did so. In the Square J5 building the north wall had extensive signs of burning. Both rooms are small; Square M5 was no more than 2.5 x 4 m inside, and Square J5 3.8 x 4 m. The differences are few, but perhaps significant in terms of the ritual. In M5,

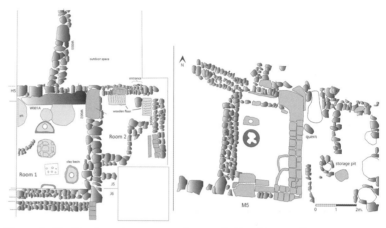

Figure 6a.10 Ritual emplacements in Squares J5/6 and M5 at Shengavit.

Figure 6a.11 Room 1 in Square J5, Shengavit and wooden floor in room 2. Inset of clay basin in Room 1.

the entryway was a set of steps with two built-in storage bins along the east wall. Neither the steps nor bins existed in J5. Also, a clay basin sat in the southeast corner of Square J5. Near the basin were a series of small holes. The ground around them were covered with what looks like melted wax. Most likely worshippers lit tall candles or candles on tall stakes. Room 2 had a wooden floor, some of which is still intact (Fig 6a.11). Both the Square M5 and J5 ritual emplacements had a narrow corridor at the short end where a shaman could enter without being seen to perform ritual practices.

Another space Simonyan hypothesizes had ritual functions were special annexes isolated from the general rectangular plan in large houses excavated in areas L-7 and I-14. He proposes that they were prayer places of

---

687   Frangipane and Palumbi 2007.

cult significance for members of an extended households. This is evidenced by the isolation of these niches from the residential sectors of houses, as well as stone and terracotta figurines found near them, which personified household gods, or ancestors. Small anthropomorphic or zoomorphic figurines can be perceived as fetishes that were intended to protect the field or home.[688] As evident in Chapter 7, this interpretation does not fit the building in Square I14.

Still, the dichotomy between public and private ritual spaces is hard to define precisely. Pam Crabtree, our archaeozoologist, reports that the animal bones found in good context within M5 and J5 resembled those in other domestic contexts (Table 6a.1), and nothing in their butchering indicated any different treatment or signs of burning (Chap 5a). Nor, unlike the case in the bones of Building 36 at Arslantepe,[689] is there any indication that the bones were from prime cuts of meat. Of the pottery of M5, 28.6 percent of diagnostic and non-diagnostic pottery was fine ware, 27 percent were utility wares, and 44.5 percent were cooking wares. For Square J5, 5 percent of diagnostic and non-diagnostic potsherds were fine ware, 42 percent were utility wares, and 53 percent were cooking wares.

The assumption we have made is that animals were sacrificed. However, the bins contained burned grain, and the hearth contained burned grain seeds. As Koşay suggested, the substance poured on altars, given the shape of the hearths, could be wine and animal blood. Simonyan thinks it was animal fat,[690] but, in any case, the altars were too small for sizeable cuts of meat. Perhaps fires were set with vegetable sacrifices in the bins.

How do we define these ritual spaces? For Simonyan, they are fire temples reminiscent of later Persian and Greek temples.[691] He interprets what he calls Shengavitian society after Bayburtian as a class society with the development of differing social statuses and wealth accumulation. To Rothman, the problem with that view is that such temples are typical of public worship in the Great Tradition religions of state-level societies. The focus on the hearth, the orientation of the ritual space to the middle of the room, and other elements of society portrayed in the economic activities of Chapters 5a to 5h simply do not speak of a state or even very complex society. Like the term we use, the variations in symbol and ritual may in part be related to whether the ritual is purely domestic or to some degree public. Sagona sees the rituals of the Kura-Araxes as private and domestic. He further sees them as rituals that seem to emphasize economic activities. Lastly, he points to a lack of human symbolic presence.[692] Theoretically, a ritual and divine symbolic system of a more centralized society should reflect a public aspect as well. A dichotomy between public and private ritual is evident in later state societies. In the shamanistic religions, like the pre-temple Mesopotamian period, the only human forms, which we have interpreted as shaman, are not fully human; they have animal features.[693] The emergence of both the state and Great Tradition religions is marked by imagery that must have been based on myths that make their way into people's consciousness later in time. The human hero controlling wild bulls or lions was clearly one of these ideological and mythological images in Mesopotamia. This became the very definition of the social perception of the positive attributes of the king that validate his authority as ruler.[694] Certainly, the appearance of many male

---

688   Mirimanov 1973, 311.
689   Palumbi et al. 2017.
690   Simonyan 2015.
691   Simonyan 2013, 2015.
692   Sagona 1998.
693   Rothman 2002.
694   Winter 1987, 1997.

and female human figurines (idols?) late in the Shengavit occupation implies somewhat of a different mental map of what was important. Perhaps, it implies a subtle move toward a figure of influence, but not necessarily those with authority.

Conclusions

Symbols and the rituals in which they are displaced are of a number of types. One is regular prayer or shamanistic connection with divine spirits. This may include divination. The ritual can be private (domestic) or public. The hearth is the clearest focus of this type of ritual. If one agrees with Simonyan that the installations like those in Squares J5 and M5 were fire temples, this ritual was largely directed toward pubic worship. That may be the use of the ritual space by many small groups, or a congregation in a public space outside the building. Rothman, on the other hand, sees the duplication of the same ritual emplacements at neighboring houses at Pulur Sakyol, and the large percentage of houses at Shengavit with ceramic hearths directed toward the middle of the room as signs of a more egalitarian, domestic ritual, at least in the earlier levels. There appears no clear evidence of a dedicated priesthood. Except for installations like the tower at Mokhrablur, there do not seem to be public spaces. We really do not know whether there was a public plaza or a different kind of public space.

At the same time, there does appear in the designs on pots some kind of agreement on the nature of how all Shengavit residents viewed their divine and society. The picture painted by symbol and ritual of sacred places is one rich in imagery. That imagery we believe refers to nature and to mystical forces that are associated most clearly with the home and literally, the hearth. The birds appearing on the Shengavit painted pot circling the tripartite hearth is the same bird that appears on a pot with a design like the spiritual face on andirons (Fig 6a.2). Fire is its transformative symbol, as its power to alter the world became a key metaphor in myths of which we can only guess.

Whether public or private, what were the steps of the ritual process? Certainly, food and drink played a part. At Pulur (Sakyol) the hearth and decorated andiron were surrounded by the large jar with an incised face and many small cups. Squares M5 and J5 at Shengavit and the Godin IV feasting center had many bones of butchered (and cooked) animals, mostly sheep/goat and cattle. According to our archaeobotanist, Roman Hovsepyan, "There was a lot of wheat and barley in the bins of M5. There were no other crop remains of any quantity."[695] Participants ate and drank. They sacrificed plant remains by burning them. Whether they sacrificed animals, blood, or fat, as Simonyan suggests,[696] remains to be tested.

Rites of passage both of individual maturation and of new roles and statuses no doubt occurred. Simonyan will detail one of those, mortuary practice, in Chapter 6b. At its end in the Early Kurgan Period the focus of ritual changed from the house to the grave, and many of the symbols were abandoned in favor of a few, such as Design 6.

There is much more to learn about these rituals and symbols that more publication of the details from other sites will help us understand.

---

695   Hovsepyan e-mailed information.
696   Simonyan 2015.

References

Adler, M. 1993 Why is a Kiva? New interpretations of prehistoric social integrative architecture in the Northern Rio Grande Region of New Mexico. *Journal of Anthropological Research* 49: 319–346.

Areshian, G. 2005 Early Bronze Age settlements in the Ararat Plain and its vicinity. *Archäologische Mitteilungen aus Iran und Turan* 37 (2005): 71–88.

Badalyan, R., Smith, A. T., Lindsay, I., Harutyunyan, A., Greene, A., Marshall, M., Monahan, B., Hovsepyan, R. 2014 A preliminary report on the 2008, 2010, and 2011 investigations of Project ArAGATS on the Tsaghkahovit Plain, Republic of Armenia. *Archäologische Mitteilungen aus Iran und Turan* 46: 149-222.

Badalyan, R., Ovsepyan, S., and Khachatryan, L. 2015 *Shengavit: Catalog of Archaeological Material and Collections in the History Museum of Armenia*. Yerevan: Museum of the History of Armenia. (in Russia).

Batiuk, S. 2013 The Fruits of Migration: Understanding the 'longue duree' and the socio-economic relations of the Early Transcaucasian Culture. *Journal of Anthropological Archaeology* 32: 447–477.

Batiuk, S., Rothman, M. S, Samei, S., Hovsepyan, R. 2022 press Unravelling the Kura-Araxes Cultural Tradition Across Space and Time. *Ancient Near Eastern Studies* 59: 235-325.

Bayburtian, E. 1938. A cult hearth from the excavations of the Shengavit settlement in 1936–1937. *Herald of Ancient History* 4 (5): 255–259. (in Russian).

Bayburtian, E. 1939 The succession of ancient cultures of Armenia, on the basis of the archaeological material, Unpublished manuscript, *The Archive of the Institute of Archaeology and Ethnography, RA*. 90:148, Yerevan. (in Russian).

Bayburtian, E. 2011 *The sequence of the oldest cultures in Armenia based on archaeological material*. Unsubmitted dissertation. Yerevan: Museum of the History of Armenia. (in Russian).

Berthon, R., Erdal, Y., Mashkour, M., and Kozbe, G. 2016 Buried with Turtles: the symbolic role of the Euphrates soft-shelled turtle (*Rafetus euphraticus*) in Mesopotamia. *Antiquity* 90 (349): 111-125.

Child, A. and Child, I. 1993 *Religion and Magic in the Life of Traditional Peoples*. Englewood Cliffs, NJ: Prentice-Hall.

Eliade, M. 1958 *Rites and Symbols of Initiation*. New York: Harper Torch books.

Eliade, M., ed. 1987 *The Encyclopedia of Religion*. New York: Macmillan.

Fogelin, L. 2007 The archaeology of religious ritual. *Annual Review of Anthropology* 36: 55-71.

Frangipane, M. and Palumbi, G. 2007 Red-black ware, pastoralism, trade, and Anatolian-Transcaucasian interaction in the 4th-3rd millennium BC, in *Les Cultures du Caucase*, edited by B. Lyonnet, 232–255. Paris: CNRS Editions.

Frangipane, M., DiNocera, G-M., Hauptmann, A., Morbidelli, P., Palmieri, A., Sadori, L., Schultz, M., and Schmidt-Schultz, T. 2001 New Symbols of a new power in a "Royal Tomb" from 3000 B.C Arslantepe, Malatya (Turkey). *Paléorient* 27(2): 105–139.

Gardiner, A. 2008 Agency. in *Handbook of Archaeological Theories*, edited by R. A. Bentley, H. D. G. Maschner and C. Chippindale, 95–108. Lanham, MD: AltaMira Press.

Geertz, G. 1973 Religion as a cultural system. in *The Interpretation of Cultures*. New York: Basic Books.

Gell, A. 1998 *Art and Agency: An Anthropological Theory*. Oxford: Clarendon Press.

Gilman, P. and Stone, T. 2013 The role of ritual variability in social negotiations of early communities: Great Kiva homogeneity and heterogeneity in the Mogollon Region of the North American Southwest. *American Antiquity* 78: 607–623.

Hauptmann, H. 1982 Die Grabungen aud dem Norşun-Tepe 1974, in *Keban Project 1974-75 Activities*, edited by S. Pekman, 13–70. Ankara: METU.

Hodder, I. 1986 *Reading the Past*. Cambridge: Cambridge University Press.

Ishoev, S. and Greenberg, R. 2019 Khirbet Kerak Ware (Kura-Araxes) Andirons at Tel Bet Yerah: Functional Analysis and Cultural Context. *Tel Aviv* 46: 21–40.

Koşay, H. 1976 *Keban Projesi Pulur Kazisi 1968-70*. Ankara: Middle East Technical University.

Mirimanow, W. B. 1973. *Kunst der Urgesellschaft und traditionelle Kunst Afrikas und Ozeaniens*. Dresden: VEB Verlag der Kunst.

Moore, O. K. 1957 Divination – a new perspective. *American Anthropologist* 59: 69–74.

Netting, R. 1978 Sacred Power and Centralization, in *Population Growth*, edited by B. Spooner, 219–244. Cambridge, MA: MIT Press.

Palumbi, G 2008 *The Red and the Black: Social and Cultural Interaction between the Upper Euphrates and South Caucasus Communities in the Fourth and Third Millennium B.C*. Rome: Università di Roma, La Sapienza.

Rappaport, R. 1968 *Pigs for the Ancestors*. New Haven: Yale University Press.

Redfield, R. 1971 *The Little Community: Peasant Society and Culture*. Chicago: University of Chicago Press.

Romain, W. 2009 *Shamans of the Lost World*. Lanham, MD: Rowan and Littlefield Publishers.

Rothman, M. S 2021 Perspectives on the Kura-Araxes: The View from Shengavit. in *Archaeology of Armenia in Regional Context*, edited by P. Avetisyan and A. Bobokhyan, 52-68. Yerevan: Publishing House of the Institute of Archaeology and Ethnography.

Rothman, M. S 2017 Explaining the Kura Araxes. in *Fitful Histories and Unruly Publics*, edited by K. Weber, E. Hite, L. Katchadourian, and A. Smith, 217-257. Leiden: Brill.

Rothman, M. S 2015a Early Bronze Age Migrants and Ethnicity in the Middle Eastern Mountain Zone. *Proceedings of the National Academy of Science* 112(30): 9190-9195.

Rothman, M. S 2015b The Changing Organization of Kura-Araxes Culture. in *International Symposium on East Anatolia South Caucasus Cultures, Vol. 1*, edited by Mehmet Isikli and Barol Can, 121-131. Cambridge: Cambridge Scholars Publishing.

Rothman, M. S 2014 Kura Araxes Culture Areas and the Late 4th and Early 3rd Millennia BC Pottery from Veli Sevin's Surveys in Malatya and Elaziğ, Turkey. *Origini* XXXVI: 37-91.

Rothman, M. S 2011 Migration and re-settlement: Godin Period IV, in *On the High Road: The History of Godin Tepe, Iran*, edited by H. Gopnick and M. S Rothman, 67–138. Toronto: ROM Press/ Mazda Press.

Sagona, A. 2000 Sos Höyük and the Erzurum region in late prehistory: a provisional chronology for northeast Anatolia, in *Chronologies des pays du Caucase et de l'Euphrate aux IV-III millénaires*, edited by C. Marro and H. Hauptmann, pp. 329–337. Istanbul: IFEA; Paris: De Boccard.

Sagona, A. 1998 Social identity and religious ritual in the Kura-Araxes cultural complex: Some observations from Sos Höyük. *Mediterranean Archaeology* 11: 13–25.

Sagona, A. 1984 *The Caucasian Region in the Early Bronze Age* (BAR International Series 214). Oxford: BAR.

Sagona, A. and Sagona, C. 2009 Encounters with the divine in Late Prehistoric Eastern Anatolia and South Caucasus. in *A Life Dedicated to Urartu, On the Shores of the Upper Sea*, edited by H. Sağlamtımur, E. Abay, Z. Derin, A. Erdem, A. Batmaz, F. Dedeoğlu, M. Esdalkıran, M. Bastürk, E. Konakçi, 537-563. Istanbul: Arkeoloji ve Sanat Yayinlari.

Sagona, A. and Sagona, C. 2011 The Mushroom, the Magi and the Keen-Sighted Seers. in *Anatolia and Europe in the First Millennium B*C, edited by G. Tsetskhladze, 387-436. Leuven: Peeters.

Sardarian, S. H. 1967 *The Primitive Communal System in Armenia*. Yerevan: Publishing House "Mitk." (in Armenian with Russian and English summaries).

Sardarian, S.H. 2004 *Armenia, Cradle of Civilization*. Yerevan: Hamalsarani Hratarakjch'ut'yun. (in Armenian).

Simonyan, H. 2013 Shengavit: An ordinary settlement or an early city? *Hushardzan* 8: 5–53.

Simonyan, H. 2015 The Archaeological Site of Shengavit: An Ancient Town in the Armenian Highland, *Fundamental Armenology* 1. http://www.fundamentalarmenology.am/Article/8/102/THE-ARCHAEOLOGICAL-SITE-OF-SHENGAVIT:-AN-ANCIENT-TOWN-IN-THE-ARMENIAN-HIGHLAND.html

Smith, A.T. and Leon, J. 2014 Divination and Sovereignty: The Late Bronze Ages Shrines at Gegharot, Armenia. *American Journal of Archaeology* 118(4): 549–563.

Smith, A. 2005 Prometheus unbound, South Caucasia in prehistory. *Journal of World Prehistory* 19: 229–279.

Smith, A., Badalyan, R. and Avetisyan, P. 2009 *The Archaeology and Geography of Ancient Transcaucasian Societies*. Vol. 1. *The Foundations of Research and Regional Survey in the Tsaghkahovit Plain, Armenia* (University of Chicago Oriental Institute publications, v. 134). Chicago: Oriental Institute.

Smogorzewska, A. 2004 Andirons and their role in Early Transcaucasian Culture. *Anatolica* 30: 151–177.

Sosis, R. 2004 The adaptive value of religious ritual. *American Scientist* 92(2): 166–172.

Takaoğlu, T. 2000 Hearth structures in the religious pattern in Early Bronze Age Northeastern Anatolia. *Anatolian Studies* 50: 11–16.

Turner, V. 1973 Symbols in African Ritual. *Science* 179: 1100–1105.

Turner, V. 1969 *The Ritual Process*. New York: Aldine de Gruyter.

Turner, V. 1967 *The Forest of Symbols*. Ithaca, NY: Cornell University Press.

Van der Toorn, K. 1996 Domestic Religion in Ancient Mesopotamia, in *Houses and Households in Ancient Mesopotamia*, edited by K. Veenhof, 69–78. Istanbul: Nederlands Historisch-Archaeologisch Instituut.

Van Gennep, A. 1960 *The Rites of Passage*. London: Routledge and Kegan Paul.

Waters, F. 1963 *Book of the Hopi*. New York: Ballantine Books.

Webster, D. 1976 On Theocracies. *American Anthropologist* 78: 812–828.

Whiting, J. and B. Ayres. 1968 Inferences from the shape of dwellings, in *Settlement Archaeology*, edited by K. C. Chang, 117–133. Palo Alto CA: National Press Books.

Wills, W. H. 2000 Political leadership and the construction of Chacoan Great Houses, A.D. 1020-1140, in *Alternative Leadership Strategies in the Prehispanic Southwest*, edited by B. Mills, 19-44. Tucson: University of Arizona Press.

Winter, I. 2007 Agency marked, agency ascribed: The affective object in Ancient Mesopotamia, in *Art's Agency and Art History*, edited by R. Osborne and J. Tanner, 42–69. Oxford: Blackwell Publishing.

Winter, I. 1997 Art in empire: The royal image and the visual dimensions of Assyrian ideology. in *Assyria 1995*, edited by S. Parpola and R. M. Whiting, 359–381. Helsinki: University Press.

Winter, I. 1987 Legitimization of authority through image and legend: Seals belonging to officials in the administrative bureaucracy of the Ur III Period. in *The Organization of Power: Aspects of Administration and Bureaucracy in the Ancient, Medieval, and Ottoman Near East*, edited by M. Gibson and R. Biggs, 69–106. Chicago: Oriental Institute Press.

Wobst, H. M. 1977 Stylistic Behavior and Information Exchange. in *For the Director: Essays in Honor of James Griffin*. Anthropology Papers 61, 317-342. Ann Arbor: Museum of Anthropology University of Michigan.

6b | Mortuary Practice at Shengavit

Hakob Simonyan

As discussed in Chapter 6a, ideology is an integral part of the culture of any society. In the previous chapter, we discussed the ritual associated with the cult of the hearth, around which people performed either a household or possibly a public ritual. More data will be needed before we can tell one from the other.

Another class of rituals, certainly a public one, was funeral rites or burial practices. This rite of transition from the world of the living is critical for modern researchers to understand.[697] As of 2014, archaeologists had recovered 111 Kura-Araxes sites with burials throughout the South Caucasus region.[698] The details of this ritual for the Kura-Araxes cultural tradition are very diverse (see below).

Cemetary Location

In Armenia in such Kura-Araxes sites as Talin, Jrvezh/Avan, Maisyan, Karnut, the large mound of Gorayk large cemeteries can't be associated with any nearby occupation sites. We do not know whether these burial grounds represent: 1) sacred places remote from the settlements, 2) the seasonal habitation of mobile pastoralists leaving few archaeological remains, or 3) the traces of settlements that were destroyed or buried under alluvial deposits over time. The large mound of Gorayk is the basis for the hypothesis that the burial grounds indicated above were formed in high-mountainous regions in alpine pastures, where animal breeders probably lived in the summer season, descending back to settlements in the lower elevations when the cold weather came. We await future research to decide which groups buried their dead there. On the other hand, the burial grounds of Kura-Araxes Shengavit, Berqber/Jogaz, and Köhne Shahar in the Lower (Araxes River) Province of the homeland rested on the outskirts of settlements (see Fig 3.1).

Method of Recording

The following method was used to record the finds. Each collection was assembled by quadrants and elevations (loci). In the labeled artifacts 0 is the initial digit for computer classification, 1-12 is the number of the square, 0-9 is the number of the locus that each cultural layer recovered from this square.

The method of mapping burials and grave goods makes it possible to determine the area occupied by the Shengavit necropolis, the density of burials, the ratio of individual types of burials and burial rites, as well as the chronological relationships of the graves located in different parts of the necropolis.

---

697 Renfrew et al. 2015.
698 Poulmarc'h et al. 2014, 233.

Our analysis used the method of archaeotanatology[699]: "an accurate record of the position of each bone as well as a record of any artifact in of the tomb (jewelry, tools, offerings, etc.). Thus, archaeotanatology allows a reliable interpretation of the decomposition process of the body, paying close attention to its skeletal remains."[700] Thanks to these methods it is possible to reconstruct funerary practices (initial position of the body, post-depositional practices, etc.). In addition, the analysis of bone movements inside the grave may permit us to discover the architectural elements or containers with perishable material. This approach also permitted us to identify previously unknown burial practices (for example, the use of cords to preserve the position of the body, storage of bodies in containers of perishable material, post-burial practices, etc.).

We used typological and historical-comparative method of analyzing artifacts and grave construction to date the burials, because we do not have radiocarbon analyses to accurately date the necropolis.

Typology of Graves

Researchers have attempted to characterize different grave constructions of the Early Bronze Age, Kura-Araxes cultural tradition. They have classified the characteristic elements of funerary structures using as few as four criteria[701] to as many as 21.[702] Poulmarc'h proposes to divide the burial structures of the South Caucasus into six types: cists, stone burials built in various shapes including horseshoe-shaped tombs, pit graves without above-ground structures, tombs marked on the surface with small piles of stones, and kurgans (Fig 6b.1).[703]

Another typology defines the diverse Kura-Araxes burial structures to include:

1) "surface" burials, in which the corpse was laid on the cleared surface of the earth, surrounded by masonry and covered with a mound made of stone and soil (for example, at Jrvezh/Avan, Mashnaari). Sometimes, on the eve of the burial, builders covered the surface with pebbles, which lay under the mounded earth;[704]

2) rectangular or oval grave pits (for example, at Elar, Arich, Jogaz, Kiketi, Amiranis Gora, Samshvilde, Kalavan, Jrarata, Aradetis Gora, Natsargora, Kvatskhelebi, Lchashen, and Tsakhkalanga). Sometimes, the graves were filled with river stones. This type of graves was especially common in Shida Kartli, where single and double burials were common.[705]

3) rectangular (for example, at Berkaber/Jogaz,[706] Shengavit,[707] Karnut) and horseshoe-shaped crypts (at

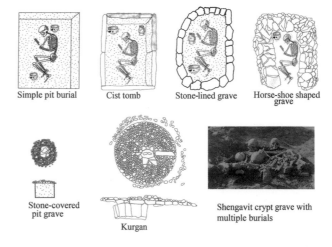

Figure 6b.1 Kura-Araxes grave types.

699   Duday 1990 and 2009; Duday et al. 1990.
700   Polmarc'h et al. 2014, 231.
701   Palumbi 2016.
702   Kalantaryan 2007, 72.
703   Poulmarc'h 2014.
704   Dedabrishwili 1979, 56, 57. Backfilling the grave bottoms with pebbles is characteristic of the Maikop culture; *Archaeologu USSR*, 1994, 34.
705   Kushnareva, 1970, 75.
706   Simonyan 2009, 215-232.
707   Sardaryan 2004, 370-378.

Elar), built of large and small raw stones or boulders (for example, at Maisyan,[708] Harich, Elar, Tamarisi, Naxçivedi, Chobareti, Kiketi, Amiranis Gora, Khorome, Gegharot, Keti, Karnut, Lanjik, Aragats, Dzori Berde, Samshvilde, and Ozni);

4) rectangular cists made of tufa and basalt slabs (for example, at Samshvilde, Shengavit, Talin, Takhtidrizi, Kiketi, Treli, Kode, Elar, Teghout, and Karchaghbyur). The average size of the graves is 2.5 x 1.5 meters;

5) crypts, the walls of which are lined with mud bricks (only in the burial grounds of Shengavit and Tsikhia Gora-Gudabertka); and,

6) kurgans with a circle of stones most common in Azerbaijan at the end of KA1 and throughout the KA2 into the Early Kurgan period.

The use of all these types of structures can be traced in a number of burial grounds (for example, at Elar, Berqaber, and Shengavit). For the burials intended for multiple use (see below), builders made *dromosi* with corridor-like passages (for example, at Jrvezh, Talin, Tsaghkalanj, Mentesh Tepe). Builders sometimes decorated the entrances with two stone pylons and the threshold with a slab (for example, at Karnut, Gegharot, Horom, Keti, Samshvilde, Kiketi, Chobareti, and Balichi-Dzedzvebi). Two types of graves existed at Berkaber (Joghaz): pit graves with single burials and crypts with stone walls for periodic burials of deceased members of a group, perhaps members of an extended family.

Some differences among graves goods are evident from the burial goods from these graves. For example, some ceramics from the crypts, as at Shengavit, are relatively uniform and poorly ornamented, while ceramics from the pit burials have a carefully made, highly burnished finish. According to my observations, richly ornamented pottery, characteristic of the early period of the KA2, precedes the simple, uniform pottery from stone crypts. The latter occur in the transitional phase from KA2 to the Early Kurgan culture. This suggests that the rite of individual burials precedes the rite of family burials in some places. It is possible that the change in the funeral rite reflects new ideas about what was important to symbolize in the ritual. Perhaps, the change represents a change in emphasis from the symbols on the pots to the materials that were in the pots.

I believe, overall, that the most important criteria for burials in the Kura-Araxes of the South Caucasus divides them into two main groups: a) above-ground structures and b) pit graves or other below ground structures for placing the remains of the deceased. Above-ground structures include ones that have mounds, *cromlechs* (stone circles), *dromos* (entryways), *stele*, or "grave statues." One can imagine that these reflect an idea of what the transformation of death meant. In that light, the mound could protect the remains of the buried; for example, the *cromlech* may have been a magic circle to prevent the penetration of evil spirits into the grave. *Dromos* could have served as a pointer to the corresponding sacred side of the world where the soul of the deceased was supposed to go. The mound and *stele* were intended to perpetuate the memory of the deceased. In some sense they were a representation of the person's status in life. Presumably, the higher the status of the buried person in the social system, the larger and more visible were the tomb structures (kurgan, cromlech). Alternatively, it could represent the role the person played more than that the status of individuals, like people buried at the death pits at Ur.[709] Grave goods might reflect some aspects of the dead person's activities in life. The existence of clear social differentiation for individuals in the Kura-Araxes remains unverified, as authors discuss in other chapters of this book.

---

708   Areshian 1987, 558, 559.
709   Moorey 1977.

Mounds in the South Caucasus appear as early as the Eneolithic or Chalcolithic period.[710] In Kura-Araxes times earthen mounds averaged one and a half to two meters high and covered small shaft graves five to fifteen meters in diameter. These were common at Maisyan, Sachkhere, Trialeti, Khachbulak, Shamkhor, Astara, Natsargora, Tkviavi, Akchakale, Hasankent, and Bozkent in Eastern Turkey.[711] Archaeologists recovered *cromlechs* under some burial mounds, which had earthen pits or quadrangular stone boxes in the center, as well as large (3 x 5 m) rectangular burial chambers.[712] The ancients buried up to 34 people in these tombs. I believe that, in contrast to the ancestral crypts in which they buried deceased family members in turn, they may have buried their dead in these kurgan crypts at the same time. This suggests a communal ritual. What the circumstances were that created this ritual still need to be explained. Rarer among the burials were barrows with a diameter of up to 35 to 40 meters, whose surface the ancients lined with mud bricks and under which there were graves with wooden floors (for example, at Mentesh Tepe and Uzun Rama).[713]

In 2019-2020 my team excavated at Gorayk, a large mound (height 3.3 m, diameter 40 m). In the center of the mound lay an egg-shaped burial chamber, the walls of which consisted of flat-laid basalt slabs. They covered the bottom of the tomb with a light yellow-colored clay. From above large, flat basalt slabs covered the burial chamber, which formed a false vault. Basalt flat slabs lined the barrow itself, somewhat reminiscent of the barrows of Mentesh Tepe and Uzun-Rama, where mudbricks lined the mounds. The mound of Gorayk was possibly the burial place of a person of importance, perhaps the elder of a clan or a person of influence. The grave contained about 15 thousand obsidian items, as well as raw materials in the form of river pebbles and pieces of obsidian, broken, unfinished objects, finished tools, and arrowheads. Here one can clearly see the locale of making tools, which would be used in rituals of the transitions of the dead. According to radiocarbon analysis, the mound dates back to Kura-Araxes times,[714] that is the first half of the 3rd millennium BC.

Grave pits or structures for placing the ashes of the deceased, grave goods, carcasses of sacrificial animals, and even people, were diverse. This diversity was due to both to the effort expended in making the grave and the nature and meaning of the funeral rite of passage. It, like variations in the styles of pottery, shows the degree of heterogeneity in the cultural landscape of the Kura-Araxes. Of great structural importance was also the covering of graves, which were built from logs (for example, at Osmanbozu), stone slabs (for example, at Elar,[715] Shengavit,[716] and Gorayk), or backfilled with cobblestones (for example, in Shida Kartli).[717]

The Treatment of the Body in the Funeral Ritual

The rite of processing the corpse and the method of burial have a separate and very important meaning as does grave construction and form. Archaeologist have uncovered: 1) individual (single) burials (for example, at Amiranis Gora, Elar, Shengavit, Jogaz, Karnut), 2) paired burials (for example, at Shengavit, Elar, Amiranis Gora),[718] 3) collective burials or family tombs (for example, at Samshvilde, Kiketi, Shengavit, Jogaz, Haghtanak, Karnut). Bodies have

710   Gummel 1948, 15-22; Munchaev 1975, 64, 65.
711   Archaeology 1994, 34.
712   Kesamanli 1978 and 1981.
713   Poulmarc'h et al. 2014.
714   Simonyan 2021.
715   Khanzadyan 1979.
716   Sardarian 2004, 373.
717   *Archaeologi USSR,* 1994, 34.
718   Kushnareva, Chubinishvili, 1973, 66.

undergone 1) cremation (for example, at Osmanbozu),[719] 2) inhumation with bent legs and outstretched arms (for example, at Elar), 3) dismemberment and decapitation[720] (for example, at Shengavit and Kiketi), 4) inclusion of a secondary body with the deceased[721] (for example, at Shengavit), 4) the body in a sitting position (for example, at Gorayk), 5) the attachment of limbs with harnesses and straps in a special position (for example, at Shengavit), and 6) secondary burials. To determine the original position of corpses, which, after the decomposition of soft tissues, altered the original position of the bones, the French school of archeology developed a special method: archeothanatology (see above).[722]

The burial rite also included the cleansing of the burial chamber with the help of fire and stones; flakes of obsidian, flint, and jasper scattered on the surface of the barrows and the grave pits (for example, at Gorayk, Dzogaz, Shengavit, and Elar). One can imagine that in the view of Kura-Araxes people, obsidian and flint had magical properties to drive away evil spirits.[723]

To isolate the corpse from the ground, builders smeared the bottom of the grave with plaster (for example, at Gorayk, Elar, and Shengavit),[724] covered it with sand (for example, at Elar), or laid wooden boards on top (for example, at Osmanbozu[725]). They also practiced the ritual of cenotaph burials, where there was no body (for example, at Osmanbozu, Maisyan, Kakhetia, and eastern Georgia: Melegele, and Mashnaari).

An essential element of the funeral rite was the sacrifice of animals (for example, at Elar and Shengavit) and even people, as well as the placement of grave goods, which were located a) at the head, b) at the feet, c) along the body, d) in front of the face, e) under the head, or f) above the corpse. According to the composition of the inventory, the burials of the Early Bronze Age can be divided into the following groups: 1) no grave goods (for example, at Kiketi), 2) only ceramic pots, 3) burials with metal objects (for example, at Shengavit and Elar), and 4) burials with precious metal objects (for example, at Shengavit and Gorayk).[726] I believe that grave goods included symbols of status (for example, at Shengavit and Gorayk) (see below).

As a rule, the bodies were laid on their sides with bent legs. Also, more and more examples show the practice of burials of dismembered corpses (for example, at Shengavit, Tsakhkalanj, Talin, Gegharot and Aparani-Berd). The person buried in Gorayk had a peculiar posture; the corpse was seated with their legs bent under the pelvis.

These different types of grave structures, burial methods, along with grave goods and the handling of the corpse, are symbolic clues to the possible meaning of burial rituals in the KA2.

Shengavit Burial Ground

Description of the Burials excavated by Sardarian
Sardarian excavated 9 burials, of which five are partially described in his 2004 book.[727]

---

719 Kcsamanli 1981, 514.
720 *Archaeologi USSR,* 1994, 35.
721 The deceased could take other family members with them. If after a funeral someone from the family of the deceased died immediately, the grave of the deceased was opened and disinterred (decapitated, chopped up, or have heavy stones put on it, etc.). This was also the case with the sacrificed individuals.
722 Duday et al. 1990; Duday 2009.
723 Simonyan 1988, 79-81.
724 Simonyan 2021.
725 Kesamanli 1981, 514.
726 Archaeologi USSR, 1994, 35.
727 Sardaryan 2004, 370-379. This book was actually written by his daughter based on his field notes.

Unfortunately, Sardarian did not describe the location of the burial ground in detail in his publications, except that they were located outside the settlement wall. Analyzing the scattered information from the archival documents, we tried to reconstruct the area where the burials excavated by Sardarian were located and put it on the map.

Burial 1

Sardarian dug this grave in 1958. It is square in plan, measuring 3.6 x 3.3 meters and 1 meter deep from the surface of the ground. The skeletons of both men and women occupied the tomb. Ninety-eight whole and fragmentary pottery vessels lay in the burial.[728] At the bottom of one bowl, decorated on the outside with finely carved rows of triangles and menanders, was a trace of red ochre which Badalyan mistook for traces of red paint.[729] Also in the burial lay a gold pendant (Fig 6b.2., A), an earring or hair ring (Fig 6b.2.,B), silver rings, a bronze axe with herringbone engraved ornament on the surface of the spherical handle (Fig 6b.2., F), a flat axe with expanding blade (Fig 6b.2., E), arrowheads, a pin for clothing (a fibula?) with a riveted figurine of a marten with hooked heads (Fig 6b.2., D), copper bracelets (Fig 6b.2., C), a flat leaf-shaped dart tip, bronze tall rings, a scroll, a stone casting mold, stone maces, and bone arrowheads.

The pottery was mostly from the Shengavit Kura-Araxes typology (see Chapter 5e; Fig 6b.3). Two large storage vessels, however, appear to be from the Early Kurgan Period. Burial 1 therefore represents the transitional phase between these two South Caucasian time periods and cultural phases.[730]

According to Sardarian, this burial, corresponds to the 4th horizon of the settlement, which he believed was post-Kura-Araxes. Despite the many skeletons buried there[731] he thought it was the grave of a leader. He asserted that these luxurious objects testify to the established institution of chieftaincy, private property, and accumulation of wealth in the hands of the upper class.[732] The interpretation of the social structure represented by these graves

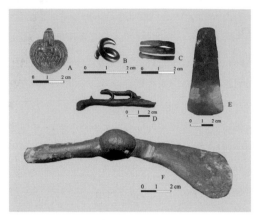

Figure 6b.2 Some of the grave goods from Burial 1.

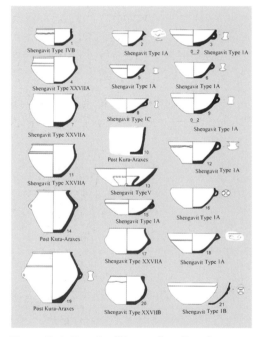

Figure 6b.3 Sample of Pottery from Burial 1.

depends in part on what school of archaeology one belongs to. I believe that these exotic goods represent a class society. My colleague Rothman sees many more levels of social evolution. Rothman believes the evidence in this volume suggests a more vertical egalitarian society.[733] In such a society one sees groups with greater influence as

---

728   Badalyan et al. 2015, 144-159.
729   Badalyan et al. 2015, 146, tabl. 64, Fig 599.
730   Simonyan and Rothman in press.
731   In our chronology it is the transition of Strata 0 and I of more than four distinct architectural layers.
732   Sardarian 2004, 371.
733   Rothman 2021.

opposed to leaders with the authority to say, "do this or else." True class society, which in anthropological theory comes only with state-level complexity, does not fit Shengavit. This may be the grave of an extended family with such influence, in which the beginning of social differentiation, limited control by would-be leaders, and some coordination of activities[734] occurred.

Burial 2

Sardarian's team excavated this tomb in 1960. River stones lined the walls of the burial in a single row, and earth covered it. Square in plan, measuring 3.0 x 2.5 meters, 0.75 meters deep from the ground surface, the ancients built the burial on the surface on a floor of small pebbles. Three skeletons occupied it. One skeleton had a gold ring on its finger (Fig 6b.4, A), next to the other skeleton was a single handled, red, burnished vessel with a tubular spout covered with a highly polished slip and small raised bumps at the base of the handle and the spout (Fig 6b.4). According to Sardarian this vessel is similar in type to the teapot-shaped vessels from Tepe Sialk.[735] I disagree with this opinion, as only the Sialk Early Iron Age vessels had beak-shaped protuberances. Widespread at that later time in Iran and the South Caucasus, they had a completely different structure and shape. In addition, there were nine whole vessels (Fig 6b.5), eight with a black and one with a red surface, as well as a gold ring,[736] a stone mace-head, and arrowheads of bone.[737] Without giving any justification, Sardarian believes that Shengavit had already been destroyed at the time of the construction of this tomb.[738] According to Sardarian the vessels from this burial correspond in typology to the ceramics from the 4th horizon[739] of the settlement; in fact, on the surface of Stratum 0. There is little evidence of willful destruction. As Figure 6b.5 shows, a number of the vessels match types from the Shengavit Kura-Araxes occupation levels, and like Burial 1 it was likely built during the transitional Kura-Araxes to Early Kurgan phase.

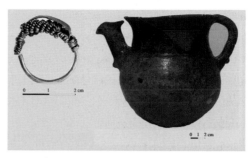

Figure 6b.4 A ring and a pot from Burial 2.

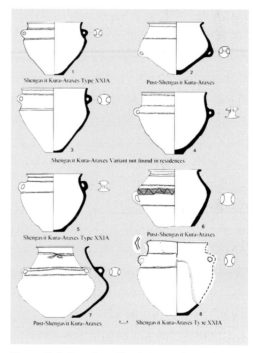

Figure 6b.5 Pots from Tomb 2.

Burial 3

Sardarian excavated this burial in 1962.[740] River stones lined the base of the walls of the burial over which the builders erected raw adobe. In plan the rectangular structure had dimensions of 3.6 x 1.5 meters. The depth from the surface

---

734   Rothman 2002.
735   Sardarian 2004.
736   Badalyan et al. 2015, 160-163.
737   Sardarian 2004, 373.
738   Sardarian 2004.
739   What Sardiarian calls the fourth horizon, we term Statum 0 (see Chapter 3).
740   Sardaryan 2004, 373; Badalyan et al. 2015, 165.

of the ground was one meter. An embankment of earth covered the grave, which builders then covered with clay mortar. In the grave near the walls and in the center of the chamber lay several skeletons of men and women with bent legs. The skeletons were oriented differently. In the grave lay 30 whole vessels: 29 with black surfaces and one red, as well as about 25 fragments of pottery (Fig 6b.6),[741] a flat copper axe, a spearhead, a four-sided arrowhead, and a long ring of one and a half turns (a hair ring?). One bowl was decorated with a mesh field, and the one goblet contained red ochre.[742] In my opinion, the shapes and ornamentation of the pottery indicate that this burial predates Burials 1 and 2, placing it solidly in the KA2.

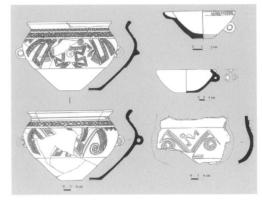

Figure 6b.6 Sample of decorated pots from Burial 3.

Burial 4

This burial was in a small ravine.[743] Sardarian excavated it in 1962.[744] Stones lined the walls of the burial chamber, which were overlaid with large tufa slabs. The rectangular structure had dimensions of 4 x 3 meters, 1 meter deep from the ground surface. The skeleton was lying facing the wall. Resting in the tomb were 45 pots with black exteriors and three with red ones.[745] Near the skeleton was a black, polished vessel with a round body and narrow neck, decorated with deeply impressed triangles, and with a red interior (Fig 6b.7., A). The shape fits well within the typology of the Kura-Araxes pottery at Shengavit, although the designs remind one of the Early Kurgan Period. An unusual element is raised cones

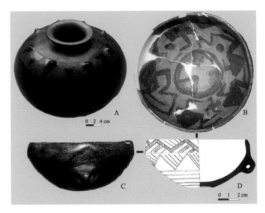

Figure 6b.7 Two pots from Burial 4.

around the neck. Nearby there was a pot with a rounded body and two lugs. At the base of the neck of the pot "three-row belt [double carinated] with sickle-shaped ornament [Fig 6a.1., 12?]."[746] It is from this burial that the often illustrated painted bowl emerged (measuring 7.2-5.3 cm at the base, 17.0-19.1 cm at the rim) (Fig 6b. 7., B-D). It had a slightly concave bottom, covered inside with light brown engobe, on which a scene is painted in dark-red-brown paint.[747] In the center is depicted a round, three-lobed cult hearth around which unfolds a scene of struggle between snakes and humpbacked birds. These are usually described as storks.[748] A swastika and circles are

741 Badalyan et al. 2015, 164-171, plate 71-73.

742 Sardarian 2004, 373.

743 This message suggests the location of tomb 4, which we have plotted on the map.

744 Sardarian 2004, 373; Badalyan et al. noted that the burial was excavated in 1964 (See Badalyan et al. 2015, p. 173).

745 Badalyan et al. 2015, 172-181.

746 These two vessels described by Sardarian either are not in the catalog due to poor illustration or are absent from the funerary inventory of tomb 4 in the published catalog, Badalyan et al. 2015.

747 Badalyan, for reasons unclear to us, attributes this bowl to collection 2392 from a settlement excavated in 1966 and preserved in the collection of the State Museum of Armenia. He highlights several swastikas in the painting, and is skeptical about the central image as a hearth (Badalyan et al. 2015, 119-121, Table 50/496). Sardarian, on the other hand, made another mistake, seeing frogs in storks' beaks together with snakes (Sardarian, 2004, 373), which do not appear to be there.

748 Sardarian 1967, 187.

drawn around the hearth (Fig 6b.7., B, C). Sardarian correctly noted the drawing of the cult hearth, which Badalyan questions.[749] On the outside of the pot is a horizontal belt of geometric motifs. The top row consists of a zigzag intersected with diagonal crosshatched lines (Fig 6a.1., 11). This design is associated with ritual spaces (Chapter 6a). Below that is a series of incised triangles facing downwards (Fig 6a.1, 6). Four rows of horizontal lines circle the pot near its base. A hemispherical handle with a horizontal hole is attached near the bottom (Fig 6b.7., D).

Sardarian considers a decorative ornament on the surface of the painted bowl in the form of engraved corners to be a characteristic feature of the upper or fourth, post-Kura-Araxes layer of Shengavit.[750] In the tomb lay 51 whole vessels: 47 with black exteriors and 4 red,[751] a copper flat wedge-shaped axe with an arc-shaped blade and a convex back side (11. 3 cm. in length), a copper bracelet (6.5 cm. in diameter), a pin with a hooked head, an earring or hair ring of one and a half turns, a stone mace, and stone beads.[752]

Burial 5

Excavated in 1965,[753] large stones (Fig 6b.8) made up the walls of the rectangular tomb with an entryway on one side. Inside the masonry sat two burial pits. At the bottom of one of the pits, measuring 3.4 x 2.6 meters and 1.2 meters high, the skeletons of the dead lay facing the walls.[754] Next to the skulls were vessels with black and red exteriors.[755] In the center of the tomb stood nine vessels, of which six had thin walls and three were roughly shaped. Four of the vessels had decorations in the form of rectangles, rhombuses, and reticulated fields. They lay interspersed around the skeletons. A total of twenty-seven whole vessels rested on the floor of the tomb: pots and bowls decorated with geometric patterns, twenty-three with black and four with red exteriors. On one of the vessels, the ornamentation was applied as a wide belt, which was divided into three parts: arched bands at the top, a cross-shaped ornament at the bottom, and triangles along the edges. From the central circle emerged three ribbon-like lines. Inside the bowl lay red ochre. Another burnished black exterior vessel at the neck had a spiral-shaped ornament on the outside. There was also a three-legged pot (a receptacle for burning incense?), a rare form at Shengavit (Type IX, C). Also, in the tomb remained a half-turn copper ear or hair rings with pointed ends, and two beads.[756]

Figure 6b.8 Burial 5 measured by Yu.A. Tamanyan.

749   Badalyan et al. 2015, 121.

750   Sardarian 2004, 373.

751   Badalyan et al. 2015, 173-181.

752   Sardarian 2004, 373.

753   Badalyan et al. 2015, 183.

754   Tomb 5 resembles the Gegharot grave, excavated by the Armenian-American expedition.

755   Tomb 5 pots illustrated in Badalyan et al. 2015, 182-187.

756   Sardarian 2004, 374.

Burial 6

Sardarian's team excavated Burial 6 in 1965. They recovered a total of 36 whole, single-handled open and closed vessels: 35 with black and one with red exteriors.[757] Some of them are decorated with geometric patterns. The vast majority are open-shaped vessels. These are identical in form to the pottery from Berkaber burials (Jogaz tombs NN 1-3).[758]

Burial 7

Excavated in 1965, it yielded four or five whole and 58 fragments of vessels all with red exteriors (Fig 6b.9).[759] Some of them are richly decorated with geometric patterns. The vast majority are open-form vessels. In all likelihood, this burial was destroyed before the excavation, as a result of which most of the vessels were broken.[760] In style the pottery of this tomb lacks any of the Post-Kura-Araxes, Early Kurgan characteristics; hence, I believe it is earlier than Burial 1, thus in the KA2.

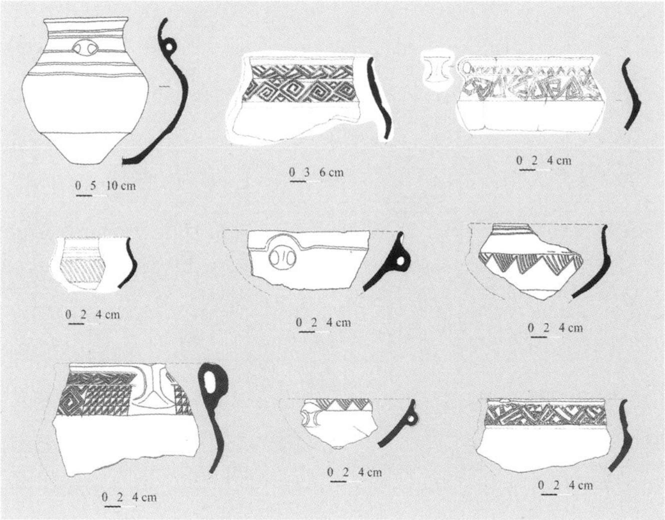

Figure 6b.9 Pots with designs from Burial 7.

Burial 8

Sardian's team excavated it in 1966. Grave goods included a total of 31 whole, single-handled, closed and open vessels: 14 with black and 17 with red exteriors.[761] Some of them are decorated with exquisite geometric patterns. The vast majority are open-shaped vessels.

Burial 9

Excavated in 1966 it yielded ten or eleven whole and six fragments of pots, mostly with red exteriors. Some of them are richly decorated with geometric patterns (Design 18a, Fig 6a.1).[762] The vast majority are open-form vessels. In all probability, before excavations this burial was partially destroyed, as a result of which half of the vessels were broken. There are six more vessels in storage at the Armenian History Museum: three closed and three black surfaced, open forms, that came from the destroyed burials.[763] We have no information about the number and structure of the ruined graves.

---

757   Sardarian does not describe the excavations of Tombs 6-9. We will cite data on the collection found in these graves from Shengavit's catalog (Badalyan et al. 2015, 189).

758   Simonyan 2009, 215-232.

759   Badalyan et al. 2015, 196-203.

760   Badalyan et al. 2015, 189.

761   Badalyan et al. 2015, 205.

762   Badalyan et al. 2015, 212-215.

763   Badalyan et al. 2015, 216-219.

Burial 10[764]

Researchers found two vessels from a ruined burial on the bank of the river Hrazdan River opposite Shengavit. The finds are preserved in the personal collection of the artist Hakhtanak Shaumyan. An official typewritten document given to the artist by the Academy of Sciences of the Armenian SSR testifies, "This jug was found in April 1967 during the construction of the Yerevan Lake on the Hrazdan River. It belongs to the Shengavit excavations of 3000 B.C. During the construction of the dam wall, elevation 900.5, 40 meters above the dam barrier wall (against the stream) in contact under the columnar basalt." There is no other information about the design of the grave or the burial rites from this burial.

The inventory of this burial consists of two exterior black intermediate types of vessels, one intermediate type, and one cup. The intermediate 1 vessel has a three-part structure of the body: narrow, concave bottom, convex-spherical body, almost straight, slightly concave neck and widening to the neck (intermediate form 1, between Types XX-XXIII (pot for eating)). The neck has a hemispherical, "deaf" handle with an expansion at the top and bottom of the handle surface and no hole (Fig 6b.10). This vessel is a typical example of KA2 ceramics.

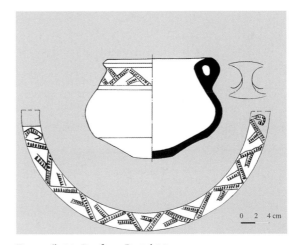

Figure 6b.10 Pot from Burial 10.

Another vessel has a similar three-part structure of the body created by two carinations: a narrow, slightly convex bottom, a convex-spherical body, and an almost straight part tapering to the top of the shoulder, with a dihedral, sharply out-turned rim, like the one described above . A hemispherical handle with a horizontal hole is attached to the neck (Fig 6b. 11). On the shoulder is a design incised with a zigzag ribbon, filled with dashes (Fig 6a.1. Design 25). Inside these dashes are white paste. Short ribbons, also filled with dashes and white paste, protrude from the central parts of the zigzag lines. At the ends of the zigzag lines are scrolls, which may represent the stylized tail and head of a snake. A vessel with the same neck shape and with an identical, rarely occurring ornament in Shengavit we found in Square O9 during excavations in 2003 (SHGT 2003, loc. 012, Fig 6b.12., A). Another potsherd with a similar ornament, depressions filled with white paste, came from the ruined burial site 19 (Fig 6b.12., B). Both vessels are made by hand and this

Figure 6b.11 Pot from Burial 10.

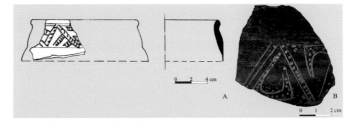

Figure 6b.12 Pottery from Burial 10.

---

764 We will group this ruined grave with the graves excavated by Sardarian, since it was discovered at the time when Sardarian was excavating in Shengavit.

techniques of filling in incisions with white lime is typical of the western Zagros diaspora sites. It is called Yanik Ware and is especially typical in the north and central Western Zagros sites.[765]

DESCRIPTION OF BURIALS EXCAVATED BY SIMONYAN 2004-2010.

In 2004, plans to build a bank building on the southwestern section of Shengavit received preliminary approval from the Architectural Council of Yerevan City Hall. The Shengavit protection zone, drawn up in 1992, did not consider this area as a site worth preserving. With great difficulty we managed to convince an interested businessman partially to finance exploratory excavations to determine the presence or absence of cultural layers.

Site III

We identified the excavation area on the southwestern side of Shengavit as Site III. It is bounded on the north by a path lined with large concrete slabs for tourists, on the west by an asphalt road built on the site of an irrigation canal that was in operation until 1960, on the south by a highway connecting Shengavit district with the Ararat massif of Yerevan, and on the east by rubble from the Sardarian excavations, which was dumped outside the settlement wall (Fig 6b.13., A, B).

Site III is not a grave per se, but an area where mixed and largely destroyed graves had been. It has a slope from east to west. It extends northward behind the concrete walkway, where someone did unauthorized construction in 2003. There are concrete bases and rows of tufa block walls (Fig 6b.13., A). As a result, the cultural layer at the construction site was destroyed, and the soil of the cultural layer accumulated under the wall of the transformer substation. In 2006-2008, we screened this soil, in which we discovered many interesting artifacts from the ruined graves.[766]

Figure 6b.13 Area of graves dug in 2004-2005.

To define the border of the Shengavit mound and to ascertain where the ritual remains existed outside the settlement wall, we excavated two 5 x 5 meter squares in 2004 on Site III. The one in the northeast part of Square C15 corresponded to Squares 2 and 6 of the 2005 excavations; the other was in the southeast (part of square C18). In the northeast quadrant of Site III, Square C15; the thickness of the cultural layer was more than one meter. We collected terracotta statuettes, flint elements of complex sickles, obsidian tools, bronze adornments, ornamented pots

Figure 6b.14 Objects from destroyed burials outside the Shengavit wall: A. sieve, B. bronze earing or hair piece, C. terracotta amulet, D. sickle elements, E. foot of terracotta figurine foot, F. Middle Bronze pot.

---

765 Rothman 2011.

766 The reports of the excavations of Shengavit settlement in 2006-2008 which are kept in the archive of the Scientific Research Center of Historical and Cultural Heritage of the RA Ministry of Education, Science, Culture, and Sports.

of black/ red design of the Early and Middle Bronze Ages (Fig 6b.14., A-F), human, and animal bones. The thickness of the cultural layer in the southeast quadrant C18 was less deep. Individual artifacts of the Early Bronze Age lay there on clay soil. However, part of a crushed early Middle Bronze Age vessel with archaic painting emerged (Fig 6b.14., G). It most likely came from a ruined burial. This vessel is displayed in the exhibition hall of Shengavit Museum.

The unequivocal evidence of the cultural layer made the entrepreneurs abandon the program to build the bank. The site was saved.

In 2005, we continued the excavations of the Site III with the financial support of the Shengavit Charitable Foundation (Martin Sarkisyan, President). We divided the excavation area into 12 squares of 5 x 5 meters with 50 cm. baulks. Squares 1, 2, 3, and 4 (partially) had arbitrary dimensions, bounded on the north side by a concrete path built during the Soviet regime (Fig 6b.15).

In 2005, we had time to excavate only the top layers to a depth of one meter from the ground surface in squares 1-9. They partly coincide with Squares A15, B15, C15 and part of Square D15 on the general plan that we made in 2009 at the beginning of the joint Armenian-American expedition (Fig 3.1). It turned out that there were burials in this area, which continued into Squares A14, B14 and C14, located on the north side of the concrete path.

The surface of the Necropolis was covered with stones and grass. The upper layer, 10-15 centimeters deep, consisted of turf, river stones, and loose earth. We found fragments pottery with black, red, and gray exteriors, obsidian flakes, fragments of basalt tools, and animal bones while clearing it as Locus 060. The next layer, 10-20 centimeters deep, had a similar structure. At a depth of 30 to 40 centimeters we found fragments of pottery with black, red, and gray exteriors (sometimes richly ornamented), obsidian flakes, bones of small and large cattle. The thin-walled, ornamented potsherds of small vessels, obsidian tools with two-sided retouch, and especially a blood-red fragment of an andiron with a ram's head in relief came from Locus 061.

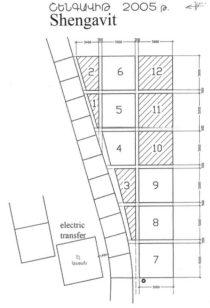

Figure 6b.15 Layout of squares in Necropolis 2005.

In the northeast corner of the square a platform made of river stones measured 170 x 85 centimeters. We discovered an ash pit between the stones and the eastern wall of the square during the 2004 excavations from which a fragment of a terracotta female statuette (Fig 6b.16, A), a copper earring (or hair ornament) of one and a half turns, and a fragment of a black polished vessel depicting goats ramming their horns against one another (Fig 6b.16, B). We recovered several other artifacts. They were all probably part of a ritual, or artifacts from a ruined burial.

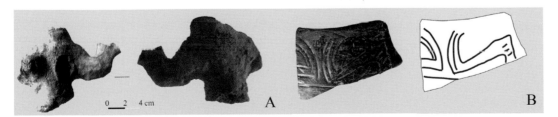

Figure 6b.16 Grave goods from ash pit with Locus 061.

Burial 11,[767] Square VI (C15)

The bones of the skeleton in Burial 11 appeared 50 centimeters below the surface in the central part of the southern wall of the quadrant (Fig 6b.17). The inhabitants placed the body and burial accessories on a flat platform of hard clay soil that rose 50 centimeters above the surrounding loose earth. The walls of the burial were not preserved except in the northeast corner of the tomb. In the northern part of the tomb lay two fragments of clay bricks, which were probably from the ruined walls of the tomb. They suggest that the tomb was rectangular in plan. Builders of the tomb plastered the floor like a house. On it lay a skeleton whose bones they stacked on top of each other in several rows. The skull and tibia were at the very top (Fig 6b.18, A).

Physical anthropologist Ruzan Mkrtchyan[768] examined the skeleton. According to her, this was the skeleton of a male between 25 and 30 years old. The facial part of the skull, including the frontal bone, temporal bone, and parietal bone were intact and in proper anatomical alignment. Some parts of the parietal bone were fractured and displaced. The skull was missing the occipital bone and mandible. The head was lying on the left cheek, facing northeast. The top of the head was facing northwest. The ancients placed a polished basalt mallet and a fragment of obsidian where the occipital bone should have been. In ancient conflict, crushing the occipital was a common way to kill. To the south of the skull was a black burnished bowl with a small handle (Fig 6b.18, B). Inside the bowl laid a long bone of small cattle, perhaps part of a memorial feast.[769] Next to the bowl rested a black, perfectly burnished, broad-necked intermediate type of pot with two carinations and a decorative handle in the middle of the body. This is a very typical Kura-Araxes style of handle and body form (Fig 6b.18, B). On the northern side of the pot sat fragments of black pottery. A black ceramic cup rested at the bottom of the pot, as if people at the funeral were dipping it and consuming whatever was in the pot.

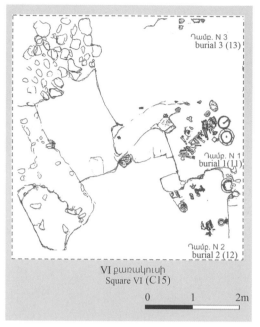

Figure 6b.17 Burials 11, 12, and 13.

Figure 6b.18 Shengavit Burial 11.

---

767 In order not to mix up the graves, we decided to change the numbering of the graves we excavated in the following order. As the number of graves excavated by Sardarian is 10, we will continue numbering from 11. With this approach, the numbers of graves will simply be renumbered as follows – Burial 1 of our excavations will be renumbered as Burial 11, Burial 2 as 12, and so on. This approach works, because so far only one article about the graves excavated by us has been published in the Armenian language (Simonyan 2008), which is not widely known to the world community it was written in a local journal in Armenian.

768 We are grateful to Ms. Mkrtchyan for determining the sex and age of those buried at Shengavit.

769 In the Early Bronze Age, in the Elar burials (NN 9, 14, 15, 1718, 20, 24,), there was also a ritual of lowering vessels filled with food with meat food into the grave (Khanzadian, 1979, 39-43).

A few centimeters to the northeast of the skull we recovered a human rib, a matching tibia and fibula (Fig 6b 19). To the northeast of them lay foot bones (metacarples) and fragments of long bones of small cattle. Ten centimeters west of the occipital bone rested the

Figure 6b.19 Evidence of intentional dismemberment of bodies.

second vertebra of the neck. Between the skull and the spine sat a cylindrical shaft sharpener made of river stone. Just to the north, a carpal bone lay under the skull. Beneath it, just below the skull, was the person's lower jaw resting on the ground. A hyoid bone protruded from the jaw, which indicates that the lower jaw had been covered with tissue during burial and had been deliberately separated from the head. The skeleton of the deceased with strongly bent limbs lay in the third horizon of the bone cluster on the hard and level clay floor. We found a whole femur on the floor, and above and to the south of it the ribs and humerus. The anatomically correct location of the skeletal bones suggests that the bones had a muscular sheath at the time of burial, and the heavily bent thighs were attached to the body.

Judging by the anatomically correct combination of the individual bones of the skeleton, I suggest that decapitation and dismemberment were part of the burial ritual. When buried, the ancients buried the leg of a sacrificed animal and three pottery vessels with the human bones. To the south of the femur bone, they placed a sharpened piece of obsidian. It was most likely associated with the funerary ceremony. The body was covered with a mat, traces of which are preserved on the ends of the lower thigh bones.

To the northwest lay the lower jaw. Associated with it 30 centimeters to the northwest lay the left humerus bone with the folded arm and wrist, the left femur, and in the bend of the knee lay the small and large shin bones of another person. The key bones of the ribs, vertebrae, wrist bones, foot bones, and fragments of black pottery scattered among the anatomically correctly positioned bones (Fig 6b.19, A). Five centimeters northeast of the humerus sat the neck of a clay bowl, inside of which were human foot bones. On the diaphyses of the femur bones and on the long (humerous) bone we observed traces of sawing, clear signs of deliberate dismemberment of the corpse (Fig 6b.19, B). Our expert determined that the second individual was a tall man of strong build, 35 to 45 years old judging by the size of the humerus (H1=322 mm). The burial rite again included dismemberment of the corpse.

The grave goods of Tomb 11 included three or four black-clay vessels discussed above, a shaft sharpener, and two pieces of obsidian. We found a bone bead with two holes for attachment just east of the first skeleton. A large number of fragments of black burnished pottery, obsidian pieces, and bones of small and cattle lay on the southern side of the area. However, the connection of these artifacts with the burials is questionable.

Burial 12, Square VI (C15)

On the slope of the mound, in the neighborhood of Burial 11 in the southwestern corner of square VI, Burial 12 appeared 50 centimeters below it. Builders made the south wall of unbaked bricks. Part of the north wall was preserved adobe (Fig 6b.20).

Figure 6b.20 Burial 12.

The western and eastern walls did not survive. Remains covered an area of 150 x 150 centimeters and consisted of ashy, soft earth.

On the floor of the grave lay bones of an individual. Among them was part of the skull, the right half of the lower jaw with well-preserved teeth, one spine, and part of a femur. Directly opposite them, under the western wall, lay one half of the lower jaw of a ram and one half of the upper jaw of a cow. The burial of the halves of the jaws, which the ancients cut off on purpose, must have had some meaning. For a number of these burials the ritual consisted of dismembering the corpse and placing it in the grave as separate parts of the body.

The grave goods consisted of two black, burnished pots (Locus 065). The small, intermediate type of vessels sat in the western part of the grave, next to the jaws of the sacrificial animals (Fig 6b.21). Pieces of a human skull lay next to it. At about 130 centimeters to the east and 30 centimeters from the floor in a specially made niche of small stone slabs inside the south wall rested a broad-necked pot. It is similar to the pot from Grave 11 (Shengavit Pottery Type XXX) in its shape and had a design like our Design 25 (see Fig 6a.1).

Figure 6b.21 Pot from Burial 12.

Burial 13, Square VI (C15)

We found this tomb in the southeast corner next to the eastern and southern walls of quadrant VI (Fig 6b.7). At a depth of 65 centimeters from the surface it consisted of collapsed pebbles and unbaked bricks, which probably constituted the ruined part of the lower wall of the tomb. The wall extended from south to north, then to the middle of the square (length 320 centimeters, width 20 to 40 centimeters, with a preserved height of 15 to 25 centimeters). On the northeast side of the square, we discovered a cluster of mud bricks 25 centimeters high and 40 centimeters long. The preserved part of the twelfth burial opened on the southern side of this cluster.

Figure 6b.22 Pot from Burial 13.

Among the grave goods were two black, burnished ceramic open forms with hemispherical handles, Type XXIV) (Fig 6b.22.) (Locus 064). Fragments of Kura-Araxes pottery, obsidian fragments, and bones of small mammals and cattle also nestled there (Locus 062). We did not find any human bones. Most likely, the main part of the grave was destroyed or is located in the unexcavated southeastern part of the area (Square D15).

Burial 14, Square II (C14)

We excavated the upper layer of the square back in 2004. In 2005, at a depth of 30 centimeters from the surface, we discovered a flint tool or core resembling a Palaeolithic hand-held chopper possibly a harrow (Fig 6b.23, A). Up to a depth of 50 to 60 centimeters, the cultural layer was a soft fill with interspersed layers of ash. A large number of Kura-Araxes pottery sherds, bones of small and large mammals, and obsidian fragments (Locus 021) remained there. At a depth of 50 centimeters, directly above the grave, we found a bronze pin with a spiral hooked head and a long rod, the upper half of which was covered with spirals, which were formed as a result of rotation of the rod around its axis during its manufacture (Fig 6b.23., B).

In the center of the square next to the concrete walkway, we found Grave 14. Compacted earth surrounded it on the outside and there was a soft, ashy embankment on the inside. The walls of the preserved lower part of the grave were round in shape. Builders made the walls out of river stones and fragments of mudbricks. Its entrance was on the west side, but a probable wall was missing (Fig 6b.24).

Figure 6b.23 Artifacts from Burial 14.

We found human body parts, sacrificed animals, and grave goods arranged in a circle (Square C14). At the top was half of a single handled open vessel form, under which lay the lower jaw of a woman, divided into two parts (Fig 6b.24., A). A little to the north of it rested half of an exquisitely decorated clay bowl with fine engravings. To the west of the bowl sat a human scapula, obsidian and flint serrated sickle elements (Fig 6b.24., B),[770] and a worked horn, probably a harrow or digging stick weight (Locus 022). A human rib and a cow rib lay a little further away. Levigated clay covered the bottom of the grave.

According to Ruzanna Mkrtchyan, only some parts of the corpse were in the grave, including: a) the lower jaw of a woman 25 to 30 years old, divided into two parts, b) two shoulder blades, lying one on top of another, c) one hand bone next to the shoulder blades, and d) one rib. Under the pile of these bones lay the right half of a child's pelvis. Below the child's pelvis lay the woman's clavicle. Along with human bones we found cattle ribs and a polished tool made of animal bones.

Figure 6b.24 Burial 14.

Apparently, this burial marks a complex ritual of dismemberment of the body or rather, a special ritual of splitting the lower jaw, as in Burial 12, and pottery into two parts, as in Burial 13. This ritual in all probability is connected with ancient beliefs about treatment of the deceased. This ritual practice was widespread among many peoples on the vast territory of Eurasia.[771] It is difficult to interpret the presence of the half of the child's pelvis. Is this a sacrifice or a burial of a woman with a child in accordance with the funerary practice of dismembering and making the spirit of the deceased less dangerous?

Tomb 15, Square IX (B15)

On top of the square lay a sod layer consisting of dried grape roots and soft earth mixed with stones, 30 to 40 centimeters thick (Locus 090). Under it was an intact, cultural layer with rich artifacts: fragments of black and brown pottery, obsidian, flint, and basalt tools (Locus 091).

---

770 The sickle elements of obsidian were also placed in burials 17, 18, 20 and 24 of Elar, see Khanzadian 1979, 41-45, Fig 50, 52, 57, 58. Interestingly, female burials with obsidian tools occurred at both Shengavit and Elar.

771 Naasov et al. 2018.

Tomb 15 lay on the west side of the square, 93 cm below the surface. It was a rectangular grave with stone walls. The walls were made of two rows of river stones. The stone vault, which continued to the west and went under the unexcavated layers of Square A15, probably consisted of two sections separated from each other by a wide partition (Fig 6b.25).

The tomb was filled with hard earth mixed with crushed bones (Loci 092-094). Four black pots remained by the western wall. The first of these was a pot whose shoulders were decorated with rows of hatched triangles pointing downwards (Fig 6b.26., A, Type XXI). An intermediate 1 form pot rested on it. Half a meter to the south an open form with the bottom upwards, and a vessel with two horizontal relief bands under the neck remained.[772] We have not yet found human or animal bones; most likely, they are in the unexcavated part of the western section. Modern agricultural work disturbed the grave.

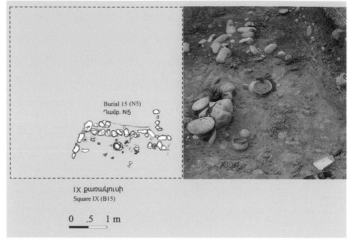

Figure 6b.25 Tomb 15.

In the excavated part of the crypt we found half of a perfectly polished axe (a weapon?) (Fig 6b.26., B), a copper bead, which had an undulating shape (Fig 6b.26., C).[773] These artifacts are dated to the KA2.

To complete the excavation of Tomb 15, we also dug in the Shengavit necropolis in 2010. We excavated the entire area of Square IX, as well as nearby layers in Square X (B/C15). Expanding the incompletely excavated part from 2005, the western side of Burial 15 revealed only a few ground stone tools and one flint flake (Locus 10002). In the eastern half of 2000-2008 Square IX, outside of the western wall of Burial 15 at a depth of 55 centimeters from the surface of the ground, sat an oval area of fine-grained, dark ground about 20 centimeters thick (Locus 10003). We did not excavate it (Locus 10005). From the western wall southwestward, we recovered a flint tool and crushed animal bones (Locus 10010). Fragments of pottery, obsidian, flint, and animal bones lay to the south of Burial 15 (Locus 10004), as well as a large (10.2 x 4 centimeters) flint flake (Locus 10023). This excavation helped define the eastern wall made of cobbles of Burial 15.

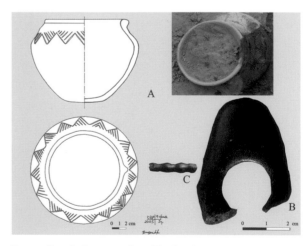

Figure 6b. 26 Grave goods in Tomb 15.

<hr />

772 We have only working photos of the three pots, because the vessels left in place were stolen at night, even though there was a watchman who pledged to preserve the burial until the final excavations. The act of vandalism had inevitable consequences. We suspended work, because there was no guarantee that the new finds would not also be stolen. In our haste, we took working photos of the unfinished excavations of burials 13, 15, and 16 and filled in the excavation site.

773 According to Valery Markarian's diary, a cylindrical copper object, 3.5 cm. wide, we found on the west side of square 5, at a depth of 85 cm., 30 cm. from the man's jaw.

Burial 16 (6), Square I (C14)

The main part of this square spread under the walkway for tourists built of large concrete slabs in 1967. The walls of the grave are not preserved, but probably the buried man lay under river stones (Fig 6b.27). Its grave goods included fragments of pottery (including Pottery Type III, Fig 6b.28), obsidian flakes, flint fragments, spherical ground stone tools the size of a human fist, a tufa loom or net weight (Fig 6b.29) and the bones of small and large domesticated mammals to a depth of 30 centimeters (Locus 010). At a depth of 50 centimeters from the surface, in the northwestern part of the area, we found three quarters of a basalt disk, fragments of black exterior, thick-walled Kura-Araxes pot (Locus 010). At a depth of 60 cm from the surface, in the center of the excavation and covered with a thick layer of river stones, we unearthed a burial. It contained fragments of human, small and large mammal bones. A black-burnished open form vessel lay upside down in the center (Fig 6b. 28, B). Nearby lay the long (leg) bones of cattle, flint sickle elements, a sharpening tool of river stone (seven centimeters long) (Locus 011). We could not excavate all of Grave 16, because the main part of the grave goes under the concrete walkway.

Figure 6b.27 Tomb 16.

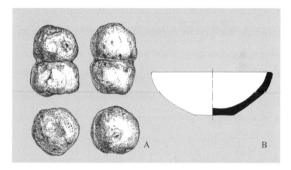

Figure 6b.28 Weights and pot from Burial 16.

Burial 17, Square V (C15)

River stones covered the entire surface of this square at a depth of 35 centimeters from the surface, especially the central, eastern and northern parts, which most likely represented a ruined crypt. The nearby parts of the southern and western boundaries of the square lacked the accumulation of stones (Fig 6b.29).

Among the river stones rested fragments of clay vessels with black, brown, and red colored exteriors, including closed forms with sides up to two centimeters thick, two round sling stones, five fragments of stone grinding stones (27 cm thick), obsidian flakes, flint scrapers, a half a wheel from a tufa cart model (or a spindle whorl), several animal bones and the teeth of cattle, and two legs of a fireplace stand. The fireplace stand is characterized by flat pediments and in shape is arched to the feet (see Chapter 5e, Function of the Pottery section). One leg is ornamented with raised designs like the ritual hearths (Fig 6b.30., A). A stone axe measuring 13 x 10 x 4 centimeters and

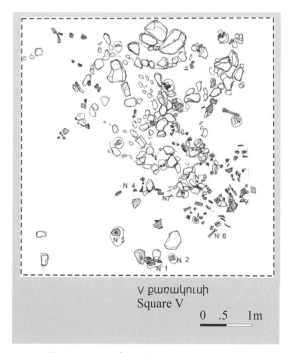

V բառակուսի
Square V

0   .5   1m

Figure 6b.29 Layout of Burial 17.

a hoe or harrower rested under the west wall of the square (Fig 6b.30., B, G). Human remains, a lower jaw on the southeast corner of the square and a fragment of an upper jaw with teeth on the north side, remained (Locus 050), 25 centimeters below the ground's surface.

At a depth of 35 to 45 centimeters, the cultural layer became harder (Locus 051). The number of bones of small and cattle increased sharply. We also found bones of a human skull and a dog's jaw. Parts of walls of river stones and mud bricks remained intact in various parts of the square, which no longer had a definite layout (Fig 6b.29). We uncovered a perfectly

Figure 6b.30 Grave goods from Burial 17.

denticulated red jasper sawing tool or sickle element (Fig 6b.30., F) and a highly corroded bronze earring or hair ring (Fig 6b.30., D). We also found another earring or hair ring with a diameter of one centimeter (Fig 6b.30., E), a piece of bitumen, a flint core eight centimeters long, a fragment of a perfectly worked knife, a 10 centimeters long shaft sharpener, an obsidian ball (Fig 6b.30., C), and an equid tooth in the central part of the western wall (Locus 051).

At a depth of 65 centimeters under the rubble of river cobbles we dug up a 60 centimeters wide remained a fragment of unbaked brick wall and next to it a section of the floor coated with plaster. There we found black and red exterior, burnished vessels with large, hemispherical handles, chevron ornaments, a thin-walled, perfectly polished sherd of small vessel with a stylized image of an equid. Flint sickle elements and scrapers, a fragment of a knife, spherical river sling stones, bones of small and large cattle, fragments of human skulls also rested there.

Under the northern wall of the square, at a depth of 70-85 centimeters (Locus 052), we uncovered large stones. Near them were the upper part of a skull, an obsidian ball (Fig 6b.31., B), flint inlays of composite sickles and scrapers, a cylindrical stone two centimeters in diameter, and half a marble macehead 5.5 centimeters in diameter with a vertical hole (Fig 6b.31., A). Another fragment (1/3) of a macehead we found on the east side of the square (Fig 6b.31., B).

In the northeastern corner of the square we recovered earrings of copper wire, a bone awl, and half of a peculiar, triangular shaft straightener (Fig 6b.31., C). In the central part of the square lay half of a human skull, two flint blades, elements of a composite sickle and, a fragment of disc-shaped worked pot sherd with a hole drilled in the central part of the sherd, possibly a spindle whorl.

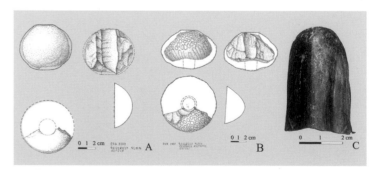

Figure 6b.31 Grave goods from Burial 17.

In the southwestern corner of the square rested a fragment of a child's upper jaw with teeth. Under the western wall of the square we found the lower jaw of a man, bones of small mammals and cattle (equid?), and broad rib bones, bone awls, a fragment of a copper needle, two flint elements of a composite sickle. A 30 centimeters wide by 380 centimeters long wall of mudbricks stretched from the south wall to the northwest. Traces of fire covered the walls.

To accurately record human remains, we divided a 25 m² square into 10 smaller squares and marked human bones on the plan, which were identified on the spot by an anthropologist. We got the following picture of the location of the bones: 1) one long (leg) bone of an animal and two large tibia bones of a human in the southeastern part of the site. The size of the bones indicates that they belonged to a very tall person; 2) a shovel made of cow bone in the eastern part towards the center; 3) the long bone and the cow bone shovel slightly south of the central part of the area. Next to them lay a woman's large tibia, one head of which was broken; 4) a cattle rib in the southeast corner of the square; 5) a man's right femur in the northwest corner; 6) the top of a human skull, a cattle vertebra, and other animal bones in the north part of the square. Next to them lay an almost complete, small, polished vessel with a black exterior; 7) the right femur and under it lay a woman's clavicle to the south of large stones in the north part of the square. To the southeast of them was a phalanx of a finger, a cattle jaw, and other bones; 8) to the east of the big stones sat the lower jaw of a man 40 to 45 years old; 9) a little further away a massive lower jaw of a man 35 to 45 years old, a lower jaw and a leg bone of cattle; 10) two shins 37 and 40 centimeters long, two lower jaws of men and the clavicle of a woman recovered in the southwest corner of the square. Flint sickle elements and a blade also rested here.

Based on the preserved parts of the walls and floor, we suggest that there was a rectangular structure about four meters long, the walls of which were made of river stones and mudbricks. The floor of the structure builders covered with plaster at a depth of 70 to 85 centimeters from the surface of the ground. The composition of the inventory and the bones of at least 10 men, women, and children (including fragments of six skulls) suggests that this was a large crypt with a collective burial and a variety of grave goods, including symbols of special status with metal ornaments in Square 5. Modern agricultural work probably destroyed the crypt. Another possibility is that after its discovery, grave robbers looted the crypt, and only ruined and fragmentary traces of the once rich burial remained.

Tomb 18, Square C18

We hypothesize that the painted vessel found in square C18 came from a partially excavated burial. Because we excavated only an L-shaped trench in this square due to a lack of funding in 2004, it is difficult to judge whether the funerary structure was preserved or not.

The jug with a spherical body and cylindrical neck is a typical specimen of the Middle Bronze Age (Fig 6b.14, F). However, the ornamentation is unique. The neck was decorated with rows of vertical dashes, and on the shoulder of the vessel were two lobed "butterflies," which are filled with intersecting straight lines (like Fig 6b.14., F). In contrast to the classical motifs of the Middle Bronze Age painting, there are no solid, filled in elements of the painting. The intersecting straight lines on the poorly slipped surface of the vessels are typical for the few samples of painted ceramics of the late Middle Bronze Age found in Shengavit squares K6, J6, M6, and N11. We believe that this vessel represents the Early Kurgan to Trialeti style of ornamentation of the Middle Bronze Age, which dates back to the boundary of the third into the second millennium BC.

Sardarian found another upper half of a painted vessel with straight and wavy lines ornamentation of the Middle Bronze Age, but he does not report anything about the location or dating of this vessel.[774]

Burial 19, Square IV and X (B/C15)

We excavated this burial in 2010, originally listed as Burial 7. We recovered a lower jaw and individual human bones, which continued to the side of Square IV, the upper, mixed layer that we excavated to a depth of 40 centimeters in 2005. At that time we already found sherds of pottery, fragments of obsidian and flint, flint tools and a sickle element, fragments of basalt millstones, human and animal bones. In the southwest corner of the square stood a large stone,

---

774   Sardarian 1967, 199.

near which we found sherds of thin-walled, perfectly burnished black pottery (Locus 040). We covered the square in 2005 with a thick layer of earth to preserve it for further excavations.

Excavations in 2010 revealed the surviving northwest corner of the tomb, which consisted of river stones and mudbrick (Fig. 6b. 32). The upper layer, 10 centimeters thick, consisted of earth with an admixture of 20th century AD glass fragments. At a depth of 15 to 25 centimeters, the cultural layer became more homogeneous. Here we excavated fragments of mudbrick, a flint sickle element, the occipital part of the skull (Locus 13006), a tibia, lower jaw, and other human bones. We also uncovered a layer mixed with clay on the southern side of the tomb, in which lay half a copper curl (2 centimeters in diameter), 2 fragments of red polished miniature "boxes" with a ledge at the rim pierced by a vertical hole (Fig 6b.33., G).

The following artifacts found at a depth of 100 to115 centimeters from the surface belonged to a ruined burial: a bronze arrowhead (bag 13053, Fig

Figure 6b.32 Burial 19.

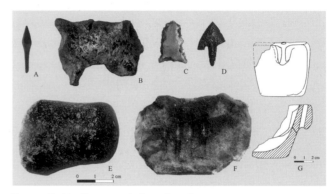

Figure 6b.33 Grave goods from Burial 19.

6b.33., A), a terracotta statuette of a bull with its head and legs broken off (bag 13060) (Fig 6b.33., B), a flint sickle element (bag 13061), a disc-shaped bead of carnelian (bag 13061), arrowheads of obsidian (bags 13101, 13104, 13109, Fig 6b.33., C&D) and flint (bag 13102, Fig 6b., C, D), a marble hammer or pestle [for metal ore preparation?] (bag 13092, Fig 6b.33., E), a ceramic fragment with painted decoration, similar to the ornament of a vessel from Burial 10. We also found a ceramic mold for casting metal pins (Fig 6b.33., F).

On the floor sat parts of two vertebrae, which were in an anatomically correct position (Fig 6b.34). This is a detail that suggests that the ancients performed an inhumation rite. For the dating of this tomb, a ceramic fragment with inlaid ornament and a bronze arrowhead, which has its analogues in the Bedeni barrows, are important. On this basis, we date tomb 19 to the 24th to 23rd centuries BC.

Figure 6b.34 Burial 19.

Burial 20, Square L20

This burial site we discovered in 2015. Construction workers were excavating between the buildings of the hospital and the former polyclinic. I was passing by and out of habit, I looked at a cross-section of the ground. There, at a depth of 60 centimeters from the surface of the ground on the southern side of the mound lay animal bones and two vessels (Fig 6b.35). This area was outside the settlement wall. I was not at all ready to excavate in this disturbed area. I took only the pots with me. The next day, when I wanted to continue the research, the builders had already put a fence up, and the cultural layer was closed off by a wall.

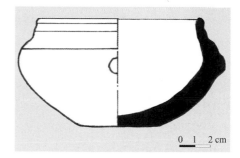

Figure 6b.35 Burial 20 Grave goods.

Conclusions

According to Sardarian and Simonyan,[775] the inhabitants of Shengavit had a special place beyond the settlement wall for burying the dead members of the community; that is, a separate cemetery. The floors were smeared with plaster or covered with small pebbles. After the burial ceremony, the ancients covered the grave with earth and then with clay mortar from above.[776] The burial ground occupied a huge territory from the south-western part of the settlement wall to the right bank of the Hrazdan River. The main part of the cemetery was on the southwestern slope of the Shengavit mound. Graves here were very densely placed. Thus, in one five-meter square we found three graves (1, 2, 3).

Most of the burial types listed by Polmarc'h existed at Shengavit. Crypts were rectangular tombs like the dwellings unearthed late in the KA2 at Shengavit. There were also cists and stone-lined graves. One burial had small pits with stone covering. Most were completely underground, unlike the above-ground tombs typical of the Early Kurgan and later Middle Bronze Age.

The skeletons found in the tombs were often in a hunched posture and lay on their sides (Fig 6b.1). According to the only surviving photograph, the ancients also practiced the ritual of dismembering the corpses (see below).

Fragmentary records from Sardarian's diaries suggest that they also practiced cremation and that human sacrifices, perhaps of captives, servants, spouses, or some other individual celebrants added to the graves of the significant dead. These they placed on the top of the graves,[777] as at contemporary Arslantepe[778] and in Northern Mesopotamia. The ritual of inhumation on the side with the bent limbs as well as the ritual of dismemberment of the corpses before burial was widespread in Eurasia and in the Kura-Araxes cultural tradition. So, too, was the rite of separating the lower jaw of the corpses. In Burials 2 and 4 the ritual involved chopping jaws in half. Sardarian writes that he saw traces of fire in one grave. This information may also indicate cremation, but we do not yet have sufficient data to know for certain. Most burials Sardarian excavated had "dozens of people."[779] Other burials had one or a pair of skeletons. Adult males and females, as well as children, were among those buried.

Grave goods added during the death ritual were primarily ceramics. Ceramics from these tombs are identical

---

775   Sardarian 2004; Simonyan 2008.
776   According to me, the floor of these burials could have been a deposition of river stones.
777   Sardarian 2004 371.
778   Frangipane et al. 2001.
779   Sardarian 1967, 180; 204, 371.

to those found in the 3rd and 4th horizons of the settlement, according to Sardarian's stratigraphy.[780] This relates to Shengavit strata IV-O in our reworking of the stratigraphy from Square K6. In addition, five burials included pots that were in the transition between the Kura-Araxes and Early Kurgan periods. According to my calculations, excavators recovered 224 samples of pottery with black exteriors and red interiors in the burials. This is a higher percentage of bichrome pots than in the settlement. We also found 72 samples of pots with brick-red exteriors (in Burial 1, 10 pieces, Burial 2, 1 piece, Burial 3, 1 piece, Burial 4, 3 pieces, Burial 5, 4 pieces, Burial 6, 1 piece, Burial 7, 28 pieces of whole and fragmentary vessels, Burial 8, 17 pieces, Burial 9, 7 pieces of whole and fragmentary vessels). More vessels had red rather than black exteriors only in Burial 7. These pots were common, but definitely in a minority in the Shengavit settlement, especially in Architectural Levels 3 to 6 (Strata IV to VIII). The most common forms were Types IA and B from our typology (Chapter 5e). Some scholars say the pots in these graves were simply made, uniform, and only 27 of the 296 pots discovered had ornamentation; that is, only one in ten vessels. The shapes of the vessels are also very uniform. Single-handled, open vessels dominated in the funerary inventory.[781] This, some say, indicates that the members of Shengavit society were equal.[782] In my opinion, such an assertion is not confirmed by the available evidence. On the other hand, as Rothman points out (Chapter 5e), the symbols of the ritual of death may be found in what was in the pots, not the pots themselves. Was there a feast as part of the ritual or were foodstuffs placed in the graves for the deceased to use on a journey into the deathly realms? Were the animal bones, some of which were in the pots, part of that feast, or were they a sign of the deceased's occupation or a belief in their mystical power? The three pots in Burial 11 are similar to pots in the ritual emplacement in Kura-Araxes Pulur Sakyol, where drinking some liquid is implied.[783] Not all the burials were contemporaneous, so the difference may represent changes over time. The quality of the pottery may not be critical signifiers of social structure, especially with so many buried individuals.

Also recovered from the graves was a rich collection of metals in the burials: copper/bronze earrings or hair rings (61), pins (27), bracelets (4), rings (1), axes (1 or 2), daggers (3), a diadem fragment; about 100 items in all. Most were items of personal adornment, as in the settlement (see Chapter 5d). These copper and bronze items existed throughout Early Bronze Age sites, but some types of Shengavit metal artifacts are unique (Fig 6.36). A uniquely shaped copper axe with a spherical shank in the central part has no known analogues in the entire South Caucasian region lay in Burial 1 (Fig 6b.2, F). We know it only from European examples. A pin with a snake head (Fig 6b.36, A) and a pin (fibula?) with an attached marten figurine (Fig 6b.2, D) are also unique. There are dozens of specimens of pins with spiral heads. Noteable are pin bodies with a wavy shape made by rotating them around their axis as artisans shaped them. The ends of these pins were sharpened by forging. I call this type of pins the Shengavit

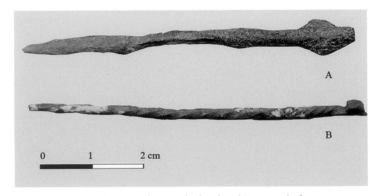

Figure 6b.36 Metal pins with A. snake head and B. twist shaft.

780   Sardarian 2004, 370.
781   Badalyan et al. 2015.
782   Badalyan et al. 2015, 371.
783   Rothman 2011, Fig 5.12.

style, because the number of such pins found in Shengavit graves exceeds two dozen, and in other Kura-Araxes sites in the South Caucasus pins of this type are either not represented or are rare. Assuming we can date the graves by their pottery, burials before the Kura-Araxes/Early Kurgan transition period tended to contain fewer metal objects, mostly beads, earrings or hair rings, and pins. Only three gold objects have survived in the graves: an amulet and a ring in Burial 1, and a ring in Burial 2, which belong to the Kura-Araxes/Early Kurgan transitional period. The increase in the number of metal objects, especially metal tools, marks this transitional period, as does the appearance of gold objects.

In addition, graves contained goods that probably reflected some aspect of the occupations or at least activities of the people buried there. Burial 1 yielded a metal and bone arrowheads, a macehead, dart tip and stone metal mold. Burial 4 contained a macehead. Site III had sickle elements, sieves, terracotta figurines, andirons, and basalt tools, Burial 14 sickle elements, worked horn, a harrow, Burial 15 obsidian, flint, basalt tools, and a polished ax, Burial 16 a loom or net weights, obsidian flakes, and flint fragments. These four burials all had one or two bodies. Burial crypt 17 and 19 with multiple bodies yielded respectively a jasper scraper, basalt harrow, obsidian ball, model cart wheel, a flint core and knife, and a macehead, and a flint sickle element, miniature clay boxes, obsidian and flint arrow points, a terracotta figurine, hammer or pestle, stone metal mold, and a carnelian bead.

According to Sardarian, who was under the control of Soviet censorship, there is no economic and social differentiation in these "tribal crypts." However, immediately after Soviet domination lessened, he claimed that social differentiation was marked in each burial by clay vessels, obsidian and flint arrowheads, copper axes, bracelets, pins, gold and silver jewelry, carnelian and jasper beads, stone maceheads, forms for casting flat axes or chisels.[784] These may represent signs of wealth and status of whatever the grouping in these multiple graves were, although we do not have what must have been hundreds of burials over the 400 plus years Shengavit was occupied to compare to them.

I believe that clear symbols of status are represented by perfectly chiseled axes and maceheads,[785] weapons, and jewelry made of precious metals. This to me indicates social differentiation in this society, while the molds for casting bronze items placed in the graves indicate the presence of professional metallurgists. This view of professionalism is not shared by my colleagues. They argue there were probably people at the site who had expertise in metallurgy, pottery making, flintknapping, etc. However, they believe in the Kura-Araxes period evidence is lacking for craft specialists who depended solely on their skill for their livelihood (professionals) and have higher status than their clan members.[786] I would call this differentiation one of class, but, again, my colleagues believe that while there was some social differentiation, certainly in the Middle Bronze Age, class as a descriptor of the organization of the Kura-Araxes society is not the right term; true class society and specialization (professionalism) represents a level of societal complexity that was millennia away.[787]

What is clear is the diversity of grave types and aspects of the ritual of death at Shengavit and across the Kura-Araxes world. From the graves with multiple bodies, to the dismembering of bodies, to the placement of animal parts among the human bodies, to the apparent difference in meanings of the grave goods, Kura Araxes cultural traditions lack strict homogeneity.

---

784   Sardarian 1967, 180.
785   Docenko 2012, 5.
786   Sagona 2018.
787   Rothman 2021; 2015.

References

Akhundov, T. 1999 *The Ancient Mounds of the South Caucasus: The Culture of Sub-Mound Vaults*. Baku: ELM (in Russian).

Akhundov, T. 2001 *North-Western Azerbaijan in the Eneolithic and Bronze Age*. Baku: Academy of Sciences of the Azerbaijan Republic, Institute of Archaeology and Ethnography. (in Russian).

Kushnareva, K. Kh., Makarov, V.I. 1994 *Archeology: Bronze Age of Caucasus and Central Asia. The Early and Middle Bronze Age of Caucasus*. Moscow: Nauka, (in Russian).

Areshian, G., Simonyan, H., Gasparqn, S. 1987 New discovered graves in Jogaz., *Theses of reports of scientific session devoted to the results of field archaeological works in the Armenian SSR in 1985-1986, April 1987,* edited by B. Arakelyan, 6-8. Yerevan: Publishing house of the Academy of Sciences of the Armenian SSR (in Armenian).

Areshian, G., Simonyan, A. 1988 Works in Ijevan district. *Archaeological discoveries of 1986*, edited by B.A. Rybakov, 469. Moscow: Nauka Publisher, (in Russian).

Areshian G., Simonyan H. 1989 Archaeological works at the Jogaz monument (in 1987). *Thesis of scientific session on results of field archeological works in Armenian SSR in 1987-1988, April 1987,* edited by B. Arakelyan, 5-7. Yerevan: Publishing house of the Academy of Sciences of Armenian SSR. (in Armenian).

Avilova, L.I. 2018 *Treasure Hoards of Metal Items in Anatolia (Eneolitic – Bronze Age)*. Moscow: Ia Ran (in Russian).

Badalyan, R., Smith, A., Lindsay, I., Khatchadourian, L., and P. Avetisyan. With appendices by Belinda Monahan and Roman Hovsepyan. 2008 Village, Fortress, and Town in Bronze and Iron Age Southern Caucasia: A Preliminary Report on the 2003–2006 Investigations of Project ArAGATS on the Tsaghkahovit Plain, Republic of Armenia. *Archäologische Mitteilungen aus Iran und Turan* 40: 45–105.

Badalyan, R., Edens, C., Gorny, R., Kohl, P., Stronach, D., Tonikyan, A., Hamayakyan, S., Mandrikyan, S., and Zardaryan M. 1993 Preliminary Report on the 1992 Excavations at Horom, Armenia. *Iran* 31: 1–24.

Boulestin, B. and Duday, H. 2005. Ethnology and archaeology of death: from the illusion of references to the use of a terminology. *Archaeologia Polona* 44: 149-169.

Dotsenko, I.I. 2012 *Mythology of Power. Royal Insignia in Beliefs and Cultures of Ancient Indo-European Peoples*. Moscow Institute of Open Education UNESCO Chair "International (Multicultural) Education and Integration of Migrant Children at School. Moscow: The Internet version of the publication is available at the IIEP website www.mioo.edu.ru (section - UNESCO Chair). " (in Russian)

Earle, T. 1997 *How Chiefs Come to Power: the Political Economy in Prehistory*. Standford, CAA.: Stanford University Press.

Frangipane, M. 2009 Non-Urban Hierarchical Patterns of Territorial and Political Organisation in Northern Regions of Greater Mesopotamia: Tepe Gawra and Arslantepe. in *À propos de Tepe Gawra, le monde proto-urbain de Mésopotamie* (Subartu XXIII), edited by P. Butterlin , 133-146. Bruxelles: Brepols.

Frangipane, M., Di Nocera, G. M., Hauptmann, A., Morbidelli, P., Palmieri, A., Sadori, l. Schultz, M. and Schmidt-Schultz, T. 2001 New Symbols of a New Power in a "Royal" Tomb from 3000 BC Arslantepe, Malatya (Turkey). *Paléorient* 27(2): 105-139.

Gabuchyan, A. V., Knyaz, V. A., Leibova, N. A., Petrosyan, R. M., Galeev, G. R., Simonyan, H. 2019 Modern methods for obtaining and analyzing three-dimensional images of anthropological materials on the example of digital odontometric study of the mandible from the burial of Shengavit. *Cultural and biological Antropology of the Caucasian and Near Eastern Populations,* 9-11. Yerevan: Institute of Oriental Studies, Russian-Armenian University.

Glonti, L., Khetskhoveli, M., and Palumbi, G. 2008 The Cemetery at Kvatskhelebi. in *Archaeology in Southern Caucasus: Perspectives from Georgia*, edited by Sagona, A., Abramishvili, M. 153–184. Louvain: Peeters Press.

Gogochuri, G., and Orjonikidze, A. 2010 The Kura-Araxes Culture Settlement and Cemetery at Tiselis Seri. In *Rescue Archaeology in Georgia: the Baku-Tbilisi-Ceyhan and South Caucasian Pipelines*. 119–132. Tbilisi: Georgian National Museum.

Kakhiani, K., Sagona, A., Sagona, C., Kvavadze, E., Bedianashvili, G., Messager, E., Martin, L., Herrscher, E., Martkoplishvili, I., Birkett-Rees, J., and Longford, C. 2013. Archaeological Investigations at Chobareti in Southern Georgia, the Caucasus. *Ancient Near Eastern Studies* 50: 1–138.

Kalantaryan, I. 2007 The Principal Forms and Characteristics of Burial Constructions in Early Bronze Age Armenia. *Aramazd* 2: 7–39.

Kalantaryan, I. 2011 The Early Bronze Age complexes of Talin cemetery. *Studii de Preistorie* 8: 123-138.

Khanzadian, E.,1967 *Culture of the Armenian Highland in the 3rd millennium B.C.* Yervan: Publishing house of the Academy of Sciences of the Armenian SSR, (in Armenian).

Khanzadian, E., 1979 Elar-Darani. Erevan, Publishing house of the Academy of Sciences of Armenian SSR (in Armenian).

Khoridze, I. and Palumbi, G. 2008 The Cemetery of Aradetis Orgora. in *Archaeology in Southern Caucasus: Perspectives from Georgia*, edited by A. Sagona, and M. Abramishvili, 125–152. Louvain: Peeters Press.

Kushnareva, K. 1997 *The Southern Caucasus in Prehistory*. Philadelphia: University of Pennsylvania Museum of Archaeology and Anthropology.

Lyonnet, B. and Guliyev, F., in collaboration with Bouquet L., Bruleychabot G., Fontuqne M., Raymond P. and Samzun A. 2012. Mentesh Tepe (in Ancient Kura 2010-2011). *Archäologische Mitteilungen aus Iran und Turan* 44: 86-97.

Mirtskhulava, G. 1975 *Samshvilde. Result of the Excavations (1968.-1970)*. Tbilisi: Metsniereba Press (in Russian).

Munchaev R.M. 1975 *The Caucasus at the dawn of the Bronze Age*. Moscow: "Nauka" publishing house. (in Russian).

Nosov, E.N., Kulunovskaya, M.E., Lazarevskaya, N.A., S.A.Yatsenko (eds.) 2018 Ancient Necropolises – Funeral and Memorial Ritualism, Architecture and Planning of Necropolises. Russian Academy of Scienses, Institut for the History of Material Culture, *The State Hermitage Museum Proceedings*. Vol. 47. St. Petersburg: Ill: Publishing House State Hermitage. (in Russian).

Palumbi Giulio. 2016 The Early Bronze Age of the Southern Caucasus. Oxford Handbooks Online.

Petrosyan, L. 1989 *Excavations of the Keti and Voskeask monuments*. Yerevan: Publishing house of the Academy of Sciences of the Armenian SSR (in Armenian).

Pkhakadze, G. 1963 *The Eneolithic of Kvemo Kartli*. Tbilisi: Academy of Sciences of the Georgian SSR (in Russian).

Poulmarc'h, M., Pequer, L., and Jalilov, B. 2014 An Overview of Kura-Araxes Funerary Practices in the Southern Caucasus. *Paléorient* 40(2): 231.

Puturidze, M., Rova, E. 2012. Khashuri Natsargora: The EBA Graves (Publications of the Georgian-Italian Shida Kartli Archaeological Project I). *Subartu* 30: 1–201.

Renfrew, C., Boyd, M., Morley, I. 2016 *Death Rituals, Social Order and the Archaeology of Immortality in the Ancient World*. Cambridge: Cambridge University Press.

Rothman, M. S 2021 Approaches to the Nature of the Kura-Araxes Societies in their Homeland. in *Pathways through Arslantepe: Essays in Honour of Marcella Frangipane*, edited by F. Balossi Restelli, A. Cardarelli, G-M Di Nocera, L. Manzanilla, L. Mori, G. Palumbi, H. Pittman. 163-172. Rome: Universitá di Roma Sapienza.

Rothman, M. S 2015 The Changing Organization of Kura-Araxes Culture. in *International Symposium on East Anatolia South Caucasus Cultures, Vol. 1*, edited by M.Isikli and C. Barol, 121-131.Cambridge: Cambridge Scholars Publishing.

Rothman, M. S 2002 *Tepe Gawra. the Evolution of a Small, Prehistoric Center in Northern Iraq*. Philadelphia: The University of Pennsylvania Museum Publications.

Sagona, A. 2004 Social Boundaries and Ritual Landscapes in Late Prehistoric TransCaucasus and Highland Anatolia. in *A View from the Highlands. Archaeological Studies in Honour of Charles Burney*, edited by A. Sagona. 475–53. Herent: Peeters Press.

Sağlamtimur, H. and Ozan, A. 2013 Başur Höyük 2012 Yılı Kazı Çalışmaları. *Kazı Sonuçları Toplantısı* 35: 514–52.

Sardarian, S.H. 1967 *Primitive Society in Armenia*, edited by M.A. Israelian. Yerevan: Publishing House "Mitk", (in Armenian, English, and Russian).

Sardarian, S.H. 2004 *Armenia the Cradle of Civilization*, Yerevan: Yerevan State University Press. (in Armenian).

Simonyan, H. 2002 Stratigraphy, Principles of Construction and Urbanism of Shengavit. in *Culture of Ancient Armenia 2. Materials of Republican Scientific Session dedicated to Emm Khanzadyan's Jubilee*, edited by A. Kalantaryan and S. Arutyunyan. 18-25. Yerevan: Gitutyun Publishing House, NAS RA. (in Armenian).

Simonyan, H. 2008 Shengavit cemetery. in *Culture of ancient Armenia, XIV. Materials of republican scientific session*, edited by A. Kalanataryan. 81-93. Yerevan, Publishing house of NAS RA. (in Armenian).

Simonyan, H. 2009 Jogaz-Berkaber. Tavush: Material and Spiritual Heritage. Proceedings of a republican scientific conference. Ijevan. Collection dedicated to the 50th anniversary of Institute of Archaeology and Ethnography, edited by A.Kalantaryan, H. Sarkisyan, 215-232 Yerevan, Publishing house of NAS RA, pp. (in Armenian).

Simonyan, H. 2013 Shengavit - an Ordinary Settlement or an Early Town? *Yearbook Monument*. Yerevan 8: 5-53 (in Armenian).

Simonyan, H. 2012 Temple of Fire in Shengavit. in *International conference dedicated to the 125th anniversary of Hovsep Orbeli. Theses of reports, October 2012*, edited by Danielyan. 103-106. Yerevan: National Academy of Sciences of the Republic of Armenia. (in Armenian).

Simonyan H. 2021 il KurganN di Gorayk, Testo e Foto Hakob Simonyan Schede Roberto Dan a Cura di Roberto Dan «L'Armenia e la Grande Steppa Onori al Principe Eroe», Archieologia Viva, Bimstrale - Poste Italiane SPA - SPED. Milano XL - N. 209 - Settemnre/Ottobre 2021 - P.I. 27.8.2021 - ISSN 0392-9426 - CM X1209W, 8-16.

Simonyan H. and Rothman M. S in press Shengavit from Kura-Araxes to Early Kurgan Periods. ARWA *The end of the Kura-Araxes phenomenon and the EB/MB transition in the South Caucasus: the chrono-cultural aspect*, edited by B. Perello and R. Badalyan.

Stöllner, T., Craddock, B., Gambaschidze, I., Gogochuri, G., Hauptmann, A., Hornschuch, A., Klein, F., Löffler, I., Mindiashwili, G., Murwanidze, B., Senczek, S., Schaich, M., Steffens, G., Tamasashvili, K., and Timberlake, S. 2014. Gold in the Caucasus: New Research on Gold Extraction in the Kura-Araxes Culture of the 4th Millennium BC and Early 3rd Millennium BC. *Tagungen des Landesmuseums für Vorgeschichte Halle* 11: 71–110.

Acknowledgements

We would like to thank the expedition participants who contributed to the comprehensive research of this complex monument: Ludwig Khachatryan - deputy head of the expedition, Valery Margaryan - team leader, Vahagn Hovhannesyan - team leader, Anna Azizyan, Arman Nalbandyan - archaeologist, Ani Grigporyan - archaeologist, Diana Zardaryan - YSU student, Tigran Alexanyan - YSU student, Hovhannes Sanamyan - architect, Ruzanna Mkrtchyan - anthropologist, Elena Atoyants - restorer, Hrachya Hakobyan - restorer, Taguhi Amayakyan - artifact artist.

6c | Figurines from Shengavit

Hakob Simonyan

Interpretations of the Meaning of Figural Art

One of the typical attributes of Kura-Araxes culture is the art of making figurines of animals and humans from terracotta and occasionally from stone. In the ancient Middle East the prototypes for such figurines appeared during the Neolithic and continued for millennia afterward.[788] Archaeologists have recovered several hundred of such statuettes, whole or fragmented, from the Kura-Araxes.[789] They are anthropomorphic, zoomorphic, or phallus-like protuberances on portable cult hearths.

The interpretation of the meanings of figural art, like other symbols, is difficult at best. There are many hypotheses about their function. They tend to fall into five categories [790]: 1) images of spirits or divine entities, 2) magical devices to guarantee successful childbirth, to drive away evil, or to ensure the fertility of people, plants, and animals,[791] 3) as teaching aides for children about sexual mores or future occupations, including use in initiation ceremonies, 4) as children's toys, and 5) to represent the dead or something related to the dead as grave goods. In Mesopotamia, sculptors made god images of wood, covered with gold leaf and semi-precious stones. People used clay copies for home worship. One can probably presume something similar happened in the South Caucasus. As magical devices to guarantee a result or to avoid evil, they were often buried, or were broken or burned in the ritual. Third millennium BC Mesopotamian texts include incantations, which later were explicitly used with figurines in magical acts. Voigt notes that the same figurine can be used for multiple functions. Its form does not necessarily correlate with its function. More critical are the contexts where the figurines were used or the way they were disposed of. Toys tend to be thrown out in trash middens. However, magical devices or figurines used in initiation rites tend to be burned or intentionally broken and deposited in houses,[792] under walls, or in water.

Shengavit Figurines

The figurines of Shengavit from the Kura-Araxes cultural tradition reflect a primitive naturalism in their construction and a tendency toward realistic presentation of forms. They are, by definition, symbols of the way the people of the Kura-Araxes cultural tradition saw their world. As part of a ritual process, which defines both the sacred and secular world, they were often used as a call to action.[793] Below I will discuss in what ways the specific types of figurines fit this process.

---

788 Voigt 1983.
789 Yesayan 1980, 9-11.
790 Voigt 1983, 186.
791 Masson and Sarianidi 1973, 47-48, 122-131.
792 Tumanyan 2012, 39, 93.
793 Simonyan and Rothman 2015.

Anthropomorphic figurines

The most expressive group of fine forms of the Kura-Araxes culture are the human figurines. Unlike seated or semi-seated anthropomorphic statuettes of Neolithic-Chalcolithic cultures, Kura-Araxes statuettes are all depicted in a standing pose.[794] In contrast to Sagona, we believe that human figures are an important part of the ritual process of KA2. By design, some anthropomorphic figurines are realistically modeled, while others are stylized.

Female statuettes

These figurines of the Kura-Araxes cultural tradition at Shengavit are usually represented by nude figures with obvious signs of the childbearing organs. The breasts and vulva are mainly represented as simple round protrusions or carved geometric motifs. Some female figurines wear necklaces. They are divided into several types depending on their shape and structure.

The first type, female statuettes, have flattened, rectangular bodies, devoid of clear anatomical modeling. Heads, arms, and in some cases, legs are represented by simple extensions (Fig 6C.1., A). They are characterized by stylized and schematic forms. The statuette shown here archaeologists recovered at Mokhrablur. Archaeologists found fragments of similar statuettes at various sites of the Kura-Araxes culture.[795]

The second type of female statuettes are depicted in a more naturalistic way. They have slightly modeled hips, long legs and open arms. Female terracotta statuettes found at the sites of Shengavit (Fig 6c.1, B) and Mokhrablur (Fig 6c.1, C) are more realistic than those of the first group.

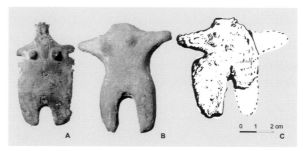

Figure 6c.1 Types 1 and 2 of figurines of women.

The third type of female statues are an intermediate variant between the first and second types and include terracotta figurines from Agarak. On the one hand, they are characterized by short protrusions of arms and legs, as the statuettes of the first group, but on the other hand, they have slightly modeled hips and buttocks (Fig 6c.2, A). The female figurines from Agarak are distinguished by lush body shapes. One figurine has a braid hanging over her shoulder as a sign of coquetry (Fig 6c.2, B). The statuettes in this group clearly reproduce female forms with full bodies

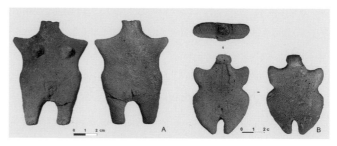

Figure 6c.2 Type 3 Figurines of women.

and wide pelvis and hips, characteristic of mothers with many children. It seems to us that there is no reason to suppose that the open arms imitate folded arms placed on the chest is a pose of invitation, as some researchers believe.[796]

The fourth type, the best example of realistic anthropomorphic statuettes, is a female figure found in Shengavit, Site 2 at a depth of 120 centimeters from the surface in 2000 in front of a niche-like ledge, which in 2010 we discovered was from Building 1, Stratum I in Squares K6, L6, and L7. Nearby, we found a large crater crushed

---

794 Tumanyan 2012, 38.
795 Simonyan and Khachatryan 2005, 57.
796 Bibikov 1953, 224; Martirosyan 1961, 39; Tumanyan 2012, 93.

in place. This small statue of black tufa depicts a nude female body with a wide pelvis and lush thighs (Fig 6c.3, A, B). While the vagina and navel are depicted according to the canons of Kura-Araxes figurines, the chest of this statuette, unlike other statuettes, is depicted in concentric circles with starburst lines, which is reminiscent of the manner of depiction on the famous idol from Mari (Fig 6c.3., C). The body of the statuette is finished by polishing, carving, and drilling.

Figure 6c.3 Type 4 Figurines of women (A, B, D from Shengavit; C from Mari).

The ancient sculptor preserved the principles (*habitus*) that defined the cultural tradition of Kura-Araxes, and at the same time showed their personal approach. The unique statuette from Shengavit is an example of this combination of tradition and individual taste. Like other female statuettes of Kura-Araxes culture, this statuette lacks arms, legs, feet, and face; the head and hands are represented in the form of cone-shaped protrusions. The shape of the statuette resembles a somewhat elongated five-pointed star. The chest is marked with dots arranged in circles. According to one hypothesis, its shape and the arrangement of the circles reflect a heavenly body. If so, it is possible that this particular form was the predecessor of Astghik, the goddess of love and beauty in the Armenian pantheon, in which a number of goddesses are depicted in the form of a star.[797]

This group also includes the pelvic part of a terracotta female figurine discovered in the Shengavit necropolis. This statuette is also characterized by a narrow waist, well-modeled pelvis and wide hips (Fig 6c.3., D).

The fifth type, the only specimen of which archaeologists found at the site of Agarak. The female statuette from Agarak differs from the others. She has a rounded body, a bloated belly and a vagina (Fig 6c.4). Her hands, folded at the elbows, rest on her bloated abdomen. This manner is characteristic of the pose of a pregnant woman. The statuette consists of two halves connected by bitumen. Most likely, the statuette was sawed into two parts in order to put grain inside, and two halves were then connected with bitumen. On the reverse artisans engraved small squares, which probably symbolized a handkerchief thrown over her back. This statuette most likely symbolizes the cult of fertility, the Great Mother, who patronized fertility, pregnancy and the well-being during the birthing process.[798] Alternatively, the figurine was used as a magic tool to guarantee success in giving birth to a healthy child and preserving the well-being of the mother.

Figure 6c.4 A Figurine of a pregnant woman or goddess.

The sixth type is represented by one specimen we found in the Shengavit cemetery. It has a characteristic rounded shape with a thin waist. The statuette is depicted in a pose of worship. The preserved left hand is raised up in a pose of prayer (Fig 6c.5., A). Similar simulations of anthropomorphic figures in the pose of prayer archaeologists found on the fragments of vessels from Norşuntepe and Vanadzor (Kosi-choter) (Fig. 6c.5., B).

Figure 6c.5 Images of women in prayer.

---

797   Simonyan 2004, 61.
798   Tumanyan 2012, 40.

Although the statuette is small, it consisted of several parts. This is evidenced by the holes in various parts of the body, which means that the parts were connected by wooden sticks or string like a puppet. The head, torso and thighs were made separately and then attached. In its pose this statuette resembles the famous statue of the "Goddess with Snakes" found on Crete, but unlike that statue it was crudely made.

The seventh type is represented by a unique female statuette archaeologists unearthed at Harich. It has broadly elongated, slightly raised up arms, a round ledge for the head, broken, round breasts and a depression for the navel (Fig 6c.6., A).[799] The construction of the hips (pelvis, thighs) and feet contrasts with the established rule of depicting statuettes in Kura-Araxes in Armenia with legs of the female figures designed as sets of raised bumps. The statuette from Mokhrablur has no legs. The figurine ends with a round hip line. It resembles the outlines of female figurines from Central Asia.[800]

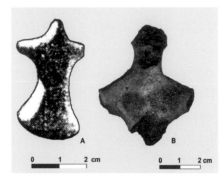

Figure 6c.6 Type 8 and 9 female figurines.

The eighth type is represented by a female statuette accidentally found at Mokhrablur. The head and part of the upper body with a conical protrusion for the arm were preserved (Fig 6c.6., B). In Yesayan's opinion the well-formed conical pelvis left no doubt that this was a statuette of a woman; however, the long strong neck ended in a flat rounded head, decorated with a protrusion resembling a cockade of feathers or rosettes along the side of a hat, which reached the tip of the nose. On either side of the nose the artisan drilled two holes for eyes. Perhaps, because of the helmet, this statuette was associated with military actions, either with a female warrior or with a goddess of war.[801]

Voigt made an apt observation that idol statuettes were used to represent the dead or something related to funerary practices as grave goods.[802] They were deliberately broken and distorted. This is the case with female statuettes found in the Shengavit cemetery. According to beliefs unknown to us, the ancient inhabitants of the site not only broke the statuettes, but also broke off the conical and hemispherical breast protrusions of terracotta statuettes we found there.

Male Statuettes

Male statuettes are rare. For a long time scholars believed that making male statuettes was not a characteristic of the Kura-Araxes cultural tradition. The absence of male statuettes was based on the notion that ancient societies were ruled by women, i.e. matriarchy was common in those times, so it would be logical that they made only female statuettes.[803] We really know little about this kind of organization of everyday life in Shengavit. However, it seems to us that this hypothesis about the social structure does not make sense based on what we do know. Perhaps, people of the Kura-Araxes were concerned with fertility, with which women are usually associated. However, in addition to female statuettes, figurine makers often formed images of the male fertility organ in the form of phallus amulets and added conical details on cult hearths and on portable altars.

Nevertheless, we have discovered several male statuettes to date, most of them from Shengavit. Unlike the female figurines, artisans modeled the male statuettes to include a head with simple facial features. You can distinguish the

---

799   Yesayan 1980.
800   Masson and Sarianidi 1973.
801   Yesayan 1980.
802   Voigt 1983.
803   Bayburtian 2011; Sardarian 1967.

nose, eyes, and mouth. The arms and legs are shaped but not detailed. Male figurines are depicted in the nude with the male genitals emphasized.

Figure 6c.7 First type male figurines.

The male statuettes can be subdivided into two types. First type includes two terracotta figurines. The first is from Harich (Fig 6C.7. A).[804] It has a straight cylindrical body, arms outstretched on either side. The head is broken. In the middle of the torso, a vertical line depicts a gash in the cloak. A staff rests on his shoulder, indicating his might be a shepherd.[805] The first male figure found by Sardarian in Shengavit (Fig 6c.7, B) has rectangular flat body with a low depression between the legs.[806] The man appears to be dressed in a long cloak covering him from shoulders to feet. His rounded head is thrown back, as if looking up. The round face has clear indentations to represent the eyes. The nose is convex, and the mouth is represented by a horizontal slit. His body is slightly curved, and he is short with a thick neck and broad shoulders, slightly wider than his torso, emphasizing the strong build of the man. His arms are attached to his well-built body. His large hands, curled into a fist, rest on his chest. A large phallus protrudes from the center of his waist, protruding from the center of his belt, and carved in relief. This simple statuette depicts a man with dignity and tremendous strength. Unfortunately, Sardarian did not deposit this statuette in the museum, and we have an idea of it only from the illustration in Sardarian's book.

Another male figure of this type from Sardarian's excavations is the most famous. It is presented in almost all catalogs and albums on the art of ancient Armenia. It is a full-length nude figure with an exaggerated phallus (Fig 6c.7., C). He has wide round legs like an elephant, his arms are crossed on his chest with his fingers open. The head is round. The flat face is rounded at the edges, with a long nose in the center. The eyes are rendered as dots. Distant examples of this statuette have also been found in other monuments of the Kura-Araxes: Hizanaant Gora, Kvatskhelebi, Amiranis Gora, and Urbnisi.

The second type is represented by two statuettes from Shengavit. One of them is intact, the other from red tufa is partially preserved, only the rounded head, which rests on straight shoulders (Fig. 6c.8., A). Archaeologists uncovered another male statuette in the same room as the black tufa female statuette, possibly of a goddess. This terracotta statuette repeats an idealized form similar to those previously described. His legs are spread wide apart, and the man appears to be depicted walking. His arms are crossed over his chest, and a protrusion in the center of his waist depicts his genitals. His head and one arm are broken. The facial features are damaged (Fig 6c.8., B).

The accompanying items of the male statuettes are phallic pendants. Crafts persons made them out of different kinds of stones: river stone, tufa, felsite, sandstone, green and white serpentine, etc. (Fig 6c.9). We found ten pendants at the Shengavit settlement and

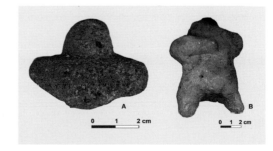
Figure 6c.8. Second type of male figurines.

804 Khachatryan 1975, 37.
805 Yesayan 1980, 11.
806 Sardarian 2004.

necropolis during the 2007 to 2012 excavations.[807] Sardarian found two more.[808] These realistic stone figurines had deep grooves at the end, as if to hang them on a string. These pendants occurred both in the settlement and from graves in the cemetery beyond the city wall.

What did they represent and what was their function? In the early Iron Age huge phallic stelae were usually erected as symbols of fertility cults and of powerful ancestors. One of the oldest phallus statues, a tufa stele, was discovered during Sardarian's excavations in 1960 inside a rectangular room in Square I16. Today this huge phallus, after a very poor restoration, is displayed near the Shengavit Museum (Fig 6c.9., D).

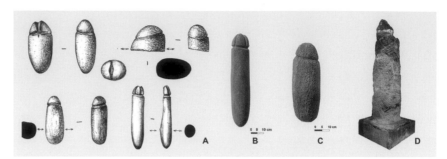

Figure 6c.9 Phallus amulets (A-C) and phallic stele at Shengavit Museum.

According to one hypothesis, small pendants of phallic shape were amulets which female acolytes wore around their necks to indicate their religious role. In order to confirm this hypothesis, it is significant that we found a model of a phallus near the altar in Room 1 of the cult structure in the Square M5 at Shengavit.[809] This hypothesis would be confirmed as true if it were possible to excavate unperturbed burials with phallus-amulets and preserved skeletons to determining their gender and other indications of the status of the women buried there.

Other human or divine figurines

There are other small statuettes. The round head of one of the idols with rectangular, flat body is separated from the body by a depression on the neck. On the face one can clearly identify the big nose, and the smiling mouth depicted by a cut (Fig 6c.10., A). We discovered an obsidian tool with what looks like an anthropomorphic shape in 2000 from Square L6 (Fig 6c.10., B).

Larger versions of these statues are 70-80 centimeters high and have flat and rectangular bodies. The protrusion representing the head is a straight cut line and is well-modeled. The drilled holes on the face represent the eyes. A depression represents the mouth. The navel is cut on the belly. Sculptors worked both sides, front and back, of these statuettes so they could be viewed from all sides. Possibly, they were attached to an altar

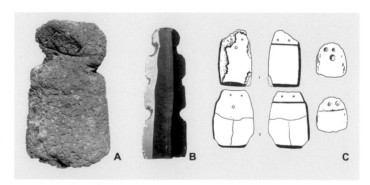

Figure 6c.10 Other human figurines.

(Fig 6c.10., C).[810] The many faces on andirons from Pulur (Sakyol), Yanik Tepe, and Bet Shean,[811] along with these statues suggest that they may have been a spirit or god. Some of the complex designs etched on pots may, too, be

---

807   Simonyan 2013, 15, Table 11.
808   Sardarian 2004, 224, tab. CXXXIV, fig. 1; 233, tab. LIX, fig. 5.
809   Simonyan and Rothman 2014, Fig. 13, D.
810   Simonyan 2013, 14, Tab. 4-6.
811   Simonyan and Rothman 2015.

abstract representations of these mystical entities (see Chapter 6a).[812]

FIGURINES OF ANIMALS

Archaeologists have unearthed figurines of animals from most Kura-Araxes sites. At Shengavit we discovered figurines of animals that could be bulls, rams, goats, dogs, equids (donkeys, horses or onagers), lion, and others. In the Kura-Araxes cultural tradition figurines of domestic animals were common. As we discussed above, their function can be variable from rituals of fertility to toys. Most of the figurines of the animals are made in primitive naturalistic style,

and as a result their different breeds (sub-species varieties) are depicted in a generalized way. However, some have rather accurate modeling.

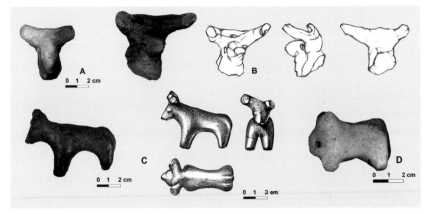

Figure 6c.11 Bull figurines.

FIGURINES OF BULLS

The statuettes of bull are realistic (Fig 6c.11). Their species characteristics are accurately modeled: thick body, short legs, long tails, strong necks, and curved horns. Two kinds of bulls are represented in the small terracotta figurines. One of them is short-horned, with a fat body (Fig 6c.11., A). The other has huge horns pointing forward (Fig 6c.11., B, C). They look very much like a variety of modern Armenian cattle .

In addition, the noses of some bulls had holes (Fig 6c.11., D). Statuettes of bulls had holes in the front legs only on one side. By putting a stick through these holes, it was possible to tie animals together. These sticks represented yokes to which residents attached plows, carts, or wagons in paired teams of animals.

In many settlements of Kura-Araxes culture we found not only bull figures with depressions in the front part of the body, but also models of cartwheels with distinct axel projections (Fig 6c.11).[813] Especially impressive are the tufa models of wheels at Shengavit (Fig 6c.12). Statuettes of bulls with holes in their sides, models of wheels and carriage bodies were also found together at Ariche.[814] Whereas these were probably model wheels, there is a possibility that they were spindle whorls. Based on the characteristics of the bull figurines and model wheels, Piotrowski aptly noted as early as 1955 that cattle were used as draught animals in Kura-Araxes societies.[815]

Yesayan suggests that statuettes of animals without holes mean that they are cows, and only bulls were used to pull carts.[816] We note that cows were also used as draught animals

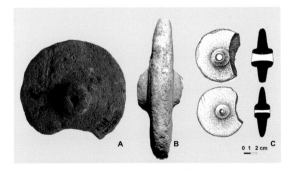

Figure 6c.12 Model wheels (or spindle whorls).

---

812   Simonyan and Rothman 2015, Fig 13, I.
813   Sardarian 2004, 217, table LXXXIX/2.
814   Khachatryan 1975, 73.
815   Piotrowski, 1955, 6.
816   Yesayan 1980, 11.

in the Kura-Araxes.[817] I believe that figurines with ring-shaped holes in the nose symbolized uncastrated bulls (Fig 6c.11., B), and statuettes with holes in the front legs symbolized farm animals, in this case oxen (Fig 6c.11., D).

Statuettes of bulls with dots (stars) on their foreheads are known from the Kura-Araxes. We propose that they the ancients perceived bulls as symbols of divinity and revered them.[818] We discovered an amulet of burnt clay in the form of a crescent or inverted, stylized head of a bull, the surface of which is covered with a dense network of holes (Fig 6c.13., A). Such a design also comes from a statuette of a bull made of fired clay from Karnut (Fig 6c.13., B). The connection of bulls with the water and the moon is reflected in many mythologies of the ancient Near East. Bulls were honored and were used in rituals. The cult significance of bulls is evidenced by the discovery of terracotta head of a black bull with long horns (Fig 6c.11., B) in the cult room with the altar in Square M5 at Shengavit. Another evidence of the cult significance of the bull in Early Bronze Age Armenia comes from Agarak. There a bull's skull was found under a ceramic ritual hearth.[819]

Bulls can also be toys, teaching young people what one of their adult tasks would be. The locations of their finds, as discussed above, may be the most important evidence of how they were used.

FIGURINES OF OTHER ANIMALS

We found figurines of rams at Shengvit. Archaeologists unearthed them at Harich, Mokhrablur, Shengavit, Kültepe I of Naxçivan, Jrahovit, Urbnisi, Arakhlo, Amiranis Gora, and other settlements.[820]

The figurines of rams can be subdivided into two groups. The first group includes realistic figurines. A fine sample of generalized realism is the figurine of a ram made of dark rosy tufa discovered at Mokhrablur. The sculpting is anatomically precise. The sculptor tried to depict the important attributes of the animal. For these details, the figurine of the ram is among the best works of generalized realism I have seen. Several statuettes of rams from Harich seem to denote dynamic movement.

Figure 6c.13 Bulls with holes portraying stars.

We found a fine example of a statuette of a ram made of terracotta in Square L4 at Shengavit in 2010. The front legs pointing forward, the curve of the back, the heavy head slightly bent downwards create a clear sense of a ram's figure. In this statuette, as well as in bovine statuettes, there are holes on the nose and depressions on the front part of the body (Fig 6c.14).

The second group of rams is on andirons (see Fig 3.23).[821] Especially impressive are the andirons discovered in Shirak Marz Province at the sites of Harich and Karnut.[822] At Shengavit in 2000 we discovered half of an andiron with a ram whose eyes were inlaid with pieces of black obsidian.

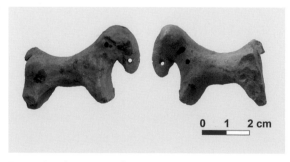

Figure 6c.14 Figurine of ram.

817   Simonyan 2013, 14.
818   Piotrowski 1949, 35.
819   Tumanyan 2012, 90.
820   Kushnarewa 1977.
821   Simonyan and Rothman 2015, Fig. 11, D.
822   Khachatryan, 1975.

The same technique, the use of obsidian for depicting eyes, was used in the twin idols from the excavations of Amiranis Gora near Akhaltsikhe (Fig 6c.15). The obsidian inlay on the place of the eyes of the statuette is also discussed in the book published by Sardarian.[823]

In Shengavit we also found a goat horn broken off from the body of the statuette, which is not preserved (Fig 6c.16). In Sardarian's book there is an image of goat with horns sticking out of the figure that looks like this clay object.[824] The clay figurine we excavated in Square L3 of Shengavit is severely damaged (Fig 6c.17). It can be cautiously considered a statuette of a goat.

Excavators found a fragment of a large storage jar with relief image of goat at Agarak.[825] Sardarian also recovered a vessel with goat motif at Shengavit.[826]

Archaeologists recovered statuettes of dogs at Harich, Mokhrablur, Agarak and Geoy Tepe sites.[827] The artisans made them from terracotta, but they lacked details denoting their breed.

During the excavations at Shengavit we found a small number of equid figures. I prefer to see them as horses, but our archaeozoologists do not believe that domestic horse existed in the South Caucasus before the Middle Bronze Age (see Chapter 5a). The body of an onager (equid) looks almost identical to that of a horse. The difference is in the head. During the excavations at Shengavit we found two statuettes in the upper layers. The head of one of them was broken, but judging from the croup and tail, it could have been a horse or onager (Fig 6c.18., A).

Another terracotta statuette of a horse had a fluttering mane. Its whole body is covered with dots, which suggests that it has some celestial origin (see above) and was most probably used in a ritual or magical procedure (Fig 6c.18., B).

During the excavations, Sardarian discovered a rather elegant horse's head.[828] Sculptors made it from burnished black fine clay (Fig 6c.18., C). The surface was

Figure 6c.15 Andiron with obsidian eyes.

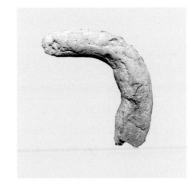

Figure 6c.16 Horn from goat figurine.

Figure 6c.17 Figurine of goat.

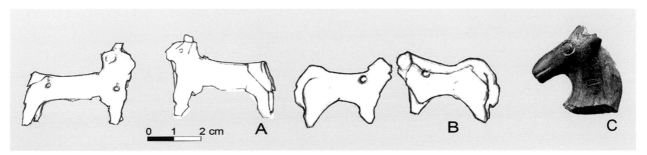

Figure 6c.18 Figurines and pot piece of equids (possible horses).

823   Sardarian 2004, 157, Tabl. XXIV.
824   Sardarian 2004, 339, tab. LXXXV/4.
825   Tumanyan 2012, 67, 78-79, table XXI/4.
826   Sardarian 1967, 186, table LX/2; Ibid. 2004, 229, table XCIX/2.
827   Yesayan 1980, 12.
828   Sardarian 1967, p. 200, table LXX/5.

polished. It has round, bulging eyes, small, protruding ears, and a well-shaped mouth in the form of a horizontal line. A cast mane is clearly distinguished on the neck. A statuette of almost the same type is kept in the museum of Regional Study in Vanadzor. That is, we have two almost identical statuettes, one in the Koytak Plateau (Shengavit), the other in the Lori region (Vanadzor). However, it remains an open question whether these statuettes were created in the Early Bronze Age or later. We believe that the quality and manner of these statuettes are more characteristic of Urartian art. Badalyan also doubts that this statuette belongs to Kura-Araxes culture and dates it to Late Urartian/Achaemenid era.[829]

The other small figurine of an equid head dated to the Early Bronze Age is very stylized with a bulging forehead, four-faceted neck, a snout, and dots for eyes.[830] Excavators unearthed another terracotta figurine of an equid head at Karaz. It has a prolonged snout, hardly visible ears, and dot-like depressions for eyes.[831] Summing up the analysis, we can state that the Kura-Araxes statuettes had dotted, small eyes, while the Urartian horse statuettes stand out with convex, large eyes.

Another animal figurine we found represented a lion. We discovered it in the upper layers in Shengavit in 2010. It is unique for the Kura-Araxes. The figurine is valuable not only from an artistic point of view, but it also suggests that lions lived in the vicinity of Yerevan at the time of Kura-Araxes.[832] These lions continued to live in Armenia until the formation of the Armenian language, because the word *aryuts* (lion), according to Acharyan, is an original Armenian word.[833] Only the front part of this terracotta figurine was preserved. The lion is standing in an aggressive pose. A rich mane decorates its head. The eyes are small hollows, the nose is a relief, and the mouth is shaped by a horizontal cut (Fig 6c.19, A). The details of the modelling are imprecise, but even so, in its abstraction the reality of a lion is reflected. No other lion figurines are known from the Kura-Araxes. However, in the subsequent epoch of the Early Kurgan Period, a perfectly modeled gold statuette of a lion archaeologists discovered in the 2nd barrow of the Alazan Valley (Fig 6c.19, B). This was clearly the grave of someone with high status.[834] That can be because of their own position or because they represent a clan or performed rituals with divine content. The ancients placed the bones of a sacrificed lion, or rather its hide, in Tomb 1 of Nerkin Naver of the late third millennium BC. [835] These findings show that the lion in the South Caucasus was already revered as a symbol of power in early days.

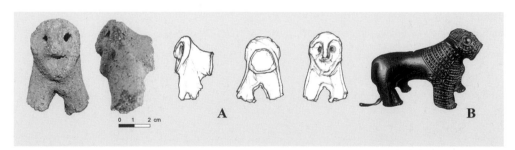

Figure 6c.19 Figurines of lions from Shengavit (A) and Alazan Valley barrow burial (B).

829   Badalyan et al. 2015, 35, 223, Table 10, Fig. 111.
830   Yesayan 1980, 12.
831   Kosay H., Turfan K. 1959, 394.
832   The earliest evidence of lions living in Armenia is recorded in the Syunik region of the Republic of Armenia in the monument of Gödedzor of the Ubaid epoch (Chataigner et al. 2010).
833   Acharyan 1971, 259-260.
834   Dedabrishvili 1979.
835   Margaret and Hans-Peter Uerpmann 2010.

The final animal represented as a figurine was a bird (Fig 6c. 20). There is only one such sample from Mokhrablur. It is a hollow figurine of a bird made of terracotta. Its body is ball-shaped, tail downward, a short, puffed-up neck; the head is broken. The bird is pictured in a sitting position. The swell craw of the bird denotes its being of pigeon species.[836] Unfortunately, we found it when screening the back-dirt, therefore no layer or square could be determined. A thousand years later, this figurine seems to repeat itself as a prototype in the form of a horn rhyton widely common in Armenia in the Late Bronze Age. The other image of a bird is from the bowl from Burial 4 (Fig 6b.7).

Figure 6c.20 Figurine of bird.

Conclusion

The largest collection of small figurines from the Kura-Araxes comes from Shengavit. The number of terracotta and stone anthropomorphic and zoomorphic statuettes is 37. We also found statuettes of large and small idols, as well as more than ten phallus-shaped amulets. The publication of the entire collection of small figurines from Shengavit significantly expands our understanding of Kura-Araxes mythology and art. Among them there are individual sculptures that are recorded only in Shengavit, such as the terracotta statuette of a lion and phallus amulets.

It is possible that the sculptures of animals had a magical meaning. This is evidenced by the traces of red paint preserved on some statues, the dotted designs on the foreheads of bulls ("stars"), as well as the andirons of a ram with eyes with black obsidian inserts found at Shengavit.[837]

All the other possible uses laid out by Voigt (see above) are possible for these statuettes as toys, magical devices, grave goods, teaching aids, etc. Their presence near the ritual the ceramic hearth in Room 1 of Square M5 at Shengavit may indicate their importance as symbols of fertility of agriculture and pastoralism. They mostly come from the buildings rather than from graves.

References

Acharyan, H. H. 1971 *Armenian Etymological Dictionary, vol. 1*, 259-260. Yerevan. (in Armenian).

Antonova, E. B. 1977 *Anthropomorphic sculpture of ancient farmers of Western and Central Asia*, Moscow, (in Russian).

Antonova, E. B. 1990 *Rituals and Beliefs of the Primitive Farmers of the Orient.* Moscow (in Russian).

Aruz, J. and Wallenfels, R. 2003 *Art of the First Cities. The Third Millennium B.C. from the Mediterranean to the Indus.* The Metropolitan Museum of Art New York. New Haven Yale University Press.

Badalyan, R., Hovsepyan, S., Khachatryan, L. 2015 *Shengavit. Catalog of Archaeological Materials from the Collection of the Museum of History of Armenia.* Yerevan: Armenian Museum of History (in Russian).

Bayburtian, Y. 2011 *Sequence of Ancient Cultures of Armenia on the Basis of Archaeological Material.* Yerevan: Armenian Museum of History (in Russian).

Bibikov, S. N. 1953 Early Tripolian settlement Luka-Vrublevetskaya on the Dniester. *Proceedings of the Institute of Archaeology* 38. Moscow-Leningrad (in Russian).

Chataigner, C., Avetisyan, P., Palumbi, G., Uerpmann, H.-P. 2010 Gödedzor: A Late Ubaid-Related Site in the Southern Caucasus. in *Beyond the Ubaid transformation and Integration in the Late Prehistoric Societies of the Middle East,* edited by R. Carter and G. Philip. 391-409. Studies in Ancient oriental Civilizations, volume 63. Chicago: Oriental Institute of the University of Chicago.

Dedabrishvili, Sh. 1969 Monuments of the Early and Middle Bronze Age. *Proceedings of the Kakheti Archaeological Expedition,* Volume 1 (in Russian).

---

836   Yesayan 1980.
837   Simonyan 2016.

Koşay, H. and Turfan, K. 1959 Ererum Karas Kasisi raporu. *Turk Tarich Kurumu Belleten* 23: 91. (in Turkish).

Khachatryan, T. S. 1975 *The Ancient Culture of the Shirak.* Yerevan: Yerevan University Press (in Russian).

Kushnareva, K. Kh. 1993 *The South Caucasus in the IX-II thousand B.C. Stages of cultural and socio-economic development.* St. Petersburg (in Russian).

Martirosyan, H. A. 1961 *The city of Teishebaini.* Yerevan: NAS RA "Gigutyun" Publishing House

Masson, V. M. and Sarianidi, V. I. 1973 *Terracotta of the Middle Asia of the Bronze Age. Attempt of Classification and Interpretation,* Moscow: Main Editorial House of Oriental Literature (in Russian).

Mirimanov, V. B. 1999 *Origins of Style.* Moscow: RGGU. (in Russian).

Piotrovsky, B. B. 1949 *Archaeology of Transcaucasia.* Leningrad (in Russian).

Piotrovski, B. B. 1955 Development of cattle-breeding in ancient Transcaucasia. *Soviet Archaeology* 23:5-15 (in Russian).

Sagona, A. 1998 Social identity and religious ritual in the Kura-Araks cultural complex: some observations from Sos Höyük. *Mediterranean Archaeology* 11: 13-25.

Sardarian, S. H. 1967 *Primitive Society in Armenia.* Yerevan: "Mitq" publishers (in Armenian).

Sardarian, S. H. 2004. *Armenia: Cradle of Civilization.* Yerevan: Yerevan University Publishers. (in Armenian).

Simonyan, H. Ye. 2004 Exclusive find of ancient Art from Shengavit. *Theses of the Symposium Devoted to the 80th Anniversary of Birth of the Academician Levon Hakhverdyan,* 59-61. Yerevan. (in Armenian).

Simonyan, H. Ye. 2013 Shengavit. An Ordinary Settlement or an Ancient Town? Annual *Hushardzan* 8: 5-53 (in Armenian).

Simonyan, H. Ye. 2016 The fine plastics of the Shengavit culture. *Yearbook N4 of Academy of Fine Arts. Studies in Art History and Humanities.* Yerevan 4: 70-80 (in Armenian).

Simonyan, H. Ye., Khachatryan L. 2005 Excavations of Shengavit in 2003. *Culture of ancient Armenia", XIII, materials of republican scientific conference,* Yerevan, 56-59 (in Armenian).

Simonyan, H. and Rothman, M. S 2015 Regarding Ritual Behaviour at Shengavit, Armenia. *Ancient Near Eastern Studies* 52: 1-46.

Tumanyan, G. S. 2012 *Agarak I. Early Bronze Age Settlement (2001-2008).* Archaeological Excavations in Armenia, No. 25. Yerevan: NAS RA "Gigutyun" Publishing Hause (in Armenian).

Uerpmann, M. and Uerpmann, H.-P. 2010 Zug-und Lasttiere zwischen Majkop und Trialeti. in *Von Majkop bis Trialeti. Gewinnung und Verbreitung von Metllen und Obsidian in Kaukasien im 4.-2- Jt. v. Chr. Beitrage des Internationalen Symposiums in Berlin vom 1-3- Juni 2006,* edited by S. Hansen, A. Hauptmann, I. Motzenbacker and E. Pernicka, 237–251. Bonn: Dr. Rudolf Habelt, GmbH.

Voigt, M. 1983 *Hajji Firuz: The Neolithic Settlement.* Philadelphia: University Museum Press.

Yesayan, S. A. 1980 *Sculpture of Ancient Armenia.* Yerevan: Armenian SSR Academy of Sciences Publishers. (in Russian).

7 | The Lifeways of Shengavit: Synthesis

Mitchell Rothman and Hakob Simonyan

Introduction

The foregoing chapters have asked core questions about a site, which are important for understanding the development of the Kura-Araxes cultural tradition and society of the homeland in the KA2 period of the first half of the third millennium BC.[838] In this chapter we look at larger patterns in the distribution of artifacts across space and time and a synthesis of the conclusions of the various authors on different artifact types to draw a picture of the nature of Shengavit's Kura-Araxes cultural tradition and society. How big was the site's population, and what were the interactions among its residents? Answering these questions involves sorting out what the activities (more broadly, functions) of the residents of the site were. We argue that Shengavit was a small center of a local polity, most of whose satellite sites were destroyed by the expansion of the modern city of Yerevan (Fig 1.1). Theoretically then, what potentially were the interactions of center and satellite sites? In what larger networks of interaction did the residents of Shengavit participate? Specifically, which of the functions we have documented reached out beyond the boundaries of this one site? If it were a center of a small polity of nearby sites, what activities defined its relationship with populations outside the site? Did some individuals or groups have control over aspects of the settlement's lifeways, production, and exchange? Did their ideology reflect some of these aspects? In other words, "settlements and the relationships and patterns they embody, provide a primary record and reading of human existence—they organize our social and productive activities in every kind of ecological settings and technical horizon. ... We can find social, productive, and cosmological order embedded in the physical structure of every human community, ..."[839]

In the following discussion, readers will notice there are differences in the approach taken by Simonyan and Rothman. Simonyan belongs to the Armenian culture history school. Rothman's approach is informed by an American New Archaeology approach[840] that emphasized a societal evolutionary, anthropological perspective.

Site Functions, Site Plan, and the Organization of Activity Areas

Understanding the lifestyles, activities, and organization of people living at an ancient site requires a significant amount of horizontal and vertical exposure along with the ability to place artifacts back into the contexts that archaeologists excavated. The advantage and problem of Mesopotamian archaeology is that early archaeologists exposed large swaths of ancient sites, although their methods were rather crude. Rothman's dissertation on Tepe Gawra, a surprisingly well

---

838   Possibly, there were some yet to be explored earlier, late KA1 levels (see Chapter 3).
839   Rykwert and Atkin 2005, 1
840   Rothman 2004, 2017.

excavated site for the 1930's, demonstrates these advantages.[841] The excavators at Gawra exposed the entirety of the mound from the top level to Level X, half the mound from Levels XA/XI to XIAB, and a third to Level XX. Showing the broad site plan for much of the site was therefore possible. As an experiment, Rothman randomly selected one quarter of the squares in the complete excavations for analysis. He found that the interpretation of the culture and society of those living on the mound would be very different if he had based his interpretation on just that sample.

Despite all the digging at Shengavit of various archaeologists from the 1930's to 2021, we can know nothing about 75% of Shengavit. Sardarian, who dug the most, did not leave us notes permitting us to determine the stratigraphy of what he dug or to put back any of the artifacts he saved. In fact, he discarded a large number of artifacts that he did not see as valuable. Earlier, Bayburtian proved a much more careful archaeologist with good notes for his time in the 1930's. So, we actually have much less than a quarter of the original mound to analyze. The excavations covered 12 percent of the entire surface, and most excavation did not expose the full stratigraphy from surface to bedrock. We can speak about what we know, but not about everything that was happening at the site. We certainly cannot discuss the site plan to any great extent. The only site with comparable exposed area for the town plan of the Kura-Araxes is Kvatskhelebi in Georgia. Even that is a limited sample in a different sub-region.

Population of the Mound

The number of people who actually lived there is a critical issue. We have written above that we interpret the size and number of the stone-lined grain storage pits to indicate that the residents of the site were producing surplus beyond that needed for food security of the population. The supposition is that the excess was used as rations for residents outside of the site to contribute to public works like the building of the settlement wall, perhaps the intensification of agriculture, or military defense. Perhaps, this surplus would feed the whole polity during inevitable years of poor yields. It created an interdependence of the whole population of the polity.

According to Simonyan, the maximum number of people living at Shengavit—presumably the number varied over time— was 3500 to 5000. His mathematical calculation serves as the basis for such a bold statement. Sardarian excavated 3,000 square meters of the territory of the upper horizon, where 50 houses were excavated. That is, he excavated on average one structure on each plot of 60 square meters. The same pattern—one dwelling on each plot of 50/60 square meters— appeared in the excavations of Bayburtian (800:14=57). Given that the same pattern can be traced in all the excavated areas of the settlement, Simonyan assumes that such dense construction was characteristic of the entire Shengavit settlement. Thus, according to this statistic, in the Shengavit settlement there were about 1000 dwellings (60000 m² /60=1000). If we factor in that the settlement had religious and household buildings, public buildings, workshops, streets and courtyards, etc., where people naturally did not live, and divided the number of all buildings by half, then the number of houses where small families and/or extended families lived was 500. According to ethnographic observations, small families consisted of five to eight people, while large families consisted of 10 to12 people (Kushnareva 1997, 25). In other words, each house had an average of 7 to10 people. If we multiply the number of houses where people lived and the number of people in the average family, the mathematical calculation of the probable number of Shengavit inhabitants at its greatest extent (500x7/10) was, indeed, 3500-5000 people.[842]

According to Sardarian, on the other hand, the houses in Shengavit were multi-room structures designed for the community, where sets of families lived together. He suggested that the population of Shengavit did not exceed a few

---

841   Rothman 2002.
842   Simonyan 2018, 7.

hundred people.[843] We do not know on what basis he made that assertion.

Rothman leans more toward Sardarian's view. He has many problems with Simonyan's calculations. To assume that the whole site was like the barely 12 percent of all areas that Sardarian and Bayburtian and we excavated is a questionable assumption, especially when the excavated areas are not all contemporaneous.

Demographers have been trying to calculate the population size of settlements, both ethnographic and archaeological for a long time.[844] They have used habitation space and when not enough of those buildings are known, as at Shengavit, they use as a proxy the size of the site. For these calculations they used an ethnographic sample of 185 societies of all kinds. They added archaeological sites with broad horizontal exposures. They estimate 100.75 up to 200 people per hectare. The smaller the site, the greater the density. So, they would estimate Shengavit's population as from 610 to 1200 people. Since the size of buildings at the lower elevations at Shengavit are smaller than those nearer the surface (later in time), the population size of the site was closest to the 1200 number later; the earliest strata would be closer to the 600 number.

The smaller number would actually support our idea of the centrality of the site. If there were 3,000 to 5,000 people, the stone-lined grain storage would probably serve only the immediate needs of the population and security against low crop yields longer term. The smaller number would indicate that surpluses would be available as rations for persons outside the site to compensate them for labor in intensifying agricultural production and performing public projects like building the settlement wall or military defense. At this period, size and control do not necessarily equate. Tepe Gawra was only one hectare when it had evidence of centralized administration, formal religion for a greater number of people, and a central role in producing and trading goods over a considerably larger area than we propose the Shengavit polity to have been (see below).[845]

Settlement Functions

Taken together, the picture we see of Shengavit's population is that of an agricultural and pastoral community living in in a highland forested zone, with largely self-sufficient production of the food, craft tools, and craft products the residents needed. The residents very likely produced some goods—salt is the most likely— in exchange for raw materials like copper ores and tempering material. According to Simonyan, Shengavit was a craft, trade, political, and religious center for a larger area[846] (see discussion below).

Agriculturally, Chapters 2b and 5b indicate that the people were producing mostly grains, more wheat than barley. The residents of Shengavit preferred free-threshing varieties, as did most of the Kura-Araxes migrants in the diaspora. The varieties they produced mostly suited the making of bread and porridges. As elsewhere in the Kura-Araxes, pulses like peas, lentils, and chickpeas existed, but in extremely small numbers. Some griddle-like pieces held up by andiron-looking ceramic feet suggest the possibility of making lavash-like flat breads or grilling as well. The palynological studies found remains of wheat gruel cooked in grape juice in one of the graves. Although Roman Hovsepyan recovered few grape pits or vegetal pieces in the floated samples of fill from pits, floors, and pots, the pollen samples analyzed by Kvavadze and Atoyants suggest significant investment in grape growing at the site. Presumably, there would be many more grape remains where the wine was made, but we did not find those places. Because we

---

843   Sardarian 1967, 174.
844   Schacht 1981.
845   Rothman 2002.
846   Simonyan 2018.

did not find wine production sites, we cannot say they did not exist. The large vat (see Chapter 5e) Simonyan's team found could have been used for wine making. However, an analysis of that pot for residues by Patrick McGovern of the Penn Museum did not produce results.

We recovered ground stone tools to process these plant crops throughout the site (see below). Primary among them were saddle querns and grinders (*manos* and *metates* in New World parlance), as well as pestles.

In the presence of a very few pulses for protein and oil, Shengavit residents' use of animals also fits the needs of the residents (Chapter 5a). By numbers, sheep were the most common animal recovered, followed by goats, cows, and much fewer pigs and equids. Domestic horses were not among the equids, as Crabtree and the Uerpemanns assert.[847] DNA analysis of equid samples from other sites— none were run on Shengavit equids— suggests the same. Crabtree and Piro also found a small number of wild animals: red and roe deer, small numbers of wild sheep and cattle, onagers, and a range of carnivore species including brown bear, European badger, and otter. Foxes and hares, although wild, are commonly found in and around cultivated fields. Fish were another source of protein (see Chapter 5a). A figurine we recovered Simonyan interprets as lions (Chapter 6c), although excavators recovered no lion bones.

The Shengavit kill-pattern of domestic animals—that is, cows, sheep, and goat— indicate that they were used primarily for their meat, milk, and/or herd security. Despite the lower numbers, the size of cattle suggests that they provided the most meat. Some cattle may have been used to pull carts or plows. Crabtree and Piro found no evidence of that, although the Uerpmanns did. Nothing in the bone remains or the pollen suggests that these animals were raised far from the site. That is to say, there is little evidence of interaction of the residents with full-time pastoral nomads to obtain meat. Clearly, crafts persons used sheep's wool, goat hair, and cattle skin (leather) for clothing and straps. This was the case, although most of the textiles Kvavadze and Atoyants observed in their pollen samples were made of flax, including some dyed pink, yellow, or orange, and other undetermined plant fibers. Flax clothing would not be very warm in winter, suggesting that woolen and leather clothing had to have been used in some seasons.

Another craft performed at Shengavit involved the use of bone. Given the amazing continuity of bone tools from the Mesolithic to the modern day, we could identify their function with some certainty (Chapter 5g). One category of bone tools was arrow heads. Experiments with these prove them to be as effective as lithic arrowheads in piercing a body. Another bone tool was used in weaving. The most common type was the awl. Among the tasks for which the ancients used different shapes of awls was piercing fabric and leather, basket making, and knitting yarn into fabric. Bone, ceramic, and stone spindle whorls and possible loom weights attest to the likely production of woolen garments. Ground stone tools (see below) verify the production of leather.

Lithics as a category (Chapter 5c) includes a wide variety of tools that represent different activities. Among them are cutting blades, awls, wedges, gravers, sickle elements, drills, and arrowheads. As a whole the craft of the flintknapper and obsidian at Shengavit was most often based on *ad hoc* use of flakes taken from pebbles of obsidian from the bed of the Hrazdan River and chunks of flint that came from a few kilometers away. Excavators found a few unfinished sickle elements at Shengavit, but not reflecting the large number of these tools found. At Mushakan, a few kilometers outside Yerevan, Gasparyan believes that flintknappers mined flint and made sickle blanks, which end users retouched and attached to wooden handles with bitumen at Shengavit. The number of sickle elements we found suggest the importance and primacy of agriculture. Artisans used other lithic tools for working wood or bone, butchering animals, incising designs into pots, etc. Of all the lithic categories, arrowheads required the most

---

847   Arbuckle et al. 2020.

skill to manufacture. In their case, experienced flintknappers would produce these, still from flakes, not the prepared blade cores typical of the Chalcolithic, but with greater care. There is no particular indication from the numbers we recovered of their being manufactured for exchange. The *ad hoc* nature of many of the tools suggests this as well. Ethnographically, farmers often produce more of these sorts of craft goods than they personally needed, especially in the off-season.[848] Exchange was arranged through networks of close kin. In some ethnographic cases part-time potters had workshops and produced pots for sale through establish networks of markets. On the other hand, late Kura-Araxes and Early Kurgan Period graves did have large numbers of very standardized, finely wrought arrowheads. Discovering how the labor of experienced flintknappers was acquired for funerary goods is a subject that needs further research. In that regard, Simonyan believes that, like the state societies of contemporary Mesopotamia, there were professionals, presumably working for some kind of leadership group. Rothman, based on ethnographic models and the distribution of activities (see below), suggests that the flintknappers and other craft makers were farmer/ herders who did this sort of activity on the side or in cooperation with kin or neighbors. The idea of extended kin who cooperated in common activities as an organizing principle makes more sense to him and seems to fit the data better. That way people with particular skills could do them as part of their contribution to small neighboring labor pools in which all subsistence and craft production was conducted.

An activity that is often discussed in regard to the Kura-Araxes cultural tradition is metallurgy (Chapter 5d). The evolution of metallurgical techniques reached a new level of sophistication by Kura-Araxes times. Smelting and making metal objects in molds became a common activity throughout the homeland and into the diaspora. We know that it happened at Shengavit (Chapter 3). Sadly, the place where Simonyan's team found evidence of metallurgical work could not be fully explored, because it was under an established wall. We really do not know if it was an organized workshop or simply a place where some smelting was done. Metal smelting can happen in a metal kiln, like the one in the craft district at Köhne Shahar,[849] or at a small, temporary installation in an open space like ones that exist ethnographically in the Middle East.[850]

The focus has to be on what the metalsmiths made, how much, and who ultimately consumed it. The metal objects we recovered were mostly in the category of adornment: beads, pins, hair rings (earrings?), and small, leaf-shaped blades. However, excavations did unearth two molds, one for metal spikes and another for a flat axe.[851] A few metal arrowheads and daggers did emerge from excavations. Simonyan et al. [852] argue that there were standardized weights for metals, implying a more centralized system of trading metal ores and objects. All but a few metals analyzed were arsenical bronze alloys. Gold really did not appear in any significant quantity until the Late Kura-Araxes/ Early Kurgan transitional period. Assessing the value of metals is hard to do. Copper sources for Shengavit metal ores range from 350 to under 100 kilometers away.[853] They had to be traded. Metallurgy is evidence at almost every Kura-Araxes site, so there was no central supplier, a conclusion that Simonyan disagrees with. Certainly, metal had enough value that it was re-smelted. The amounts we recovered do not suggest production for exchange to Rothman, but again we really do not know much about its production nor, unlike obsidian, has its source been used to trace its movement

848   Watson 1979.
849   Alizadeh et al. 2018.
850   Wulff 1966.
851   Badalyan et al 2015, 39 (110).
852   Simonyan et al. 2019.
853   Batiuk et al. 2022, Fig 6.

to any significant extent.[854] Metals at this period may be more of a marker of status than a primary producer of tools.

One of the uses for metal was for the jewelry (Chapter 5h). Jewlery is an art form that often carries symbolic messages about status, gender, or group affiliation. Still, in this category we found mostly beads made of local stones. The pieces of personal adornment we recovered came not from graves, but mostly from residential areas.

The other craft that is discussed more than any other is pottery making (Chapter 5e). Rothman argues that there was certainly a shared Kura-Araxes mental model of shapes, although we found that the same shape often came in very different sizes. Those shapes could be fine ware, utilitarian ware or cooking pot ware. There was no evidence of standardization in key measurements like body thickness, again leading to a widely shared assertion that pottery making was a domestic activity. Domestic here may mean a set of kin or neighbors, since the steps in pottery making can be quite labor intensive. Simonyan asserts that pottery making was a profession, and points to pottery kilns at contemporary Mokhrablur and Velikent and feels that the similarity in some ornaments across a wide area suggests centralized production. Ethnoarchaeological studies of pottery makers suggest that there is no correlation between kiln, pit, or bonfire firing and the structure of its manufacturers or exchange (commercial or kin exchange), except later in time when central production sites with large kilns produced pottery for a considerable area.[855] Common designs are shared, for example, during the Uruk Period, but neutron activation analysis and petrography, show that the pots with these styles were locally made.[856] In the Mesopotamian case, we are talking about state-level centralization, whereas no one we know of thinks the Kura-Araxes was the cultural tradition of a state.

A last craft category consisted of ground stone tools (Chapter 5f). These tools proved more variable and potentially important than lithic tools. Unfortunately, most site reports do not list more than querns and the grinding stones used on them. By categorizing them according to their working surface, we were able to see that first, the same tool could be used for multiple functions. Among those functions were agricultural field preparation, processing of agricultural crops, leather making, pottery making, building crafts, cutting down trees, grinding holes in stone axes, maceheads, and hammers, bead-making, metal ore processing, salt mining and refining, flintknapping, etc.

Household Activity Areas

As we mentioned at the beginning of this chapter, one of the better ways to determine who was conducting activities and how they organized them is to put evidence of those activities back into buildings and adjoining unroofed areas. We wish we were able to do so for many more spaces. Those we do have are from different architectural levels, so we cannot draw very broad conclusions from them. Nonethless, their consistency suggests some patterns that need testing in the future. Sadly, the area excavated in the lowest levels is too small to analyze in this case. The key to the artifact distribution maps that follow is in Figure 7.1. No animal remains can be associated with Bayburtian's excavations. None of Sardarian's buildings are useful for this analysis.

Among the deepest cases we have is from one of the smaller separate round houses excavated by Bayburtian (Fig 7.2). This building had two ritual ceramic hearths (probably Bayburtian conflated two strata), grain querns, grain storage, and a closed storage pot, as well as an open eating vessel and lids. A probable cooking pot also lay on the floor of the building. In addition, Bayburtian's team found a small tufa statuette, which might have been worn as a personal

---

854   Batiuk et al. 2022; According to Simonyan's calculations, only one workshop contained semi-finished metal weighing more than 150 kg (Simonyan 2013). This quantity, as well as the discovery of a mould for alloying standards to a weight corresponding to the Levantine weight system testifies to the production of copper articles for trade (Simonyan 2012).

855   Kramer 1997.

856   Minc 2016, Gopnick et al. 2016.

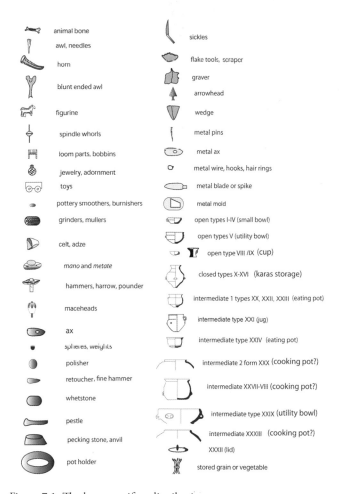

animal bone	sickles
awl, needles	flake tools, scraper
horn	graver
blunt ended awl	arrowhead
figurine	wedge
spindle whorls	metal pins
loom parts, bobbins	metal ax
jewelry, adornment	metal wire, hooks, hair rings
toys	metal blade or spike
pottery smoothers, burnishers	metal mold
grinders, mullers	open types I-IV (small bowl)
celt, adze	open types V (utility bowl)
	open type VIII /IX (cup)
mano and *metate*	closed types X-XVI (karas storage)
hammers, harrow, pounder	intermediate 1 types XX, XXII, XXIII (eating pot)
maceheads	intermediate type XXI (jug)
ax	intermediate type XXIV (eating pot)
spheres, weights	intermediate 2 form XXX (cooking pot?)
polisher	intermediate XXVII-VIII (cooking pot?)
retoucher, fine hammer	intermediate type XXIX (utility bowl)
whetstone	intermediate XXXIII (cooking pot?)
pestle	XXXII (lid)
pecking stone, anvil	stored grain or vegetable
pot holder	

Figure 7.1 The key to artifact distribution maps.

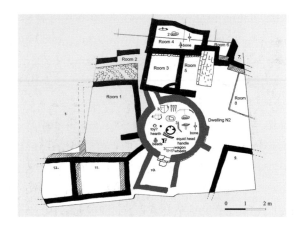

Figure 7.2 Artifact distribution in Building 22.

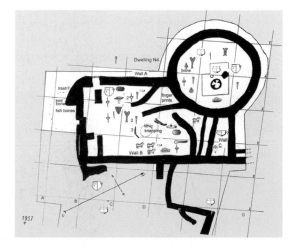

Figure 7.3 Artifact distribution in Bayburtian Building 2.

ornament. Two craft tools, a deer antler, and three grinding stones indicate possible flint retouch and processing of some substance, which microscopic surface analysis might permit us to determine. So, there was evidence of food storage, processing, cooking, and eating, and also processing of other substances.

At a higher elevation, Bayburtian's Building 2 (Fig 7.3) is from a level with round and square rooms. The focus is the small round room (only 3.25 meters in diameter). Like the previous Building (Room) 22, this room has a ritual ceramic hearth and a small copy of one that might be a toy. Three wagon wheels indicate another possible toy. Present are tools to prepare and serve food: a quern, cooking pots, and eating pots.

Also present are sickle elements for farming, a horn possibly for lithic retouch, a spindle whorl and three bone awls for working with fabric, and a hammer. A weight Bayburtian found there may be for a loom. Possibly for ritual is a small brazier. Beads mark personal adornment. Again, this space seems to provide for food processing, a place for children to play, and some economic activities: farming and cloth working.

The building at the highest elevation Bayburtian's team

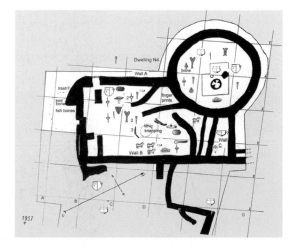

Figure 7.4 Bayburtian Building 1 with round room and unroofed courtyard.

dug was Building 1 (Fig 7.4). This is probably contemporaneous with Architectural Level 3 in Square K6, and the earlier construction of the ritual and attached room in Square J5 (the material from that building described below would have been later than Bayburtian's Building 1). In the circular room a ceramic hearth sits in the center with a flat stone near it. This could be a base for a center pole or a low table for food coming off the hearth (see Chapter 4b). Like the other rooms described above, this circular room has stored grain and a saddle quern, a cooking pot, and two eating pots. It also has a pin and another item of personal adornment. Crafts represented by tools there include a spindle whorl, awls for cloth, and a scraper type of awl for taking hair off animal skin.

The open courtyard attached to it clearly was a craft area. Bayburtian writes about a flintknapping concentration there. Three sickle elements rested near it, and again a horn retoucher lay next to the lithic debitage. Yarn making is represented by a number of spindle whorls. Awls, grinding stones, an obsidian wedge, and an awl for removing hair from animal skin all suggest cloth and leather working. A different element consisted of a number of figurines. Could the residents be making them there? A rhomboidal room with no sign of a door southeast of the round room contained a deep open pottery vessel and a macehead. Perhaps, this was a storeroom.

Again, this building appears to have been a place where people slept, ate, cooked, and conducted a series of craft activities.

We excavated a square building (2) probably a stratum after Bayburtian Building 1 in Square K6 2010 (Fig 7.5). In this case a center post base was not so near the hearth and we found no ceramic ritual hearth. However, we now have information on animal remains from Crabtree and Piro. That analysis matches the overall pattern we saw in other building above. Most of the remains came from domestic sheep and goat. Cow remains were less than half their number. A few pigs, dogs, and fish and one wild red deer made up the rest of the identifiable species. Again, the pottery included closed storage jars, cooking, and intermediate 1 eating types, and many open vessels. Querns completed the set of food processing tools. A sickle element suggests farm work, along with a small retouch hammer to sharpen the sickle blades. One spindle whorl remained to indicate cloth producing. Unlike the other building we examined, a new activity is indicated. Burnishing stones and gravers suggest that pottery making was an activity that residents of this house engaged in. The ancients could have used the hammers, abraders, and polishers for a number of activities; most would fit a builder's trade, but other activities are also possible.

So, like the other houses this one represents the basic domestic suite of activities and some other basic crafts.

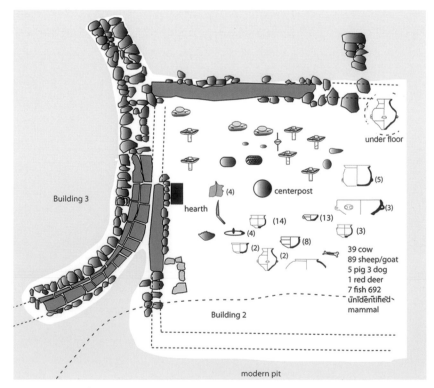

Figure 7.5 Artifact distribution Building 2 Square K6.

Another contemporary building is one in Square J5 (Fig 7.6) from Architectural Level 2. This one appears to be a two-room building. Room 1 has the pieces of a ritual emplacement, very much like the building in M5 (see below). There was a ceramic hearth, an altar, and instead of two bins, a clay basin. Residents seem to have destroyed the hearth and cut down the altar, perhaps to desacralize them when the building was abandoned. As such, analysis of its contents is not fully reliable. In terms of animal remains, the low number of animal bones recovered from Room 1 compared to the number in Room 2 and what seems to be a trash midden outside of the north wall makes this clear. Overall, however, the proportions

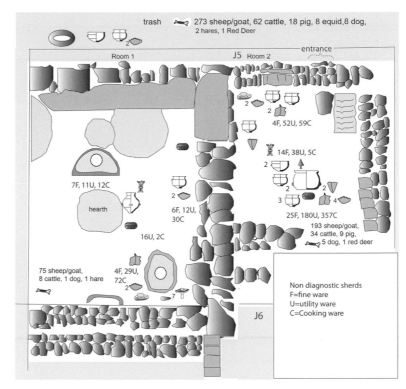

Figure 7.6 Two rooms with ritual emplacement and adjoining room.

of sheep and goat to cattle was higher than in the other residential building for which we had enough information to map their remains. Room 2 appears not to have been cleaned out. Its remains included stored grain in a small, stone-lined pit, cooking, and eating vessels, a quern built into the side of the wall. This could have been the kitchen for a ritual space like Building 3 from Kura-Araxes Level IV at Godin Tepe.[857] However, both rooms have tools that indicate other activities happened there, including gravers, wedges, abraders, a hammer, a ground stone retoucher, and an arrow head. The last was not buried near the hearth, so its presence is not likely ritual. We did not get as complete a set of measurements of all the diagnostic pots as elsewhere, but we did have the functional types of non-diagnostic pots (see Chapter 5e). Those indicate many more cooking pots, but also many more utilitarian pots than fine wares. These suggest that there was a difference between the function of the purely domestic spaces and this building, but not a completely specialized purpose.

The remaining two buildings whose artifacts we were able to map artifacts into reliably came from the last, Kura-Araxes period, Stratum I. The first was the room with a ritual space like the J5 Building in Square M5 (Fig 7.7). Like the J5 building, there was a ceramic ritual hearth and a raised platform, presumably for sacrifices (Chapter 6a). Instead of a large clay basin this room had two bins by a set of steps down into the room, filled with burned grain, similar to a feature in the Godin Building 3. There were cooking pots, closed storage pots, and intermediate eating vessels. The animal remains were closer to the domestic proportions than in the Square J5 building, Room 2. A number of querns rested on the floor. Probably ritual figurines of a bull's head and a phallus lay there as well. Imprints of a mat were preserved on the floor. Near the hearth a libation bowl lay in one of the indentations on the surface of a clay hearth. On a bench rested a polished horn of a red deer with cut-out away from the pointed end, perhaps to hang. Was it intended for piercing the neck of a sacrificial animal? A phalanx of a human finger (little finger) also lay there, covered

857   Rothman 2011.

in burnt fat or other organic material. According to Simonyan, this could have been a finger sacrifice.

However, there were a lot of tools for agriculture and craft activities: a sickle element, abraders, gravers, flake tools, pecking stones, hammers, a polisher, a husking tray, and hammers. There is little doubt that this was a ritual space and the adjoining room like Room 2 in Square J5 was a work room, but activities in this building were not restricted to only ritual activities.

The final building is the large rectangular building with an annex-in Square I14 (Fig 7.8). This building is also from Architectural Level 1 (Stratum I). Like all the other building whose artifacts we could map, this building has evidence of processing and cooking vegetables and meat. We found cooking pots, intermediate 1 eating vessels, open pots, and trays, as well as querns and grinding stones in primary or secondary context. Animal bones had a percentage of sheep/goat to cattle that was typical of the other domestic units. Sickle elements indicated farm work.

Additional craft activities are indicated: awls for removing hair from animal skin, a fine hammer for flint-knapping, gravers for potting or jewelry making, hammers and polishers for building, and flake tools for butchering. An unusually large number of wedges suggests that the residents did a lot of bone or wood working. We found no tools for cloth making.

So, this building was another domestic house. Its residents appear to have produced bone or wooden objects, but not cloth. This suggests that at this point that some nuclear households produced their own subsistence, but also some craft goods, but not others. To know this for certain, more buildings need to be excavated. That would permit us to compare a number of different buildings of the same time period, as I was able to do at Tepe Gawra.[858]

---

858   Rothman 2002.

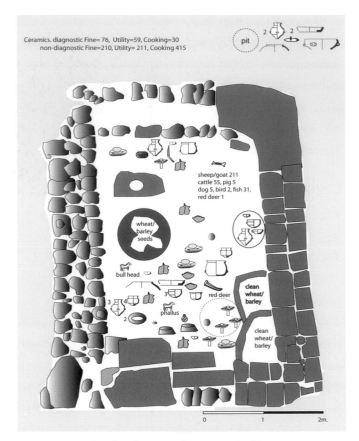

Figure 7.7 Artifact distribution in Square M5 Building.

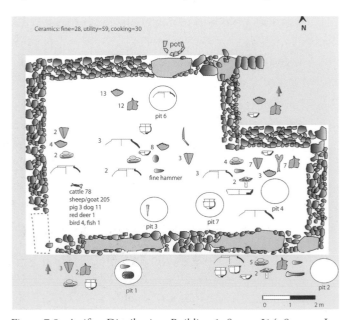

Figure 7.8. Artifact Distribution, Building 1, Square I14, Stratum I.

All the buildings in this section had elements of processing food, cooking, and eating it. All had evidence of other craft activities. Even the two buildings with clear ritual activities were not totally specialized in that one function. Few metal items or ones made of exotic materials appeared in any of them. There were no clear status differences apparent. Buildings at the same architectural level appear to have had very similar structures, so there do not appear major differences in the size of buildings, their functions, or any indication of differential access to goods. Simonyan believes that buildings like the one in Squares M5 with a ritual emplacement represent special function buildings, although domestic goods and craft tools were deposited there.

Evolution and Organization of Shengavit Society

When we put all the data we have presented together what is the picture that we can paint? As we wrote at the beginning, new data can change this picture, because of how little of the site we have available, and how much of the area that was dug is part of Sardarian's poorly recorded efforts.

The question of defining a center is critical here. A center is a place with functions like governance, craft production, markets, military planning, or formalized religion that do not exist in its satellite sites.[859] A center can be one that is a mediator with areas outside of its polity and control access of its dependent settlements to the larger world (closed), or it can be a place where unique opportunities are available to settlers in its polity, although those satellite sites can be independently part of larger trading and cultural interaction networks (open).[860] Areshian and Kushnareva saw the creation of centers of different levels of control based solely on their estimated size in the KA2 Ararat Plain.[861] This conclusion does not take into account many factors necessary to draw such a conclusion from site size hierarchies. Mostly, their claims did not measure the locational patterns at a given time, the functions that were necessary to create the network, or what and how were the networks administered.

One would expect in a situation like Areshian proposes to see concentrations of sites in easy transport distance. On the Ararat Plain, Simonyan mapped Kura-Araxes settlements on average every 3 km from each other, which to him indicates a dense and organized population during the Kura-Araxes. This does not indicate which was a center or how these equi-distant sites were controlled by a center. It seems rather like individual sites with their area of carrying capacity not allowed to overlap. The most current mapping of Kura-Araxes sites (Fig 7.9), shows the spread of KA2 and the few KA1 sites look even less centralized. However, some concentrations do appear possible. In the north of Lake Sevan, two clusters appear.

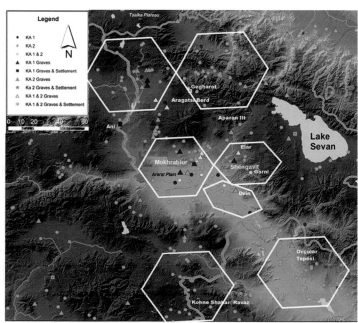

Figure 7.9 The Lower Province site distribution.

---

859   Rothman 2002.
860   Rothman 2002.
861   Areshian 2007; Kushnareva 1997.

These fit the pottery style area Badalyan describes as Ayrum-Teghut, although no single site is clearly the center. Another concentration is in the northern Ararat Plain. Mokhrablur is a possible candidate, or perhaps Aygevan. This area was dominated by the Shresh-Mokhrablur KA2 pottery style.[862] South in a more highland zone was a cluster with Köhne Shahar as a possible center. Another small cluster appeared in the southern Ararat Plain near Ovçular, although there is no particular reason to see that site as a center. The two remaining clusters are actually quite small. One is around Dvin, assuming that it is not the primate center Areshian proposes, and, of course, Shengavit in the higher elevation Koytak Plateau. There Karnut-Shengavit pottery was concentrated, although, as we demonstrated in Chapter 5e, Shengavit had within it both Shresh-Mokhrablur and Karnut-Shengavit pottery style dialects, but also style connections into the western Zagros and highland Taurus diaspora zones. Few parallels are evident with the Ayrum-Teghut pottery style cluster.

This does not suggest that Shengavit was primarily in control of many sites, but rather that it was probably part of a smaller polity that had interconnections with a much broader area of the Kura-Araxes landscape. That polity may have been a successor to Ararat Plain ones that were abandoned due to salinization of the soil. The possibility that it engaged in a larger network of economic and cultural interchange is possible. One possible reason we cannot say this for certain is because of exchange relations clearly associated with salt or other goods did not survive in the ground for archaeologists to find.

What does this say about the organization of the site itself? It is here where Rothman and Simonyan disagree most.

Simonyan sees the Armenian highlands, covering the South Caucasus and Taurus Mountain zone, as a unified area in which Kura-Araxes people were a powerful force, culturally and politically. He argues that the use of all these types in Shengavit provides a basis to suppose that many style types originated in the Ararat Valley and spread all over the northern regions of the Armenian Highland continuing from the Kura-Araxes to the Early Kurgan period. The ones with triangular incised shapes continued into the Middle Bronze Age and then to the Late Bronze Age cultures. In that region, he sees Shengavit, based largely on existence of the major wall, as a military fortress and political center. The great number of weapons, the rich assortment of arrowheads of various types and sizes, which were used for defense and attack, the ideal defensive system of the site, the layers burned and destroyed by the wars (known in different Bronze Age sites) are evidence of the uneasy situation and repeated military skirmishes in Armenia of the Kura-Araxes period. Simonyan believes that Shengavit's large population, social stratification, and centralization of power in the hands of the high stratum of society, as well as the wealth accumulated as a result of copper and salt production, enabled the center to organize military units capable of long-distance military campaigns.[863] He also points to metal production and the existence of seals and a unified system of weights[864] as proof of its export capability and administrative complexity.[865]

Rothman sees Shengavit in a very different way. The KA1, represented by a few sites like Norabats in the Ararat

---

862   According to Simonyan, Badalyan's division is accepted among Western specialists. In his opinion, however, this division has no solid basis. This requires cultural and typological analysis, which Badalyan lacks.

863   Simonyan 2015, 33-34. One of his arguments is that Kura-Araxes armies from the Armenian Highlands conquered Arslantepe, destroying the state society represented by the temple-palace complexes in 3000. Rothman points out that new data indicates that the temple-palace complex was destroyed in 3200 BC, before the founding of Shengavit. The so-called Red Black Burnished Wares of Arslantepe were more closely related to a Central Anatolian pottery style than to those of the Kura-Araxes.

864   Simonyan et al. 2019.

865   Simonian 2002.

Plain,[866] was a classic egalitarian society of farmer/herders. They were self-sufficient and shared a very homogeneous set of cultural traditions. Their technological capabilities were basic. This type of society is called a horizontal egalitarian society.[867] The transition to the KA2 was one of increasing societal complexity. The homogeneity of style in the KA1 was replaced by different style dialects in different areas of the Kura-Araxes homeland and diaspora.

Still, according to Rothman, as the information we have on production suggests, most crafts were domestic. Each of the households discussed above appear to have been largely self-sufficient with food production and processing. A group of kin or neighbors handled the basic crafts in the various areas of the site. Even residents of the two rooms with ritual emplacements conducted craft activities. The sophistication of the productive efforts certainly increased, but to Rothman that alone does not suggest that the organization became more centralized. The lack of standardization in pottery is one measure of the lack of central control or of production for export. The lack of any of the classic traits associated with societal stratification—this includes different sized buildings, evidence of differential access to exotic goods in households or in graves— again raises questions of how complex the society of Shengavit was.

The Lower Province associated with the Araxes River appears to have been one economic sphere. We can see this in the movement of obsidian from its sources.[868]

The two activities that to Rothman say that this was more complex than a horizontal egalitarian society were the construction of the settlement wall and the filling of so many stone-lined grain pits. Simonyan assumes that the wall is a defensive construction. That is certainly possible. The secret tunnel under the wall to the river certainly seems like a feature against a siege. But, there are other reasons to build a wall. One is symbolic. In order to establish a center and promote the status of the residents of that center vis-à-vis its dependent satellite sites, a great public work of some kind is one avenue to accomplish this. In the Early Bronze Age II Levant, contemporary with the end of the KA1, walls became a feature of many settlements.[869] There is little evidence there of violent military operations at that time.[870] In the South Caucasus we are still unclear who the enemies of sites like Shengavit in the KA2 would have been. The assumption has been that kurgan-building nomads were the enemy, eventually ending the Kura-Araxes and transitioning the societies of the South Caucasus to the Middle Bronze Age mobile forms, where social stratification is clearly marked in graves. If, as we considered at the beginning of this section, there were a number of centers, competition among them could have led to violent interactions within different areas of Armenian Highlands.

When did the residents of Shengavit build the wall and what does that say about the evolution of the site. Simonyan believes builders constructed the wall between 2900 and 2700 BC. Rothman believes rather that they built it between 2700-2600 BC.[871] To Rothman, the date is important because the later date correlates with new architectural forms, new pottery style dialects, and probably new social structures. This is one reason he believes that the society remained largely egalitarian, but it began a period of increasing control by subgroups within the polity. This new organization he believes is vertical egalitarian. An analogy with the Pueblo societies of the Chaco Canyon Great kivas may help us understand it.[872] There they retained all the trappings of egalitarian society, but used extended

866   Areshian 2005.

867   Rothman 2021.

868   Batiuk et al. 2022.

869   Greenberg 2019.

870   Simonyan 2021 believes the grave he dug at Gorayk in the north of Armenia has some evidence of violence and military clashes. The person buried in the elaborate tomb there had an arrowhead buried in his ankle bone.

871   Simonyan and Rothman in press.

872   Mills 2000.

networks of kin to accomplish goals and centralize planning like a chiefly society. People seeking newly promoted status could plan and carry out large public works and control a great network of trading covering hundreds of kilometers, but within but not outside the kinship structure of the society.

Like the Pueblos, the ritual life of the people of Shengavit seems to have undergone some changes during the period of the wall building. Virtually all the early round houses at Shengavit had a ceramic, ritual hearth. However, dwellings like Building 2 of Square K6, Architectural Level 2 and Building 1 of Square I14 (Architectural Level 1) lacked them. This was the time span when the residents of Shengavit built a ceramic hearth *and* an altar in Rooms 1 of Squares J5 and M5. Simonyan takes this to mean that these places were fire temples like those of more Classical times with a class of full-time priestesses. However, the square M5 ritual room was merely 2 x 3 meters inside (6 x 4.5 meters outside), and the Square J5 one not much bigger. To Rothman, this is still the ritual of a small-scale, possibly shamanistic society where only a few people at a time practiced whatever the ritual had been. Even the secret entrance to Room1 in Squares J5 and M5 mirrors the secret entrances into Pueblo ritual *kivas*. That fits the vertical egalitarian societal structure that he proposes. The other possibility is that public, group worship happened outside of ritual spaces, marked by the stele of Mokhrablur or the very large stone phallus at Shengavit. We just do not have enough information to tell.

The stored grain we discussed above. Assuming the population were small enough for there to be a big surplus would have required some at least temporary comptroller. That person or group would need to make sure who put what into storage and to whom it was released. Planning and carrying out the construction of the settlement wall would have required a similar set of comptrollers and pay masters. A vertical egalitarian society could handle these tasks. There are a few objects scholars describe as seals, but no corresponding clay sealings (locks) impressed with seals.

So, the reader has two quite contrary interpretations of Shengavit's society. It is for you, the reader, to decide which one (or another one entirely) is closer to the ancient reality.

Next Steps

That interpretation may depend on what archaeologists do in the future and how they choose to report it. The study of the evolution of the Kura-Araxes has progressed quite a bit, but it has some distance yet to go before we can fully understand it.

At Shengavit, which has the advantage of very good preservation and location close to student workers, there is a lot of potentially useful information yet to offer. Because of the 75 percent that is completely inaccessible and the idea in the Yerevan Preserve that no walls can be taken down to expose full plans underneath, however, Shengavit is not ideal. One strategy would be to expose more of the mound, especially lower levels with modern techniques. Opening the other hotspot identified by georadar in the open area to the east could be a place to start. The area around Square I14 would also be useful. Certainly, J5 and M5 could be re-opened to see what lies beneath, both the area around the ceramic ritual hearths, and in the architectural levels below. Other sites with potential for broad horizontal excavation would be worth exploring.

More sites of the KA1 and especially of the Chalcolithic/KA1 transition are important to find and excavate in the same way. Only then will we get a full picture of what happened in this critical millennium from 3500 to 2500 BC. Hopefully, more settlements of the Early Kurgan period will be excavated as well.

Wherever more digging is done, better publication with readily available, detailed databases like the one in our web archive are essential. The problem with publishing only one's own pottery typology, for example, is that these typologies change, often radically. Without the potential for statistical re-analysis, publications may have limited use in a couple of decades. Using the universally available internet makes this possible.

More source analysis is necessary for metals, obsidian, and flint. Also, use wear studies with microscopes of lithics, ground stone, and bone tools would enhance our understanding of the craft activities of the residents of Kura-Araxes sites. Residue analyses of pots, now becoming more available, should be tried on Shengavit pots from residential, ritual, and grave areas.

Using the model nomenclature of settlement, cities, towns, and villages may be detrimental our seeing the world as the ancient did. This settlement nomenclature works for Southern Mesopotamia, but it may not work for the mountains to its north. We as archaeologists always have to take the perspective of looking up from the perspective of the people of the time.[873]

Overall, reviews of how appropriate and consistent various theoretical approaches are will refine our understanding and draw the various archaeological schools closer together.

References

Alizadeh, K., Samei, S., Mohammadkhani, K., Heidari, R. and Tykot, R. 2018 Craft production at Köhne Shahar, a Kura-Araxes settlement in Iranian Azerbaijan. *Journal of Anthropological Archaeology* 51: 127–143

Areshian, G. 2005 Early Bronze Age settlements in the Ararat Plain and its Vicinity. *Archaeologische Mitteilungen aus Iran und Turan* 37: 71–88.

Areshian, G. 2007 From extended families to incipient polities: The trajectory of social complexity in the Early Bronze Age of the Ararat Plain. in *Social Orders and Social Landscapes*, edited by L.M. Popova, C.W. Hartley, and A.T. Smith, 26–54. Cambridge: Cambridge Scholars Press.

Atkin, T. and Rykwert, J. (eds.) 2005 *Structure and Meaning in Human Settlements.* Philadelphia: University of Pennsylvania Museum of Archaeology and Anthropology.

Batiuk, S., Rothman, M. S, Samei, S., Hovsepyan, R. 2022 Unraveling the Kura-Araxes Cultural Tradition across Time and Space. *Ancient Near Eastern Studies* 59:236-325.

Bayburtian, Ye 2011 *Sequence of Ancient Cultures of Armenia on the Basis of Archaeological Material.* Yerevan: Armenian Museum of History. (in Russian).

Gopnik, H., Reichel, C., Minc, L,.and R.Elendari, R. 2016 A View from the East: The Godin VI Oval and the Uruk Sphere. in *Trade and Interaction in the Uruk Expansion: Recent Insights from Archaeometric Analyses*, edited by L.D. Minc and G. Emberling), Special Section of *Journal of Archaeological Science: Reports* 7C. doi:10.1016/J.jasrep.2016.02.020

Greenberg, R. 2019 *Archaeology of the Bronze Age Levant.* Cambridge: Cambridge University Press.

Hayrapetyan, A. 2008 Some Technical Aspects of the Pottery of the Early Bronze Age Site of Gegharot (Armenia). in *Ceramics in Transitions: Chalcolithic Through Iron Age in the Highlands of the Southern Caucasus and Anatolia*, edited by K. Rubinson, and A. Sagona, 71-86. Leuven: Peeters.

Kramer, C. 1997 *Pottery in Rajasthan.* Washington DC: Smithsonian Press.

Kushnareva, K. 1997 *The Southern Caucasus in Prehistory: Stages of Cultural and Socioeconomic Development from the Eighth to the Second Millennium B.C.* Penn Museum of Archaeology. Philadelphia.

Minc L. 2016 Trace-element analyses of Uruk ceramics: Establishing a database to track interregional exchange. *Journal of Archaeological Science: Reports* 7C: 798-807.

Rothman, M. S in press Reconstructing the Lifeways of the Kura-Araxes. Avestiyan Festschrift, in *Systemitizing the Past,* edited by E. Grekyan, 410-422. Oxford: Archaeopress.

Rothman, M. S 2021 Approaches to the Nature of the Kura-Araxes Societies in their Homeland. In *Pathways through Arslantepe: Essays in Honour of Marcella Frangipane*, edited by F. Balossi Restelli, A. Cardarelli, G-M Di Nocera, L. Manzanilla, L. Mori, G. Palumbi, H. Pittman, 163-172. Rome: Universitá di Roma Sapienza.

Rothman, M. S 2018 Modelling the Kura-Araxes Cultural Tradition. in *Context and Connection: Essays on the Archaeology of the Ancient Near East in Honor of Antonio Sagona*, edited by A. Batmaz, G. Bedianashvili, A. Michalewiz, and A. Robinson, 125-146. Leuven: Peeters.

Rothman, M. S 2017 Explaining the Kura Araxes. in *Fitful Histories and Unruly Publics*, edited by K. Weber, E. Hite, L. Katchadourian, and A. Smith, 217-257. Leiden: Brill.

Rothman, M. S 2011 Migration and Resettlement: Godin IV Period. in *On the High Road: the History of Godin Tepe, Iran,* edited by H. Gopnick, and M. S Rothman, 139-208. Toronto: Royal Ontario Museum/ Mazda Press.

Rothman, M. S 2004 Studying the Development of Complex Society: Mesopotamia in the Late Fifth and Fourth Millennia BC. *Journal of Archaeological Research* 12 (1): 75-119.

Rothman, M. S 2002 *Tepe Gawra. the Evolution of a Small, Prehistoric Center in Northern Iraq.* Philadelphia: The University of Pennsylvania

---

873   Rothman 2022.

Museum Publications.

Sagona, A. 2018 *The Archaeology of the Caucasus from the Earliest Settlements to the Iron Age.* Cambridge: Cambridge University Press.

Schacht, R. 1981 Estimating Past Population Trends. *Annual Review of Anthropology* 10: 119-140..

Simonyan, H. 1984. *The Culture of the Middle Bronze Age in the Northern Regions of the Armenian Highland.* Ph. D. in Philosophy, Leningrad (in Russian).

Simonyan, H. 2012 Armenia and International Trade in the Early Bronze Age. *Armenia's Civilizing Contribution to the History of the Silk Road: Materials of international conference* (2011), edited by A. Melkonyan, 18-37. Yerevan: Publishing house of NAS RA. (in Armenian).

Simonyan, H. 2015 Observations of the Armenian-American Joint Expedition of Shengavit. *Fundamental Armenology.* http://www.fundamentalarmenology.am/issues/9/ISSUE-2,-%C2%A0-2015.html.

Simonyan, H. 2018. Shengavit - ancient settlement of Yerevan. *Yerevan* 5: 3-13 (in Armenian).

Simonyan, H., Gevorgyan, A. Bobokhyan, A. 2019. Cognitive links between mountains and lowlands: balance weights from the Early Bronze Age site of Shengavit (Armenia) in context. *Aramazd* XIII(2):34-52.

Simonyan, H. 2021. il Kurgan di Gorayk. l'Armenia e la Grande Steppa. *Archeologia Viva*, 2021.

Simonyan, H. and Rothman, M. S in press New data on the construction and meaning of the Shengavit settlement wall in *Paradise Lost: Collection of papers in honour of Ruben S. Badalyan* on the occasion of his 65th birthday, edited by A. Kosyan, P. Avetisyan, K. Martirosyan-Olshansky, A.Bobokhyan, and Y. Gekyan. Aramazd XVI (1/2): 406-428.

Watson, P. J. 1979 *Archaeological Ethnography in Western Iran.* Viking Fund Publications in Anthropology. Tucson: University of Arizona Press.

Wulff, H. 1966 *Traditional Crafts of Persia.* Cambridge: M.I.T. Press

Sources of Figures

Frontispiece Aerial photograph supplied by Hakob Simonyan.
*i.*1   Photographs by Mitchell Rothman and Hakob Simonyan.
*i.*2   Photograph from Shengavit archive.
*i.*3   Photograph by Mitchell Rothman.
*i.*4   Photograph by Mitchell Rothman.
1.1   After Batiuk et al. 2022.
1.2   Pottery images from Antonio Sagona's Powerpoint for the Toronto Kura-Araxes Workshop; map by Mitchell Rothman
1.3   Photograph by Hakob Simonyan.
1.4   After Simonyan 2013, figure 3.
1.5   Aerial photograph supplied by Hakob Simonyan.
1.6   Section drawing by Hovannes Sanamyan, colorized and details by Mitchell Rothman.
2.1   After Google Earth image modified by Mitchell Rothman
2.2   Fifth National Report of the Republic of Armenia to the Convention on Biological Diversity, 2014, Figure 1.
2.3   Supplied by Eliso Kvavadze.
2.4   Supplied by Eliso Kvavadze.
2.5   Photograph by Eliso Kvavadze.
2.6   Photograph by Eliso Kvavadze.
2.7   Photograph by Eliso Kvavadze.
2.8   Photograph by Eliso Kvavadze.
2.9   Photograph by Eliso Kvavadze.
2.10   Photograph by Eliso Kvavadze.
2.11   Photograph by Eliso Kvavadze.
2.12   Photograph by Eliso Kvavadze.
2.13   Supplied by Anahit Atoyants.
2.14   Supplied by Anahit Atoyants.
3.1   Supplied by Hakob Simonyan
3.2   Sardarian 1967, Figure 19.
3.3   Aerial photograph supplied by Hakob Simonyan.
3.4   Bayburtian 2011, pp. 28, 3
3.5   Bayburtian 2011, pp. 32, V.
3.6   Bayburtian 2011, pp. 34, VI.
3.7.   Provided by Hakob Simonyan.
3.8   Photograph by Hakob Simonyan.
3.9   Provided by Hakob Simonyan.
3.10   Provided by Hakob Simonyan.
3.11   Provided by Hakob Simonyan.
3.12   Photograph by Hakob Simonyan.
3.13   Provided by Hakob Simonyan.
3.14   Photograph by Hakob Simonyan.
3.15   Photograph by Hakob Simonyan.
3.16   Photograph by Hakob Simonyan.
3.17   Photograph by Hakob Simonyan.
3.18   Provided by Hakob Simonyan.
3.19   Photograph by Hakob Simonyan.
3.20   Photograph by Hakob Simonyan.
3.21   Photograph by Hakob Simonyan.
3.22   Photograph by Hakob Simonyan.
3.23   Photograph by Hakob Simonyan.
3.24   Photograph by Hakob Simonyan.
3.25   Photograph by Hakob Simonyan.
3.26   Photograph by Hakob Simonyan, drawings Ashot Tumanyan .
3.27   Photograph by Hakob Simonyan.
3.28   Photograph by Hakob Simonyan.
3.29   Harris matrix by Hakob Simonyan.
3.30   Photograph by Hakob Simonyan.
3.31   Photograph and Drawing by Mitchell Rothman.
3.32   Photograph and Drawing by Mitchell Rothman.
3.33   Drawing by Mitchell Rothman.
3.34   Photographs by Mitchell Rothman.
3.35   Photographs by Mitchell Rothman.
3.36   Drawing by Mitchell Rothman.

3.37   Photograph by Hakob Simonyan.
3.38   Photograph and Drawing by Mitchell Rothman.
3.39   Drawing by Mitchell Rothman.
3.40   Photograph by Mitchell Rothman.
3.41   Drawing by Mitchell Rothman.
3.42   Photograph by Mitchell Rothman.
3.43   Photograph by Mitchell Rothman.
3.44   Photographs by Mitchell Rothman.
3.45   Photograph by Mitchell Rothman.
3.46   Drawing by Hovannes Samanyan processed by Mitchell Rothman.
3.47   Photograph by Hakob Simonyan.
3.48   Drawing by Hovannes Samanyan.
3.49   Photograph by Hakob Simonyan.
3.50   Drawing by Hovannes Samanyan, colorized and edited by Mitchell Rothman
3.51   Drawing by Hovannes Samanyan.
3.52   Photograph by Mitchell Rothman.
3.53   Photograph by Hakob Simonyan.
3.54   Drawing by Mitchell Rothman.
3.55   Photograph by Mitchell Rothman.
3.56   Photograph by Hakob Simonyan.
3.57   Photograph by Hakob Simonyan.
4a.1   Areshian 2005, Figs 6 and 8.
4a.2   Palumbi 2008, Figs 2.7 and 5.18.
4a.3   Drawing from Gregory Areshian.
4a.4   Drawing from Gregory Areshian.
4a.5   Palumbi 2008, Fig 2.9.
4a.6.   https://www.barewalls.com/art-print-poster/daub-and-wattle-indian-house_bwc4746678.html
4a.7   Salzman 2000, Fig 1.3.
4a.8   Rothman 2011, (A) Fig 5.17, (B) Fig 5.11.
4a.9   Drawing from Gregory Areshian.
4a.10   Kleiss and Kroll 1979, Fig 7.
4a.11   Hauptmann (A) 1979, Pl. 40, (B) Pl. 26, (C) 1982, Pl. 35.
4a.12   Palumbi 2008, Fig 5.12; Rothman 2011 Fig 5.13.
4b.1   after Bayburtian 2011, (a) pp. 34, Fig VI, (b) pp. 32, V.
4b.2   Drawings Hovannes Sanamyan and Mitchell Rothman.
4b.3   after Sardarian 1967, pp. 180/181.
4b.4   Photograph by Hakob Simonyan.
4b.5   Photograph by Hakob Simonyan.
4b.6   Photographs by Hakob Simonyan and Mitchell Rothman.
4b.7   Photographs by Hakob Simonyan and Mitchell Rothman.
4b.8.   after Szabo and Barfield 1991, xi.
4b.9.   Bayburtian 2011, pp. 31, I.
4b.10.   Sagona 2018, Fig 5.6.
4b.11.   after Szabo and Barfield 1991, pp. 136 and iv.
4b.12.   Photograph by Mitchell Rothman.
4b.13.   after Sardarian 2004.
4b.14.   Photograph by Hakob Simonyan.
4b.15.   Photograph by Mitchell Rothman.
4b.16.   Bayburtian 2011, pp. 95.
4b.17.   Simonyan 2013, Fig 8.
4b.18.   Photograph provided by Hakob Simonyan.
4c.1.   Photographs supplied by Gregoryan.
4c.2.   Imagine drawn by M. Gregoryan.
4c.3.   From Report by Durgaryan and Gregoryan.
4c.4.   From Report by Durgaryan and Gregoryan.
5a.1.   Photograph by Mitchell Rothman.
5a.2.   Photograph by Mitchell Rothman.
5a.3.   Photograph by Pam Crabtree.
5a.4:   Histogram prepared by Pam Crabtree.
5a. 5.   Photograph by Pam Crabtree.
5a.6.   Histogram prepared by Pam Crabtree.
5a.7.   Photograph by Mitchell Rothman.
5b.1   Burney and Lang 1971, Figure 24.
5b.2   Photograph by Roman Hovsepyan.
5b.3   Photograph by Roman Hovsepyan.

5b.4   Photograph by Roman Hovsepyan.
5b.5   Photograph by Roman Hovsepyan.
5b.6   Photograph by Roman Hovsepyan.
5b.7   Photograph by Roman Hovsepyan.
5b.8   Photograph by Roman Hovsepyan.
5b.9   Photograph by Hakob Simonyan.
5c.1   Photograph by Mitchell Rothman.
5c.2   Photographs provided by Hakob Simonyan.
5c.3   Photographs provided by Hakob Simonyan.
5c.4   Photographs provided by Hakob Simonyan.
5c.5   Photographs provided by Hakob Simonyan.
5c.6   Photographs provided by Hakob Simonyan.
5c.7   Drawing by Tiziana Gallo, Photograph by Dan Rahimi.
5c.8   Photograph by Mitchell Rothman.
5c.9   Drawing by Tiziana Gallo.
5c.10 Photographs provided by Hakob Simonyan.
5c.11 After Bayburtian 2011, pp. 32, V.
5c.12 Drawing by Tiziana Gallo.
5c.13 Drawing by Tiziana Gallo, Photograph by Dan Rahimi.
5c.14 Photographs provided by Hakob Simonyan.
5c.15 Drawing by Tiziana Gallo, Photograph by Dan Rahimi.
5c.16 Photograph provided by Hakob Simonyan.
5d.1   Photographs provided by Hakob Simonyan.
5d.2   Badalyan et al. 2015, Fig 110; photograph provided by Hakob Simonyan.
5d.3   Photographs provided by Hakob Simonyan.
5d.4   Photographs provided by Hakob Simonyan.
5d.5   Graph drawn by Khatchetor Meliksetian.
5d.6   Graph drawn by Khatchetor Meliksetian.
5d.7   Graph drawn by Khatchetor Meliksetian.
5e.1   Pictures by Hakob Simonyan, Badalyan et al. 2015, Figs 580, 867.
5e.2   Photographs by Mitchell Rothman.
5e.3   Photomicrograph by Nyree Manoukian.
5e.4   Photograph by Mitchell Rothman.
5e.5   Photomicrograph by Nyree Manoukian.
5e.6   Photograph by Mitchell Rothman.
5e.7   Photomicrograph by Nyree Manoukian.
5e.8   After Manoukian 2015, Fig 15.
5e.9   Photograph by Mitchell Rothman.
5e.10 Photograph by Mitchell Rothman.
5e.11 Photograph by Mitchell Rothman.
5e.12 Photograph by Mitchell Rothman.
5e.13 Drawn by Mitchell Rothman.
5e.14 Photograph by Mitchell Rothman.
5e.15 Drawn by Rothman after Rice 2015.
5e.16 Photograph by Mitchell Rothman.
5e.17 Photograph by Mitchell Rothman.
5e.18 Drawn by Mitchell Rothman.
5e.19 Drawn by Mitchell Rothman.
5e.20 Drawn by Mitchell Rothman.
5e.21 Drawn by Mitchell Rothman.
5e.22 Drawn by Mitchell Rothman.
5e.23 Drawn by Mitchell Rothman.
5e.24 Drawn by Mitchell Rothman.
5e.25 Drawn by Mitchell Rothman.
5e.26 Photograph by Hakob Simonyan.
5e.27 Photograph by Hakob Simonyan.
5e.28 Photograph by Mitchell Rothman.
5f.1   Photograph by Mitchell Rothman.
5f.2   Photographs by Mitchell Rothman, Hakob Simonyan, and Badalyan et al. 2015, Fig 178, 509, 510, 511, 554.
5f.3   https://www.thesprucecrafts.com/how-to-burnish-pottery-2746229
5f.4   Kramer 1982, Fig 2.4.
5f.5   Watson 1979, Fig 5.51.
5f.6   Stapleton et al. 2014, Figs 2 and 5.
5f.7   Photographs by Mitchell Rothman, Badalyan et al. 2015, 515, 512.
5f.8   Adams 2014, Fig 6.2.

5f.9   Drawing by Mitchell Rothman.
5f.10   Drawing by Mitchell Rothman.
5f. 11   Photographs by Mitchell Rothman.
5f.12   Photographs by Mitchell Rothman.
5f. 13   Adams 2014, Fig 4.8.
5f. 14   Photographs by Mitchell Rothman; Badalyan et al. 2015, Fig 150, 93.
5f.15   Marro et al. 2010, Fig 7.2
5f.16   Adams 2014, Fig 7.5.
5f.17   Adams 2014, Fig 5.17.
5f.18   Photographs by Mitchell Rothman.
5f.19   Squitieri and Eitam 2016, Fig 2.
5f. 20   Photographs by Mitchell Rothman, Badalyan et al. 2015, Fig 89.
5f.21   Histogram by Mitchell Rothman.
5g.1   Photographs provided by Hakob Simonyan.
5g.2   Photographs A-G provided by Hakob Simonyan; H provided by Claudia Sagona.
5g.3   Photograph from C. Sagona 2018, Fig 2.
5g.4   Photographs provided by Hakob Simonyan.
5g.5   Luik 2006, Fig 4.
5g.6   Photographs provided by Hakob Simonyan, except C, Badalyan et al. 2015, Fig 50.
5h.1   Simonyan 2013, from Plates 12, 14, 15, 16.
5h.2   Simonyan 2013, from Plates 12 and 14; https://commons.wikimedia.org/wiki/File:Tsalka_pin.JPG
5h.3   Simonyan 2013, from Plate12.
5h.4   Simonyan 2013, from Plate 14 (1,2,4,5); Photograph by Hakob Simonyan (6); Sagona 2018, Fig 7.3 (3).
5h.5   Meliksetian et al. 2011, Fig 8.
6a.1   Drawn by Mitchell Rothman using observation and Sagona 1984.
6a.2   After Fig 6a.1; Koşay 1976; Simonyan and Rothman 2015, Figs 9; Sagona and Sagona 2011.
6a.3   Drawn by Mitchell Rothman.
6a.4   Drawn by Mitchell Rothman.
6a.5   Simonyan and Rothman 2015, Figs 9 and 10.
6a.6   Photograph by Mitchell Rothman.
6a.7   A. Sagona Toronto Workshop Powerpoint (B); Hauptmann 1982, Pl. 18,2 (C); Sardarian 1967, pp. 175, 1 (E); Photograph by H. Simonyan (F); Badalyan et al. 2015, Fig 44 (I), Fig 530 (G), Fig 298 (D), 362 (H), 363 (J).
6a.8   Simonyan and Rothman 2015, Fig 11.
6a.9   A. Sagona Toronto Workshop Powerpoint (A, B), Photograph by Mitchell Rothman (C), Simonyan 2013, Pl 9, 3 (G), 10 (D), Pl 10, 5 (H), 9 (I), Pl 11, 5 (E), 10 (F).
6a.10   Drawings by Mitchell Rothman based on original plans by H. Sanamyan.
6a.11   Photographs by Mitchell Rothman.
6b.1   Batiuk et al. 2022, Fig 5.
6b.2   Photographs by Hakob Simonyan and Vram Hakobyan.
6b.3   After Avetisyan and Bobokhyan 2008, Fig 1.
6b.4   Photographs by Hakob Simonyan.
6b.5   After Avetisyan and Bobokhyan 2008, Fig 2.
6b.6   Badalyan et al. 2015, Fig 697-701.
6b.7   Badalyan et al. 2015, Fig 579; Photographs by Hakob Simonyan and Vram Hakobyan.
6b.8   Drawing by Y. A. Tamnayan.
6b.9   Badalyan et al. 2015, Figs 846, 840, 819, 816, 818, 825, 826, 843, 842.
6b.10   Photograph by Taguhi Hmayakyan and drawing by Taguhi Hamayakyan.
6b.11   Drawing by Taghui Hmayakkan.
6b.12   Photograph and drawings provided by Hakob Simonyan.
6b.13   Photograph by Hakob Simonyan.
6b.14   Photographs provided by Hakob Simonyan.
6b.15   Map by Hakob Simonyan.
6b.16   Photographs provided by Hakob Simonyan, drawing by Mitchell Rothman.
6b.17   Drawing provided by Hakob Simonyan.
6b.18   Photographs provided by Hakob Simonyan.
6b.19   Photographs provided by Hakob Simonyan.
6b.20   Photographs by Hakob Simonyan.
6b.21   Photographs by Hakob Simonyan, drawings provided by Hakob Simonyan.
6b.22   Photograph by Taguhi Hmayakyan, drawing by Taguhi Hamayakyan.
6b.23   Photograph and drawings provided by Hakob Simonyan.
6b.24   Photographs of tomb by Hakob Simonyan, chipped stone tools.
6b.25   Photographs provided by Hakob Simonyan.
6b.26   Photographs by Hakob Simonyan, drawing by Taguhi Hamayakyan.
6b.27   Photograph by Hakob Simonyan.
6b.28   Drawings provided by Hakob Simonyan.

6b.29   Drawings by Hovhannes Sanamyan.
6b.30   Photographs by Taguhi Hmayakyan and drawings by Taguhi Hamayakyan.
6b.31   Photographs and drawings provided by Hakob Simonyan.
6b.32   Photograph by Anna Azizyan.
6b.33   Photographs by Taguhi Hmayakyan and drawing by Taguhi Hamayakyan.
6b.34   Photographs by Anna Azizyan.
6b.35   Drawing by Taguhi Hamayakyan.
6b.36   Photographs by Hakob Simonyan
6c.1   Photograph provided by Hakob Simonyan; Simonyan 2013, Pl 10,10.
6c.2   Photographs provided by Hakob Simonyan.
6c.3   Simonyan 2013, Pl 10, 2,4 (A, B, D); Margueron, J.-C. 2007 Une stele du temple dit de Ninhursag. *Akh Purattim-Les rives de Euphrate*, 123-134. Paris: MOM Éditions, Fig 1.
6c.4   Photograph provided by Hakob Simonyan.
6c.5   Simonyan 2013, Pl 10,3, Photograph provided by Hakob Simonyan.
6c.6   Simonyan 2013, Pl 10, 1.
6c.7   Simonyan 2013, Pl 5, 9.
6c.8.   Simonyan 2013, Pl 10, 7, 6.
6c.9   Drawings provided by Simonyan (A); Simonyan 2013, Pl 11, 1,2 (B, C); Photograph by Simonyan (D).
6c.10   Photographs and drawings provided by Hakob Simonyan.
6c.11   Simonyan 2013, Pl 9, 10 and 11 (A), Drawings by Gohar Telumyan (B, C)
6c.12   Photographs by Taguhi Hmayakyan, drawing by Taguhi Hmayakyan.
6c.13   Simonyan 2013, Pl 9, 2 (A), photograph by Hakob Simonyan (B).
6c.14   Simonyan 2013, Pl 9, 3.
6c.15   Photograph by Hakob Simonyan.
6c.16   Photograph by Hakob Simonyan.
6c.17   Simonyan 2013, Pl 9, 5.
6c.18   Simonyan 2013, Pl 9, 4 (A), drawing by Gohar Telumyan(B); Badalyan et al. 2015, Fig 111.
6c.19   Simonyan 2013, Pl 9,1, drawing by Gohar Telumyan (A), https://www.pinterest.com/pin/189080884342982320/ (B).
6c.20   Photograph provided by Hakob Simonyan.
7.1   Drawings by Mitchell Rothman.
7.2   Drawings after H. Sanamyan architectural sketches by Mitchell Rothman.
7.3   Drawings after H. Sanamyan architectural sketches by Mitchell Rothman.
7.4   Drawings after H. Sanamyan architectural sketches by Mitchell Rothman.
7.5   Drawings after H. Sanamyan architectural sketches by Mitchell Rothman.
7.6   Drawings after H. Sanamyan architectural sketches by Mitchell Rothman.
7.7   Drawings after H. Sanamyan architectural sketches by Mitchell Rothman.
7.8.   Drawings after H. Sanamyan architectural sketches by Mitchell Rothman.
7.9   After Batiuk et al. 2022, Fig 7.

Index

Stratigraphy of Shengavit:

Symbols, Ritual and Ideology: